Increasing Student Retention

Effective Programs and Practices for Reducing the Dropout Rate

Lee Noel
Randi Levitz
Diana Saluri
and Associates

Foreword by Theodore J. Marchese

Increasing
Student
Retention

Jossey-Bass Publishers
San Francisco • London • 1985

INCREASING STUDENT RETENTION
Effective Programs and Practices for Reducing the Dropout Rate
by Lee Noel, Randi Levitz, Diana Saluri, and Associates

Copyright © 1985 by: Jossey-Bass Inc., Publishers
433 California Street
San Francisco, California 94104
&
Jossey-Bass Limited
28 Banner Street
London EC1Y 8QE

Library of Congress Cataloging in Publication Data
Main entry under title:

Increasing student retention.

    (The Jossey-Bass higher education series)
    Includes bibliographies and indexes.
    1. College attendance—United States—Addresses,
essays, lectures. 2. College dropouts—United States—
Addresses, essays, lectures. I. Noel, Lee. II. Levitz,
Randi S. (date). III. Saluri, Diana. IV. Series.
LC148.I385 1985   378'.16913'0973   84-47992
ISBN 0-87589-624-3

Manufactured in the United States of America

The paper in this book meets the guidelines for
permanence and durability of the Committee on
Production Guidelines for Book Longevity of the
Council on Library Resources.

JACKET DESIGN BY WILLI BAUM

FIRST EDITION

Code 8541

The Jossey-Bass
Higher Education Series

Consulting Editors
Student Services and Counseling Psychology

Ursula Delworth
University of Iowa

Gary R. Hanson
University of Texas, Austin

Foreword

How can a college improve its retention of students? Researchers have tilted at the question for the last twenty years; hundreds of colleges have attempted retention programs over the last ten. Up to now, though, reliable answers were scarce.

Increasing Student Retention changes that situation, markedly for the better. Its authors have culled the research; they have scrutinized on-campus experience; they now announce, "attrition is a problem with solutions." The book moves beyond the traditions of literature review and anecdote to look at what works, why it works, and how to do it on your own campus.

The appearance of *Increasing Student Retention* is fortuitous for two reasons. First, a combination of internally felt enrollment pressures and of hard, new questions from external authority ("How come so many of your students drop out?") raises the stakes for effective action to combat attrition; a practical handbook with a better set of answers could not be more timely. Second, the book's publication signals and expands upon the emergence of a fresh set of ways to think about retention.

What is the new thinking about retention? Increasingly it is to view retention in relation to admissions, with the two functions seen as twin aspects of enrollment management. Earlier in this decade, concepts of enrollment management changed the way we thought about admissions and recruitment; now, mid-decade, a similar change is affecting our ideas about retention.

To understand these developments, consider the more familiar changes we have seen in admissions. In the sixties, admissions concerns centered on issues of student guidance and selection. By the mid-seventies, as enrollment pressures began to be felt, the emphasis turned to techniques of student recruitment. In the early eighties, as competition heated up and people got a better grasp of marketing, the emphasis shifted again—to questions about the institution itself and what it purveyed in student markets.

A similar pattern of emphasis has occurred with regard to retention. In the sixties, we began with an academic literature on issues of student persistence and attainment. During the seventies, the vocabulary shifted from "persistence" to "retention," that is, to the needs of the institution; the focus moved to techniques and program adaptations believed to retain students. Now we are in a new phase, in which the focus is less on techniques and brushing up services than it is on the overall character of the experience offered to students.

Both aspects of enrollment management then bring one to the same point: over time, it is qualities of the institution itself that attract and retain students. The repeated message of this book is that effective retention has little to do with instituting gimmicky programs, lowering standards, or manipulating students into staying; it has everything to do with providing experiences that engage student minds and energies. The effective institution commits itself to student advancement; it realizes market and holding power as a result.

From this perspective, there is nothing that might be done on behalf of retention that would not be good educationally. Whether one entertains the techniques historically associated with retention ("boost career and life planning"), or moves more fully into this book's larger questions about curriculum, staffing, and student life, the result should be a plus for students. It's a nice irony that many of the steps that fifteen years ago were the platform of student-oriented reformers are now back on the agenda as ways to strengthen the institution.

I conclude with a suggestion, aimed at academic administrators and faculty. Read this book carefully: it's full of ideas and brings you up to speed on where the thinking is. But don't over-focus on technique or use the chapters that follow exclusively to load up an agenda for a retention committee. Think also about what all this means for the character of education your institution offers. If there are agendas to be built, a crucial one will be for senior officers concerned about issues of mission and strategy. A fresher sense of "what business we're in and how it should operate" may be the first need.

Being in the talent development business, which these authors recommend, is a suggestive idea. For a companion piece on how such a business would operate, look again at the 1984 National Institute of Education (NIE) Study Group report, *Involvement in Learning*. Its themes—involve students in their learning, raise expectations for performance, front-load in the freshman year, assess and provide feedback—have research origins in the literature on retention. Read in this light, the NIE report speaks again to the strong interrelation between good education and holding power.

For that matter, *Increasing Student Retention* may be the companion you need for *Involvement in Learning*, especially because it is so much more specific and grounded in examples. With either starting point, almost anything one tries will be a plus for students, and a tonic for the institution.

Washington, D.C.
October 1985

Theodore J. Marchese
Vice-President
American Association
for Higher Education

Preface

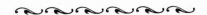

Our experience consulting with more than 375 colleges and universities over the past decade suggests that there are few institutions in this country that could not reduce their freshman-to-sophomore year attrition rate by one-third. And our success in working with these institutions indicates that this is a realistic goal.

Effective retention practices as defined in this book focus on improving campus programs, services, attitudes, and behaviors, resulting in quality educational experiences for students and, at the same time, in significant increases in enrollments. Time after time we have seen colleges with this focus thriving while their fellow institutions fall victim to spiraling college costs, decreasing federal support for education, increasing fiscal constraints, declining public confidence, and a diminishing pool of traditional-age college students.

Successful institutions know that ultimately student retention is a by-product of student success and satisfaction. As they market themselves honestly and effectively; strive to improve the quality of campus programs and services; put the most caring and competent faculty, advisers, and staff in frontline contact positions; and work hard at matching student needs with responsive services and support, they reap the benefits of full classrooms. When students find that their needs are being met, when we facilitate their success in the classroom and help them translate that success into their lives beyond the campus, education becomes a clear priority for them and they return to the campus. In short, retention is linked to student learning and the development of basic life competencies.

We see the highly successful campuses of tomorrow putting students' needs and interests squarely at the center of their organizations today. They are wrapping programs and services around the student, rather than requiring that an individual student's needs be manipulated so that they might better fit the system.

For these reasons, changes that result in improved student retention are equally important on campuses with stable applicant pools and high retention rates as on those with serious enrollment and attrition problems. Whether prompted by a sense of opportunity or threat, colleges and universities around the country have pioneered many retention improvement efforts in recent years. A variety of strategies and practices have been designed and implemented, and enough have been judged successful that we can now begin to speak of the "state of the art" in college student retention.

And retention *is* a practitioner's art. At times it seems as though we have lost sight of this basic fact. In the literature of the past fifty years there has been considerable theoretical, scholarly, and empirical work on the dropout phenomenon. Indeed, the attrition problem has been vastly overstudied: it is now time to get to work. This book fills the gap in the literature by going far beyond merely identifying characteristics associated with attrition, focusing on the programs, practices, and people who can make a difference for students today. We have brought together some of the most talented and successful practitioners in the field who share with you their approaches to helping colleges mobilize people, design interventions, and implement strategies to get results.

Because we approach retention as a campuswide effort, this book will appeal to a campuswide audience, from the president's office to the classroom, the admissions office to the placement center. The book is comprehensive in scope. Following the path of students into and through the institution, if offers proven action-oriented guidelines for those who manage the retention systems on the campus—chief executive officers, deans, directors, department heads—as well as faculty members, academic advisers, admissions, financial aid and placement counselors, nontraditional returning adult and commuter program staff members, residence hall and orientation staff members, and others working in supportive student assistance roles. Additionally, it ought to be required reading for all campus retention task force members. The book should also be an invaluable resource for faculty and students in graduate programs in higher education and student personnel administration, counseling, and many other academic fields, who want to be on the cutting edge of exemplary practice.

Overview of the Contents

This is an action-oriented book replete with examples and illustrations of successful programs now in place on campuses throughout the country. The first part of the book presents a comprehensive overview of the concepts and principles involved in student attrition and retention and illustrates the practices that we know have an impact on student retention. The emphasis in the second and third parts is on providing guidelines for practitioners interested in improving the quality of programs, services, and activities on their own campuses. The concluding part describes processes for creating a campuswide change effort to improve the quality of programs and services provided for students.

Part One focuses on the institutional factors that have an impact on student retention. Chapter One introduces the themes of attrition and forces of persistence and identifies the many benefits that accrue to institutions that strive to improve the quality of student life on campus. Chapter Two provides a conceptual basis for understanding why students drop out and for redefining the term *dropout*. Chapter Three presents an innovative and highly useful model for exploring the positive and negative forces influencing an individual student's decision to persist or drop out. Chapter Four examines the newly documented close relationship between student learning and persistence and identifies the institutional features recent research has demonstrated to be associated with growth in student learning and increased retention rates and levels of alumni satisfaction.

Targeting and better serving student populations that retention research has shown to be particularly dropout prone is the subject of Part Two. Our experience reveals that the most effective retention strategies are those that directly focus on serving specific groups of students. Chapters Five through Nine zero in on ways to better serve students who come from low-income families, academically underprepared students, students who are undecided about their majors, those who are older than traditional college age, and commuting students. Each of these chapters highlights significant research related to the academic success of a high-risk group and then identifies currently successful academic and nonacademic support services that increase retention of this group. Chapter authors draw upon their own extensive research and experience in making specific, innovative recommendations for the design of programs, services, and activities that provide support and encouragement for high-risk groups.

Institutional interventions in specific areas of campus life provide the focus for Part Three, which highlights specific practices that have a positive impact on student persistence. Each of the authors in this part has had considerable success in designing and implementing successful retention practices and strategies, and the chapters have a practical focus, building on the principles and recommendations put forth in Part Two. Chapters Ten through Seventeen follow the flow of a student's interaction with an institution, from recruiting and admitting through financial aid applications and awards, orientation, academic advising, academic reinforcement, teaching, career planning and counseling, housing, and student activities. Each chapter provides concrete information to assist practitioners in the design, redesign, and implementation of programs, activities, or services in each of the service areas. From smoothing the transition to college life to enlivening the classroom and residence halls, these interventions are designed to recruit and nurture graduates-to-be.

Across the country we see faculty, staff, and administrators motivated by the desire to enhance student success on campus, actively structuring partnerships across the campus in their search for better ways to serve their students. Part Four of the book is outcome oriented, focusing on ways of actually bringing about change on campus. Building upon the theories, principles, and practices discussed in the first three parts of the book, the chapters in this part examine the research and strategies necessary to translate knowledge into action, suggest how to motivate campus support behind retention efforts, present case studies of individual campus success stories, and—most important—show how to make campuswide participation the cornerstone of an effective retention program.

The purpose of Chapter Eighteen, on retention research, is not to cover methodology and research design in detail, since much has been done in this area already. Rather, the chapter underscores the role and importance of evaluation and research in retention efforts by providing vivid illustrations of how documented retention efforts can have an impact on campus.

Chapter Nineteen presents the basic principles for bringing about successful change efforts on campus based on current principles of organizational change and development. Chapter Twenty goes on to specifically discuss ways of involving faculty in a change effort as frontline retention agents.

Chapter Twenty-one features thirteen retention case studies from schools such as Harvard College, Jefferson Community College, Western New Mexico State University, and Notre Dame University. Although an emphasis on student success is the common thread running through all the case studies, each school has explored very different approaches to better serving its students, based on its own individual character and situation. The chapter also includes a catalogue of successful practices drawn from a nationwide survey. The catalogue includes capsule descriptions of innovative programs now in place on campuses in areas ranging from advising to academic alert systems to creating peer support and involvement experiences.

The concluding chapter pulls together the major themes introduced in the book and ends with a step-by-step process for mobilizing and organizing a retention improvement effort as a campuswide activity.

Overall, this book illustrates that the key to student retention is to help students to be more successful—to motivate, provide, and deliver experiences in which student confidence is built and student learning takes place. Campuses that provide students with this type of laboratory for developing their potential are campuses that enjoy higher retention rates. In our recent nationwide study we have found that the best retaining campuses have created tight webs of academic and student support services that assist the student in successfully accomplishing his or her objectives. Surprisingly, this is more characteristic of highly selective institutions than it is of many less selective ones. We have found that in many institutions where students need this type of comprehensive support the most, there is a feeling that it would be handholding to provide such a comprehensive and coordinated approach. Yet our experience strongly suggests that just the opposite is true. Regardless of selectivity, we measure an institution's quality on the basis of its ability to promote student success and retention by creating a supportive staying environment.

Acknowledgments

From beginning to end this project has been a team effort. We want to thank the American College Testing Program (ACT), and in particular, David Crockett, vice-president for public affairs, for his generous support and enthusiasm for the project. We also owe many thanks to Donald Clifton, president and founder of Selection Research, Inc., for focusing our attention so squarely on people as the key element in making colleges work better for students.

Collaboration with many people was needed to pull this volume together. We are indebted to the chapter authors for their willingness to share their expertise and the fruits of their experience and research. Since the beginning of this project, Ursula Delworth, Jossey-Bass Publishers' executive editor of this series, has enthusiastically provided us with much encouragement and wise editorial direction. We also want to thank the hundreds of colleges and universities that have served as our laboratory over the years and have provided us with such a rich base of experience.

We are especially grateful and indebted to Donna Appleglise, ACT National Center program secretary, whose cheerful enthusiasm, professional attitude, and superb administrative and technical skills have seen us through the preparation of numerous drafts. At every stage of the writing and editing process, her remarkable efficiency and eye for detail were invaluable and contributed much to the completion of the final manuscript.

Finally, we each want to thank our families for their constant support and encouragement.

Iowa City, Iowa   Lee Noel
October 1985   Randi Levitz
                                                     Diana Saluri

Contents

Contents

**Part Four: Guidelines and Models for Achieving
Retention Results**

The Authors

Lee Noel is cofounder and president of the Noel/Levitz Centers for Institutional Effectiveness and Innovation. He received his B.S. degree (1956) from Illinois State University in education, his M.S. degree (1959) from the University of Illinois in educational administration, and his Ph.D. degree (1969) from Northwestern University in student personnel administration. Noel joined the American College Testing Program (ACT) in 1971, and served first as regional director and later as regional vice-president. He founded the ACT National Center for the Advancement of Educational Practices in 1979 and served as its first executive director until 1984. In 1965, prior to joining ACT, Noel served as associate director of the Illinois State Scholarship Program for students. He has also been a teacher, campus administrator, and lecturer in higher education.

Noel has become a nationally recognized authority on college student retention and enrollment management and the *Chronicle of Higher Education* has identified him as a pioneer in this area. He is the author, coauthor, or editor of numerous articles, monographs, and books, including *Reducing the Dropout Rate* (1978), *What Works in Student Retention* (1980), *Mobilizing the Campus for Retention: An Innovative Quality-of-Life Model* (1981), *How to Succeed with Academically Underprepared Students* (1982), and *Organizing the Campus for Retention* (1982).

He has conducted over 100 national retention/enrollment development conferences attended by 12,000 college administrators and faculty from 1,800 campuses, served as keynote speaker at more than 200 national and regional educational meetings, and has consulted directly with more than 300 institutions.

Randi Levitz is cofounder and executive vice-president of the Noel/Levitz Centers for Institutional Effectiveness and Innovation. She received her B.A. degree (1970) in history and her M.S. degree (1972) in education from the State University of New York at Albany, and her Ph.D. degree (1982) from the University of Michigan in higher education. She was affiliated with the American College Testing Program (ACT) National Center for the Advancement of Educational Practices during 1981–1984, where she served first as research specialist and then as assistant director and director of postsecondary practices. She joined ACT's Research and Development Division as research assistant in 1978 after serving as a campus administrator and academic adviser.

Levitz's professional activities and research efforts focus on student retention through the perspectives of organizational development, staffing, teaching and advising, and marketing. In addition to consulting directly with colleges and universities across the country, she has codirected over 60 national conferences attended by more than 5,000 college administrators and faculty members from over 1,000 campuses and has been a featured presenter at more than 50 national and regional educational meetings.

She is the coauthor or editor of a number of recent articles on retention and advising and other publications including *Attracting and Retaining Adult Learners* (1980), *How to Succeed with Academically Underprepared Students* (1982), and *Organizing the Campus for Retention* (1982).

Diana Saluri is an editor at the American College Testing Program (ACT) National Center for the Advancement of Educational Practices and a visiting assistant professor of English at the University of Iowa. She received her B.A. degree (1971) from Grinnell College in American studies and both her M.A. degree (1977) in journalism and her Ph.D. degree (1980) in English from the University of Iowa. Her areas of interest include modern American fiction, the teaching of writing, and developing successful college admissions publications.

In addition to teaching literature and writing for many years, she has worked on several University of Iowa admissions publications and has written free-lance feature stories for a number of publications.

She has also worked as an adviser and learning center coordinator for high-risk student athletes at the University of Iowa and has written a study skills manual and a student handbook for student athletes.

She has published journal articles on the fiction of novelist Wright Morris and on teaching underprepared students, and has coauthored a book on community colleges, *Beacons for Change* (with John E. Roueche, George A. Baker, and William M. Jaap, 1983).

Edward "Chip" Anderson is the director of preparatory programs at the University of California at Los Angeles. He received his B.A. degree (1964) in speech and history and his M.A. degree (1966) in adult education from Pasadena College and his Ph.D. degree (1970) from UCLA in educational psychology and counseling. While working on his doctorate, he designed and directed one of the first college preparatory programs for Vietnam veterans. He has also directed a UCLA academic support program for low-income and minority students, the freshman and transfer summer instructional programs for underprepared students, and three tutorial centers on campus.

Lorraine C. Carpenter most recently served as a graduate research associate in education at the Ohio State University. She received her B.M. degree (1968) in music education and her M.M. degree (1972) in vocal performance from the University of North Carolina at Greensboro, and her Ph.D. degree (1984) in educational administration from the Ohio State University. Carpenter has been a music instructor at the elementary, junior high, and community college levels and has frequently performed as a soprano soloist. Her major professional interests are community college administration and strategic planning within colleges and universities.

David S. Crockett is vice-president for public affairs at the American College Testing Program (ACT). He received his B.A. degree (1957) in history and physical education from Ohio Wesleyan University and his M.A. degree (1958) in higher education from the University of Maryland. He has served as editor of two major resource documents designed to assist college personnel in improving the advising process and has contributed to numerous other publications including the second National Survey on Academic Advising (1983). He has directed more than 50 national academic advising seminars and was the recipient for ACT of the first Research Award for Outstanding Contribution to the field of Academic Advising from the National Academic Advising Association in 1982.

Aubrey Forrest is the director of instructional design and assessment at the American College Testing Program (ACT). He received his B.A. degree (1956) from Nebraska Wesleyan University in political science, his M.A. degree (1958) from Northwestern University in political science, and his Ph.D. degree (1959) from Northwestern University in educational psychology, higher education, and counseling. Since 1976, he has directed the ACT College Outcome Measures Program (COMP). He has held numerous college teaching and administrative positions and has directed seminars on educational program evaluation, served as a consultant, and authored articles, books, and assessment instruments.

Virginia N. Gordon is coordinator for academic advising in University College at the Ohio State University and adjunct assistant professor in the College of Education. She received her B.S. degree (1949) in education, her M.A. degree (1973) and Ph.D. degree (1977) in guidance and counseling from the Ohio State University. Gordon is a national consultant in the areas of academic and career advising. She has written numerous journal articles, is the author of *The Undecided College Student* (1984), and is coauthor of a text for alternative advising, *Academic Alternatives: Exploration and Decision Making* (with Susan Sears, 1984).

Eric V. Gravenberg is assistant dean of academic affairs in the Office of the Chancellor for the California State University system. He received his B.A. degree in black studies (1972) and his M.P.A. degree (1974) from California State University at Chico. Gravenberg has directed outreach and retention programs at Humboldt State University and authored a number of reports documenting the effectiveness of nontraditional retention approaches.

William Ihlanfeldt is vice-president for institutional relations and dean of admissions at Northwestern University. He received his B.A. degree (1959) in general studies from Illinois Wesleyan University, and his M.A. degree (1963) in counseling psychology and his Ph.D. degree (1970) in educational psychology from Northwestern University. Ihlanfeldt has published widely, and his book *Achieving Optimal Enrollments and Tuition* (1980) is the primary source on student recruitment and college costs in the field.

Ronald Lippitt is professor emeritus of sociology and psychology at the University of Michigan. He received his B.S. degree (1936) in group work from Springfield College and both his M.A. degree (1938) in child psychology and his Ph.D. degree (1940) in social and child psychology from the University of Iowa. His book *Dynamics of Planned Change* (1957) linked the discipline of social psychology with the professional practice of change-agentry. He is senior partner of Planned Change Associates, which provides consultation to colleges, businesses, and human service agencies.

Rosalind K. Loring, a consultant on lifelong learning, has formerly served as associate provost and as dean of the College of Continuing Education at the University of Southern California. She received her B.A. degree (1940) in art and her M.A.degree (1956) in adult education from the University of California at Los Angeles. In addition to a number of articles and book chapters on adult education, she has coauthored two books, *Breakthrough: Women into Management* (1972) and *New Life Options* (1976). In the past she has served as a member of the National Advisory Council on Extension and Continuing Education and as president of the Adult Education Association/USA. Currently she specializes in the management and financing of continuing education programs in higher education and in public libraries and museums.

A. Dallas Martin, Jr., is executive director of the National Association of Student Financial Aid Administrators. He received his B.A. degree (1965) in theatre arts and his M.A. degree (1969) in counseling and guidance psychology from Colorado State College, and his Ph.D. degree (1971) in college student personnel administration from the University of Northern Colorado. He has served as director of financial aid at a community college, as associate dean of student services at a four-year university, and as director of program planning and administration for the American College Testing Program. He has published numerous articles on student financial aid, including a chapter in *Handbook of Student Financial Aid* (Robert H. Fenske and Robert P. Huff, eds., 1983).

Martha C. Merrill is dean of the humanities division at the County College of Morris in Randolph, New Jersey. She received her B.A. degree (1974) in Russian literature from the University of Michigan, her M.L.S. (1977) in liberal studies and creative writing from Boston University, and her M.A. and Ph.D. (1982) in college administration from the University of Michigan. Merrill's current interests include writing across the curriculum, international and intercultural studies, remedial education, and the changing role of the community college in a changing society. A published poet, Merrill lectures frequently on the Soviet Union and is working on a novel.

William Moore, Jr., is professor of higher education administration at the Ohio State University. He received his B.A. degree (1952) in education from Stowe Teachers College and his M.A. degree (1958) and Ph.D. degree (1964) in educational administration from St. Louis University. He has held administrative posts at several colleges and universities and has written numerous articles and books on working with students who are academically deficient. His best known works are *Against the Odds: The Disadvantaged Student in the Community College* (1970) and *Blind Man on a Freeway: The Community College Administrator* (1971).

James P. Pappas is associate dean of continuing education, director of correspondence study, and professor of educational psychology at the University of Utah. He received his B.A. degree (1961) from the University of Utah in psychology, his M.S. degree (1964) from the Ohio University in counseling and student personnel administration, and his Ph.D. degree (1968) from Purdue University in clinical psychology. He recently coauthored a workbook titled "Promotional Techniques and Practices for Recruiting Adult Students" (1983). In 1982, he was the corecipient of the NUCEA (National University Continuing Education Association)/ACT administrative award.

John H. Rivers is associate dean of students and special services at Monterey Peninsula College in Monterey, California. He received his B.A. degree (1968) in sociology from California State University at Chico, his M.A. degree (1970) in psychology from California State University at Sonoma, and his Ph.D. degree (1973) in psychology from the Union for Experimenting Colleges and Universities. Rivers was the founding director for the Educational Opportunity Program at California State University at Chico and has designed other programs for disadvantaged students at Monterey Peninsula College. His book *From the Bottom Up to the Bottom* (1972) details historical accounts of experiences in administering programs for disadvantaged students during the turmoil of the 1960s.

John E. Roueche is professor and director of the Community College Leadership program of the University of Texas at Austin. He received his B.A. degree (1960) in history from Lenoir-Rhyne College, his M.A. degree (1961) in history from Appalachian State University, and his Ph.D. degree (1964) in education administration from Florida State University. Roueche has made presentations to more than 1,000 colleges and universities and has published several books and articles. His latest study, with George A. Baker and Suanne D. Roueche, is *College Responses to Low-Achieving Students: A National Study* (1983). His study with George Baker of teaching excellence in American schools and colleges will be published in late 1985.

Suanne D. Roueche is editor of *Innovation Abstracts*, a weekly publication of the University of Texas National Institute for Staff and Organizational Development (NISOD), and senior lecturer in the department of educational administration at the University of Texas at Austin. She received her B.A. degree (1964) in English from North Texas State University and her M.A. degree (1967) and Ph.D. degree (1976) in education administration from the University of Texas at Austin. She is the author of five books and numerous articles and has served as consultant to many colleges on serving underprepared students. Her most recent study, conducted with John E. Roueche and George A. Baker, is *College Responses to Low-Achieving Students: A National Study* (1983).

Laurence N. Smith is vice-president for university marketing and student affairs at Eastern Michigan University. He received his B.A. degree (1960) from the University of Rochester in history and his M.Ed. degree (1961) from the State University of New York at Buffalo. He also serves as a management consultant. In his work with colleges he stresses marketing, retention, managing limited resources, and using new volunteer resources. He is a coauthor of *Mobilizing the Campus for Retention:*

An Innovative Quality-of-Life Model (with Ronald Lippitt, Lee Noel, and Dorian Sprandel, 1981). Also scheduled for publication in 1986 are two books: *Adventures in Self-Management: Action Planning for Personal Success*, with Ronald Lippitt, and *Higher Education Marketing for Adult-Learners*, with Carol Aslanian.

Dorian Sprandel is associate vice-president for student affairs at Eastern Michigan University. He received his B.A. degree (1963) from Albion College in English and history, his M.A. degree (1965) from Michigan State University in counseling, and his Ph.D. degree (1969) from Michigan State University in psychology and higher education. Sprandel has published articles on organizational change and curriculum development and was coauthor of *Mobilizing the Campus for Retention: An Innovative Quality-of-Life Model* (1981). He also serves as a consultant to business and service organizations and as an enrollment management specialist.

Hazel Z. Sprandel, a counseling psychologist in private practice, most recently served as associate director of student educational services at Washington University in St. Louis, Missouri. She received her B.A. degree (1942) from the University of Nebraska in mathematics and English, and her M.A. degree (1965) and Ph.D. degree (1969) from Washington University in counseling psychology. Sprandel is coeditor of *Serving Handicapped Students* (with M. R. Schmidt, 1980) and *Helping the Learning-Disabled Student* (with M. R. Schmidt, 1982). She is the author of *The Psychoeducational Use and Interpretation of the Wechsler Adult Intelligence Scale-Revised* (1985), as well as various articles.

Sylvia S. Stewart is assistant to the vice-chancellor for administrative affairs at the University of Maryland at College Park. She received her B.A. degree (1968) from Berea College in history and her M.S. degree (1972) from the Ohio University in journalism. Stewart has served as director of commuter affairs and the National Clearinghouse for Commuter Affairs at the University of Maryland at College Park. She is the editor of *Commuter Students: Enhancing Their Educational Experiences* (1983).

Vincent Tinto is associate professor of sociology and education at Syracuse University. He received his B.S. degree (1965) in physics and history at Fordham University, his M.S. degree (1967) in physics at Rensselaer Polytechnic Institute, and his Ph.D. degree (1971) in sociology of education at the University of Chicago. Tinto has consulted widely with colleges and private state and federal agencies on matters concerning student retention, institutional assessment, and inequality in higher education. He has published numerous articles and reports and is currently completing a major book on student departure in higher education.

Bonnie S. Titley is director of academic advising at Colorado State University. She received her B.A. degree (1959) and M.A. degree (1962) in English from the University of Colorado and her Ed.D. (1976) in higher education from the University of Northern Colorado. Her research interests center on the undecided student and students who change majors. She has published several articles and has consulted with several institutions on the improvement of advising and the training of faculty advisers.

Terrence J. Toy is associate professor of geography at the University of Denver. He earned his B.A. degree (1969) and M.A. degree (1970) from the State University of New York at Buffalo and his Ph.D. degree (1973) from the University of Denver, all in the field of geography. Toy has published extensively in the areas of geomorphology and climatology. Since directing the Retention Project at the Unversity of Denver, he has been a faculty member at numerous American College Testing Program retention workshops and has spoken at several campuses on organizing retention efforts. In 1982 he received the University of Denver Distinguished Teaching Award and has been further recognized by other segments of the university for his outstanding contributions as a faculty member.

M. Lee Upcraft is director of the Division of Counseling and Health Services, associate professor of education, and cofounder of the Total Alcohol Awareness Program at Pennsylvania State University. He received his B.A. degree (1960) in history, and his M.A. degree (1961) in guidance and counseling from the State University of New York at Albany, and his Ph.D. degree (1967) in student personnel administration from Michigan State University. Upcraft has served as a consultant and has published several journal articles. He is the principal author of two books, *Residence Hall Assistants in College* (1982) and *Learning to Be a Resident Assistant* (1982), and is associate editor of the New Directions for Student Services sourcebooks for Jossey-Bass Inc., Publishers.

Leonard A. Valverde is the director of the Office for Advanced Research in Hispanic Education and professor of educational administration at the University of Texas at Austin. He received his B.A. degree (1966) in liberal arts and history at California State University at Los Angeles, and both his M.A. degree (1971) and his Ph.D. degree (1974) in education from the Claremont Graduate School. Valverde's professional interests and publications concern the access and retention of ethnic and racial minority student populations and the equality issues institutions face in serving these students.

Increasing Student Retention

~~~~~~~~~

*Effective Programs
and Practices for Reducing
the Dropout Rate*

1

Increasing Student Retention: New Challenges and Potential

Lee Noel

The excitement ahead in higher education lies in what an institution can do to deliver learning—student growth and success—that leads to reenrollment, to the desire on the part of students to come back. Recent national reports on the status of education suggest that the key in the 1980s is going to be quality. The more students learn, the more they sense they are finding and developing a talent, the more likely they are to persist; and when we get student success, satisfaction, and learning together, persistence is the outcome.

Reenrollment or retention is not then the goal; retention is the result or by-product of improved programs and services in our classrooms and elsewhere on campus that contribute to student success. If retention alone becomes the goal, institutions will find themselves engaged in trying to hold students at all costs. Pressuring students to stay when it is not in their best interests to do so is not only wrong morally but also counterproductive; it often results in an accelerated attrition rate. Pressuring or trapping behavior from institutional personnel has a spreading effect: dissatisfied students who are leaving take others with them. There are no magical tricks. Gimmicks to attract and retain students in the 1980s simply will not work over any extended period of time. We are finding that what really encourages students to enter and to persist is the institution giving them the chance to think through their futures, to discover their talents, to grow and develop. This takes hard work and resources—human and financial—on the part of the institution.

As the bottom line, we find that students reenroll when they are having an exciting, substantive learning and personal growth experience that they can relate to their future development and success. We need to be more specific in interpreting for our students and potential students how the outcomes of education, the competencies they will develop with us, will be useful in adult roles beyond the classroom. Boyer and Levine (1981, p. 20) note, "On campus after campus, there is no agreement about the meaning of a college education. We are more confident about the length of a baccalaureate degree program than we are about its substance." We convey set notions to students about the time it takes to complete a degree, but in too many institutions we are not really sure what we want our students to know when they finish and whether they will have acquired the skills to put that knowledge to work.

This need to emphasize and measure outcomes will require that we in higher education increasingly think of ourselves not as being in the education business but as being in the talent business—talent identification and talent development. If an institution creates the environment where a student's talents can be identified and developed, an amazing degree of learning and personal growth can take place. This growth can be in a classroom, on a stage, on an athletic field, in a club, in an organization—anywhere an institution is responsive to the specific needs of students, helping them in very individualized ways to identify and develop their talents, to get hooked into and involved with some significant individual or group on campus.

Emphasizing outcomes also means we will need to move away from some of the more traditional indicators of quality and excellence—such as admitting only the top half of one percent of students—to new indicators, such as increasing the competency base of students. As Astin (1980, p. 132) notes, "Quality is equated here not with physical facilities or faculty credentials but rather with a continuing process of critical self-examination that focuses on the institution's contribution to the students' intellectual and personal development." The recent National Institute of Education report, *Involvement in Learning* (1984), similarly encourages us to replace proxy measures of educational excellence that are really nothing more than input measures with evidence that "demonstrable improvements in student knowledge, capacities, skills, and attitudes" take place between beginning and completing college.

This value-added notion of education puts the emphasis on the outcomes of the education process—student learning, growth, and development—where it ought to be. If we can help students find their talents and help those talents grow, then we will have a right to consider ourselves part of a quality institution.

Further, a wise retention strategy is the best alternative to pressures facing education. For as we look at the future, at the dwindling number of high school graduates, we see twin challenges ahead. If we want to keep our colleges and universities viable through an adequate level of enrollment, the challenges are to encourage enrollment for the first time and, more important, to encourage reenrollment. As Green (1983, p. 3) points out, "Stable enrollments ultimately depend on the retention of currently enrolled students as well as the steady inflow of new students. According to a recent Carnegie Council report, increased attrition—not recruitment difficulties—is the cause of enrollment problems among institutions that actually experienced enrollment declines during the past decade."

This introductory chapter will first look at three factors in the environment of higher education today: the threat of dwindling enrollments, current myths about attrition, and how today's students weigh the costs and benefits of college going. In this context I consider the themes of attrition—why students leave and why they stay—and how a campuswide effort to promote student success, satisfaction, and retention is dependent upon a people-oriented approach that emphasizes the careful selection and encouragement of teachers and staff members who key in on students' individual talents to counter attrition.

The Current Environment

The need for identifying and interpreting for students the benefits of a liberal education is made all the more pressing by the threat of three storm clouds hovering over higher education today. These clouds are in the forms of a diminishing student pool, attrition rates, and students' analyses of the cost-benefit of their educations.

The Student Pool. First, there is a decline in the number of high school graduates. In 1963 we had slightly over four million births in this country: today's potential students. But by 1975, the annual birth rate dropped to just over three million—a 26 percent decline (*Statistical Abstract of the United States*, 1984). Declining numbers of high school graduates in all but ten states are forecast for the period between 1979 and 1995. The Rocky Mountain states, Texas, and parts of the Southwest will experience a 0 to 58 percent gain in the numbers of high school graduates. But in the Northeast, those numbers will decline by 31 percent or more; in the Midwest by 17 to 28 percent; and in the South by 2 to 15 percent ("Changing Numbers in High-School Graduating Classes," 1980).

Second, there has been a decline in the college-going rate among eighteen- to nineteen-year-old male high school graduates. In 1978 50 percent were enrolled in college, compared to 58 percent in 1970 (Frances, 1980). Although this represents a decrease, it may be that we have reached the bottom and that the future does not look quite as grim. As Frances notes, the college-going rate among women of all ages increased slightly from 45 percent in 1970 to 47 percent in 1978 and there was an increase in attendance among men twenty five years old and older in the same period. There is some indication that perhaps the economy and limited alternatives in the job market have been positive influences on student attendance.

Third, our data, based on ten years of intensive research, indicate that dropout rates experienced only minor fluctuations from the moderately high rate experienced in the mid 1970s. In our nationwide study, 944 institutions were asked, "Of your full-time entering freshmen who entered in the fall, how many are not enrolled one year later?'' These data for the years 1975, 1976, and 1977 were converted to attrition percentages. At the two-year public institutions, on average, 44 percent of the full-time entering freshmen were not there the second year; at the four-year public institutions, 33 percent; at the two-year private institutions, 37 percent; at the four-year private institutions, 29 percent. Over all types of institutions, the freshman-to-sophomore attrition rate increased slightly from 33 percent in 1975 and 1976 to 35 percent in 1977. When we aggregated the data, we found that 34 percent of our full-time entering freshmen across America were not at the same institution one year later. Of these, some transferred and some completed educational objectives; many others simply dropped out of higher education altogether (Beal and Noel, 1980).

In 1983, a secondary analysis of data annually provided to American College Testing (ACT) Program by all U.S. colleges and universities was conducted. These self-reported data, which include freshman-to-sophomore year attrition rates, reflect the percentage of full-time freshmen who entered college in the fall of 1981 who returned to that same college in the fall of 1982. Data were available by degree level and control for 2,432 institutions. As seen in Table 1, the dropout rate across all types of institutions was 32 percent; overall, very little change occurred since the study several years earlier.

Table 1. National Attrition Dropout Rates.

Degree Level/Control	Freshman-to-Sophomore Year Number of Institutions	Percentage
Two-Year Public	767	46
Two-Year Private	165	30
B.A./B.S. Public	77	30
B.A./B.S. Private	592	26
M.A. Public	207	31
M.A. Private	359	22
Ph.D. Public	144	26
Ph.D. Private	121	15
	2,432 total	32 percent

Source: Adapted from Noel and Levitz, 1983.

Investigation revealed a relationship between admissions selectivity and attrition rates. Actual freshman class average ACT/Scholastic Aptitude Test (SAT) scores were available for 1,473 colleges and universities. The information in Table 2 demonstrates the linear relationship that exists between ability

Table 2. ACT/SAT Scores of Entering Freshmen
and Freshman-to-Sophomore Year Attrition Rate.

Average ACT/SAT Scores of Entering Freshman		Freshman-to-Sophomore Year Attrition Rate	
		Number of Institutions	Percentage
ACT	SAT V & M		
≥26	≥1100	89	10
22–25.9	931–1099	275	18
18–21.9	800–930	656	29
15–17.9	700–800	363	39
15	700	90	41
		1,473 total	29 percent

Source: Adapted from Noel and Levitz, 1983.

levels of entering students and attrition at the end of the freshman year. As we had expected, institutions admitting the most able students—ACT Composite of 26 or above, SAT (Verbal and Math) of 1100 or above—experienced the smallest attrition rates; an average of 10 percent. Essentially open-door institutions, those in which the average ACT score was below 15 and the SAT below 700, experienced an average attrition rate of 41 percent. The relationship between entering ability-level and attrition was further explored among four-year institutions in the data base. Institutions were asked to report the selectivity of their admissions policy according to five categories: (1) Highly Selective—majority of accepted freshmen in top 10 percent of high school graduating class; (2) Selective—majority of accepted freshmen in top 25 percent of high school graduating class; (3) Traditional—majority of accepted freshmen in top 50 percent of high school graduating class; (4) Liberal—many accepted freshmen from lower half of high school graduating class; and (5) Open—all high school graduates accepted to limit of capacity.

Table 3. Freshman-to-Sophomore Year Attrition Rates in Four-Year Institutions.

Self-reported Admissions Selectivity	Public Institutions			Private Institutions		
	B.A./B.S. (%)	M.A. (%)	Ph.D. (%)	B.A./B.S. (%)	M.A. (%)	Ph.D. (%)
Highly Selective	21[a]	15	13	7	11	8
Selective	16	25	22	15	17	16
Traditional	24	27	27	24	22	21
Liberal	30	34	33	31	29	27[a]
Open	44	37	31	35	24	15
	(N = 77)	(N = 207)	(N = 144)	(N = 591)	(N = 353)	(N = 119)

[a]Mean based on <5 institutions.

Source: Adapted from Noel and Levitz, 1983.

Self-reported admissions selectivity classifications were available for 1,491, or 99 percent, of the four-year institutions in the data base. These data are displayed in Table 3.

As institutions admit students more selectively, they are likely to experience increased persistence rates. Yet the real test of quality lies not with an assessment of the abilities of students on entering an institution, but with the degree of improvement in student learning and success on campus as reflected in the institution's retention rate. Our experience indicates that institutions focusing squarely on student success experience significantly higher persistence rates than the type and selectivity of the institution might suggest.

Dispelling Myths About Attrition. In order to begin thinking of retention in terms of identifying the benefits of a quality education, we need to consider and dispel some of the myths about the causes of attrition. One myth is that retention means lowering standards. Our experience suggests that this is absolutely incorrect. On one campus where I later consulted, faculty had responded to the president's directive to "retain students at all costs" by giving students higher grades than they deserved. In one year the attrition rate actually increased 11 percentage points. On average, students who left had higher grade point averages than those who stayed. Inflated grades and watered-down expectations and requirements clearly have an adverse effect on some of our more capable students. If what students get is not substantive—if they don't sense they are learning, growing, and building skills that are preparing them for the future—they are likely to say it is not worth it.

Dropouts are flunkouts—another myth. When we look at confidential data supplied to us by many institutions, it is not at all uncommon to find that the mean grade point average of students who drop out is equal to or greater than the grade point average of students who persist.

A third myth is that students drop out because of financial problems. Research suggests that financial need and availability of financial aid have more to do with college access and choice than with persistence (Cope and Hannah, 1975). Student data that Levitz and I have examined at two colleges indicate that little difference exists between persisters and dropouts in the amount of money already borrowed or anticipated to be borrowed. Once students get to college, factors other than financial considerations seem to take over. If those other factors are positive, the students are willing to pay the price, to find ways to finance their education. Although recent changes in federal financial aid regulations may now be affecting persistence, data on this effect are not yet available.

Finally there is the feeling at many campuses that retention is the responsibility of student services; student success is someone else's concern. A fallacy that exists among many faculty is that enrollment maintenance is a function of the admissions office. The message to the admissions office is, "Go out and bring in some more students, and while you're at it, make them a little smarter." Too often retention activities are carried out almost exclusively by student services, even though it is now clear that the key people on campus in a retention effort are those on the academic side of the institution: classroom teachers, academic advisers, and academic administrators.

The Cost-Benefit Scale. A third factor in today's environment is that students are becoming better informed and more sophisticated consumers. This is particularly true of adult returning students, but all students are more demanding than they have been. They are scrutinizing their options. They are not taking requirements for granted simply because they are listed in the college catalogue. They are asking more and tougher questions: "Why is this important? How do you know it will help me? What is your evidence?" To understand how students judge whether their educational experience is preparing them for the future and living up to their expectations, we can use the cost-benefit theory of private industry. With it we can visualize how students weigh the benefits of their educational experience, why they leave, and why they stay.

We can envision students coming onto our campuses with very finely-tuned scales in their heads. On one side of their scales are the costs: tuition, housing, transportation, time, forfeited income, and effort. On the other side are the benefits: job entry skills, transferable job skills, self-satisfaction, money, upward

mobility, status, life-style, and respectability. These benefits can
be split into economic benefits and non-economic benefits. Taken
together, the non-economic benefits are the quality-of-life skills,
the outcomes we need to identify for students because, although
they may not talk about it in these terms, students are making
decisions on a daily basis that involve some interpretation of
the weight on both sides of the cost-benefit scale. They drop
out when the costs are heavy, when they do not sense that the
benefits are being delivered or that they are very important,
when education becomes less than a major priority in their lives.

This brings us back to interpreting outcomes, to the need
for additional resources, additional help to interpret and explain
to students the curricula and the options available on our campuses. The process of identifying the benefits that tip the cost-
benefit scale needs to begin in the advising offices and in the
classroom. Faculty need to identify rather specifically what it
is they have to offer the students in their classes and how this
information is going to be useful to them. This should happen
in general education classes as well as in more vocationally
oriented courses. As Bean (1983, p. 32) notes, "While institutional fit is very much the outcome of social forces, institutional
commitment comes from personal assessments of the institution's value to [students] and their own educational goals."

Identifying the Themes of Attrition

When it comes to getting beyond the current myths and
identifying just who the dropout-prone student is, just what tips
the cost-benefit scale, we find that it is almost impossible to pinpoint the single, specific reason why a student leaves. Dropping
out of college is a complex decision that is nearly always the
result of a combination of factors. We therefore have come to
think in terms of the themes of dropping out, the forces of attrition, and what we can do to counter them. The major themes
we have found are academic boredom and uncertainty about
what to study, transition/adjustment problems, limited and/or
unrealistic expectations of college, academic underpreparedness,
incompatibility, and irrelevancy.

Academic Boredom and Uncertainty. Two of the key themes we have isolated are academic boredom and uncertainty about major and career goals. These themes are intertwined; at the root of academic boredom is uncertainty about career goals. Students without specific goals cannot have the same drive that others, moving toward a goal, have. One of the first objectives of an institution ought to be to help students think through, in a very rational, informed way, the kinds of careers or majors that are most appropriate for them. This does not have to be accomplished in the first week, the first term, or the first year. It should be a process that begins in and continues throughout the first year, perhaps even throughout the second.

Academic boredom sets in for undecided students because learning is not quite as relevant to those who do not have a goal. Tests, courses, and curricula lack meaning to students who question the worth of requirements, who ask, "Why do we have to take these three units in the humanities?" To guide these students, we need to provide not only career counseling, but the resources and personnel to interpret for them the value of course requirements. We need, for instance, to give a good, sound rationale for a solid course in literature, to explain how that course is going to contribute to their skill bank and be meaningful to them beyond graduation. This kind of guidance takes top-notch frontline teachers in the classroom and academic advisers in the advising office who are willing and able to interpret the curriculum for students. To serve as such an "educational interpreter" requires very sophisticated marketing skills; educators must continue to point out and explain to many students, even after matriculation, what educational advantage the institution has to offer them.

Another root of academic boredom is lack of challenge. If we neglect to test basic skills and consequently place students in courses for which they are overprepared, putting them through the same paces as in high school, they are not going to stay. Without appropriate intake data, institutions are forced to process students as standard objects moving through the institution on an assembly line. We need to provide opportunities for accelerated studies through advanced placement, credit by examination, portfolio assessment, and course bypass examinations, as well as through more opportunities for individualized instruction.

Finally, academic boredom sets in when students encounter poor teaching and advising. Good teaching and advising is what they contract for when they come to the institution. If they do not get them, the benefits will not outweigh the costs.

My experience indicates that the second major theme of attrition, uncertainty about what to study, is the most frequent reason talented students give for dropping out of college. Levitz and I have found that students who drop out without having decided on a major often have higher grade point averages than other dropouts at their colleges, sometimes even higher than those who persist. Other studies that Levitz and I have reviewed have corroborated that some form of uncertainty and tentativeness about career choice exists in three out of four entering freshmen (see, for example, Titley and Titley, 1980). The options a student has today upon leaving college and entering the career world are vastly expanded over those of a few years ago. The scope of these options can be overwhelming. Of the one million students who take the ACT Assessment each year, two out of three indicate that they are not fully sure of their vocational choice (*American College Testing Program High School Profile Report*, 1984). It is estimated that 75 percent of students who enter college with a declared major change their minds at least once during their four years on campus (Gordon, 1984).

As Gordon demonstrates in her chapter on undecidedness, students are clearly dropout prone unless they get help with the decision-making process involved in declaring a major. We thus ought to be treating each one of our entering freshmen as being undecided and in need of some help with career and personal future planning. That is the best way to put into place the kind of motivation that will make those students attentive and productive in the classroom. They need comprehensive career planning and placement services to assess their academic abilities and career interests. We need, in a thoughtful, systematic way, to help them arrive at a chosen goal through our courses and support programs. This may require the use of intrusive methods to get students involved in career exploration and to communicate to them the links between course/program outcomes and career opportunities. In academic advising and career planning offices as well as in their classrooms during freshman year, students need to encounter the mentor, the faculty member, the adult, the trained professional who can facilitate student decision making on a one-to-one basis. In our extensive work with campuses over the years, Levitz and I have found that institutions where significant improvement in retention rates has been made, almost without exception give extra attention to career/life planning and to academic advising; they often combine the two functions.

Transition/Adjustment Difficulties. Recent high school graduates have spent four years putting into place a series of support systems in their high schools. There they were known, they performed, they were rewarded; suddenly, overnight they are in a new environment. They have to start all over. It is not difficult for them to become lost—to say, "I'll just retreat to my past group"—unless we provide comprehensive, ongoing orientation activities that begin before the first class session and continue throughout the first year. These students will also benefit from a campuswide awareness of typical new student needs reflected in concerned, competent advisers and well-trained caring staff in residence halls and campus offices and a campuswide alert-referral system.

Limited or Unrealistic Expectations of College. Another important theme grows out of the growing numbers of first-generation college students. Through the 1980s and beyond there will be an increasing percentage of low-income students coming out of our high schools who do not have the benefit of a parent or sibling who has already gone to college. As Valverde points out in his chapter on low-income students, to pave the way for these students we need orientation programs that link with advising. We need programs to carry these students through the registration process and through the critical first term. The programs must address the theme of uninformed or unrealistic expectations about the demands of college learning and college life.

Academic Underpreparedness. A nationwide study of the decline in literacy rates points to a related theme in attrition rates:

academic underpreparedness. The average high school graduate today is graduating with better than a *B* average and yet reads below the eighth-grade level (Roueche, Baker, and Roueche, 1984). As Cross pointed out to me in our discussion in 1983, "We have no more right to expect a student without reading skills to be an effective learner than we do to expect a carpenter without a hammer to be effective at pounding nails." We now know that you cannot overcome twelve years of learned failure through one course in reading and writing. To accommodate these students, we will need more assessing of basic skill levels for course placement as well as a more comprehensive set of academic/learning support services and a supportive learning environment that attends to the affective as well as academic development of students.

Incompatibility. A form of incompatibility occurs when an institution that does a good job with average and below-average students expends time and energy recruiting students from the top 3 percent of their high school classes. I have seen many fine institutions around the country, not equipped to serve the exceptionally bright student, put together recruiting packages to attract National Merit semifinalists. Retention begins with recruitment, with a good match between what the institution has to offer and what the student needs. To promote this kind of compatibility, institutions need to review their mission statements and target their recruiting efforts on the type of student they are best equipped to serve. The goal is to create honest, informative admissions materials that emphasize the institutions' distinctive merits and that will foster an informed decision on the part of the prospective student. The essential concept of market segmentation and carefully targeted recruitment are treated in detail in the chapter by Ihlanfeldt.

Irrelevancy. To counter irrelevancy, teachers should review their course content and instructional design to ensure that they are providing students with a concrete rationale for course requirements, a rationale that defines outcomes in relation to effective functioning in adult roles. In presenting material on a daily basis, they need to communicate these benefits in a vivid, effective, and realistic fashion.

Finally, as we attempt to design academic and student support services to counter these themes of attrition, it is very important that we reach out to those students who need the programs and services, and not merely wait for them to come to us. The importance and effectiveness of intrusive strategies and mandatory approaches have been reinforced in our studies, *What Works in Student Retention* (Beal and Noel, 1980) and *How to Succeed with Academically Underprepared Students* (Noel and Levitz, 1982), as well as in a number of unpublished, single-institution studies. One point is particularly clear: when student participation is mandatory, a quality experience *must* be provided. I can think of no more potent force of attrition than requiring a student to sit through or participate in a "helping" experience that does not contribute, in a very positive way, to that student's personal and educational growth.

Recognizing Retention as a Campuswide Responsibility

One of the most difficult challenges that I encounter as I visit campuses across the country is to convince faculty and staff that the enrollment level of the institution is a campuswide responsibility; I must dispel the myth that retention is the function of admissions or student services. To maintain enrollment on any campus, to identify and develop students' talents, takes at least three key ingredients: satisfied students and alumni; competent, caring faculty and staff; and concerned, aware administrators.

Critical Factors. First, enrollment is dependent upon satisfied students and alumni; they are, after all, an institution's best recruiters. This satisfaction is manufactured in classrooms by competent, caring faculty who believe that their mission is to reach individual students and have a positive impact on their lives. This is particularly true at a commuter institution where 90 to 98 percent of the contacts by students with that institution occur in the classroom. And promoting good teaching, in turn, takes a lot of reinforcement from concerned, aware administrators who recognize the importance of the relationship between teacher and student and look for ways to recognize and to reward faculty who make individualized contact with students.

Further, good teaching must be supported by "talent developers" on campus—those staff members responsible for meshing the institution's programs, services, and curriculum in such a way as to maximize success for individual students.

Next to caring faculty and staff and high-quality teaching, high-quality advising, counseling, and career planning services are rated as critical retention factors (Beal and Noel, 1980, p. 43). Again, these services involve the same kind of individualized support and attention students need from faculty. They involve helping students in an individual way think through who they are, getting them to answer for themselves such questions as: Who am I? What can I do? Where can I go? What is open to me? Where am I likely to be successful and satisfied? What will it take to get there?

Four Stages. The study of student retention has progressed through a number of stages over the past decade and a half. First, as retention became recognized as a key factor in enrollment management, researchers turned attention to the design of conceptual and predictive models of dropouts, focusing on personal, environmental, and social forces contributing to the phenomenon (Spady, 1971; Tinto, 1975; and Astin, 1975). Next, the emphasis shifted to more action-oriented responses, to what worked. Researchers documented colleges' attempts to counter the forces of attrition with constructive programs, strategies, and approaches (Beal and Noel, 1980). The third major thrust centered on principles of organizational development; campuses began to organize and mobilize campuswide retention efforts (see, for example, Noel and Levitz, 1982, 1983; and Smith and others, 1981). I can draw one clear conclusion from these recent efforts: the best, most thoughtfully designed curriculum, the most perfectly designed program or delivery strategy will be just another curriculum or program if one has not paid attention to those people who will be executing it. In my opinion, staffing will be squarely at the center of the fourth generation of work in student retention.

People as the Key. Keller (1983) reminds us that we are in the people business. It should not be surprising to learn that it is people who make a difference. It is people on campus—

teachers, advisers, staff members—those who come face-to-face with students each day, who provide the positive growth experiences for students that enable them to identify their goals and talents and learn how to put them to use. As our study establishes (Beal and Noel, 1980), caring attitude of faculty and staff is viewed as the most potent retention force on campus. Requiring courses does not guarantee learning, but competent, caring teachers in the classroom who are motivated to deliver learning can.

On the occasion of his retirement, Theodore Von Laue, professor of European history at Clark University in Worcester, Massachusetts, reflected on the "moral communication and moral attitudes" associated with teaching. He noted that "understanding, charity, goodwill . . . are the lubricants on which the subject matter slides more easily into student minds" (1983, p. 8). Teachers who feel, as does Von Laue, that teaching involves the whole beings of teachers and students in joint venture are really teachers. I make a distinction between this type of teacher and those information dispensers who believe that the art of teaching depends solely on one's competence in a discipline.

If we want to create a staying environment, this responsiveness to student needs must extend to everyone on campus—the telephone operator, the receptionist, the clerk at the cashier's window. Keller (1983, p. 136) illustrates this receptivity to others in his description of the attitude of the staff of the University of Maryland, Baltimore (UMBC) library, where "The librarians treat everyone—pimply farmboys; ghetto youths; nonbookish young scientists; adult mothers working on a graduate degree; bearded professors—like visiting ministers of education, the way professional waiters at New York's Russian Tea Room treat everyone from shop girls to Isaac Stern." This attitude, evident to Keller as he researched, is apparently evident to many others as well, for UMBC is reported to have the highest rate of library usage by students of any college or university in the state of Maryland.

In short, we need people working in frontline positions on our campuses who have a mission, a burning desire, to help students become all that they can become. Further, we need people who have a tremendous drive to establish rapport with students, people who are able to woo students, who make them feel that they are the most important people on campus—not the interruption of their work, but the purpose of it. The quality and responsiveness of our faculty and staff may be the most powerful resources available to us as we strive to have an impact on student satisfaction, success, and retention. We need competent receptionists, faculty, advisers, and librarians who are also able to woo students, who get turned on instead of turned off when a student comes for assistance. Finding these people is the challenge we face. As Baldridge (1981, p. 12) notes, some of the most important decisions involve staffing.

Staffing—An Approach for Getting the Right Person in the Right Place. To find the people who are truly responsive to others' needs, we are going to have to get more serious about selecting the right people for the right responsibilities on campus. We need to realize that when we take professors whose courses are cancelled because of insufficient enrollments and give them the academic advising assignments, we put ourselves in double jeopardy. We need to become more serious and more systematic about whom we hire and whom we assign to what tasks. As Keller (1983, p. 64) observes, "Two-thirds or more of any college's budget goes for academic, staff, and executive salaries. A college or university is usually judged by the quality of people it has. Yet many campuses have strangely paid relatively little attention to the quality and productivity of their people." And as President Cyert of Carnegie-Mellon University notes (in Keller, 1983, p. 137), "One of a manager's most important and time-consuming tasks is judging people. Like most managers, I think I'm an excellent judge of other human beings. Yet I estimate I haven't beaten random chance by much in my appointments." We need to devote more effort to this task.

On far too many college campuses I see two cardinal principles of management violated regularly. First, we continue to expect people to perform well outside their main talent areas. We expect people to do everything to the same level of competence—teach, advise, and simultaneously research. Second, as managers, we generally spend more time with those who perform poorly than in reinforcing those who excel.

Keller (1983) estimates that within the next decade the average university may experience a 40 percent turnover in faculty and staff positions. A recent study by Bowen and Schuster indicates that over the next twenty-five years, American colleges and universities will need to hire 500,000 faculty members, replacing virtually the entire professoriat. In thinking through what will be needed to deal with the oportunity this turnover presents, Bowen emphasizes teaching, saying that "writing books, jurying articles, and fundraising are add-ons," and not necessary qualifications (Evangelauf, 1984, p. 29). Bowen, a member of the National Institute of Education panel reporting in *Involvement in Learning* (1984), sums up that effort, saying that seventeen of their twenty-seven recommendations centered on the faculty and that the bottom line will be "greater attention to teaching" in the future.

The time to pay attention to staffing and to managing people is clearly upon us. This will require that administrators believe in and understand individual talents, match the talents of individuals to the responsibilities of positions, and create a climate conducive to the development of these talents, a climate in which recognizing faculty and staff who contribute to student development is foremost in the reward structure.

Selecting the right person for the right position will require that administrators give more thoughtful and systematic attention to staffing than they have in the past. One of the systematic selection methods currently in use was designed by Donald Clifton, a former professor of psychology at the University of Nebraska at Lincoln. Clifton's approach is centered on a structured interview process that identifies the patterns of thought, feeling, and behavior—life themes—of outstanding practitioners in the field. When staffing organizations, this process is used to identify talent, reliably and with validity in the selection, reassignment, and development of people. The process, available through Noel/Levitz Centers and in use for more than fifteen years, is making quantitative and qualitative improvements in more than 600 business, industrial, and health care organizations and more than 400 school districts nationwide.

If we on college campuses decide to take advantage of the theme strengths of individuals—if we make the most of the talents of the people we already have on campus, systematically hire more like our very best, and then manage them in a way that really develops their talents—think what a difference that will make. In some ways this will require a conceptual change of major proportion. In hiring people to put in front of our classes, in our advising offices, in our registrar's offices, and in libraries we must begin to look at factors in addition to degrees and publications—factors such as understanding, charity, and goodwill. This shift will require valuing the importance of actual performance in one's position as well as one's credentials. It means assessing outcomes as well as inputs.

If people are the key and staffing is the vehicle for putting the right person in the right place, the formula is incomplete without a concern for timing; we must make sure that these "right people" come into contact with students at the right time. *Involvement in Learning* (1984) focuses attention on the importance of the first year, when many new students are not now well served: they find themselves closed out of classes, given lower priority in advising and scheduling, and treated impersonally. The panel's first recommendation centers on a "front-loading" strategy: the reallocation of faculty and other institutional resources to better serve our entering students.

Critical Time Period. We have, in fact, found that the critical time in establishing the kind of relationships and one-to-one contacts between students and their teachers and advisers that contribute to student success and satisfaction occur during the first few weeks of the freshman year. It is not uncommon to find that of the students who drop out *during* the terms of the freshman year (not between terms), 50 percent drop out during the first six weeks (Myers, 1981). If students make it through that high-risk first year and return for the sophomore year, experience indicates the attrition rate begins to drop off by almost 50 percent each succeeding year.

Many institutions are now concentrating retention activities on that critical transition period of the first two, three, or six weeks of the first term. A three-year Minnesota study concluded that more than 50 percent of those students who did not have some kind of significant contact with an adviser, dormitory counselor, or teacher during the first three weeks would not be enrolled the succeeding year (Myers, 1981).

To encourage this kind of initial contact, many institutions are now urging their academic advisers to meet with each of their freshman advisees three times during that first term. In other institutions, ongoing orientation classes led by advisers meet weekly throughout the first term. Another strategy being employed is to urge faculty to give a substantive examination during the second or third week of the freshman year. For some students this is reality therapy: Goodbye high school, hello college. For others it provides the important reinforcement needed to overcome the anxiety of encountering a new level of competition.

A key step in improving retention is then recognition of the fact that those first sessions taught in freshman courses are probably the most important class sessions students will encounter during their college days. In line with a cost-benefit emphasis on positive outcomes, conscious efforts must be made in those first class meetings to reach students, to identify in specific ways the importance of that course, and how it is going to have value to them later on. To promote this kind of interaction campuswide, we need to get across to the entire campus community the changing needs of students, the changing demographics, and the changing demands students are bringing to our classrooms.

Measuring Outcomes

The link between retention and academic quality and concern for the individual student's development is borne out in a project currently being conducted by ACT's College Outcome Measures Project (COMP). As Forrest (1982) explains, COMP is concerned with identifying the outcomes of general education and determining how successfully these outcomes are achieved.

Essentially, what we are finding is that those programs and services that are linked to the delivery of the outcomes of general
education also contribute to persistence.

The COMP study divides these general education outcomes into two categories: (1) helping students develop the skills
and motivation necessary to graduate and (2) helping students
acquire the skills and abilities to read, think, and compute—
the abilities needed to function effectively in adult roles after
graduation. The emphasis in the second category is on adult
roles because today's students want to know how we are going
to help them be better employees or employers, friends, neigh-
bors, spouses, parents, citizens, policymakers, lifelong learners.
These are the outcomes that will be attractive to students. As
University of Iowa President James Freedman said at his in-
augural address (Oct. 25, 1982) in Iowa City, "The mission
is to prepare young men and women, not for the first year of
their first job, but for the next fifty years of their lives."

The concept of preparation for a variety of roles is becoming increasingly important in interpreting and promoting the
outcomes of general education. Bisconti and Solmon's six-year
follow-up study of more than 4,000 graduates of the class of 1965
indicated that one-half of the women and two-thirds of the men
chose their present occupation after completing college. Only
17 percent of the men and 31 percent of the women had chosen
their present careers before entering college (1976). Previous
studies have shown considerable career instability for the first
few years after college and have indicated that long-run occupational difference between individuals is most accurately assessed
after ten years in the labor force. Research also indicates that
people today experience a significant number of career changes
in their lives. About 33 percent of men and 67 percent of women
college graduates had to accept jobs unrelated to their college
majors in the 1970s, compared with only 10 percent of men and
13 percent of women in the early 1960s (Freeman and Hollomon,
1975). And the labor market is changing. "Research suggests
that pupils now in public schools will enter a labor market where
60–70 percent of the jobs are unknown" (Bennis, 1978, p. 100).

The world is clearly changing too rapidly to allow us to

realistically focus narrowly on career preparation. Yet students today are career-driven. To attract and retain these students, we need to make clear to them, to interpret for them, the importance of achieving those career transferable skills which are the outcomes of general education: thinking, writing, communicating, computing, applying scientific principles, and conceptualizing.

Conclusion

One of the problems we face today in structuring this value-added argument for attending college, in addressing our real worth and value as "talent developers," is one we in higher education created. In years past we advised students to go to college because they would earn more money; we perpetuated that idea very effectively through the 1950s and 1960s. In relying on that argument, we were doing a rather careless job of promoting our worth. This is not to suggest that increased earning potential is not good reason to go to college. However, all these years the public has heard one thing: going to college means more money.

Now there is some indication of a slight downward shift (7 percentage points in recent years) in the variance in earning power between college graduates and nongraduates. In some occupations, the relative earnings of college graduates have changed over time. For example, graduates employed in managerial jobs or in the federal government in 1970 earned relatively more than their counterparts in 1980 (Rumberger, 1983). Some forecasters paint an even bleaker picture for the future. Kerr (1984), for instance, indicates that some economists predict a decline in enrollment beyond 23.5 percent (the decline in the size of the college-going age cohort by 1997). They add to the impact of the demographic depression the fact that the rate of return on a college education—what economists call the private economic rate of return on what it costs a student to go to college, including lost income—has gone down by 50 percent in the last fifteen years. Now that our chief selling point has lost some of its appeal, we need to work together to begin convincingly identifying for prospective students the benefits of higher education, the competencies and talents that they can expect to develop with us.

We in higher education feel that we are doing an exceptional job of marketing and recruiting; we are half right. We have highly skilled professionals who are doing a good job of recruiting. We are not, however, doing a very good job with a basic task of marketing: helping students identify in advance the outcomes, the competencies they can expect to develop in one term, two terms, or sixteen terms with us. When we become more specific about the outcomes, the admissions staff can then take the next step and convert those outcomes into more specific benefit statements that connect directly with a particular student's needs.

The emphasis on outcomes and the emerging themes of attrition mean that the key to attracting and retaining students in the 1980s is going to be quality. Finn (1981, p. 21) notes that "quality is almost certainly going to turn out to be the foremost educational concern of the 1980s much as equity was the premiere issue of the sixties and seventies." As we have seen, quality on campus begins with selecting, nurturing, and rewarding faculty, advisers, and other staff who are committed to creating a quality environment for students. As Keller (1983, p. 64) points out, "Without new monies and additional students, a university's chief hope for increased productivity, higher levels of academic quality, and better management is to improve the performance of the people already at the college and make every new appointment count."

In short, I have found that the real excitement today is taking place in institutions that understand the needs of their students who are coming in and then set into place programs, services, people, and attitudes designed to increase the competency base, knowledge, and skills of those students. Retention is highest at institutions that are committed to delivering the kind of educational experience that leads to learning and success. That is not surprising, for when students sense that they are learning, growing, developing, maturing, they will keep returning term after term for more of the same.

References

American College Testing Program High School Profile Report: Students Tested 1983-84. Iowa City, Iowa: American College Testing Programs, 1984.

Astin, A. W. *Preventing Students from Dropping Out.* San Francisco: Jossey-Bass, 1975.

Astin, A. W. "Proposals for Change in College Administration." In A. W. Astin and R. A. Scherrei (eds.), *Maximizing Leadership Effectiveness: Impact of Administrative Style on Faculty and Students.* San Francisco: Jossey-Bass, 1980.

Baldridge, J. V. "Higher Education's 'Jugular Vein Decisions.'" *American Association for Higher Education Bulletin,* 1981, *33* (10), 1, 6, 11-13

Beal, P. E., and Noel, L. *What Works in Student Retention.* Iowa City, Iowa: American College Testing Program and National Center for Higher Education Management Systems, 1980. (ED 197 635)

Bean, J. P. "Interaction Effects Based on Class Level in an Exploratory Model of College Student Dropout Syndrome." Paper presented at annual meeting of American Education Research Association, Montreal, Canada, April 1983.

Bennis, W. G. "Toward a Learning Society: A Basic Challenge to Higher Education." In D. W. Drew (ed.), *Competency, Careers, and College.* New Directions for Education and Work, no. 2. San Francisco: Jossey-Bass, 1978.

Bisconti, A. S., and Solmon, L. C. *College Education on the Job— The Graduates' Viewpoint.* Bethlehem, Pa.: CPC Foundation, 1976.

Boyer, E. L., and Levine, A. *A Quest for Common Learning: The Aims of General Education.* Washington, D.C.: Carnegie Foundation for Advancement of Teaching, 1981.

"Changing Numbers in High-School Graduating Classes." *Chronicle of Higher Education,* Jan. 7, 1980, p. 8.

Cope, R., and Hannah, W. *Revolving College Doors: The Causes and Consequences of Dropping Out, Stopping Out, and Transferring.* New York: Wiley, 1975.

Evangelauf, J. 'Colleges Must Hire 500,000 Professors in the Next 25 Years, New Study Finds." *Chronicle of Higher Education*, Nov. 7, 1984, pp. 1, 29.

Finn, C. E., Jr. "Toward a New Consensus." *Change*, 1981, *13* (6), 17–21, 60–63.

Forrest, A. *Increasing Student Competence and Persistence: The Best Case for General Education.* Iowa City, Iowa: American College Testing Program National Center for Advancement of Educational Practices, 1982.

Frances, C. *College Enrollment Trends: Testing the Conventional Wisdom Against the Facts.* Washington, D.C.: American Council on Education, 1980.

Freeman, R., and Hollomon, J. H. "The Declining Value of College Going." *Change*, 1975, *7* (7), 24–31, 62.

Gordon, V. N. *The Undecided College Student: An Academic and Career Advising Challenge.* Springfield, Ill.: Thomas, 1984.

Green, K. C. "Retention: An Old Solution Finds a New Problem." *American Association for Higher Education Bulletin*, 1983, *35* (8), 3–6.

Involvement in Learning: Realizing the Potential of American Higher Education. Final report of Study Group on Conditions of Excellence in American Higher Education. Washington, D.C.: National Institute of Education, Oct. 1984.

Keller, G. *Academic Strategy: The Management Revolution in American Higher Education.* Baltimore, Md.: Johns Hopkins University Press, 1983.

Kerr, C. "Impressions 1984: Higher Education Once Again in Transition." 1984 Earl V. Pullias Lecture in Higher Education, University of Southern California, Los Angeles.

Myers, E. Unpublished attrition research studies, St. Cloud State University, St. Cloud, Minn., 1981.

Noel, L., and Levitz, R. 'Mobilizing a Campuswide Retention Effort." National Conference Series, American College Testing Program National Center for Advancement of Educational Practices, 1981–82, 1982–83.

Noel, L., and Levitz, R. (eds.). *How to Succeed with Academically Underprepared Students: A Catalog of Successful Practices.* Iowa City,

Iowa: American College Testing Program National Center for Advancement of Educational Practices, 1982.

Noel, L., and Levitz, R. "National Dropout Study." Iowa City, Iowa: American College Testing Program National Center for Advancement of Educational Practices, 1983.

Noel, L., Levitz, R., and Kaufmann, J. (eds.). *Organizing the Campus for Retention.* Iowa City, Iowa: American College Testing Program National Center for Advancement of Educational Practices, 1982.

Roueche, J. E., Baker, G. A., and Roueche, S. D. *College Responses to Low-Achieving Students: A National Study.* San Diego: Harcourt Brace Jovanovich Media Systems, 1984.

Rumberger, R. W. *The Job Market for College Graduates, 1960–1990.* Project Report, no. 83-A3, Stanford, Calif.: School of Education, Stanford University, 1983.

Smith, L. N., and others. *Mobilizing the Campus for Retention: An Innovative Quality-of-Life Model.* Iowa City, Iowa: American College Testing Program, 1981.

Spady, W. G. "Dropouts from Higher Education: Toward an Empirical Model." *Interchange,* 1971, *2* (3), 38–62.

Statistical Abstract of the United States. Washington, D.C.: United States Bureau of Census, 1984.

Tinto, V. "Dropout from Higher Education: A Theoretical Synthesis of Recent Research." *Review of Educational Research,* 1975, *45,* 89–125.

Titley, R. W., and Titley, B. S. "Initial Choice of College Major: Are Only the 'Undecided' Undecided?" *Journal of College Student Personnel,* 1980, *21,* 293–298.

Von Laue, T. "In Honor of Teaching: Reflecting on Forty Years as a College Professor." *Change,* 1983, *15* (6), 7–10.

2

Dropping Out and Other Forms of Withdrawal from College

Vincent Tinto

Defining dropout is no simple matter. There are many forms of student departure from higher education. They arise from a variety of sources, involve a range of different students, and lead to a diversity of educational outcomes. Some arise very early in the student's career; others occur much later. Each reflects the unique experience of a particular individual with specific intentions, commitments, and skills.

Not all forms of student departure deserve the label "dropout." Nor do they all require institutional action. We must decide which forms of student departure are to be considered dropout and therefore require institutional action and which are to be viewed as perhaps the unavoidable outcome of institutional functioning. In the process, we must be sensitive both to the variety of individual experiences which lead to departure and to the sometimes conflicting interests which mark student and institutional views of this complex issue. Our definition of dropout must accurately reflect the views of both parties. If it does not, we may formulate policies seeking to remedy those forms of student departure that are largely immune to institutional intervention or peripheral to our own educational interests.

28

I will consider this issue from the perspective of the institution and ask how institutions should go about formulating effective policies on student retention. I will describe what is known about the scope and variability of student withdrawal from college and investigate the various individual and institutional factors that appear to give rise to those withdrawals. I will propose a way of defining dropout and will argue that if the term is to be used at all, it should be limited to those situations in which there is failure on the part of both the individual and the institution, a failure of the student to achieve and of the institution to facilitate the achievement of reasonable and desired educational goals.

Finally, in reflecting on the issue of promoting the essential educational interests of both students and institutions, I will argue that the primary goal of effective retention programs should not be merely that more students be retained but that they be further educated. An institutional concern for retention, without regard to the question of the education of students, is a misplaced concern. It leads institutions to consider their own immediate interests—keeping students—without regard either to their own long-term educational interests or those of students. It is striking, though not surprising, that those institutions concerned with student welfare and with the quality of students' social and intellectual development retain students and attract those students more likely to be retained.

Patterns of Departure Among First-Time Entrants

There are a variety of forms of student departure from college. Some lead to permanent withdrawal from higher education, others to transfer, and still others to stop-out. The National Longitudinal Survey of the High School Class of 1972 indicates that nearly 60 of every 100 first-time entrants to the four-year college sector will leave their first institution of registration without completing their degree program (Eckland and Henderson, 1981). Of these institutional departures, slightly less than half, or approximately 29 of every 100 first-time entrants, will immediately withdraw from all forms of formal participation in higher education. Another 40 percent will transfer to other institutions of higher education. The remainder, or approximately 8 to 10 percent of all institutional departures, will leave higher education for a relatively brief period of time to reenroll later at the same or a different institution. This last form is referred to as stop-out or delayed transfer.

Thus, of every 100 first-time entrants to the four-year college sector, nearly 65 will eventually obtain a four-year college degree; approximately 44 of those entrants will do so from the institution of initial entry. This figure is understandably lower in the two-year college sector since a great many two-year college entrants do not seek to obtain four-year college degrees. Nearly 13 percent do, but a much larger percentage (approximately 25 percent) obtain two-year degrees. Given patterns of entry to the two- and four-year college sectors, it is therefore estimated that between 40 and 45 of every 100 first-time entrants to all forms of higher education will eventually obtain four-year degrees. Another 15 will obtain two-year degrees. Taken together, it follows that between 40 and 45 of every 100 first-time entrants will leave without earning a degree of any sort.

Of those who eventually obtain four-year degrees, an increasingly large share are taking more than four years of continuous enrollment to do so. The so-called standard form of college progression—taking four years to earn a four-year degree—is no longer the standard. It may soon become the exception. Students are taking a variety of disparate routes to four-year degree completion; many of these routes involve at least one departure from an institution. Continuous enrollment to degree completion in one's first institution is simply not as common as we are wont to believe. Perhaps it never was.

The Roots of Student Departure:
Voluntary and Involuntary Student Withdrawal

Student withdrawal is a uniquely individual event. The decision to withdraw reflects the experiences of a person with given intentions, skills, and commitments to particular educational goals within a specific institution made up of distinct social and academic communities, each with its own characteristic patterns of interaction among its students, faculty, and staff. Nevertheless, the literature on attrition reveals important similarities in causes of withdrawal (Tinto, 1975). It is to these common roots of individual departure, not their institutional-specific variations, that we now turn our attention.

In order to describe the roots of student departure we must first distinguish between those forms of departure which arise voluntarily and those which are forced or involuntary in nature. Public impressions to the contrary, the great bulk of student institutional departure is voluntary in character. On the average, no more than one-quarter of all leavers depart because they are or will soon be forced to leave their colleges. Most leave of their own accord.

Involuntary Departure. Involuntary departure most often takes the form of academic dismissal. It typically results from the individual's inability or unwillingness to meet the minimum standards of academic performance required to maintain enrollment. Only rarely is it due to a violation of institutional rules and regulations; social dismissals do occur, but not frequently.

For many individuals, involuntary departure is most often associated with insufficient intellectual competence or a lack of the skills required to meet the demands of college work. Though often related, these two factors do not always occur together. True, there are many students who fail to maintain minimum levels of performance because they do not possess the intellectual competence to do so. But there are many others for whom academic dismissal is largely the result of a lack of the study skills and habits required for college work (Demitroff, 1974). Because high school work does not always adequately prepare individuals for the more complex demands of college study, even the brightest students sometimes find the adjustment to college-level work difficult. Programs aimed at improving the study skills and habits of students are therefore often quite effective in reducing the frequency of academic dismissal. This is particularly true of programs designed specifically for academically underprepared students.

But not all student fail because of an inability to meet the demands of academic work. Some are simply unwilling, lacking either the motivation or interest to apply their skills to meet even minimal standards of academic performance. Though institutions may formally record such departures as academic dismissals, they are more the result of voluntary decisions by the students not to assert themselves.

Even in a rather specific form of student departure, such as academic dismissal, some cases, most notably those caused by inadequate skills, may be properly viewed as matters of institutional concern, while others, such as those arising from insufficient motivation or intellectual ability may not be. Although there are good reasons for open-door admissions policies, it does not follow that a minimum level of intellectual competence and individual motivation should not be expected of all college entrants. At some point we must be willing to assert the principle that individuals as well as institutions must be held responsible for student performance. To not do so is to deny the very educational principles upon which higher learning is founded.

Voluntary Departure. Nearly 85 percent of student institutional departures are voluntary. They occur despite the maintenance of adequate levels of academic performance. In fact, such withdrawals may involve many of the brightest and more creative students on campus, individuals whose grade point averages often exceed those of the average persister.

In these and other forms of voluntary departure, difficulty in meeting academic demands appears to have little to do with the decision to withdraw. Instead, such departures are primarily the result of the individual's intentions and commitments and the nature of personal experiences in the academic and social communities of the college.

The Role of Individual Intentions and Commitment

Of the many attributes associated with voluntary withdrawal from college, the two most important prove to be the intentions or goals and commitments or motivations with which students approach higher education. Formed prior to college entry, intentions reflect the educational and occupational goals

that lead students to invest in a particular form of higher education. Commitments or motivations indicate the degree to which
individuals are willing to commit themselves to that effort as
opposed to alternative investments of time and energy.

Student Intentions. Among any group of entering college
students the range of educational or occupational intentions may
be quite varied. Not all intentions or goals are clearly held or
expressed. Nor when clearly held are they necessarily consistent with degree completion or compatible with the educational
goals of the chosen institution.

Some individuals enter college with educational goals that
are either more limited than or more extensive than those of
the institution. Students with more limited educational goals
may attend the institution to accumulate credits for occupational
certification or job promotion. Part-time working students may
seek a specific, rather than general, set of skills needed for on-
the-job promotion. For these students, as for others, completion of a degree program may not be a desired end. Short-term
rather than full-term attendance may be sufficient to achieve
their educational goals. Short-term attendance may also be sufficient for individuals whose educational goals exceed those of
the institution. In two-year colleges particularly, large numbers
of students enter with the intention of transferring to other institutions to complete their degrees. For those students, entry
to the two-year college is a means to educational ends whose
attainment requires transfer.

In either situation, we should expect that students will
leave prior to degree completion: they have accomplished what
they came to the institution to do. To label such departures as
dropout, and representing a form of failure, is both inaccurate
and misleading. It is inaccurate because such a definition misrepresents students' intentions and misleading because it distorts
the meaning they attach to their behavior. Equally important,
labeling such departures as dropout does not account for the
many institutions and programs whose mission it is to serve such
individual needs and interests.

All this assumes that students enter college with clearly
defined goals. In fact, as noted by Sprandel in Chapter Sixteen,

this is not the case. Many students begin their college careers with only the vaguest notions of why they do so. For many high school graduates the process of deciding to attend college and selecting a particular college is quite haphazard. Often it is based upon limited information derived from a variety of secondhand sources (for example, friends and relatives). Little wonder that early in their college careers many students question their reasons for being in higher education or in a particular institution. The inevitable process of goal clarification which occurs during college will invariably lead some of these students to withdraw from higher education altogether or to transfer to other institutions or programs. These departures will occur whether or not the institution invests heavily in career counseling for new students.

Some students will alter their initial intentions during their college careers. For some this change will reflect the natural process of maturation. For others it will mirror the impact of the college experience on their judgments and preferences. In either instance, changes in goals may lead students to leave higher education altogether or to transfer to other institutions that provide for these redefined goals. Again, labeling such departures as dropout misrepresents them and denies the importance of the effect of social and intellectual maturation and the hoped-for impact of the college experience upon maturing youth.

Student Commitment. Even when a student's goals are compatible with those of the institution, finishing a college degree program requires a considerable amount of effort and therefore commitment to the goal of college completion (Hackman and Dysinger, 1970). As noted earlier, not all entering students possess that commitment. Their leaving, whether forced or voluntary, indicates their unwillingness to expend the effort required to attain the goal of college completion.

Completing a degree program at a particular college also requires a commitment on the part of the student to obtaining a degree at that institution as opposed to another institution. Some students enter college with a firmly established institutional commitment because attendance there is necessary to achieve their occupational goals (for example, attendance at one of the military academies is required for certain military careers). For many others, however, institutional commitment either develops or does not develop largely as a result of their experiences at the institution following entry. For these students, departure is not due to a lack of goal commitment as much as it is due to the absence of institutional commitment. By extension, such departures are more a reflection of experiences following entry than of events or predispositions prior to entry (Terenzini, Lorang, and Pascarella, 1981).

Social and Intellectual Integration Within College Communities

Evidence mounts that experiences that promote students' social and intellectual integration into the communities of the college are likely to strengthen their commitment and therefore reinforce persistence. The absence of integrative interactions is likely to lead students to disassociate themselves from those communities and eventually to voluntarily withdraw (Terenzini and Pascarella, 1977).

In a very real sense, the process of persistence in college is very much like that of establishing competent membership, that is, becoming integrated in the communities of the college. By contrast, the process of voluntary withdrawal reflects the failure or unwillingness of persons to become integrated, that is, establish competent membership within the college. In this regard colleges are very much like human communities elsewhere and the process of voluntary withdrawal is not substantively different from the process that leads to departure from human communities generally.

Colleges are composed of academic and social communities, each with its own characteristic patterns of interaction and norms of behavior. Achieving membership in college involves participating in its academic and social communities; departure may arise from the failure to become integrated in either of those spheres. Failure to become integrated and establish competent membership in either the academic or social life of a campus appears to arise from two interrelated, yet quite distinct, phenomena: personal incongruency or individual isolation from the academic and social communities of the college.

Congruency and Student Withdrawal. Congruency involves the match or fit between the needs, interests, and skills of the individual and those of the communities of the institution. This applies to the more formal climate of the classroom and to the informal day-to-day interactions among students, faculty, and staff.

In the academic realm, incongruency may arise when students perceive the academic or intellectual demands of the institution as being either too difficult or too easy. When those demands are viewed as excessive, academic dismissal may result. When they are viewed as not demanding or stimulating enough, voluntary withdrawal and transfer to other institutions may follow. Thus the observations that voluntary withdrawal is often related to the lack of adequate academic support and that it is sometimes directly related to individual ability and academic boredom growing out of poor teaching.

Withdrawal may also occur when students, having found the academic or intellectual climate of the institution not to their own preferences, choose not to seek out intellectual membership. They decide to leave because they see the intellectual climate of the college as being at odds with their own intellectual preferences. Not surprisingly, such withdrawals often involve some of the more intellectually demanding students whose commitment to the intrinsic rewards of college attendance is high.

The same imbalance may apply to the social communities of the institution, but social mismatch is more likely to be the result of differences in social values and preferences than of excessive or insufficient social demands imposed by those communities. Presumably the more varied and numerous the social communities on campus, the more likely is it that differing students will find a social niche within the institution. The more socially homogeneous the campus, the more likely is it that mismatches may arise.

The intellectual climate of the institution can, in a similar way, give rise to matches and mismatches. Thus the finding among studies of successful programs for disadvantaged minority students, and applicable to other groups as well, that program success is very much a function of there being a "critical mass" of similar students on campus.

Isolation and Student Withdrawal. Isolation also proves to be an important element in the process of voluntary withdrawal from college. Though it may reflect a prior lack of congruency, a sense of isolation may also arise when there is insufficient day-to-day personal interaction between the student and other people on campus. In these cases, students are unable to establish the personal bonds that promote community membership. Students who might otherwise establish membership are unable to do so because the institution has not provided appropriate and necessary support for individual integration into new intellectual and social surroundings.

Frequent contact with faculty outside the classroom appears to be one of the most important forms of interaction impacting upon student persistence (Pascarella and Terenzini, 1977). More importantly, it has also been shown to be instrumental in student intellectual and social development (Endo and Harpel, 1982). The more frequent and rewarding those contacts, especially when they go beyond the requirements of academic work, the greater the likelihood of persistence and high levels of individual growth. It does not follow, however, that faculty behavior within classrooms is unimportant to student persistence. Quite the contrary. Not only do teaching and classroom style influence student judgments of the educational quality of the institution, they also affect student perceptions of the receptivity of faculty to further contact outside the classroom. Nevertheless, the occurrence of largely informal contacts with faculty outside the classroom appears as a consistent factor distinguishing those who stay from those who voluntarily withdraw.

Membership in one of the social communities made up of their peers is another important element in student persistence in college. For maturing youth in particular, the social rewards of such membership may be an especially important part of their college careers. The absence of social integration and the social membership it engenders may, in turn, be a significant element in individual decisions to withdraw. But peer contact can have its drawbacks. When the peer group opposes the academic communities of the college or demands a great deal of participation, the student's persistence may be hindered. The same is generally not true for contact with the faculty.

Of the two forms of integration, academic integration proves to be somewhat more important than social integration. This is especially true among the more able members of the student body. Though frequent and rewarding contacts with other students may offset a lack of contact with the faculty and at least partially integrate students into the college, such contacts do not promote the same degree of intellectual development as do interactions with faculty. Though such students may persist, they do so at the price of achieving lower levels of intellectual development. Of course, when social contacts with one's peers take precedence over academic efforts, they may prove to be counterproductive and result in academic dismissal.

We should also note that integration into the academic domain of the college without social integration may lead to withdrawal. Though the intellectual rewards of persistence may be great, the personal costs of social isolation may prove excessive for some individuals. Many students who withdraw are academically very able, but tend to be isolated socially; they rarely report significant relationships with other persons on campus (Husband, 1976).

The interplay between the intellectual and social life of college communities points up the fact that colleges, like other types of human association, are systems of interactive and interdependent parts, intellectual and social. The process of withdrawal reflects the student's experience in the total system of the institution. Policies designed to retain students must be sensitive to both domains of individual experience and to the manner in which experiences in one domain interact with and influence experiences in the other.

Redefining Dropout

In revising our concept of dropout we should keep in mind that among students, at least, the very act of withdrawal does not necessarily carry the stigma of personal failure that we, as college teachers and administrators, normally associate with it. The meaning that withdrawing students attach to their actions depends very much on their educational intentions and their perceptions of their experiences within the institution. Among administrators, however, there is a tendency to view all institutional departures as representing forms of student and institutional failure. Whether a person leaves to transfer to another institution or to depart higher education entirely, to the institution each departure represents a loss of a potential graduate and much-needed tuition revenue. Accordingly it is not surprising that colleges often label all forms of departure as dropout and treat each as a matter for institutional concern and action. This is particularly true for those institutions, now in the majority, which admit virtually everyone who applies for entry. At these institutions, retention of students, all students, is frequently viewed as crucial to institutional survival.

Such a view of student departure is, however, both incorrect and unwise. It is incorrect for it fails to distinguish between the variety of influences on student actions and fails to take into account the distinct patterns of individual experiences which give rise to these departures. It is unwise for it assumes, in effect, that all forms of departure are equally treatable or of equal importance to the educational mission of the institution. This, as we have seen, is simply not the case. Many forms of departure arise from conditions not easily modified by institutional action. Moreover, of those that may respond to such action, not all are equally deserving of institutional attention.

How then should one define dropout? Should all forms of departure be so labeled? Or should the term be restricted to certain modes of withdrawal? My view is that the term dropout should be applied, if at all, only to those forms of departure involving individuals who are unable to reasonably complete what they came to the institution to achieve. Dropout may be seen as occurring when individuals of sufficient skill, competence, and commitment fail to achieve reasonable educational goals consistent with those of the institution or fail to receive sufficient institutional support to enable them to achieve those goals. In this sense, the term dropout acknowledges that there is a commonality of interests between the individual entering student and the institution. For the individual, departure represents a personal failure to achieve a reasonably held goal. For the institution, that departure is a failure to help the student who possesses sufficient skills and commitments achieve what he or she initially came to the institution to achieve.

Thus it is possible to understand dropout as occurring even when the student's educational goals are less extensive than those of the institution. For dropout is not so much a reflection of goals as it is of the inability of the student to attain those goals within the institution. The inability of a student to complete the one course for which he or she enrolled is as much an educational failure as is the withdrawal of a student prior to completing a desired four-year degree program. On the other hand, as I have argued, the simple act of leaving should not be defined as dropout when that departure represents the attainment by the student of a sought-after goal.

It would also be incorrect to label as dropout all those forms of departure that arise from substantial forms of incongruency between the individual and the institution. It is simply unreasonable to expect all entering students to be sufficiently informed of the character of the institution to accurately assess congruency before matriculation. So too is it unreasonable to assume that individual preferences, beliefs, and values will not change during students' college careers. Indeed it is a presumed aim of higher education to so change individuals. Mismatches between the individual and the institution should be viewed as an expected part of institutional functioning, not as a result of imperfect selection procedures. The expectation that more scientific or rigorous selection procedures will eliminate departures is, in my judgment, quite mistaken.

Institutions would be better served if they took it as part of their educational mission to more effectively assist students to find their proper niche. When that niche is determined to be elsewhere, the institution should, within reason, encourage departure. It is not by chance alone that those institutions that tend to guide individuals in this way also tend to have higher rates of retention; maturing youth will most readily seek out helping educational environments.

Dropout, as defined here, primarily involves cases of academic dismissal and voluntary withdrawals arising from insufficient intellectual and social integration of the individual into the communities of the college. Academic dismissal may occur when motivated individuals are not provided reasonable access to the resources needed for the development of college-level skills. Voluntary withdrawal may arise when an insufficient number and variety of contexts are provided for the interaction of students, faculty, and staff within the institution.

The responsibility of the institution to educate, not merely train, its students does not end at the classroom door. Colleges are intellectual and social communities whose maintenance is primarily the responsibility of the faculty and staff. What takes place in the classrooms of the institution is but one part of the daily life of these communities. The broader task of the institution is to involve students in the learning enterprise.

Conclusion

The proper question to ask regarding departure and retention then is not who leaves and who stays, but what do individuals learn as a result of attending the institution. The goal of high retention rates may be more effectively achieved by establishing a genuine concern for the education of all students and the implementing policies designed to achieve that end. The question institutions should first ask themselves is not how many students they should seek to retain, but how to best meet the educational responsibility they have assumed in admitting these students. By extension, the beginning point of an effective retention policy is the raising and answering of the questions: What are the educational goals of the institution? and What educational needs can the institution successfully address? In the final analysis, the development of institutional commitment among students is a direct reflection of the institution's own commitment to its students and to the educational goals it is established to serve.

Finally, we should observe that when we speak of leaving other types of human communities, we rarely label such departures in a punitive manner, representing a form of personal failure. Perhaps the unrestricted use of the term dropout in higher education reflects our own underlying belief that the only proper place to acquire education is within the formal boundaries of the higher educational system and that other forms of learning are less desirable. Such a stance may reflect self-interest in protecting the enterprise within which we have staked out our personal careers. But, this belief is not only unfounded and contradicted by a wide range of evidence, it is also contrary to experience. Can we believe that only those persons who go to and complete college are educated and that the notion of life-long education is a foolhardy one? Such a view requires us to deny the talents of many of our most truly educated and creative citizens—artists, writers, and the like—who did not participate in higher education and whose contribution to our society is without measure. With this in mind, perhaps it would be better to greatly restrict our use of the term dropout, as I suggest here, and to consider striking the word from our educational vocabulary altogether. We should talk, instead, of individual learning and of the various ways we can, during the college years, promote learning throughout the individual's lifetime.

References

Demitroff, J. F. "Student Persistence." *College and University*, 1974, *49*, 553–567.

Eckland, B., and Henderson, L. *College Attainment Four Years After High School.* Washington, D.C.: National Center for Educational Statistics, 1981.

Endo, J. J., and Harpel, R. L. "The Effect of Student-Faculty Interaction on Students' Educational Outcomes." *Research in Higher Education*, 1982, *16*, 115–138.

Hackman, J. R., and Dysinger, W. S. "Commitment to College as a Factor in Student Attrition." *Sociology of Education*, 1970, *43*, 311–324.

Husband, R. L. "Significant Others: A New Look at Attrition."
Paper presented at 7th annual meeting of Association for In-
novation in Higher Education, Philadelphia, February 1976.
(ED 124 056)

Pascarella, E. T., and Terenzini, P. T. "Patterns of Student-
Faculty Informal Interaction Beyond the Classroom and Voluntary Freshman Attrition." *Journal of Higher Education*, 1977,
48, 540-552.

Terenzini, P. T., and Pascarella, E. T. "Voluntary Freshman
Attrition and Patterns of Social and Academic Integration
in a University: A Test of a Conceptual Model." *Research
in Higher Education*, 1977, *6*, 25-43.

Terenzini, P. T., Lorang, W. G., and Pascarella, E. T. "Predicting Freshman Persistence and Voluntary Dropout Decisions: A Replication." *Research in Higher Education*, 1981, *15*,
109-127.

Tinto, V. "Dropout from Higher Education: A Theoretical Synthesis of Recent Research." *Review of Educational Research*,
1975, *45*, 89-125.

3

Forces Influencing
Student Persistence
and Achievement

Edward "Chip" Anderson

We, as educators, tend to view the factors involved in students' academic success as fortunate but somewhat nebulous and mysterious. Fifteen years of directing academic support programs have led me to a different view: we can identify the forces that produce either academic achievement and persistence or academic failure and attrition.

While it may seem a bit mechanistic to view academic success as the result of related causal forces, a force field analysis provides an excellent model for assessing academic programs. Using such a model, program planners can determine the types of students who are likely to succeed and the types of academic support services, policies, and procedures needed to produce the desired result—academic achievement and persistence. And, as we shall see, a force field analysis also helps distinguish between those forces that promote persistence generally and those that promote academic achievement, an important distinction in resource allocation.

Lewin (1951) pioneered the kind of theoretical model used here for analyzing academic forces. His model reasons that all behavior is caused, that the causes of behavior are multiple and interrelated, that these causes vary in strength and direction, and that behavior can be predicted by correctly analyzing the strength and direction of these forces. Any change or movement toward a new future is accompanied by forces that promote and impede it. Forces that push toward the fulfillment of goals are called driving forces. Forces that resist and impede change are called restraining forces. If these forces are in equilibrium, there is no movement. If restraining forces are stronger than driving forces, the situation may regress. If driving forces are stronger than restraining forces, positive change may occur. Once these forces have been identified, it is possible to discover the key to increase driving forces or decrease restraining forces to achieve a desired change. In designing academic support systems, I have applied Lewin's model to student achievement to better understand the forces that promote or impede the fulfillment of students' goals.

Forces Influencing the Decision to Attend College

Considerable research has been done on the decision to attend college. Findings indicate that this decision results from a complicated interaction of external and internal factors or forces (Trent, 1970). These influencing forces vary in intensity and strength from student to student, yet there is a clear pattern of external and internal forces involved in choosing to attend college.

Among the external forces that may influence students' decisions to attend college are:

- Parents who value a college education and stress its importance
- Peers from similar socioeconomic groups who have aspirations toward college and value a college education
- Cultural values that emphasize learning, intellectual achievement, and higher education
- Information on college opportunities that explains how to gain admission and discusses financial aid, programs of study, and opportunities for intellectual and personal development at college in general and at specific colleges

- Teachers and counselors who have expressed confidence in a student's potential to succeed in college
- Information on the benefits of college that examines the ways a college education will help a student clarify and reach personal goals
- Exposure to college educated people who have benefited from college and who provide role models

Internal forces that may influence students' decisions to attend college include:

- Academic skills that make college admission and achievement possible
- Motivation to succeed and persist in academic undertakings
- Interest in gaining a college education for personal and intellectual development
- Career aspirations for which a college education is necessary
- Enjoyment of learning that allows a student to derive satisfaction from satisfying personal intellectual curiosity
- Self-confidence enough to accept the challenge of learning at the college level and adjusting to the college experience
- Values that recognize the importance of a college education
- Identification with college educated people who have functioned as positive role models

Forces Militating Against Achievement and Persistence

We must temper this analysis of the factors involved in the decision to attend college with the knowledge that nearly 40 percent of those who enter higher education never attain a bachelor's degree. To attain such a degree a student must overcome steep obstacles and perform at the high levels demanded by colleges and universities. These obstacles and requirements include:

1. Completing institutional procedures—applying for admission, registering, enrolling in classes, filing petitions, obtaining financial aid, procuring campus housing, and so on.

2. Selecting appropriate courses—fulfilling graduation require-
    ments by completing 45–60 courses in proper sequence and
    combination.
3. Reading and analyzing college-level texts—informal surveys
    indicate that a college student is assigned from 24,000 to
    40,000 pages of reading in courses leading to the bachelor's
    degree.
4. Achieving on tests—taking and achieving on examinations,
    estimated by informal surveys to number from 100 to 200.
5. Completing library research and written assignments—
    meeting academic standards and professors' expectations.
6. Performing in laboratories and studios and completing other
    out-of-class assignments—demonstrating ability and moti-
    vation and budgeting time.

These obstacles, which vary in difficulty depending on
the institution and major, are formidable and call upon students'
preparation, academic skills, motivation, adjustment skills, and
frustration tolerance. Clearly, students who are underprepared
and have weak academic skills will encounter more frustration
and need to spend more time on their studies than those who
are prepared. Accordingly, those with weak motivation and adjustment skills will be less likely to overcome the obstacles that
the college experience presents than those who are highly motivated and adjust easily.

The obstacles account for some of the reasons that students
leave college, but they cannot fully explain poor student performance and high attrition rates. Just as there are external and
internal forces that influence a student's decision to go to college,
there are external and internal forces that tend to push a student out of college or at least militate against academic success.
The negative external forces can include:

- Lack of money to meet educational, living, and personal
  expenses
- Housing problems that make it impossible for students to
  find convenient and affordable housing or force them into
  living arrangements that interfere with their learning

- Roommate problems that interfere with learning or consume time and energy needed for academic performance
- Transportation problems that consume time and energy and create additional financial pressures on students who cannot afford to live on or near campus
- Work demands and conflicts that consume time and energy needed for achievement, particularly for those who work off campus or for those who must work long hours to meet financial obligations
- Social demands, including personal relationships, involvement in organizations, or other social demands that might be distracting and detrimental to academic achievement
- Rejection by family or friends because they do not value a college education or because they are threatened by the decision to go to college
- Discrimination by which particular ethnic groups perceive that they are discriminated against and in which certain majors cater more to one gender than the other
- Family obligations that may consume time and energy necessary for academic achievement or parents who may have difficulty letting go and thus hinder performance and persistence

In addition to overcoming institutional obstacles and other negative external forces, college students must cope with negative internal forces. In general, these negative internal forces fall into two categories: (1) self-defeating perceptions and behavior patterns, and (2) confusion or indecision. They include:

- Procrastination and other self-management problems. These self-defeating patterns consume a student's most precious commodities: time and energy.
- Loneliness. Going to college usually results in a separation from friends and family and forces students to meet new people and adjust to a new social and physical setting. Feeling lonely is a source of discouragement and causes some college students to question their original decision to go to college.

- Inability to assert needs and seek help for problems. While learning to cope with the independence college allows and with an environment that values self-sufficiency and self-reliance, many college students fail to make their needs and problems known. If those needs and problems were addressed, students could increase their achievements and persistence.
- Self-doubt. Students, particularly during their first year, frequently doubt their ability to succeed in college; they view others as smarter, more able, or better prepared than they are. They may think: "What's the use!" and not put forth their best effort.
- Fear of failure. This fear often goes hand-in-hand with self-doubt. There are, however, usually other factors involved: students fear that failure will cost them someone's love or esteem.
- Fear of success. Oddly enough, some students fear success in college. They perceive that success in college could result in additional responsibilities or expectations for which they feel inadequate. Students may also fear that success in college means acculturation into a system that is antithetical to their own values and beliefs, acculturation that could result in separation from or conflict with valued friends, family members, or potential mates.
- Fear of rejection. Students may feel that both success and failure can lead to rejection. Some family members and friends may reject a student just for going to college; this may make persistence very unlikely.
- Value conflicts. Attending college produces internal value conflicts for some students. For example, students from low-income homes may experience conflict because college keeps them from working to help support their families. Some students perceive college primarily as a way to get a good job and do not see the value of a liberal arts education. Others resist the acculturation college demands.
- Career indecision. Some students who are undecided about their college major and career goals may conclude that they should not be in school because they have no direction in their lives.

- Boredom. Some students find the instruction they receive uninspired or unchallenging. Also, college itself may be less exciting than expected because the student is unable to find a way to become involved.

Upon entering college, students may lose contact with many of the positive external forces (parents, peers, teachers, counselors) that were originally the influences for attending college. Students may drift away from these positive forces just at the time when they must, through their own devices and with minimal external support, contend with a host of new forces that work against persistence, all the while endeavoring to meet the demands of bureaucratic procedures, classes, reading assignments, examinations, library research, and laboratory experiments. Not easily done.

Figure 1 presents a summary of those forces with which students must contend, the pressures to which students must adjust, and the obstacles which they must overcome.

Explaining Attrition or Persistence by Using the Force Field Analysis

The forces acting upon students and affecting attrition and persistence vary in intensity and in type. The intensity or strength of each force varies in magnitude from person to person and from group to group. Some students will have many, others will have few forces acting either for or against them as they strive for their degrees. Thus, when using the force field analysis scheme to analyze and predict persistence or attrition, we must take individual and group differences into account. We must also take institutional differences into account. Clearly, demands and difficulties vary from college to college; degree requirements, curricula, assignments, professors' expectations, competition, resources, services, and general environment all vary. Thus, we must analyze both the student and the individual institution in order to predict and explain attrition rates.

This scheme assumes that all behavior is caused. Identifying the exact cause of a particular behavior (in this case attrition)

Figure 1. Force Field Analysis of College Persistence.

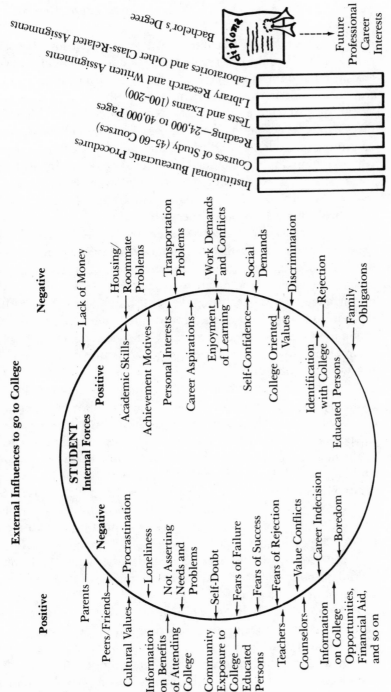

is complicated. There is seldom a single cause for any human behavior; rather, the causes are multiple and interrelated. We look at attrition as a caused event, yet there is no single factor responsible for it. Instead, a complex mesh of causal factors, forces, or obstacles is responsible. Nevertheless, as we identify the various forces acting upon and within particular students or groups of students, and assess the intensity of those forces while recognizing the unique characteristics of the institution we are studying, we can begin to analyze the causes of attrition and to plan programs, implement services, change policies, and alter procedures to promote persistence.

Socioeconomic Influences. A force field analysis provides a good explanation of the high attrition rates among certain groups of students; it demonstrates that for some students the forces against persistence accumulate in geometric progression. Think, for instance, of low-income students. Proportionally fewer students from low socioeconomic groups enter college and persist to graduation than do students from higher socioeconomic groups; a force field analysis provides a graphic means of understanding why this occurs.

Parents of low-income students may want their children to attend college, and yet may not stress its importance, either because they do not think college tuition can be paid or because the potential income from their children's employment is needed in the home. They may not have—likely did not—go to college and they may fail to see the benefit of attending college. Since relatively few low-income students go to college, there is little peer pressure to do so. In addition, the sociocultural environment of low-income students provides minimal information on college opportunities and the benefits of a college education. There are relatively few college educated people with whom such a student can identify and who can explain what is involved in attending college.

Seen in this light, it is quite obvious why relatively few students from low socioeconomic groups attend college. In the higher socioeconomic groups, parents are likely to have attended college and to value a college education; more of the students' friends plan to go to college; information on college opportunities and benefits is more readily available; and there are simply more college educated people in the immediate environment with whom students can identify and from whom they can learn about college. Thus, students raised in a higher socioeconomic community have many forces influencing them to attend college, whereas students from low socioeconomic environments encounter relatively few such forces.

These accumulative influences are not just external, they are also internal. Students from low socioeconomic groups tend to have lower academic skills than students from higher socioeconomic groups. They either attended schools with inferior instructors and curricula or their general environment distracted them from academic achievement or placed demands on them which left little time for skills acquisition. Moreover, as we have seen, students in a low socioeconomic environment are less likely to develop an interest in college; the careers to which they aspire less frequently demand higher education and the role models they seek to emulate are less likely to be college educated. By contrast, students from higher socioeconomic groups usually attend schools with better instructors and better curricula; as a result, they have higher academic skills. The higher socioeconomic environment also encourages students to acquire interests and aspirations that promote college attendance.

Clearly, the difference in college attendance rates between socioeconomic groups is not coincidental—it is the result of predictable external and internal forces. The socioeconomic influence remains prevalent even after students are actually in college.

While students from all socioeconomic groups encounter the same obstacles to attaining their degrees (bureaucratic procedures, classes, reading loads, tests, library research, and so on), the effects of those obstacles differ dramatically between the low and higher groups. In essence, the performance and persistence differences between students from low and higher socioeconomic backgrounds stem from differences in preparation and available time and energy to deal with college demands.

As noted, students from low socioeconomic backgrounds have almost always attended inferior schools which turn out students with lower academic skills. These students will need to spend more time and energy on the academic demands of college—more time reading, studying, preparing papers, and completing assignments—than the better prepared students who generally come from higher socioeconomic groups. Low-income students are often underprepared in other ways as well. They are usually unfamiliar with the nature of a college education and thus either do not know what to expect in college or have false expectations. Bureaucratic procedures, student life, professors' expectations, and the numerous other pressures of the college experience which affect all students may thus present more difficulties for low socioeconomic students. This academic and experiential underpreparation means that low-income students will need to spend more time and energy studying and adjusting to college than students who come from higher socioeconomic backgrounds.

Another dynamic in the performance and persistence differences between students from different socioeconomic backgrounds involves differences in time and energy available for academic demands and general adjustment issues. By definition, students from low socioeconomic groups lack money to meet education, living, and personal expenses. Even with financial aid, these students usually have to work to meet expenses. And the demands and scheduling conflicts of work consume precious time and energy needed for study. In addition, students from low socioeconomic backgrounds frequently live some distance from campus or are unable to afford on-campus housing or housing near campus. Again, precious time and energy must be expended getting to and from campus and to and from work.

In addition to the time and energy consumed by work, housing, and transportation difficulties, low-income students frequently have greater family responsibilities than their wealthier classmates. These responsibilities may include helping out at home, caring for brothers and sisters, and making a financial contribution to the home.

We can now begin to see that the performance and persistence difficulties of students from low socioeconomic backgrounds grow geometrically. The process goes something like this: students from low socioeconomic backgrounds generally attended inferior schools and have lower academic skills, they must therefore spend more time reading, studying, and preparing for their courses; at the same time, more of their time and energy is required to fulfill financial, work, housing, transportation, and family responsibilities. The bottom line is that those students who need the most time and energy to succeed academically have the least time and energy available to devote to their studies.

Other Influences. The force field analysis scheme can be applied to help explain the causes of attrition and poor performance among other student populations as well. Of course, when doing so, the strength and direction of the various forces need to be reexamined and additional forces may need to be added (for example, when analyzing the performance and persistence of student athletes). There may also be particular obstacles and forces that must be added or adjusted because of institutional differences and the demands of certain majors. With the necessary modifications, however, this scheme provides (1) a way of graphically viewing the forces that push and pull students toward persistence and achievement or attrition and failure, (2) a means of representing research findings on the impediments to persistence and achievement, and (3) a basis for planning academic support services and directing institutional changes to increase academic performance and persistence.

Promoting Persistence and Academic Achievement

In designing specific strategies to promote persistence and achievement, it may be useful to reflect upon how powerful various treatment variables, services, or programmatic efforts are. Moreover, it may be instructive to differentiate those treatments or services that tend to promote persistence from those variables that tend to promote academic achievement. This distinction may be artificial—persistence and achievement are, after all, interrelated—but such a distinction can help us make resource decisions and identify areas which deserve our attention. Without first developing a hierarchy of persistence and achievement variables, institutions may address secondary variables but miss primary ones. A hierarchy of institutional activities is described in the following sections.

Persistence Factors

1. Individuals who take a personal interest in students and relate to them as persons can promote persistence in a variety of ways, including:

- Helping students identify and clarify purposes for attending college and the anticipated outcomes of the college experience. Motivation to persist is in large measure a function of the meaning a student ascribes to the college experience and how college relates to future aspirations, careers, and desired areas of personal, social, and intellectual development.
- Affirming students as persons in terms of potential, abilities, skills, gifts, talents, worth, and uniqueness.
- Helping students deal with patterns of self-defeat and sources of anxiety.
- Replacing or substituting for some of those positive forces that influenced students to attend college in the first place (for example, parents, with whom students often have reduced contact once they enter college).

2. Financial support that adequately fulfills basic maintenance needs for food, housing, transportation, books, supplies, and personal expenses contributes to student persistence. Sufficient financial support is important: when it is not available, students must expend time and energy, which are not available for academic demands, to earn money.

3. Assessment and referral procedures that initiate interviews with students to identify needs and problems as well as to stimulate student use of appropriate campus resources and services in a timely manner contribute to students' perseverence.

4. Orientation activities that begin soon after admission and continue through the student's first term on campus encourage student persistence. Such orientation should have multiple stages and might include:

- Telephoning students and their parents within two weeks of acceptance to congratulate them, answer immediate questions, and leave a name and telephone number to call if additional questions arise.
- Inviting entering students and their parents to conferences in the winter and spring. Through these conferences, information and procedures concerning registration, enrollment, financial aid, housing, parking, academic advisers, and support services could be explained and diagnostic examinations administered.
- Providing preparation for entering students by means of summer programs. For some students, a two-day on-campus orientation to academic departments, curriculum options, student life, and support services may be sufficient. For others, a six- to ten-week summer program with instruction in basic skills may be needed.
- Providing, during an entering student's first week on campus (usually registration week), activities and assistance to ease the confusion of that transitional period and help students begin to form relationships.
- Conducting assessment interviews with referrals and follow-up throughout a student's first term on campus. In addition to identifying student needs and problems, these interviews should cover the cycle of deadlines, procedures, and activities of that term and the academic year. Also, the final stage of orientation should attempt to stimulate student involvement on campus through faculty contacts, student organizations, and identification of a resource person in the event of future problems.

5. Counseling services can help students resolve personal problems and interpersonal conflicts and gain greater control of themselves, their time, and emotional reactions. Counseling designed to promote persistence is not only a problem-solving, self-clarifying, and conflict-resolving process, it is also an educational process that teaches students self-management, assertiveness, decision making, and self-reinforcing methods to foster persistence.

6. A support system within the college environment which

fulfills students' needs to belong and through which they can feel they are members of the campus community also contributes to students persevering in college. Such a support system may include faculty, counselors, campus jobs, student clubs and organizations, residence halls, or athletics. It can counter negative forces, including loneliness; build support; and encourage persistence.

Achievement Factors

1. Diagnostic testing of student skills and preparation can help students achieve. In order to succeed, students must enroll in courses for which they are adequately prepared.

2. Offerings of courses and curricula consistent with students' diagnosed skills and preparation also contribute to student achievement. Not only should courses begin at students' diagnosed skill levels, but some courses should be available which directly attempt to improve skills and preparation. Offering appropriate courses and curricula strengthens and reinforces the all-important internal positive forces (for example, academic skills and confidence).

3. Comprehensive educational planning and academic advising are also important to student achievement. Well-informed, properly directed educational planning is a complex process of selecting appropriate courses based on a thorough understanding of a liberal arts education, academic skills, course requirements and demands, personal interests, career aspirations, and university requirements. Moreover, it involves an ongoing process of redefining and clarifying desired outcomes of the college experience based upon exposure to courses, faculty, extracurricular activities, and the world of work. Educational planning designed to promote academic achievement should

- Discuss the purposes of a liberal arts education and how those purposes are reflected in academic departments, course offerings, and graduation requirements.
- Explore academic interests, career aspirations, and desired outcomes of the college experience.

- Explore academic strengths and weaknesses in terms of preparation, background, learning skills, and performance skills.
- Refer students to campus services to identify or clarify career interests, academic preparedness, and learning/study skills as needed.
- Have students consult the professor or teaching assistant of each course in which they are enrolled to obtain feedback on performance, academic skills, areas of needed development and exposure, and readiness for subsequent courses of study.
- Synthesize information and insights gained through the foregoing process, and show students how needs and interests can be addressed through courses of study and independent learning activities.
- Help students develop four-year degree plans based on interests. These plans should (1) remediate skill deficiencies, and (2) fulfill university and major requirements and use elective credits to explore alternate majors, pursue interests, and prepare for graduate schools or careers.
- Refer students to sources of information (for example, course abstracts, syllabi, previous examinations, texts, professor evaluations, instructors, and diagnostic/placement examinations) on the courses in which they are considering enrolling.
- Confirm with students their final program of study to assure that courses are consistent with learning and are in accord with college and departmental policies. Course combinations that maximize learning between courses and take extracurricular demands into consideration should be sought.

4. Assessments of study skills and needs for tutorial assistance are important to student achievement. These assessments should include:

- Course- or discipline-specific tests of presumed background knowledge and information.
- Tests of reading comprehension, ability to identify main points, and vocabulary levels.
- Inventories to identify study habits, learning strategies, and

dysfunctional reaction to learning, study, or performance tasks (for example, test anxiety, procrastination, writer's block).

- Procedures to assess performance skills on multiple-choice tests, essay examinations, reports, and term papers.

5. Learning skills instruction and course content tutoring. Learning skills instruction and tutorial assistance should be based on the assessment described earlier and should be provided in a course-specific manner. The emphasis in tutoring should be both on understanding course concepts and on learning study and performance skills necessary for achievement.

6. Monitoring of student progress and performance. When students receive incomplete grades, withdraw, take courses randomly or out of sequence, enroll in reduced loads, or are on academic probation, interviews should be initiated with appropriate referrals and intensive follow-up.

7. Recognition of academic achievement and reinforcement of progress. Through personal letters, telephone calls, and publications, recognize student achievement and improvements in performance.

When designing academic support services, we must keep this hierarchy of services in mind. Failure to identify and implement the most significant services will result in frustration among faculty, students, and staff. For example, many programs have implemented tutorial services, yet few employ diagnostic procedures, courses based on the actual level of students' skills, or an organized approach to academic advising. As a result, students enroll in courses for which they are unprepared and then seek a tutor out of desperation. At this point, the tutor must simultaneously try to supply the needed and overdue background information and help the student understand the content of a course that was ill-chosen to begin with. Both the student and the tutor are likely to become frustrated; there is too much to do and too little time. Such impossible situations frequently occur when program planners do not organize services in a way that takes into account the hierarchy of services which students need.

Conclusion

The intent of this chapter was to present a model for analyzing the causes of attrition and low performance among college students; a force field analysis provides a way of picturing the forces that militate against academic achievement and persistence. By identifying those forces that push students toward attrition and failure, planners can begin to develop support services to target specific problem areas. A force field analysis also makes it very clear that the most effective support services are those that counter the forces leading to attrition and promote the internal and external forces leading to academic achievement and persistence.

References

Lewin, K. *Field Theory in Social Science*. Chicago: University of Chicago Press, 1951.

Trent, J. W. *The Decision to Go to College: An Accumulative Multivariate Process*. Center for Study of Evaluation, report no. 64, Los Angeles: University of California Press, Nov. 1970.

4

Creating Conditions
for Student
and Institutional Success

❦❦❦❦❦❦

Aubrey Forrest

Virtually all colleges and universities have felt pressure in recent years to convince students and the public alike that general education programs successfully prepare students to function effectively in adult society. They are, in other words, under pressure to demonstrate the relevance of general education. As Levine (1983, p. 8) points out, "For too long we have told students self-righteously to study the humanities because it's 'good for you.' They don't believe us anymore."

There are at least two other reasons for the growing interest in demonstrating the relevance and usefulness of our programs through assessing educational outcomes. Many institutions desire to reshape their curricula and design more effective learning activities to help students obtain the knowledge, skills, and attitudes necessary for functioning in adult roles after graduation. Others are concerned with helping students use existing general education programs in ways that will best prepare them to achieve their personal and professional goals as well as to meet the expectations of society. These institutions involved in revamping their programs find that only through assessment of educational outcomes can they ensure that students are achieving the goals of the general education program and are receiving appropriate credit and recognition for doing so. In its 1984 report, *Involvement in Learning*, the National Institute of Education's Study Group on the Conditions of Excellence in American Higher Education recommends that "postsecondary institutions be less grandiose in their statements of goals and far more specific about their objectives" (p. 39). The group recognizes that even though not all of the outcomes of an undergraduate education can be easily quantified, we have a responsibility to define the knowledge, capacities, and skills we expect students to obtain.

This emphasis on defining outcomes means that general education can no longer afford to be what Boyer and Levine (1981, p. 33) call the spare room of academia: "The one consistent and persistent use to which both general education and the spare room have been put is the least satisfying: they are simply storage spaces, places to keep odds and ends . . . Like most spare rooms, general education is chronically in a state ranging from casual neglect to serious disrepair. Sporadic efforts at dusting, rearranging, and sprucing up absorb a great deal of effort and bring little return. All in all it's much easier to keep the door closed than to rethink the room's uses." In a survey of general education programs, respondents often refer to the hodgepodge quality of their programs. One respondent notes that "only through a combination of unusual maturity, exceptional advising, and high determination could a student acquire a truly liberal education" (Gaff, 1983, p. 21).

The need for reassessing the goals and outcomes of general education programs has become increasingly urgent in a time of scarce resources and retrenchment. As Keller (1983, p. 133) points out: "In a time of enrollment growth, access is the key word; but in a time of enrollment decline—at least in the traditional eighteen-to-twenty-two-year-olds category—competition increases, and schools that give great intellectual value and superior training for their tuition will fare best. Quality throughout a college's operation is therefore a condition of survival and a must for academic management." Hardison (1983, p. 5) also sees a positive side to retrenchment: "The fact that education can no longer afford to do everything will provide an incentive to decide what, in fact, it should be doing. If retrenchment leads to a better, more coherent humanities curriculum, that will be good for students, for the humanities, and for democracy in general."

Finally, Gaff (1983) concludes that "All the debate about general education, all the changes in the philosophy, curriculum, courses, teaching, governance and financing—however persuasive the various cases may be and however promising the changes are—lead to a single question: Do they make a difference in the education of students?" He then points out that it is only through evaluation that we can "shift the grounds of the decision about general education from a normative to an empirical basis . . . Curricular reform can best proceed on the basis of empirical findings that elicit the credibility of all constituencies" (pp. 146–147).

Much of the current emphasis on reevaluating and assessing the outcomes of general education programs, however, has been focused purely on curriculum. But a general education program is much more than a curriculum. As Noel and Saluri (1983, pp. 11–12) point out: "Successful general education programs extend beyond the classroom attending to both the affective and the cognitive needs of students and encompassing services ranging from orientation activities to remedial programs. Moreover, as the notion of general education expands to include a whole range of student programs and services, measurement of its impact or effectiveness becomes even more complex. A number of dimensions related to student achievement of general education outcomes need to be considered, including how courses are taught, what kinds of advice students receive about academic offerings, and what happens to students outside the classroom."

Key Variables

This chapter will look at two separate studies in which a number of variables related to student learning, student persistence, and graduate satisfaction were studied. One study is based on the American College Testing (ACT) Program's College Outcome Measures Program (COMP) and the other on ACT's Alumni Survey. Of the variables studied, only a small number emerged as indicators of institutional quality. And, in both studies, two variables—comprehensive orientation and advising and individualized instruction focused on development of relevant skills and knowledge—emerged as key indicators of student performance and satisfaction. That is, at institutions with strong orientation and advising programs and with emphasis on individualized instruction, students learn more and are more satisfied with what they learn.

After first explaining the designs of the two studies, I will review the findings of both studies as they relate to orientation and advising and then as they relate to individualized instruction. I will present recommendations for action in these two critical areas. It is heartening to note that these two key variables are factors over which an institution has some control. It is also encouraging to note that the findings come down squarely on the side of quality. The findings strongly suggest that some of the practices we might consider implementing to improve retention are the same ones we should consider if we are interested in improving student learning and graduate satisfaction.

COMP Study: Design and Findings. Recent studies have verified that these two program features—comprehensive orientation and advising of new students and individualized instruction focused on development of relevant skills and knowledge— are not only important to student retention, but also to student learning and graduate satisfaction. In one study, forty-four institutions that had administered COMP tests were reviewed. Included from various regions of the country were five liberal arts colleges that are units of large public research universities, five public community colleges, eight small private colleges that are above average in wealth and admission selectivity, six small public colleges, eight small private colleges below average in wealth and admission selectivity, five small private universities, and seven large public comprehensive universities.

The forty-four institutions involved in the COMP study

vary considerably in the percentage of entering full-time freshmen who graduate in five years (at senior colleges) or in three
years (at community colleges). The percentages range from 40
percent to 70 percent with an average of 52 percent. The significance of these persistence-to-graduation rates may be seen
by comparing two senior institutions with rates of 47 percent
and 60 percent respectively. This difference may not seem great
until the percentage rates are translated into numbers of students. If each institution admitted 1,000 freshmen, one would
retain 600 students for all four years, the other only 470. The
difference in revenue generated from 130 students over several
years would be considerable, not to mention the educational
and financial losses suffered by the students and society.

The COMP tests are designed to measure student learning in six general education outcome areas.

- Communicating—can send and receive information in a
  variety of modes (written, graphic, oral, numeric, and sym-
  bolic), within a variety of settings (one-to-one, in small and
  large groups), and for a variety of purposes (to inform, to
  persuade, and to analyze)
- Solving problems—can analyze a variety of problems (scientific, social, and personal), and can select or create and implement solutions to problems
- Clarifying values—can identify personal values and the values
  of other individuals, can understand how values develop,
  and can analyze the implications of decisions made on the
  basis of personally held values
- Functioning within social institutions—can identify social
  institutions (religious, marital, and familial institutions; employment; and civic, volunteer, and recreational organizations), and can analyze own and others' functioning within
  social institutions
- Using science and technology—can identify those activities
  and products which constitute the scientific/technological
  aspects of a culture (transportation, housing, clothing, health
  maintenance, entertainment and recreation, communication,
  and data processing), can understand the impact of such en-
  tities on the individuals and the physical environment in a

culture, and can analyze the uses of technological products in a culture and personal use of such products

- Using the arts—can identify those activities and products which constitute the artistic aspects of a culture (music, drama, literature, dance, film, and architecture), and can analyze uses of works of art within a culture and personal use of art

The groups to which COMP tests were administered at the forty-four institutions ranged from 30 to 191 students and averaged 75 students. A total of 3,318 students were tested. An average COMP total score was computed for each group of seniors (or sophomores at the community colleges). Using the average ACT Assessment or Scholastic Aptitude Test (SAT) score (obtained when entering freshmen) for each group, an estimate was made of what the average COMP total score would have been had the group taken COMP tests as entering freshmen. By subtracting a group's estimated freshman average COMP total score from that group's senior (or sophomore) average COMP total score, an estimated total score gain was computed.

It was appropriate to compare freshman-to-sophomore COMP total score gains at community colleges with freshman-to-senior gains at four-year institutions since research has shown that most of the total score gains on COMP tests in a four-year period occur in the first two years. In fact, students in a four-year program show virtually no gains in their junior and senior years. This is to be expected since the COMP tests are designed to measure the outcomes of general education (usually completed in the first two years of a four-year program) and not the outcomes of any particular major field of concentration (the focus of the last two years).

The forty-four institutions in this study exhibit a wide range of gains (0–20.0) in average COMP total scores from entering freshman status to graduation. The typical score gain was 7.0. An institution with a score gain of less than 3.0 is viewed as having no significant impact on student growth, while one with a score gain of 11.0 or more is viewed as having great impact.

I then analyzed the data to determine the relationships

among student learning (as measured by the COMP tests), rates of persistence to graduation, orientation and advising of new students, and instructional style.

Alumni Study: Design and Findings. The ACT Alumni Survey is designed to help an institution evaluate the impact that a college has had on its graduates. One question asks: "How much did your education at this college contribute to your personal growth in each of the following areas?" Areas such as writing effectively, speaking effectively, understanding written information, working independently, managing personal and family finances, learning on your own, and understanding graphic information are then listed.

In this 1984 study, I reviewed forty institutions that had administered ACT's Alumni Survey form to recent graduates within four years after graduation. Included from various regions of the country were twenty-two small private colleges, nine regional state universities, six large public universities, two private universities, and one small public college. At the forty institutions, the groups responding to the survey ranged from 31 to 1,262 graduates and averaged 240. An aggregate of 9,609 graduates responded. An average score was computed for this section of the survey for each group and these scores were converted to a ten-point scale. I then analyzed the scores to determine the relationships among graduate satisfaction (as measured by the ACT Alumni survey), rates of persistence to graduation, orientation and advising of new students, and instructional style.

Orientation and Advising of New Students

COMP Study Findings. All forty-four institutions in the COMP study could identify ways in which they informed prospective and new students about the curricular objectives and requirements of their general education program. All the institutions provide some printed information about general education. They also provide information about support services.

These forty-four institutions differed widely, however, in at least two important respects: (1) the number of formal orientation contact hours required of all freshmen, and (2) the degree to which freshman academic advising is administered as a distinct function.

At one extreme are the eight institutions I identified at which the required orientation program lasts more than one day. This group of eight institutions includes a large public research university, two small private universities, two regional public universities, one selective private college, one public college, and one nonselective private college. In some cases, the orientation activities take place for two to five days before fall classes begin. In others, orientation continues as a credit course throughout the fall term. Several institutions use selected upperclass students as peer counselors. All eight institutions require entrance tests and collect high school performance data on entering freshmen. They then use this data to systematically place students in appropriate general education courses.

All eight of these institutions also administer freshman advising as a distinct function through one of the following means: (1) providing a formula for reducing the expected teaching loads of faculty members who are assigned advisees, (2) providing additional compensation for faculty members who serve as advisers, or (3) assigning freshmen to a special group of advisers or counselors not identified with regular academic departments. Furthermore, all eight institutions support general education advising as a special function by clearly identifying an administrator and faculty committee as having the responsibility for coordinating the general education program.

At the other extreme are the sixteen institutions at which freshman orientation either is not required or is at most a single-day affair. This group includes a mix of all types of institutions. Special course placement is generally done at the initiative of the student (in the case of well-prepared students) or without consulting the student (in the case of the underprepared ones). None of the sixteen institutions recognizes freshman advising as a distinct function; advising is considered just another duty assigned to all faculty members. In addition, none of the sixteen institutions has clearly identified an administrator or faculty committee as having the responsibility for coordinating the general education program. Whatever leadership is provided is at the initiative of the chief academic officer and/or the faculty committee on general academic or curricular affairs, who usually are involved in many other concerns.

The remaining twenty institutions in the total group of forty-four have some, but not all, of the orientation and advising characteristics attributed to the eight institutions having the most comprehensive orientation and advising programs.

The three groups do not differ significantly in average ACT/SAT scores for entering freshmen. Apparently, decisions made at these institutions about the degree of comprehensiveness of orientation and advising are not influenced by the level of ability of entering students. Some institutions receiving high-ability students apparently regard extensive orientation and advising as unnecessary because of their selective admission practices; others, receiving the same level of students, view all students as in need of guidance in meeting the challenges of their new environments. One might expect that the more comprehensive orientation and advising efforts would be found at institutions where such efforts might be most needed, that is, those institutions attracting low-ability students. But these institutions are just as likely to neglect this part of their general education program as those institutions attracting the better students.

Does orientation and advising make a difference? How do the two groups, one having the most comprehensive set of services and the other having the least comprehensive set, compare in COMP score gains and persistence-to-graduation rates? The group of eight institutions having the most comprehensive orientation and advising program shows an average of 60 percent of the full-time freshmen graduating in the three-to-five-year period, while the group of sixteen institutions with the least comprehensive program has an average persistence rate of 47 percent. The group of eight has an average score gain of 9.5, the group of sixteen an average of 6.2.

Alumni Study Findings. Using the same definition of a comprehensive set of orientation and advising services as in the COMP study just described, I identified the nine institutions that had the most comprehensive set of services and the nine institutions with the least comprehensive. The two groups do not differ significantly in average ACT/SAT scores for entering freshmen. The group with the most comprehensive orientation and advising services includes six small private colleges and three regional state universities. The group with the least comprehensive services includes four regional state universities, two small private colleges, two large public universities, and one small public college.

In the group of institutions having the most comprehensive set of services, and average of 56 percent of the full-time freshmen graduated within a five-year period; in the group with the least comprehensive set of programs, that average was 47 percent. The group with the most comprehensive programs has a graduate satisfaction index of 5.8, while the group with the least comprehensive programs has an index of 3.6.

As does the COMP study, the graduate study indicates that a relationship exists between programs of orientation and advising and persistence rates among students. Such programs also appear related to graduate satisfaction. It seems logical to conclude that students will learn more and be more satisfied with a program that affords them with a good start by providing guidance on how individuals can make the best of what the institution has to offer.

Conclusions. The data from these two studies are not enough to determine that a more comprehensive program of orientation and advising will produce greater intellectual growth, persistence, and satisfaction among students, but it does seem probable that such a relationship exists. Freshman orientation and advising do seem likely times and places for students to come to an understanding of the objectives of the general education program and make appropriate decisions about how best to benefit from the program. These are also convenient times to carefully diagnose individual learning interests and abilities. Furthermore, initial orientation and advising offer early opportunities for freshmen to establish working relationships with faculty, staff, and upperclass students. Administering freshman advising as a distinct function stresses the importance of advising to all concerned, facilitates the training and motivating of advisers, and probably strengthens the commitment of both faculty and students to the general education program. It therefore seems logical to conclude that a well-developed orientation and advising system makes a significant and positive contribution to student acquisition of general knowledge and skills, to the persistence of students to graduation, and to their satisfaction as graduates.

Instructional Style

COMP Study Findings. The forty-four institutions in the COMP study were found to differ widely in terms of the degree to which they attempted to individualize instruction in their general education courses and to focus on the development of skills and knowledge relevant to completing advanced courses.

I was able to identify nineteen institutions at which students are systematically placed into remedial, regular, or advanced general education courses, according to current ability levels. Instructional style in these courses could generally be characterized as involving

- Discussions about the applications of the skills and knowledge upon which the courses focused
- Out-of-class assignments that required students to apply what they read or heard in lectures
- In-course examinations that required students to reason and solve problems rather than engage in simple recall of specific facts and concepts and principles

I could also identify thirteen institutions in which varying levels of general education course work (remedial, regular, and advanced) were generally not available. Also, the general education courses placed heavy reliance on reading assignments, lectures, and simple recall-type examinations. The remaining twelve institutions were judged to be somewhere in between the other two groups.

There are no significant differences among the three groups as to average entering ACT/SAT scores. The commitment to individualized instruction focused on the development of relevant knowledge and skills is apparently not influenced by the academic abilities of the entering freshmen at these institutions. All three groups are highly diverse in the types of institutions represented, except that four of the five community colleges are in the group with the most focus on individualized instruction in developing relevant skills and knowledge.

In comparing the group of nineteen institutions having the individualized, practical instructional style, and the thirteen not so characterized, I found that the group of nineteen has a persistence-to-graduation rate of 55 percent, while the other group has a rate of 46 percent. The first group has an average score gain on the COMP tests of 8.8, the second a gain of 4.6.

Thus, although one cannot affirm a definite cause-and-effect relationship between instructional style and score gains or persistence rates, it does seem likely that the institution's degree of success in individualizing instruction and focusing it on relevant, practical skill building within the structure of the formal general education program is an important factor in student persistence.

If we can take this to mean that such instruction is consistent with the diagnosed skill levels of entering students and that all students in general education classes are provided with opportunities to practice relevant skills and use relevant knowledge, we can assume that it probably results in greater motivation and self-confidence in students. It would appear that students are more motivated to learn and persist to graduation if they believe that the general education program is providing knowledge and skills that promise to be important to effective functioning at the institution.

Alumni Study Findings. Again, using the same definition of instructional style as used in the COMP study, I identified the nine institutions that had the greatest focus on individualized instruction in developing relevant skills and knowledge. I also identified the nine institutions most lacking in this focus. The two groups do not differ significantly in average ACT/SAT scores for entering freshmen. The group with the most instructional focus includes five regional state universities, three small private colleges, and one large public university. The group with the least instructional focus includes eight small private colleges and one public university.

The group having the most focus on individualized instruction in developing relevant skills and knowledge shows an

average of 58 percent of the full-time freshmen graduating within
a five-year period, while the group with the least emphasis on
individualized instruction has an average of 50 percent. The
group with the most focus on individualized instruction has a
graduate satisfaction index of 5.8, while the group with the least
has 4.2.

Conclusions. There is evidence that a relationship exists
between instructional style and learning and persistence rates
among students. It also appears that instructional style is related
to graduate satisfaction. Students will learn more, will be more
likely to persist to graduation, and graduates will be more satisfied when the instruction is individualized and develops relevant skills and knowledge. These conclusions support the suggestions set forth in *Involvement in Learning* (1984) for making
learning an active, individualized process through internships
and other forms of experiential learning, in-class presentations
and debates, simulations in appropriate subjects, and using practitioners as visiting teachers.

Recommendations

Based on COMP study results on the importance of orientation and advising and individualized instruction, I reiterate and
continue to support my earlier recommendations concerning ways
to increase student competence and persistence. Probably the
single most important move an institution can make to increase
student persistence to graduation is to ensure that students receive
the guidance they need at the beginning of the journey through
college to graduation. This early guidance can also assist students
in acquiring the competence that they will need to complete their
courses of study and function effectively after graduation.

At its best, this guidance system should include the following features.

- Orientation of new students should begin well before their
  arrival on campus and should continue as a formal course
  during the first term.
- Faculty should be specifically selected, trained, and compensated for academic advising.

- An administrator and a faculty committee should coordinate orientation and academic advising.
- Orientation and academic advising should, at a minimum, include exploring the value of general education, course placement based on tests and academic records as well as on student and institutional objectives, career planning, and services and policies of the institution.

Probably the single most important move an institution can make to simultaneously increase student competence and persistence is to adopt an institutional commitment to individualized instruction focused on relevant skill development through the formal academic program. The payoffs of such efforts to the students and the institution can be enormous. Top priority should be given to the following:

- Systematic placement into general education courses for all students. Many entering freshmen need to improve their academic survival skills—reading, writing, computing, and so on. Special remedial courses should be provided to them. Those students ready for advanced courses should be placed in courses appropriate to their current ability level.
- All general education courses should require students to apply what they have learned rather than merely recall information. Throughout the general education curriculum, ample opportunities should be provided for students to practice applying theoretical knowledge to at least realistic simulations of situations commonly encountered after graduation. After the freshman year, off-campus learning experiences should be strongly encouraged, if not actually required. (Forrest, 1982, pp. 44–45).

Conclusion

In considering the findings of the two studies presented in this chapter, it is clear that improving new student orientation and advising as well as the instructional style of the general education program increases both student learning and student satisfaction. These findings, which point to the advantage of involving students in the advising and instructional processes, correspond with the finding of the Study Group on the Conditions of Excellence that "more learning occurs when students are actively engaged in the learning process" (*Involvement in Learning*, 1984, p. 19). Indeed, the study concludes that: "The most important implications of this fact can be stated in two fundamental principles about the conditions of educational excellence everywhere: (1) the amount of student learning and personal development associated with any educational program is directly proportional to the quality and quantity of student involvement in that program, and (2) the effectiveness of any educational policy or practice is to increase student involvement in learning" (p. 19).

The COMP findings suggest further that an emphasis on outcomes is beneficial because it forces us to articulate the objectives of our general education programs. For it is true that if students are to become more responsible for learning, colleges must be more specific about their exit standards. As the Study Group notes, "Research on effective elementary and secondary schools strongly suggests that clearly communicated, detailed statements of this kind are positively related to student achievement" (p. 39).

As Astin points out, "Universities must monitor what they get paid to do. It is irresponsible for an institution not to know what the students are learning, what impact the college is having, what suggestions the students have for change" (in Keller, 1983, p. 132). After all, in defining and evaluating outcomes we are only giving our students their due. It is, and has long been, the time for us to focus on outcomes.

References

Boyer, E. L., and Levine, A. *A Quest for Common Learning: The Aims of General Education.* Washington, D.C.: Carnegie Foundation for Advancement of Teaching, 1981.

Forrest, A. *Increasing Student Competence and Persistence: The Best Case for General Education.* Iowa City, Iowa: American College Testing Program National Center for Advancement of Educational Practices, 1982.

Gaff, J. G. *General Education Today: A Critical Analysis of Controversies, Practices, and Reforms.* San Francisco: Jossey-Bass, 1983.

Hardison, O. B., Jr. Reply to "The Shattered Humanities" by W. J. Bennett. *American Association for Higher Education Bulletin,* 1983, *35* (6), 5.

Involvement in Learning: Realizing the Potential of American Higher Education. Final report of Study Group on Conditions of Excellence in American Higher Education. Washington, D.C.: National Institute of Education, Oct. 1984.

Keller, G. *Academic Strategy: The Management Revolution in American Higher Education.* Baltimore, Md.: Johns Hopkins University Press, 1983.

Levine, A. Reply to "The Shattered Humanities" by W. J. Bennett. *American Association for Higher Education Bulletin,* 1983, *35* (6), 8.

Noel, L., and Saluri, D. "Setting and Assessing Learning Outcomes: A Fresh Approach." In J. E. Roueche (ed.), *A New Look at Successful Programs.* New Directions for College Learning Assistance, no. 11. San Francisco: Jossey-Bass, 1983.

5

Low-Income Students

❦❧❦❧❦❧❦❧

Leonard A. Valverde

Beginning in the late 1960s, American public institutions were forced, mainly through public demand, to address the multifaceted issue of equal opportunity. One tenet of the equality movement was that disadvantaged groups be provided access to higher education. Initially the emphasis was on recruiting more students from ethnic and racial minority groups and economically depressed backgrounds. In the seventies these efforts expanded to include retention of these students. At the same time, the number of different disadvantaged groups to be served increased; the term "nontraditional" student was coined to include older persons, women, language-handicapped persons, underachieving white youths, physically handicapped, and so on, as well as ethnic and racial minority students. In line with this changing student population and increased emphasis on retention, institutions developed new action programs to meet changing demands and needs and to provide a staying environment for all students.

The emphasis of equality programs shifted from access to retention and multipurpose programs evolved to serve more categories of nontraditional students, but the process of carefully defining each of the targeted groups did not keep pace. One particular group not distinguished sufficiently from the global category of high-risk students is low-income students. Reports by institutions of higher education on their efforts to retain high-risk students indicate that the low-income variable is one characteristic attributed to nontraditional, high-attrition students. Further scrutiny of the literature reveals that ethnic and racial minority students are viewed as being low-income students as well. In short, the attrition studies are replete with discussions referring to minority and low-income students as one group.

This confusion is understandable. It is fairly well documented that the majority of black, Hispanic, and native American families in the United States are of low socioeconomic status and that a high percentage of students from such ethnic and racial groups who are attending institutions of higher education are low-income students (Cross, 1971). In a 1968 nationwide study involving some 243,000 college freshmen, of whom 12,300 were black, Bayer and Boruch (1969) found that 56 percent of the blacks as opposed to only 14 percent of the non-blacks were from homes in which the parental income was less than $6,000 per year. While it is thus not surprising that the low-income and ethnic and racial factors have been viewed as one classification by educators, it is now important that low-income students be carefully identified and defined so that educators can design programs tailored to meet their special needs.

This chapter will present underlying principles and guidelines that college personnel can use to better define the characteristics and needs of low-income students in their efforts to enhance the recruitment and persistence of these students. After profiling the characteristics or indicators of low-income students, and their likely outcomes, the chapter will consider models for understanding the needs of these students; it concludes with a typology of three intervention strategies characteristic of current retention programs.

Indicators of Low-Income Students and Likely Outcomes

What indicators will assist in identifying low-income students? The word "indicator" is used intentionally since what follows is a compendium of phrases commonly found in the literature, dissected out and patched together in order to form a profile of low-income students. It should be noted that in my research, I found no published study that attempted to purposefully catalogue low-income students.

Non-Minority Low-Income Students. It has already been established that most low-income students participating in specially designed retention programs are members of minority groups. However, not all low-income students are minorities. It is estimated that at least one-fourth to one-third of low-income students are non-minority with regard to ethnicity or race. Rovezzi-Carroll and Thompson (1980) report that of the low-income students they studied, 70 percent were ethnic/racial minorities and 30 percent were white. The Bayer and Boruch study (1969) finds that 25 percent of college freshmen who were non-minority came from blue-collar families (skilled, semiskilled, or unskilled workers) while 46 percent of black college freshmen came from blue-collar families.

Faculty Stereotypes of Minority Students. One last word regarding the ethnic/racial indicator of low-income students. Faculty often have a tendency to assume that nearly every minority student is a special admission, that is, a student who did not meet the standard academic requirements of the university. These faculty view minority students as needing more remedial help than other students. Thus some capable minority students are incorrectly labeled as being deficient while very few white students, who may actually be academically underprepared, are so stereotyped. These assumptions, although difficult to verify, may influence faculty interaction with and behavior toward low-income students. Later in this chapter, in the discussion of intervention strategies, the importance of faculty attitudes and assumptions about high-risk students to their retention and success in college will be considered in greater detail.

First-Generation College Students. Aside from being mostly ethnic minority persons of lower social class and in need of economic support, low-income students are often children of parents who have relatively little education. They are usually the first members of their families to attend college; prior to attending college they are likely to have attended poor public schools and experienced higher rates of failure while in school. They also probably received insufficient positive feedback or encouragement from teachers and classmates. As a result of such experiences, low-income students are persons whose psychological makeup may be characterized by low self-confidence, low motivation levels, a tendency to be less assertive verbally, low confidence in their ability to learn new tasks, and a lack of career goals. (For background on these factors, see, among others, Friedlander, 1980; Meyers and Drevlow, 1982; Maynard, 1980; and Beal and Noel, 1980.)

Outcomes and Manifestations. The descriptions just listed manifest themselves in likely outcomes. Because low-income students are in financial need, they are likely to be off-campus workers or part-time students and to select an institution on the basis of proximity to home or low tuition. Because community colleges fit these criteria, the first higher education experience for a great many low-income students is with a community college (Roueche and Snow, 1977; and de los Santos, Montemayor, and Solis, 1980). When low-income students initially select four-year institutions or transfer to four-year colleges or universities, they are likely to live off campus and thus tend to enroll in commuter colleges rather than major state universities or prestigious research institutions.

Because they are the first generation to attend college and their parents cannot provide them with guidance in coping with college life and its daily academic and social problems, low-income students are likely to perceive higher education institutions as foreign or even hostile, and certainly as unresponsive (Adolphus, 1979). Their values often differ from university norms and values which are rooted in the upper- and middle-class value system. The role of colleges and universities as socializing agencies with implicit norms of behavior, expectations, and regulations and policies that students are expected to live by thus creates conflict for those students who live off campus, low-income students, and minority students.

The foregoing discussion of descriptors and the resulting circumstances should present a picture of incompatibility between low-income students and postsecondary institutions. Obviously if low-income students are to be attracted to and retained

by such institutions, new student services and curricular approaches must be developed. Recruitment and retention programs must eliminate the incompatibility that potentially exists
between low-income students and institutions or such special
programs are doomed to fail.

Relevant Theoretical Constructs and Models

In addition to basing programs and services on likely descriptors of the population and the conditions that result from
these descriptors, college personnel should be familiar with theoretical constructs that can help them understand low-income
students. These constructs aid in understanding the factors involved in the persistence of low-income students, delineate their
problems in adjusting to campus life, and explore the learning
styles of low-income students.

Persistence of Low-Income Students. As a result of conducting
a number of studies on college dropouts versus persisters, Astin's
construct addresses the degree of involvement or intensity of
exposure students who dropped out had during their college experience. Astin finds that students with poor academic skills are
less likely to engage in relationships with faculty and other students. Uninvolved students are also less likely than involved
students to persist in college, to improve their skills, and to implement their career plans (1975 and 1977). Similarly, Turner
(1970) finds that potential withdrawers display certain identifiable characteristics such as disinterest and lack of involvement
in college affairs, doubtful vocational goals, unrealistic images
of college life, and unsatisfactory attendance.

In trying to distinguish involved students from uninvolved
students, Astin (1977) establishes a criterion, intensity of exposure, as the basis of a continuum on which to place students.
Students at the low end of the involvement continuum live off
campus, come on campus only to attend classes, devote minimum effort to their academic pursuits, and center their lives
primarily around persons and events outside the institution. The
description of uninvolved students thus parallels closely the indicators of low-income students. Astin's research also indicates

that living in a dormitory increases the chances of student success by 12 percent, and that involvement in the campus environment enhances persistence rates, as does working on campus and participating in extracurricular activities. These involvements not only enhance persistence but intensify the impact of the college experience on the students' personality, behavior, career progress, and general level of satisfaction.

Role of Adjustment to Campus Life. Organizations, no matter what their primary purpose, act as socialization agencies; that is, every organization has a set of ethics and preferred set of behaviors which its members are expected to honor. Organizational socialization is the process by which new members learn the value system, norms, and required behavior patterns of the organization or group they are entering (Schein, 1970). Colleges and universities are no exception; they too have norms and values to which students are expected to conform (Wheeler, 1966; and Merton, 1968). Once admitted to the system, students are expected to pass through predesignated phases that lead to successful exit. Upon exiting, they are expected to be better than when they entered college, that is, educated, mature, responsible, and acculturated.

Postsecondary institutions thus attempt in many ways to get students to conform to particular life-styles and communication patterns. Conflict develops when students' values, norms, and behavior are different from the college's values, norms, and expectations. Those students who differ from the majority on these points are often considered to be different, difficult, and even defiant.

Because colleges and universities are predominately white, middle- to upper-class social systems, low-income students come with socioeconomic need dispositions that are different from and generally in contrast to the institution's expectations of students. For example, Hannah (1969) finds that dropouts had strong neighborhood peer ties while in college and high needs for independence which resulted in conformity conflict. Rose and Elton (1966) observe that anxiety, hostility, maladjustment, nonconformity, and value conflicts are significantly related to leaving college. Many low-income students, particularly those who are also ethnic minorities, find adjustment to be a one-way street: they, not the institutions, must change. This creates a stressful situation that is often detrimental to academic performance.

Attempts to encourage low-income and minority students to accept middle-class values have been fruitless undertakings (Hampton, 1980). Yet the main aspiration of low-income and minority students has been and continues to be the same as that of other students, that is, to improve their economic status. College personnel must keep this simple fact in mind. Low-income students should be exposed to an expansive curriculum but not forced to accept it or penalized if they do not communicate certain expected values. Moreover, the burden of adjustment should not be placed entirely on the shoulders of low-income students; postsecondary institutions should compromise in adjusting to a changing student population.

Problems of Academic Adjustment. Equally important as social adjustment is academic adjustment (Ramist, 1981). Full integration into any environment depends upon a person's motivation. Because low-income students' previous educational experience in public elementary and secondary schools was, for the most part, unrewarding and lacking in encouragement from peers and teachers, they are not likely to be motivated to devote themselves to the traditional curriculum beyond what is minimally necessary. To maximize low-income students' learning, colleges and universities will need to adopt a theory of motivation to increase these students' desire to learn.

According to Atkinson and Birch's theory of achievement (1970), the probability that individuals will participate in learning activities is dependent on their previous experiences. That is, if such previous experiences have been positive, then the learning activities will be pursued. If past experiences have been mostly negative, individuals will not choose to engage themselves—it would be a risk to do so. Thus if one changes students' expectations about the consequences of participating in learning activities that have in the past been associated with failure and frustration, the likelihood that they will participate in learning will increase. Once expectations of positive outcomes and success are confirmed, then a mind-set of wanting to engage in learning will be established.

In practice then, postsecondary institutions need to create new expectations of acceptance and success for low-income students. Retention programs must incorporate activities which facilitate attaining incremental and achievable objectives, communicate that individuality with its inherent differences is all right, and demonstrate that deficiencies are not lasting detriments but are surmountable. In addition to designing special retention activities, colleges and universities need to recognize that to offer only the traditional curricula that low-income students encountered in public schools is to play to their weaknesses and to the strengths of traditional students. Low-income students need to be given opportunities to build on the learning strengths they do possess while bolstering learning skills that are less well developed.

Institutions also need to recognize that adjustment to campus life is crucial to academic success and social integration, which are, in turn, necessary for success in college. As Tinto (1975, p. 92) indicates, "A person can conceivably be integrated into the social sphere of the college and still drop out because of insufficient integration into the academic domain of the college."

Tinto's model of dropout, as presented in Chapter Two of this book, reinforces the observations made at the beginning of this chapter: a major shortcoming of previous research on dropouts is the inadequate attention given to questions of definition and to the development of theoretical models that explain rather than merely describe why students withdraw. His model goes beyond the social and academic dimensions to include individual characteristics and dispositions relevant to persistence as well as educational expectations and the individual's commitment to the institution. These interrelated factors can help to predict persistence and thus can be used in designing retention programs for low-income students.

A discussion of constructs that can provide the groundwork for retention programs for low-income students should include theories involving their learning styles and academic potential. A substantial body of information supports the premise that a majority of low-income students are victims of poor elementary and secondary schooling (Coleman and others, 1966). Since the quality of education students receive depends upon the wealth of the communities in which they reside (*San Antonio Independent School District* v. *Rodriquez*, 1973), it is logical to assume that low-income college students attended poor public schools. Therefore, their problems in competing academically with better prepared college students in a traditional college curriculum are not due to innate lack of ability but to inadequately developed skills and low self-concept resulting from poor school environments and negative attitudes on the part of their teachers.

Not all low-income students are academically deficient, but even those who are have the capability to succeed in college if methods of instruction and expectations are changed. Postsecondary institutions should not merely adopt the compensatory educational approach often employed by public schools; such an approach will not transform high-risk students into traditional college students. Remedial laboratories in community colleges and universities often do not go far enough. Their efforts frequently are directed toward keeping students who were in the bottom third of their graduating high school class in the bottom third of their graduating college class, instead of trying to develop students' abilities to compete in—rather than just cope with—college.

Because many students with acceptable levels of skills were still having learning problems in classes, Nisbet, Ruble, and Schurr (1982) seek a way of accurately profiling the learning behaviors of individual students to provide a better fit with various educational situations and delivery systems. They use the Myers-Briggs Type Indicator—which identifies sixteen learning types based on eight factors (extroversion, sensing, thinking, judging attitude, introversion, intuition, feeling, and perceptive attitude)—to determine the learning styles of high-risk students at Ball State University. In administering the test, the researchers found that high-risk students prefer formalized instruction, teacher-directed lessons, predictable academic routine, group-directed learning goals, and certain types of tests and reading assignments; they also desire immediate closure in teacher-announced projects and test dates. It is logical to assume that students with such preferences would have negative experiences in classes that are informal, flexible in instructional routine, and rely on open-ended assignments, student-directed discussions, and independent reading assignments. Thus, the Myers-Briggs Type Indicator is a valuable tool in diagnosing learning behaviors and can provide a basis for action in redirecting failure-prone students, such as low-income students, into learning experiences which are more compatible with their learning styles.

An alternative method of determining learning styles has been developed by Ramirez and Castaneda (1974). Their work in determining the cognitive learning styles of Mexican-American children is based on earlier research conducted by Witkin and others in 1962, which produced the concepts of field dependence and independence. After examining public school teaching styles and classroom environments, these researchers concluded that public school curricula were almost exclusively focused on field independent cognitive development. Very briefly, a field independent person favors independent work, likes to compete and gain individual recognition, is task oriented, favors formal interaction with teachers, prefers the discovery approach, and focuses on details of concepts. On the other hand, a field dependent person likes to work with and is sensitive to the feeling of others, desires a more personal relationship with teachers, works cooperatively, seeks guidance and demonstration in learning lessons, and focuses on global aspects of curriculum. Ramirez and Castaneda (1974) find that Mexican-American students coming from traditional families tended to be field dependent. The implication of their research is that students with cognitive styles incompatible with traditional college teaching methods and curricula are at a disadvantage. Ramirez and Castaneda provide instruments for assessing cognitive styles and advocate bicognitive development for all students, including the favored field independent students, because their development has been restricted by the continued emphasis on this style at the expense of the field dependent mode.

Learning can be enhanced not only by matching teaching styles, classroom environment, and curriculum to the learner but also by concentrating on improving the learner's motivation. There is a direct correlation between motivation and learning; how much one learns is dependent on how much one wants to learn. In addressing the issue of improving the motivation of high-risk students, Roueche and Mink (1979) employ the concept of locus of control. Through their extensive involvement in community colleges, they conclude that many high-risk students feel they have little or no control over their lives. They therefore postulate that if students could be helped to develop control over their behavior, they would be able to succeed as college students.

Locus of control is a personality variable developed from Rotter's (1954) social learning theory in which a continuum is used to define externals (where control over payoffs is seen by the learners to be outside of their control) and internals (where the learners believe that their behavior can control payoffs). According to Roueche and Mink's composite profile (1979, p. 7), internals have a higher self-concept; are generally better adjusted, more independent, more successful, and more realistic in their aspirations; are more open to new learning, more creative, more flexible, and increasingly self-reliant; show more initiative in controlling their environment; are less anxious; have higher grades; and show more interest in intellectual and achievement matters than externals. Considering these two profiles, the best strategy would seem to be to somehow convert externals to internals. Roueche and Mink offer instruments which identify internals and externals and discuss ways in which others have attempted to develop internal attitudes in students. They advocate the changing of attitude by work approaches rather than by word approaches.

Hampton (1980) recommends applying Maslow's need priority theory to increase the motivation level of low-income and minority students. Maslow's (1954) hierarchical set of needs, from low to high, are physiological, safety, belongingness and love, esteem, and self-actualization. In order for an individual to move from one level of need to the other, the lower order need must first be satisfied. Hampton maintains that because low-income students are often preoccupied with satisfying low-level needs, college personnel should focus on meeting the emotional and sensory needs of students before attempting to satisfy their conceptual and learning needs. To do so, Hampton recommends that external incentives be provided to low-income students making it materially worthwhile for them to learn. His logic is that if low-income students are paid for learning, they will have the chance to experience success and thus gradually build the internal initiative and motivation to carry on independently.

A Three Tier Typology of Intervention Strategies

With these theories about the persistence, adjustment to campus life, and learning styles of low-income students as a foundation, we can set forth a three tier typology of retention intervention strategies for such students.

Intervention Type I: Need-Specific Intervention. Intervention Type I, or need-specific intervention, is characteristic of retention programs which focus on one or more specific sets of student needs. An Intervention Type I retention program is made up of recruitment, admission, and orientation services focused on the specialized needs of nontraditional students. After such a program is established, a remedial laboratory to help students develop their basic skills might be added. A related but not necessarily coordinated service could be financial aid.

Intervention Type I retention programs are usually initiated to respond to federal requests for proposals (RFPs) and are thus drafted and designed to match specific criteria described in the RFP. The guidelines are often inconsistent with the needs of the student population to be served and available funds inadequate to provide the aid required by students. The Intervention Type I approach to retaining low-income or other nontraditional students is therefore inadequate because it is not comprehensive enough in providing the coordinated services needed by students and is usually unable to provide services to all students requiring or desiring help. Even more detrimental is the fact that such services are not designed on the basis of a thorough knowledge of the students to be served or the theoretical constructs discussed earlier. Intervention Type I strategies can only be effective if the student population to be served is in need of only minor remediation or assistance in developing coping skills. If, however, there are more than minor deficiencies to overcome, such retention programs are of little worth and should be implemented only after institutions have thoroughly assessed and prioritized their students' needs and when they have only limited resources to apply.

Intervention Type II: Comprehensive Strategies. The evolution of retention programs, the growth of research on high-risk students, and the accumulation of program evaluations have made it apparent that Intervention Type II, or comprehensive strategies, should be designed and implemented for low-income students. Successful retention depends upon numerous factors such as learning styles, financial need, social adjustment, and so on, and a college retention effort must be equal to all these factors. Consequently, an Intervention Type II retention program should include the following components: (1) recruitment; (2) admissions; (3) orientation; (4) a diagnosis and prescriptive center; (5) an academic skill development laboratory; (6) a counseling unit directed at personal development, career interest identification, and goal setting; (7) financial aid; and (8) a unit which deals with social integration via extracurricular involvements. A retention program with such an all-inclusive scope is essential if the multiple factors which influence retention are to be addressed.

Two programs which employ Type II intervention strategies are Project Pride at Tuskegee Institute in Alabama and the Summer Bridge Program at the University of California at San Diego. Project Pride is characterized by nearly all of the components identified as being part of a Type II strategy. Even though the Summer Bridge program is not as comprehensive in terms of components, it is cited here because it is designed on the basis of the theoretical constructs discussed earlier in this chapter.

Adding specialized services, even if they are comprehensive in nature (Type II approach), appears to be only a temporary solution, however. The increase of nontraditional students continues and there is no end in sight. The academic skills of these students may improve, but their attitude of remaining independent and faithful to their value system appears not to change. In fact, the history of American society demonstrates that cultural diversity will remain as long as there are different ethnic and racial groups residing here. Consequently, colleges and universities will need to go beyond temporary solutions and modify their norms and customs campuswide to accommodate this diverse student body.

Intervention Type III: Systemic Solutions. Intervention Type III entails a systemwide approach. Instead of retention efforts being limited to particular units, add-ons, and temporary programs, Type III intervention involves a systemic solution, that is, faculty changing their teaching methods, curricula being altered, administrators changing their attitudes, and governing boards modifying their admissions criteria and rules and regulations to make admissions and retention of nontraditional students possible. These changes should reflect the view that all students are equally qualified when we are willing to look at their situation from an alternative perspective.

Type III, or institutionwide intervention, is probably viewed by institutions as the most radical and most difficult to accomplish of the three, and rightfully so. Because it calls for a major overhaul of the campus operation and of the established means of conducting campus life, such revamping will require the initiative and constant support of the regents and chief executive officers. They will need to fashion a new mission statement which returns to the original purpose of universities—to provide a liberating experience for tomorrow's leaders. This will mean turning away from a preoccupation with gatekeeping (letting in only the best and brightest students). With a new mission statement which has learning as its centerpiece, admission requirements can be rewritten to legitimately qualify a larger number of students.

Faculty will alter their attitudes to be in accord with the revised mission statement and the new makeup of the student body. They will have to be retrained and provided with an alternative structure that will permit them to learn new teaching methods. Curriculum sequence and presentation will have to be examined and modified to fit the new mission and new students. A new type of faculty member will be attracted; already-employed faculty who do not change their expectations, and thus feel uncomfortable, will leave.

The colleges and universities likely to be first to establish Type III intervention are minority dominated. Although it is likely that the willpower to establish Type III intervention currently exists at such institutions, limited financial capability will more than likely slow its advent for the next two decades.

Conclusion

Attracting and retaining low-income students to higher education will be more successful and fruitful when institutions design and implement comprehensive (Type II) programs or, better still, when they evolve into Type III institutions. Whatever the intervention strategy now employed, the theoretical constructs discussed in this chapter addressing persistence, adjustment to campus life, and learning styles should be incorporated into retention efforts. But above all, it is fundamentally necessary for colleges and universities to be aware that their students vary in background, future aspirations and abilities, motivation, and academic skills. If we in higher education honor the research on and literature about low-income and other nontraditional students—students whom community colleges, four-year colleges, and major universities are receiving in greater numbers, new students who are different in many respects from the traditional college students of the past and not simply less capable academically—then we need to go beyond the current approach of making special adjustments to accommodate such students and consider revamping institutions as a whole.

References

Adolphus, S., and others. *Guidelines for the Design of Developmental Education Programs.* Washington, D.C.: Institute for Services to Education, 1979. (ED 193 346)

Astin, A. W. *Preventing Students from Dropping Out.* San Francisco: Jossey-Bass, 1975.

Astin, A. W. *Four Critical Years: Effects of College on Beliefs, Attitudes, and Knowledge.* San Francisco: Jossey-Bass, 1977.

Atkinson J. W., and Birch, D. *The Dynamics of Action.* New York: Wiley, 1970.

Bayer, A. E., and Boruch, R. F. *The Black Student in American Colleges.* Washington, D.C.: American Council on Education, 1969.

Beal, P. E., and Noel, L. *What Works in Student Retention.* Iowa City, Iowa: American College Testing Program and National Center for Higher Education Management Systems, 1980. (ED 197 635)

Coleman, J. S., and others. *Equality of Educational Opportunity.* Washington, D.C.: U.S. Office of Education, 1966.

Cross, K. P. *Beyond the Open Door: New Students to Higher Education.* San Francisco: Jossey-Bass, 1971.

de los Santos, A. G., Jr., Montemayor, J., and Solis, E. *Chicano Students in Institutions of Higher Education: Access, Attrition, and Achievement.* Austin: Office for Advanced Research in Hispanic Education, University of Texas, 1980. (ED 205 360)

Friedlander, J. "Are College Support Programs and Services Reaching High-Risk Students?" *Journal of College Student Personnel,* 1980, *21,* 23–28.

Hampton, P. J. "Innovative Strategies for Teaching Low-Income and Minority Students." *Teacher Educator,* 1980, *15* (4), 15–23.

Hannah, W. "Withdrawal from College." *Journal of College Student Personnel,* 1969, *10,* 397–402.

Maslow, A. H. *Motivation and Personality.* New York: Harper & Row, 1954.

Maynard, M. "Can Universities Adapt to Ethnic Minority Students' Needs?" *Journal of College Student Personnel,* 1980, *21* (5), 398–401.

Merton, R. K. *Social Theory and Social Structure.* New York: Free Press, 1968.

Meyers, C., and Drevlow, S. "Summer Bridge Program: A Dropout Intervention Program for Minority and Low-Income Students at the University of California at San Diego." Paper presented at annual meeting of American Educational Research Association, New York, March 1982. (ED 216 630)

Nisbet, J., Ruble, V., and Schurr, T. "Myers-Briggs Type Indicator: A Key to Diagnosing Learning Styles and Developing
Desirable Learning Behaviors in High-Risk College Students." In L. Noel and R. Levitz (eds.), *How to Succeed with
Academically Underprepared Students.* Iowa City, Iowa: American
College Testing Program National Center for Advancement
of Educational Practices, 1982.

Ramirez, M., and Castaneda, A. *Cultural Democracy, Bicognitive
Development, and Education.* Orlando, Fla.: Academic Press, 1974.

Ramist, L. "College Student Attrition and Retention." College Board Report no. 81-1, New York: College Board, 1981.
(ED 200 170)

Rose, H. A., and Elton, C. F. "Another Look at the College
Dropout." *Journal of Counseling Psychology,* 1966, *13*, 242–245.

Rotter, J. B. *Social Learning and Clinical Psychology.* Englewood
Cliffs, N.J.: Prentice-Hall, 1954.

Roueche, J. E., and Mink, O. *Improving Student Motivation.* New
York: Media Systems Corporation, 1979.

Roueche, J. E., and Snow, J. J. *Overcoming Learning Problems:
A Guide to Developmental Education in College.* San Francisco:
Jossey-Bass, 1977.

Rovezzi-Carroll, S., and Thompson, D. L. "Forecasting College Success for Low-Income Students." *Journal of College Student Personnel,* 1980, *21*, 340–343.

San Antonio Independent School District v. *Rodriguez,* 411 U.S. 1
(1973).

Schein, E. H. "Organizational Socialization and the Profession of Management." In A. O. Elbing (ed.), *Behavioral Decisions in Organizations.* Glenview, Ill: Scott, Foresman, 1970.

Tinto, V. "Dropout from Higher Education: A Theoretical Synthesis of Recent Research." *Review of Educational Research,*
1975, *45*, 89–125.

Turner, H. J., Jr. "The Half That Leaves: A Limited Survey
of Attrition in Community Colleges." Gainesville: Institute of
Higher Education, University of Florida, 1970. (ED 038 127)

Wheeler, S. "The Structure of Formally Organized Socializing Settings." In O. G. Brim and S. Wheeler (eds.), *Socialization After Childhood: Two Essays.* New York: Wiley, 1966.

6

Academically
Underprepared Students

William Moore, Jr.
Lorraine C. Carpenter

In an attempt to be what some call innovative in working with
academically underprepared students, educators have employed
reality therapy, behavior modification techniques, value clarification exercises, management-by-objectives strategies, activities
to improve students' self-concept, and so on. Three limitations
are immediately discernible in such methods. The first is that
they do not relate directly to the improvement of instruction
in any measurable way. The second is that such techniques are
based on assumptions which suggest that there is something
wrong in the psychological condition, behavior, or makeup of
students who are academically underprepared. Ryan (1976)
calls this blaming the victim. And, third, we can find no evidence to suggest that instruction is more effective with the use
of such techniques. Indeed, ''spending an inordinate amount
of time linking academic skill deficiencies in adults to self-
worth, cultural factors, race, economics, family dysfunction
and disorganization, and past performance has not proved to
be a useful exercise in terms of information that will help . . .

teachers improve the teaching and learning process'' (Moore, 1983, p. 33).

Quality instruction, as we view it, has nothing to do with so-called innovations. Instead, such innovations, established under the concept that understanding the class and psychosocial pathology of students contributes to the instructor's ability to help them, are interventions and intrusions into the privacy and life-styles of academically deficient students.

In this chapter we will examine the limitations of traditional characterizations of underprepared students; consider the two main approaches currently used in working with these students—support services and curriculum adjustments—and suggest new foci for truly innovative research that would put the emphasis on improving the quality of instruction, on institutional change and true innovation, rather than on the psychosocial characteristics of underprepared students.

Defining the Academically Underprepared

Academically underprepared students are those students with distinctive characteristics that are perceived by the academic community to place them at a disadvantage in contention with the vast majority of students who enter college with the acdemic skills necessary for success in college (Roueche, 1967, 1972; Roueche and Kirk, 1973; Moore, 1970, 1971, 1976; and Kraetsch, 1980). These characteristics are usually portrayed on two dimensions. The evident and measurable dimensions include, but are not limited to, erratic academic performance both in high school and as college freshmen, unimpressive standardized test scores, low socioeconomic background, race, gender, and rate of persistence and withdrawal from college. The vague and speculative dimensions which cannot be measured with precision include depressed motivation; poor abstract and conceptual skills; low self-esteem; poor self-concept; unclear goals; and being culturally deficient, verbally passive, and educationally disadvantaged.

Waterhouse (1978, p. 39) summarizes both of these dimensions by saying that underprepared students are ''unsure of themselves; need success—cognitive and/or affective; need financial assistance; need tutoring and basic skill development; possess minimal knowledge of career and educational opportunities and skills related to taking advantage of both; and need to feel comfortable within the learning environment." Green (1977) is more specific. He targets minority group students in particular as including many underachievers who are dysfunctional because they do not have the confidence and academic self-esteem to perform in college.

Misleading Characterizations. Characteristics just described can be misleading. They can lead one to believe that academically underprepared students are confined to lower-class and minority students. Researchers in higher education began to focus on these groups in the early 1960s; since then, they have continued to highlight and restate, if not update, their characteristics.

There are, in fact, many other students who make up the pool of academically underprepared students. More specifically, the academically underprepared students of the late 1970s and early 1980s represent a diverse population. Included are older women (widows, divorced women, and those at particular junctures in the life cycle), war veterans, workers whose jobs have been changed or eliminated, persons who are attempting to change careers, others who are being subjected to rapid and extreme social and technological change, and still others who chose not to enter college immediately after completing high school. Only half of the college going population at the end of the 1970s entered directly from high school (Henderson and Plummer, 1978, p. 25).

The New Underprepared. Cross (1971, 1981) identified some of these new underprepared students at the beginning of the seventies and again at the beginning of the eighties. They have special persistence problems. Some were not poor achievers in high school, did not score low on standardized tests before they left high school, and were neither culturally nor educationally disadvantaged. There is little reason to believe that most of them suffer the psychological maladies (low self-esteem, poor self-concept, low motivation) that those in the academic community associate with underachievement and underpreparation. There are upperclass students who are academically underprepared, but their lack of academic preparation and high dropout rates have not received a large amount of attention.

Research Findings Consistent but Limited. Because of the limited character of the underprepared population studied, researchers' findings on retention have been remarkably consistent. They consistently demonstrate, for example, that the lack of social cohesion in the external environment of many students and the perceived lack of psychological cohesion in the internal environment are important factors in the persistence or withdrawal of underprepared students. We must, however, look at underprepared students today. If we see who and where they are, and see their pervasiveness at every level of higher education institutions, we can begin asking the right questions in our research.

Where and in What Types of Institutions Do Academically Underprepared Students Enroll?

Academic underpreparedness among students in the nation's colleges and universities is widespread and a major concern. "The fastest growing college and university programs in the nation are in developmental education" (Roueche and Armes, 1980, p. 21). Underprepared students can be identified in surprisingly large numbers in such diverse institutions as some of the most prestigious Ivy League Colleges; in large land-grant institutions; in small sectarian and independent liberal arts colleges; and in community, junior, and technical colleges. At Stanford, Ohio State University, University of California at Berkeley, Louisiana State University, University of Texas, and many other senior institutions nationwide, programs are provided for students with academic deficiencies. In a study conducted by the American College Testing Program, over half of the 300 colleges and universities surveyed had programs for the academically underprepared (Noel, Levitz, and Kaufmann, 1982). It must be noted, however, that underprepared does not mean the same thing at Harvard and Stanford as it does at the local community, technical, or state college.

Declining standardized test scores as well as statistics indicating that 30 to 40 percent of entering freshmen are deficient

in college-level reading and writing skills have been used by
educators to demonstrate that a significant number of students
come to school academically deficient and that the need for
remedial education is pervasive throughout American colleges
(Wharton, 1979, p. 39). Community colleges report that "more
than half of the entering freshman class read below the eighth-
grade level" (Roueche and Roueche, 1982, p. 32). Kissler (1980,
p. 8) complains that the undergraduate division of the University of California is threatened by the decline in the quality of
students in its traditional feeder institutions. Kissler's observation confirms that of Cohen and Lombardi (1979).

Increased College Attendance Among Minority Students. Of the
4.8 million students who attend community colleges, one fourth
of them are representative of minority groups. And 40 percent
of the ethnic minorities attending colleges attend community
colleges, with the majority being blacks (Cohen and Brawer,
1982, p. 42). There are many reasons why such students have
found their way into college, and why their presence is so widespread. For those characterized as culturally and educationally
disadvantaged and often considered discriminated against, the
reasons are clear: the passage of federal laws opening up equal
educational opportunity for more citizens; the provisions in state
laws guaranteeing admission to state schools for all students who
earn a high school diploma or its equivalent; the open-door
policies and accessibility of community colleges; targeted recruitment by many institutions who need the tuition dollars; pur-
suit of government funds with their stipulations that specified
populations be served, and so on.

Influence of Social Promotion. One can also point to the
prevalence of all forms of social promotion, beginning in public
schools and ending in graduate schools. these conclusions are
consistent with the findings of national studies and editorial com-
ment (National Commission on Excellence, 1983; and Stone,
1981). The underprepared status of those who did not suffer
such social maladies may be due to poor education, changes
in job and specific skill requirements, and so on. They may also
be among that group of students who are older and who are
attempting to make significant changes in their lives.

Growing Professional Interest. There is further evidence of the prevalence of underprepared students in the nation's colleges and universities. The National Developmental Education Conference was originally designed for community college personnel, and two-year college people attended its first national meeting in 1972. Within three years, more than 20 percent of the meeting registrants were from senior colleges and universities, including prestigious private colleges. By 1982, the number of participants had increased threefold and senior college and university people accounted for one in three participants. From this conference were spawned state and regional conferences focusing on exchanging ideas on understanding and teaching underprepared students.

It might be concluded then that the academically underprepared student pool is large and diverse in terms of age, socioeconomic condition, previous academic performance, standardized test scores, and emotional health, and is enrolled in colleges and universities of all types nationwide. This suggests that the old assumptions about who withdraws and who persists and what we can do to help may need reexamining.

Specific Programs and Pracices: Some Suggestions

Many approaches have been employed to increase retention of underprepared students, but only two are in widespread use and have repeatedly been described as successful, although attrition rates seem to remain constant. The first is to buy professional and support services for underprepared students. The second is to make minor adjustments in the curriculum.

Support Services. Under the first approach, providing support services, counselors have been hired, tutorial services provided, special preenrollment provisions established, and summer preenrollment orientations initiated.

Despite the fact that counseling is often viewed as crucial to the retention of high-risk students, those students still approach it only as a last resort (Gordon and Hutson, 1971; and Benedict, Apsler, and Morrison, 1977). Students go to others before they go to counselors (Christensen and others, 1976). In fact, counseling center programs to counteract attrition have failed to alter the withdrawal rate (Garni, 1980). Counseling effectiveness with high-risk students is negligible (Gallagher and Demos, 1970). Groves and Groves (1981, p. 312) suggest areas that need improvement in counseling, including (1) personalizing the experience, (2) evaluating students, (3) helping students improve skills necessary to achieve academic standing, (4) helping students assess college major choice, and (5) helping students evaluate and understand long-range educational goals.

Tutorial services provided often include group tutoring courses, peer tutoring, and dial-a-tutor programs. Success has been noted in institutions where this type of resource is available. As part of a program called Supplemental Instruction at the University of Missouri at Kansas City, a group tutoring course, Studying for Biology, is taken by students concurrently with freshman biology. A follow-up of students taking biology and Studying for Biology in fall of 1982 indicated that 20 percent more students passed biology (and with higher grades) than in the year before when Studying for Biology was not offered (Martin, Blanc, and De Buhr, 1982). In the peer tutoring programs at Bellevue Community College in Washington and the University of Alabama in Huntsville, tutors work not only on developing skills that will generalize to all courses, but on tutoring for success in specific subjects. Dial-a-tutor is used during evenings and weekends when tutors are not available in person.

Special preenrollment processes enable counselors and developmental studies staff to identify and meet with underprepared students and begin counseling and academic support prior to enrollment. This early and continuing contact with high-risk students has had a positive impact on student success and retention (Noel, Levitz, and Kaufmann, 1982). Through one such program, Assistance in Development, in use at Onondaga Community College in Syracuse, New York, students who have graduated in the lowest quarter of their high school class participate in a one-semester program designed to help them integrate general career exploration and increased personal awareness with specific skills. A reading and study skills program may be offered for students admitted on probation. ''If the student who is deficient in reading and study skills is also motivated to improve such skills, the intangible variables of self-discipline, persistence, appropriate counseling when needed, and maturity will also contribute to his or her ultimate success in the completion of a college degree'' (Sheridan, 1982, p. 141).

Summer preenrollment orientation is one of the oldest and most widely used programs to increase the success rate of conditionally accepted freshmen. There is evidence that some skill enhancement and development of higher aspirations toward education takes place in these programs (Scherer and Wygant, 1982). Critics maintain that little remediation of the basic academic skills can take place in a summer. Etzioni (1971, p. 115) reviews the findings of 150 studies of compensatory programs and concludes that putting high-risk students through a few courses such as those offered in summer programs could not remedy the academic disparity that separates those students from their academically prepared classmates. What *can* take place in that time is acquainting students with the institution, and with the services and resources that can help them negotiate and adjust to the system.

Curriculum Adjustments. With regard to the second main approach to helping underprepared students, minor adjustments in the curriculum have included developmental and remedial programs. Essentially, these programs constitute review courses in the basic academic areas such as English, reading, mathematics, and the social sciences. In a follow-up study of dropouts from developmental programs, it was found that students drop out of these programs for many reasons, including the amount of time required; leaders' lack of empathy; and dissatisfaction with the program and its leaders (Barrow, 1980).

There are a number of issues associated with curriculum adjustments about which the academic community has not achieved consensus. Should academically deficient students be required to take remedial courses or should their participation be voluntary? Should students receive credit for remedial courses successfully completed? Should the credit earned be included on their transcripts to meet graduation requirements? Should students' writing be evaluated across the curriculum by all their instructors regardless of subject? What about entry-level assessment and placement?

A major question is whether remedial courses should be voluntary or mandatory. Should academically deficient students be able to decide whether or not they enroll in remedial courses? We say no for several reasons. Academically deficient students have already demonstrated that their academic skills are below the minimum required to succeed in college-level courses. It follows that to correct those deficiencies, some type of remediation must take place. While it may be perceived as arrogant or authoritarian and may be human relations heresy, the fact is that in this case, the professionals do know what is best for students. This is not to suggest that professionals always do what is best for students. However, even open-door institutions have a right and responsibility to set minimum standards that students must meet in order to take courses, enter programs, and fulfill degree requirements.

The transcript credit versus noncredit issue is another consideration that generates controversy. We believe that a student who pays for a remedial course and successfully completes that course should have something to show for it. This does not mean that the credit received for a remedial course will satisfy the requirements for a nonremedial course. The successful completion of a remedial course only qualifies or helps the student to qualify for a course or program whose criteria he or she could not initially satisfy. In short, remedial courses are not at a sufficient level of academic rigor to meet degree requirements. They are corrective, compensatory, and preparatory courses. It is not unusual, however, for some institutions to permit students to use credit earned in such courses to fulfill their elective requirements.

Institutions should establish policies that are educationally sound and provide the best opportunities for the student. Give the student the appropriate credit for all of the educational experiences provided and mastered, but make sure that any restrictions imposed on the use of that credit are understood. Students must understand that remedial credit provides them with only a limited warranty.

Closely related to the question of mandatory enrollment in remedial courses is the issue of assessment and placement. Assessment is crucial to any program of remediation. It is the point of departure, the rationale for what is taught to whom and for what reason. It provides academic profiles of the students which serve as the basis for making instructional prescriptions to assist them. It provides the rationale for placement of students in a curriculum appropriate to the level of their demonstrated achievement. The placement of students in programs based on objective assessment makes educational sense. McCabe (1981) maintains that academic skills should be assessed and a total assessment of the student's abilities, values, career orientation, and so on made.

New and Innovative Approaches?

In reviewing programs that fall under the two major approaches to helping underprepared students—support services and curriculum adjustments—we were unable to find any approaches to the remediation of high-risk students that we consider totally new or innovative. Preenrollment programs, tutorial services, counseling, peer counseling, the use of programmed texts, skill laboratories, writing laboratories, cognitive matching, special courses on how to study and how to succeed in college, and the placement of students in special and supportive programs cannot be considered new or innovative.

Consider, for example, the English workshop model. It was designed and implemented at Stowe Teachers' College in Saint Louis, Missouri in 1947, by the late Dr. Ruth M. Harris. The biology tutorial program described by Martin, Blanc, and De Buhr (1982) is very similar to one conceived and implemented by Dean Dunbar, professor of biology at Saint Louis Community College at Forest Park, Missouri in 1966. Both writing laboratories and mathematics laboratories were part of the Programmed Materials Learning Laboratory implemented at the same college in 1965. Skill laboratories have been in wide use for more than two decades. Cognitive matching has been used at Mountain View College in Dallas, Texas for almost ten years. Special orientation courses for freshmen have been a curriculum staple for both two- and four-year colleges for decades. Claude Ware and his associates at Los Angeles City College raised peer counseling to the level of an art during the early 1970s. A dial-a-tutor program was introduced by Ben Standifer at Dunbar High School in Fort Worth, Texas in 1982. During the late 1960s, Experiment in Higher Education, designed to take underprepared students and guide them through a special program to the baccalaureate, was implemented at Southern Illinois University at Edwardsville. Both mandatory and self-selection remedial programs have been in effect for many years.

The Truly Innovative. In sum, after examining sources that listed hundreds of programs designed for underprepared students, we could not find a single one that could now be considered innovative. Perhaps the problem is that what may be truly innovative may also be inconceivable from the point of view of many college personnel. They may not, for example, consider hiring elementary school teachers to teach basic skills to underachieving students at the university level. This has, however, been done at community colleges. Roueche mentioned this strategy in the late sixties, but it was by no means original with him (Roueche, 1967). During the early years of special programs for working with the educationally disadvantaged, elementary school teachers were actively recruited. It is rather common for community colleges to hire part-time teachers from all levels of education as well as from business and industry. Seattle Central Community College in Washington used elementary teachers to provide instruction to academically deficient students in 1969. In the late 1940s and early 1950s, Stowe Teachers' College assigned substitute teachers from the ranks of elementary school teachers.

The logic of employing elementary school teachers to teach remedial courses is axiomatic: they teach most Americans how to read and write. They know about how people learn the basic skills, and their focus is on the subject matter and the students, not on research, publication, and other factors that are a part of the higher education community. As elementary teachers they are not a part of the college and university ethos and the established reward system. Since most of them work in open, non-selective systems, they are accustomed to working with students with widely varying ability levels and appear to be tolerant of students who perform at lower levels.

Attitude Change Needed. There is clear evidence that academically deficient students will be a part of the higher education population for some time to come (Hodgkinson, 1983). There are little data to suggest that those who deliver instructional services will be able to successfully accommodate this reality. Most of what we believe to be truly innovative has little to do with one particular teaching method or another, but with attitudes. Will academic personnel voluntarily change their attitudes or, at least, some of their practices with regard to who is qualified to teach or be their colleague, which students deserve and are eligible for or entitled to their services, and which activities—teaching, research, or service—will receive priority?

True Innovation Means Good Teaching

We believe that the most innovative thing that an institution can do to help academically underprepared students is to furnish them with teachers who can provide quality instruction irrespective of students' age, race, gender, economic situation, psychological perspective, previous test scores, and past performance.

Promoting and Rewarding Good Teaching. In order to promote this kind of good teaching we believe that it is necessary, first, to recognize it, and then to reward it. The most impressive recognition that a program can receive in an institution is that which comes from the president, the administrator(s) in charge of academic affairs, and the deans. (Department chairpersons are not included here because they are usually more representative of the faculty and less involved with resource allocation.) Persons in control of resources can encourage teaching improvement efforts without apparent force or direct command. Recognition means public and private advocacy; it entails adequate publicity and support in terms of receiving the same level of staff facilities, materials, and benefits available to other programs in the institution.

With regard to rewarding good teaching, we suggest that some individual, group, or organization in the institution must initiate the proposal, seek wide participation in the community, identify the resources, and develop the processes for implementing the reward system. Distinguished teaching awards are given at the Ohio State University in Columbus each year. The eight recipients come from all parts of the university and represent a diversity of programs. They have included distinguished professors who teach theoretical physics and junior professors who teach beginning photography. They have been nominated by their students for this award, which carries with it a cash prize of $1,500 in addition to a plaque, and a dinner attended by university officials, the families of the recipients, the students who made the nominations, and others in the university community.

Joseph P. Cosand, former president of Saint Louis Community College at Forest Park, did it differently. He convinced his board of trustees that exemplary programs and teachers should be recognized and rewarded. The board agreed that 4 percent of the instructional budget should be set aside to carry out this strategy. As it turned out, most of the rewards went to teachers and administrators associated with the General Curriculum Project, a program for academically deficient students.

Elements of Good Teaching. When institutional leaders and faculty focus on instruction, fair and equitable distribution of resources, and equal recognition of all programs, they create an atmosphere in which good teaching can flourish. Good teachers are teachers who (1) believe instruction to be their first academic priority, (2) focus on content, (3) engage in problem-solving activities with their students, (4) understand the importance and application of the basic academic skills and insist that their students have command of those skills, (5) design academic exercises to develop conceptual skills, (6) recognize the significance of good academic habits, (7) understand the principles of learning, (8) have some command of instructional technology, (9) have the patience to work with students who are academically deficient, (10) are willing to develop their own approaches and trust their own instincts, and (11) continue to grow professionally by updating their skills, and by staying abreast of changes, new knowledge, and trends in their field. We stop short of prescribing any specific method; it is our experience that all methods can be effective. We do, however, note that all of the above activities suggest direct involvement with learners and with knowledge, planning, and design as well as some control of instructional elements. (See also the criteria Roueche and Roueche set forth in their chapter on teaching.)

Conclusion

The Reality: The Existing Situation. From every indication, educators do not really know what makes high-risk students persist or drop out of college. Identifying and understanding their motives or the particular circumstances that trigger their withdrawal or sustain their persistence has eluded scholars and practitioners. The voluminous information and prodigious research on attrition in higher education does not provide conclusive evidence of what causes students to persist or withdraw. Many variables have been identified and correlated with persistence and nonpersistence but the study of such relationships reveals very little about causality. Moreover, even the most recent research has omitted a large and growing population of academically underprepared students.

The Seekers: The Researchers. Most researchers who investigate the retention and voluntary withdrawal of high-risk students from college have not broken with the traditional approach of concentrating on lower-class social and psychological pathology—paths already trodden for more than two decades with high-risk students. There exists yet another concern about researchers who study underprepared students: they often seem to design their studies to assert certain positions, refute others, omit still others, and to carve out a particular point of view. Understandably they approach their subjects from the perspectives of their own discipline. Such judgments and choices may be unavoidable; they may even be appropriate, but they also demonstrate why researchers often cannot extricate themselves from the social phenomena studied.

Moreover, researchers are affected by the ever-present

political and social forces to which they must be sensitive. The choice of variables included or omitted in the study of high-risk students is a case in point. Some variables are sacrosanct. Researchers do not often choose, for example, to correlate the variables of faculty attitudes about the race and gender of high-risk students with persistence and nonpersistence. The correlation of such variables is, to be sure, controversial, politically sensitive, and methodologically troublesome for researchers, but might provide significant information about the influence of faculty attitudes and behavior. Pascarella and others (1981, p. 347) may be correct in their assertion that "voluntary withdrawal is less a function of preenrollment traits than postenrollment experiences."

The Inquiry: Research. The research on retention and withdrawal is plentiful and has been reported and published in the social and behavioral science journals, in the literature of college admissions and financial assistance reports, in federal documents, in the general higher education literature, and in the popular press. The research data have been broadly disseminated, but the data tend to confuse rather than clarify, are more descriptive than experimental, and more speculative than theoretical. Contradictions between and among these data are inevitable since they originate from a multiplicity of sources. The statistical procedures used to quantify the relationships and other conditions examined in the research have become increasingly complex and sophisticated, often receiving as much attention as the phenomena studied. This fine tuning of statistical procedures may have improved the quantification process but has done little, if anything, to assist the investigator in finding answers to why high-risk students drop out or persist.

The Proposal. Since poor retention has not been responsive to most of the past remedies, its causes have not been determined definitively, and workable solutions and targeted research are still being sought, it may well be that new foci are needed. Focusing on traits, on conditions that the institution and its agents cannot modify, and on other variables designed to show how different underachievers are from other students seems counterproductive.

A starting point is to correct some of the research omissions. As Tinto notes in his chapter on defining dropout, a high-risk dropout must be clearly defined. Presently all students who leave voluntarily and without officially withdrawing are classified as dropouts; there are not provisions for what could be described as legitimate reasons for withdrawing. Indeed, there does not appear to be any situation where a student can withdraw and not be considered a nonpersister, a term which holds negative connotation and implies that the student is a quitter and could not make it.

Suggested Guidelines. Some suggested ways to improve the research methodology include treating success in college as a sequential process rather than emphasizing graduation after a four-year period. With an older, part-time student population and one increasingly engaged in working, lifelong learning over many years needs to be studied. The need for making a distinction between permanent and temporary withdrawal becomes increasingly apparent. Research has shown that part-time students are less likely than full-time students to progress to the sophomore year and working students are less likely to progress to the sophomore year than non-working students (Kohen, Nestel, and Karmas, 1976). However, a portion of that heterogeneous working group shows an extraordinarily high commitment to their goals and views work as the only means of meeting the expense of college attendance.

Kohen, Nestel, and Karmas also find that as students advance from freshman status, the likelihood of their completing a subsequent year of schooling generally increases. It is uncertain, however, whether the factors determining successful completion of the freshman year would cause similar success in subsequent years. More longitudinal research in this area is needed. Their findings further indicate that those students who were enrolled in the college preparatory curriculum in high school and who receive scholarship assistance in college were also less likely to leave college early. Their principal conclusion was that factors important to understanding persistence vary with the stage of the undergraduate career and are not significantly related to socioeconomic status, race, marital status, or age.

The retention findings to date are not readily generalized because they are frequently institution specific. Comparative studies of several colleges might reveal similar strains and characteristics which would be helpful in analyzing factors contributing to retention. At the very least, these research possibilities might be examined. Researchers might also consider asking different questions.

Questions We Need to Ask. Although much research has been done and many questions asked about the personal characteristics, aptitudes, aspirations, environmental conditions, and collegiate experiences of the high-risk underprepared student, additional questions should be asked. What causes the lack of persistence among low-risk, privileged students? Is persistence or withdrawal a clear choice of the individual involved? What students persist to avoid job responsibilities, to receive veterans' benefits, or to participate in other financial assistance programs? What other individuals have very private motives for persisting which are never revealed? Older women appear to persist or not persist for special reasons; what are they?

Much of the research deals with a "typical" student, but this student is no longer typical. An increasingly large percentage of students in the enrollment pool are nontraditional students. Should checks be made to determine whether or not their behavior matches what is considered to be normal? Further, most of the published research focuses on students at traditional, residential universities. How different might the results be at nontraditional, commuter, and community colleges?

Another suggestion concerns closing the gap between the students' expectations of what college will be and what it really is. Comparison studies of counseling procedures in various feeder schools might reveal which students are receiving realistic college advising and which students are not. Articulation between and among the high schools and other levels of higher education to increase awareness and communication about what is actually occurring in these institutions is a crucial idea whose time has certainly come.

Finally, putting faculty members back into the role of advising and teaching undergraduates is strongly suggested.

Teaching assistants are frequently inadequate substitutes for veteran, experienced, successful faculty members.

In short, all the studies deal with the necessity of the students changing if they are to persist. Instead, we should be asking if changes are needed in the structure and design of educational institutions to ameliorate existing persistence and withdrawal patterns. We should consider if research should be concentrating on variables, such as instruction, that have a direct relationship to achievement. It is only through such new questions that we can develop truly innovative approaches to working with a growing and ever-changing population of underprepared students.

References

Barrow, J. C. "Follow-up of Dropouts from Developmental Programs: A Supplemental Program Evaluation Approach." *Personnel and Guidance Journal*, 1980, *59*, 186–189.

Benedict, A. R., Apsler, R., and Morrison, S. "Student Views of Their Counseling Needs and Counseling Services." *Journal of College Student Personnel*, 1977, *18*, 110–114.

Christensen, K. C., and others. "Where Clients Go Before Contacting the University Counseling Center." *Journal of College Student Personnel*, 1976, *17* (5), 396–399.

Cohen, A. M., and Brawer, F. B. *The American Community College*. San Francisco: Jossey-Bass, 1982.

Cohen, A. M., and Lombardi, J. "Can the Community Colleges Survive Success?" *Change*, 1979, *11* (8), 24–27.

Cross, K. P. *Beyond the Open Door: New Students to Higher Education*. San Francisco: Jossey-Bass, 1971.

Cross, K. P. *Adults as Learners: Increasing Participation and Facilitating Learning*. San Francisco: Jossey-Bass, 1981.

Etzioni, A. "The Policy of Open Admissions." In G. K. Smith (ed.), *New Teaching, New Learning: Current Issues in Higher Education 1971*. San Francisco: Jossey-Bass, 1971.

Gallagher, P. J., and Demos, G. D. (eds.). *The Counseling Center in Higher Education*, Springfield, Ill.: Thomas, 1970.

Garni, K. F. "Counseling Centers and Student Retention: Why

the Failures? Where the Successes?" *Journal of College Student Personnel*, 1980, *21*, 223–228.

Gordon, L., and Hutson, J. "College Student Attrition and the Counseling Factor." *Public Affairs Bulletin*, 1971, *10* (2).

Green, N. "Do I Belong in College?" *Community College Frontiers*, 1977, *5* (2), 20–25.

Groves, S. L., and Groves, D. L. "The Academic Assistants Adviser Program." *College Student Journal*, 1981, *15* (4), 309–314.

Henderson, C., and Plummer, J. C. *Adapting to Changes in the Characteristics of College-Age Youth.* Policy Analysis Service Reports, *4* (2). Washington, D.C.: American Council on Education, 1978.

Hodgkinson, H. L. "Guess Who's Coming to College: A Demographic Portrait of Students in the 1990s." *Academe*, 1983, *69* (2), 13–20.

Kissler, G. R. "Trends Affecting Undergraduate Education in the University of California." Paper presented to Board of Regents of University of California, Berkeley, Oct. 1980. (ED 194 138)

Kohen, A. I., Nestel, G., and Karmas, C. *Success and Failure in College: A New Approach to Persistence in Undergraduate Programs.* Columbus: Center for Human Resource Research, College of Administrative Science, Ohio State University, Feb. 1976.

Kraetsch, G. A. "The Role of Community Colleges in the Basic Skills Movement." *Community College Review*, 1980, *8* (2), 18–23.

McCabe, R. H. "Now Is the Time to Reform the American Community College." *Community and Junior College Journal*, 1981, *51* (8), 6–10.

Martin, D., Blanc, R., and De Buhr, L. "Supplemental Instruction: A Model for Increasing Student Performance and Persistence." In L. Noel and R. Levitz (eds.), *How to Succeed with Academically Underprepared Students.* Iowa City, Iowa: American College Testing Program National Center for Advancement of Educational Practices, 1982.

Moore, W., Jr. *Against the Odds: The High-Risk Student in the Community College.* San Francisco: Jossey-Bass, 1970.

Moore, W., Jr. *Blind Man on a Freeway: The Community College Administrator.* San Francisco: Jossey-Bass, 1971.

Moore, W., Jr. *Community College Response to the High-Risk Student: A Critical Reappraisal.* Horizons Issues, no. 1. Washington, D.C.: American Association of Community and Junior Colleges, 1976. (ED 122 873)

Moore, W., Jr. "Special Roles with Special Students." In A. S. Thurston and W. A. Robbins (eds.), *Counseling: A Crucial Function for the 1980s.* New Directions for Community Colleges, no. 43. San Francisco: Jossey-Bass, 1983, 29–47.

National Commission on Excellence in Education. *A Nation at Risk: The Imperative for Educational Reform.* Washington, D.C.: U.S. Government Printing Office, 1983.

Noel, L., Levitz, R., and Kaufmann, J. "Campus Services for Academically Underprepared Students." In L. Noel and R. Levitz (eds.), *How to Succeed with Academically Underprepared Students.* Iowa City, Iowa: American College Testing Program National Center for Advancement of Educational Practices, 1982.

Pascarella, E. T., and others. "Preenrollment Variables and Academic Performance as Predictors of Freshman-Year Persistence, Early Withdrawal, and Stop-Out Behavior in an Urban, Nonresidential University." *Research in Higher Education,* 1981, *15* (4), 329–349.

Roueche, J. E. "Gaps and Overlaps in Institutional Research." *Junior College Journal,* 1967, *38* (3), 20–23.

Roueche, J. E. *A Modest Proposal: Students Can Learn.* San Francisco: Jossey-Bass, 1972.

Roueche, J. E., and Armes, N. R. "Basic Skills Education: Point-Counterpoint." *Community and Junior College Journal,* 1980, *50* (6), 21–24.

Roueche, J. E., and Kirk, R. W. *Catching Up: Remedial Education.* San Francisco: Jossey-Bass, 1973.

Roueche, J. E., and Roueche, S. D. "Literacy Development: Foundation for General Education." In B. L. Johnson (ed.), *General Education in Two-Year Colleges.* New Directions for Community Colleges, no. 40. San Francisco: Jossey-Bass, 1982, 31–37.

Ryan, W. *Blaming the Victim*. New York: Vintage Books, 1976.

Scherer, C., and Wygant, N. S. "Sound Beginnings Support Freshmen Transition into University Life." *Journal of College Student Personnel*, 1982, *23* (5), 378–383.

Sheridan, E. M. "Traditional Skills for Nontraditional Students." *Improving College and University Teaching*, 1982, *30* (3), 138–141.

Stone, M. "Soon, a Nation of Illiterates?" *U.S. News and World Report*, Sept. 7, 1981, p. 76.

Waterhouse, P. G. "What's So Nontraditional About Nontraditional Students?" *Community and Junior College Journal*, 1978, *48* (5), 39–40.

Wharton, C. R., Jr. "The Darwinism of Basic Learning." *Change*, 1979, *11* (8), 38–41.

7

Students with Uncertain Academic Goals

Virginia N. Gordon

College students with unclear, unrealistic, or uncertain academic and vocational goals have been identified in several attrition studies as a dropout-prone population (Abel, 1966; and Astin, 1975). Undecided students have been the subject of numerous research studies for over fifty years (Crites, 1969), but they have only recently been recognized as a target group for retention programs. Some of the general factors identified as causing attrition have also been used to describe the undecided student population. These characteristics include lack of career objectives, unsure degree expectations, selection of certain majors (for example, science majors are more persistent than many other majors), absence of or a change in career goals, and a lack of adequate advising services (Astin, 1971; Cope and Hannah, 1975; and Pantages and Creedon, 1978).

A great deal of research on undecided students over the past fifty years has examined a variety of personal variables such as interests, abilities, values, family background, risk-taking tendencies, levels of anxiety, and self-identity issues (Ashby, Wall, and Osipow, 1966; Baird, 1967; Elton and Rose, 1971; Lowe, 1981; and McGowan, 1977). Many of these studies describe

116

students who enter college undecided; others examine the changes that students make as they progress through the college years. Many researchers have concluded that students entering college undecided are a heterogenous group and that it is difficult if not dangerous to make generalizations about them. The voluminous research does, however, permit the following characteristics to be noted as typical of this important student population:

1. Undecided students constitute a large number of students. The number and type of uncommitted students on a given campus will reflect the institution's policy toward exploration. This policy can be discerned in what is said or not said at orientation, the organizational or delivery systems used to accommodate undecided students, and the type of advising and career services that are provided specifically for them.

2. Because their aptitude levels and interest patterns reflect those of the general student population on a given campus, entering undecided students at most colleges provide a microcosm of the freshman class. Many undecided students have multiple interests and the aptitude to succeed in many areas just as do many decided students.

3. Some undecided students may feel anxious about making an educational or vocational choice, but in most cases, this level of anxiety is quite healthy and not debilitating. Goodstein (1965) identifies students who are indecisive. Those students for whom anxiety is debilitating and permeates every decision, minor or major, require more in-depth counseling than those expressing normal anxiety about selecting a major.

4. Many undecided students are quite aware that they need concrete information about their interest areas before making a choice. They feel free to admit this and are usually open to, and indeed expect, advising assistance to help them explore their options.

5. Some students require help in understanding the decision-making process itself and assistance in identifying and acquiring the skills needed to make satisfying, realistic, and long-reaching decisions.

Recent research findings indicating that multiple subgroups exist within the undecided population have led to the development of diagnostic schemes to identify the multidimensional reasons for indecision. These new diagnostic instruments provide a structured way to identify specific causes for indecision such as vocational identity issues, informational problems, career salience, lack of motivation, or external barriers that students perceive to be blocking a choice (Hartman and Fuqua, 1982; Holland and Holland, 1977; Jones and Chenery, 1980; and Osipow, Carney, and Barak, 1976). It is assumed that once certain reasons for indecision can be ascertained, specific interventions may be initiated.

This chapter will discuss different factors in indecision and explore how student and career development theory has given us a clearer understanding of the way these students progress through the decision-making process. It will then consider developmental approaches to advising and programming which can provide a framework for designing interventions to help retain undecided students. Finally, specific components of a model program for retention will be outlined.

Two Types of Undecided Students

Major Changes. Students who enter college declaring a major are assumed to have chosen their academic area on the basis of accurate and realistic information about themselves, curricular requirements, and occupational fields. Since, however, it is estimated that up to 75 percent of all students change their major at least once before they graduate (Foote, 1980; Kojaku, 1971; Slaney, 1980; and Titley, Titley, and Wolff, 1976), all initial decisions must be considered tentative at best. Students who are in transition from a former major to a new one need as much academic and career advising as those who enter college undecided.

Students change majors for many reasons. Some may have been influenced or pressured by family or friends in making their first choice; they may approach the curriculum with some misgivings because they are not truly committed to their choice. Other students change majors because they realize they had unrealistic ideas about their academic strength and ability to succeed in a given area. Still others choose a major because of the practical applications of the curriculum to the job market (that is, business, engineering, and the health areas) and then find that their abilities do not match the curricular requirements in the area. Students with weak backgrounds in mathematics and science often find themselves in this dilemma during their freshman year. Others who change their major have the ability to perform in the area they chose initially, but discover they no longer have an interest in the curriculum or have changed their vocational goals after a period in college.

Undecided students entering two-year technical schools often find that they do not know enough about the programs offered and so make a forced choice that often does not satisfy them as they become more involved in the curriculum. Many of these students spend more than two years in school because of the decision to change majors. Switching majors is not always as critical in a four-year degree program because many offer more flexibility.

When planning retention programs and services for uncommitted students, it is essential to include the students who are in the process of changing majors and who comprise an often unrecognized and neglected category of undecided students.

The New Undecided. An increasing phenomenon in higher education today is students who enter college very much decided about a particular major such as business, engineering, or nursing, only to find they are closed out of the program because they have fewer credit hours than are required for admission or lack a certain grade point average in specified courses. This is becoming more prevalent as student demand for certain majors becomes intense and many departments limit enrollment because of a shortage of faculty or facilities.

These students need special support and advising approaches to help them reestablish or revise their initial vocational goals and generate alternatives that fit their abilities and interests. Some campuses provide academic alternative workshops where students can review their strengths and interests through self-assessment inventories and learn about other groups of majors that might be as satisfying as their initial choice. If such special advising is not provided, many of these students will drop out or transfer to other institutions.

Reasons for Indecision

Regardless of the specific factors involved in a student's indecision, certain basic causes of indecision can be identified in order to construct a theoretical framework upon which programs and services may be built. These basic causes of indecision include lack of personal, academic, and career information; lack of developmental skills such as those required in decision making; and personal or social concerns which may be blocking the student's progress.

Lack of Information. As any academic adviser knows, many students do not have the information required to make realistic educational and vocational decisions. Such students often lack (1) information about their personal strengths and limitations—interests, abilities, values, and needs; (2) information about academic majors, curricular requirements, and relevant course work; and (3) information about the tasks involved in and requirements for success in specific occupational fields. Many students are also unaware of or do not understand the relationship between specific college majors and occupational groups.

Lack of Developmental Skills. Other students lack appropriate decision-making skills and have not acquired a consistent and realistic means for making choices. Others have not been involved in enough decision-making experiences to have practiced using their skills. Still others do not know how to implement a decision once it has been made. These students have not identified their own personal styles or strategies for approaching a decision once they are confronted with it and may adopt counterproductive habits and approaches over and over again.

Personal and Social Problems. Some students have personal or social problems which impede progress toward a career decision. They may experience self-conflict in several ways including: (1) values-goals conflicts when their values do not match the work values implicit in the occupations they have chosen, (2) interest-abilities conflicts when their interests and abilities are not matched or are in different areas or at different levels, (3) interest-energy level conflicts if they do not have the energy level required to obtain their goal, or (4) conflicts with other people whom they admire or want to please. Any one or a combination of these conflicts may block a choice (Carney, 1975).

Working with undecided students can be a challenge since each one will have different reasons for being undecided, and will bring different personality factors, attitudes, levels of motivation, work experiences, and academic interests and strengths to the decision-making process. Retention efforts will need to take these individual differences into account while developing programs that will meet the needs of all students.

Developmental Issues

As indicated, entering college freshmen often lack the maturity to identify and resolve conflicts that may be impeding their progress. They simply do not have the developmental skills needed to approach career and life decisions in a mature way. In his chapter on academic advising, Crockett advocates a developmental approach. It is clear that certain developmental tasks must be accomplished before these students are capable of making the types of decisions that will have far-reaching impact on their lives (Gordon, 1981).

Chickering's Stages. Chickering (1969) places college students' development within stages or vectors involving certain developmental tasks which students need to accomplish if they are to move confidently into adulthood. There is a directionality and content to these developmental tasks that greatly influences when students can be expected to make career decisions. According to Chickering, students must achieve intellectual, physical, and social competence; learn to manage their emotions; and become independent before they have the capacity to establish their self-identity. Although these issues are usually not resolved until the sophomore or junior year in college, students are often forced or expected to make choices at the beginning of or during their freshman year; thus is created a stressful and confusing situation for many.

Link with Self-Identity. Identity issues are not only closely

tied to career development (Crites, 1981), but are often related
to indecision (Maier and Herman, 1974; and Resnick, Fauble,
and Osipow, 1970). Developing and identifying one's self-concept
are critical components of the choice process. Rose and Elton
(1971) conclude that all freshmen entering college experience
varying degrees of identity confusion and some undecided students who drop out of college may do so because they find the
identity issue too confusing to resolve at that point in their lives.
Students who are able to resolve identity issues while in college
are more apt to persist to graduation.

Super's Five Stages. Super (1957), who postulates that there
are certain tasks, attitudes, and behaviors associated with different stages of career development, identifies five life stages
in establishing a career identity. These stages are growth (birth
to age fourteen), exploration (age fifteen to twenty-four), establishment (age twenty-five to forty-four), maintenance (age forty-
five to sixty-four), and decline (age sixty-five and older). Inherent in each of these stages are certain developmental tasks that
need to be accomplished. The tasks that college students are
concerned with are crystallizing a vocational preference, specifying it, and implementing it.

Many undecided students enter college in the exploration
stage, still trying to crystallize and specify a vocational choice.
Since they can formulate and specify academic and occupational
choices only after a period of purposeful exploration, they need
to test their tentative ideas through course work, field experiences, personal contact with workers, or actual work experience.
According to Super, these are normal developmental tasks that
all students experience during the college years.

Dualistic State. Another developmental theorist whose work
has great relevance for understanding undecided students is
Perry (1970). In outlining the natural evolution of cognitive
development during the college years, Perry contends that many
entering freshmen are incapable of understanding a relativistic
world. Because they tend to approach events and decisions in
a very dualistic way, they are looking for the one right major
or career field. Since it limits the amount and type of exploration and knowledge a student is capable of undertaking and

assimilating, this dualistic state of reasoning often frustrates academic advisers, career counselors, and faculty.

Many dualistic students who select a specific major as they enter college, viewing it as *the* right choice, do, however, eventually discover that there are multiple alternatives for reaching their goals. As these students develop a more relativistic view of their world, they may radically change decisions that they made as dualistic, dependent freshmen. Perry's theory thus helps explain why so many students change their majors.

A strong developmental emphasis must be an integral part of any retention effort geared to undecided students. To ensure that students receive the help and support they need at critical decision points, especially during their first few months in college, Sheffield and Meskill (1974) suggest that retention programs include an ongoing orientation program, a strong academic advising component, and a greater emphasis on counseling effort. Teaching, advising, and counseling efforts should be coordinated to provide the type of developmental approach that is responsive to undecided students' needs at every juncture of their search.

Intervention Design

Beal and Noel (1980) conclude that the services most related to the retention of undecided students are orientation, advising, and career assistance. Since undecided students comprise such a large group with few distinct characteristics, a program designed to retain them must encompass a variety of elements if it is to be effective. The following principles apply to designing retention interventions.

1. Undecided students must be identified, studied, and analyzed to determine the factors contributing to their attrition or retention.
2. An all-college committee or task force should be established to make recommendations for establishing special services for all groups targeted for retention efforts and for undecided students in particular.

3. Retention efforts for undecided students must intercept them during recruitment, admissions, and orientation. Identifying them immediately is crucial so that a series of activities may be set in motion.

4. An institutional commitment, positive administrative and faculty attitudes toward exploration, and a well-coordinated effort are three necessary elements in maintaining a strong program. The full support and cooperation of all campus units is essential to the retention of undecided students.

5. Specific responsibility for retention efforts should be assigned to qualified individuals such as academic advising coordinators, student personnel professionals, or appropriate faculty or administrators.

6. The delivery system for advising undecided students must be comprehensive and intrusive in nature. An effective program sets attainable objectives, provides specially designed services, and regularly monitors students' progress until they have chosen realistic and satisfying academic programs.

7. Selecting advisers who want to work with undecided students is essential if the students' needs are to be identified and met. Special training programs should be required of all advisers working with undecided students.

8. Retention efforts must be based on developmental principles if they are to succeed. Acknowledging the developmental needs of college students means integrating an awareness of those needs into all teaching and advising efforts.

These principles are incorporated into the model program that follows.

A Model for Retention

As undecided students enter college, they need to become involved immediately in an organized academic and career-advising program. A model program for the retention of undecided students will encompass students from the first admissions contact through orientation and advising until they select their majors. The institution's acknowledgment of the need for some students to explore and its commitment to providing the services to accomplish this task will have great impact on the success of retention efforts.

Recruitment and Orientation. Serving undecided students successfully begins with recruitment and orientation. Attracting qualified students has become an increasingly important function of admissions offices. Because the undecided group has been shown in many instances to be a bright, highly qualified population, assuring parents and students that there are special programs and advising services for students who are not ready to commit themselves to a specific direction is an excellent recruiting tool.

A detailed description of advising services for this group can also be an important recruiting factor. A positive attitude toward being undecided and positive statements about the resources available to help undecided students explore the avenues open to them may be provided in admissions brochures, college catalogues, or in a separate document describing the institution's policies toward exploration and the services provided for this important task. The message that admissions office personnel convey in their contacts with students and parents can also be a powerful recruiting tool. The fact that undecidedness as students enter college is considered to be a healthy, normal, developmental condition should be conveyed during these personal contacts.

Orientation can be a critical time to reinforce the positive aspects of wanting to explore career goals. Because many students change their minds about a major during orientation but are sometimes hesitant to admit it, the institution's philosophy on undecidedness should be offered during this period. Separate advising sessions for undecided students can become an important part of orientation and set the tone for future contacts. Since some parents feel apprehensive because their students are undecided, a special session for all parents in which the developmental tasks and needs of college students are discussed is an excellent way to prepare them for the changes that will take place in their children during the college years.

Academic Advising. Advising undecided students is the most important component of any program designed to help them. Because these students often see the choice of major as the first decision they will make in college, advising that encourages them to explore many major fields can be one of the most helpful of all interventions from the students' perspective. Many of the general guidelines for an effective advising program set forth by Crockett in his chapter on advising also apply to advising undecided students. Here we will consider how different delivery models, adviser training methods, and so on can best serve the undecided student in particular.

Any system to advise undecided students must adhere to an advising philosophy and establish objectives for the program, offer career exploration and planning services, provide the essential materials and resources—including an academic and career library—for carrying out its functions, and select and train competent advisers.

Although retention is an important consideration when working with undecided students, the primary responsibility of any institution is to provide the best possible academic experience for all students. When students benefit, the institution benefits as well. An advising philosophy that accepts an exploration period as normal, healthy, and even desirable will benefit the student and the institution in many ways. Having the opportunity to explore is the right of every student. If a student has already made a choice, this exploratory time may be spent confirming that decision.

Well thought-out objectives that are clearly stated in writing are absolutely essential if advising programs for undecided students are to be effectively developed and evaluated. Objectives should include consideration of such factors as the time frame in which information is gathered and processed by students, students' awarenesss of the factors involved in making decisions, students' personal decision-making styles, and students' satisfaction with the advising help they received during the exploration process. Objectives will need to be unique for each institution or program unit which provides advising services for undecided students.

At this writing, the main approaches for delivering academic advising services for undecided students are faculty advising programs, advising centers, and advising units specifically created to advise undecided students.

Perhaps the oldest and most widely used approach is the faculty adviser system in which undecided students are assigned an academic adviser upon entering college. Advisers are either assigned randomly or chosen from faculty who volunteer to work with undecided students. The undecided students remain with their assigned advisers until they have decided on a major. It has been demonstrated that quantity and quality of faculty-student interaction has a direct impact on retention (Baldridge, Kemerer, and Green, 1982; Lenning, Beal, and Sauer, 1980; Pascarella and Terenzini, 1980; Tinto, 1975; and Spady, 1971), perhaps because interaction with faculty increases social and academic integration. If there is an active, involved, ongoing relationship between students and faculty advisers, a faculty advising system can be an important ingredient in the retention process.

According to several studies, student interaction with faculty is more important in the student's academic major area than in other areas (Miller and Brickman, 1982; and Tinto, 1982). Since undecided students have no major, arranging for faculty contact immediately upon entering is essential. Such contact may be established during orientation programs or through structured group meetings just before or after classes begin. Faculty may conduct exploratory meetings introducing their academic disciplines to small groups of undecided students or meet with students individually on a referral basis. This is not to suggest that faculty advising systems are the most effective, but it does seem that the opportunity for undecided students to interact informally and socially with faculty is important and that this interaction needs to be planned and structured rather than left to chance.

A second delivery mode, the advising center, is increasingly being viewed as an excellent vehicle for providing focused, coordinated advising services, particularly for undecided students. In the advising center, advising is often performed by full-time professionals who are trained as career specialists and have a general knowledge of all the academic programs on campus. Faculty may be involved as center advisers for their particular academic disciplines and as points of referral for students needing more in-depth information about specific fields. Advising center personnel often engage in research and evaluation as well as advising.

Some institutions have created special units for the sole purpose of advising undecided students and have appointed a full- or part-time professional to coordinate all efforts for this particular group. Like advising centers, these units are generally staffed by professionally trained academic and career counselors. Because retention efforts can be focused in a very specific, concentrated way, special units are probably the most effective way of identifying and monitoring undecided students' needs and progress.

Regardless of the delivery system used for advising undecided students, providing an opportunity for exploration is critical. These students need to be exposed to as many academic alternatives as possible so that they can explore their varied interests in an open and organized fashion. A generalist adviser can help students identify a few realistic alternatives which incorporate their interests and abilities; guide them to primary information sources to explore these ideas in depth; and help them compare the positive and negative aspects of each option. Academic areas can be tested by taking a course or a series of courses in one area. Options can be kept open for an extended period of time if adviser and student meet on a regular basis, eliminating certain majors while continuing to investigate others.

Up-to-date and comprehensive advising materials are another critical component of an advising program for undecided students. If a student has three alternatives and can see specific requirements for each, part of the mystery which often surrounds the creation of a degree program is dispelled. Because college bulletins which provide this information in a condensed form are sometimes not as current or clear as they should be, separate curricular worksheets for each major are invaluable tools for advising undecided students. When students can study curricular sheets, understand how the general requirements overlap, and see what is involved in upper-level requirements for specific majors, they have a solid basis for comparison that may help them eliminate an option or generate some new ideas.

Other elements of successful advising programs for undecided students include the identification of one professional who is responsible for coordinating the program and accountable for its outcomes, a system for monitoring undecided students' progress on a regular basis, and an ongoing and responsive evaluation process to gauge the effectiveness of the program in meeting its objectives.

Career Advising. Another important but often overlooked advising service for undecided students is an organized approach to career exploration. Many students lack understanding of the relationship between academic work and careers. The connection between a physical therapy major or an architecture major and their respective occupational fields is fairly well defined. Such a connection is not as obvious for a business major, but an occupational environment may be identified. It is more difficult, however, to pinpoint occupational opportunities relating to liberal arts majors such as English, history, or sociology. The liberal arts degree has never been vocationally oriented, of course, but many students need help in understanding how the skills they acquire in liberal arts courses can be applied to specific occupations, as well as serve as a general preparation for life.

In addition to needing academic and occupational information, many undecided students need to be guided through a self-assessment phase. Helping them identify their interest patterns is a starting place for the self-exploration process. An interest inventory is only one of the self-assessment tools that may be used; it will provide students with information that is structured and personal. Because many undecided students have difficulty in setting goals and valuing is an important part of this process, helping them identify, clarify, and prioritize their work values is a critical part of the career choice process.

An adviser should help students identify the career information resources available on campus and should emphasize the benefits that these resources can provide. The wide variety of career resources necessary for undecided students include counseling services, testing services, and library resources. A career library is essential if printed materials are to be convenient and useful. Because there are so many printed resources available and students are often overwhelmed by them and confused about where or how to start their search, they need the structure of a system in order to explore in an orderly, logical way. Career libraries need to be organized so that students may learn how careers are set apart by personal factors such as work activities and aptitudes and by work environments and tasks. There are many systems for organizing career libraries, including the Department of Labor's worker trait group classification and the American College Testing Program's occupational information system. Some career libraries have found it convenient to organize by Holland's codes classification system (Gottfredson, Holland, and Ogawa, 1982).

One of the newest and most effective resources for career exploration is the computerized career information system. Computerized systems such as DISCOVER and SIGI provide a very personalized approach to self-assessment, occupational exploration, and decision making as well as voluminous current, and frequently updated, occupational information. They also provide the structure necessary for students to integrate the information as they collect it and the opportunity to make tentative decisions and try them out in a risk-free environment. Because the outcomes of different sets of variables can be projected through a complex system, students can try on many different occupational hats before selecting options to explore further. Computerized systems may be only one part of a total program but they will become an increasingly vital tool as their capabilities are integrated into a comprehensive system for helping undecided students explore.

Training Advisers for Undecided Students

Not only are positive attitudes toward exploration on the part of advisers essential, but different types of advising techniques need to be learned for different types of undecided students. A pre-service training program for advisers learning to work with undecided students should emphasize that an understanding of student and career development theory and practice will help advisers recognize differences among individual students. Campus experts or outside consultants can be brought in to identify and discuss individual differences and advising techniques geared to these differences. All advisers need good communication skills, such as being attentive listeners, but advisers for undecided students need basic counseling skills as well. They also need to understand some conceptual frameworks for decision making. As Crookston (1972) points out, advising is often teaching. Advisers can teach students the most effective approaches to career exploration, decision making, and planning; and can help them examine their own strategies for making decisions in different situations. And, since exploring students may be delving into several perhaps totally unrelated fields, advisers of undecided students need to have broad knowledge of academic and career fields at their disposal.

In-Service Programs. In addition to pre-service training, in-service programs for experienced professional or faculty advisers are essential if high levels of competency are to be maintained. In-service sessions are especially important in providing advisers with new and up-to-date information about academic majors, program requirements, and occupational opportunities in various fields. The updating of materials in advising manuals can provide an organized agenda for such in-service sessions. Other in-service programs can deal with refinements of the pre-service topics already mentioned or new topics which are more applicable to local situations. Such programs might employ a lecture-discussion format or focus on experiential learning through a case study approach. Asking experienced advisers for their suggestions for in-service topics will provide more personally relevant content.

Regardless of content and method, advisers working with undecided students need ongoing opportunities for training. Sharing problems and expertise with colleagues will provide support and a climate for refining old skills and learning new ones.

Encouraging Openness. Overall, because many students enter college with no real sense of their aptitudes, skills, or talents, a critical role for advisers is to encourage students to take a broad, open approach to testing their aptitudes and skills. Some possibilities may be eliminated early on if the student finds the academic work too difficult or uninteresting. Students often need to realize that their goals may be reached in many different ways. They are also often unaware of the import of time itself in making an informed academic and career choice and expect a decision to happen overnight without much effort on their part. These students need time to gather information and to reflect upon what they have learned. They should be encouraged by advisers to take risks and to enroll in courses and take part in experiences that may be totally new to them. Advisers who offer their personal support while students are taking these risks are providing a service of inestimable value. Consistent and frequent contact with such an adviser is absolutely essential during undecided students' first year in college.

Freshman Orientation Courses

A freshman orientation or seminar course is probably one of the most effective ways of helping entering undecided students begin the exploration process. Such courses have been taught on college campuses for almost 100 years. The content has varied among institutions, yet traditionally, the purpose has been to help students adjust to new surroundings and to provide the support they need during the first few months on campus. A freshman orientation course designed specifically for undecided students can provide many advantages, including:

1. Undecided students are identified and receive attention immediately in a structured format and on a regular basis during their first weeks in college.
2. If academic advisers teach the course to their own undecided advisees, immediate and consistent contact and rapport may be established.
3. In a class composed of students who are exploring, the undecided discover that there are other students who are unready to commit themselves to an educational or voca-

tional decision upon entering college. This peer support can be very positive.

4. The self-assessment activities that are essential for career planning may begin in an organized classroom format. Self-information, including knowledge about personal interests, values, needs, and types of aptitudes may be gathered, organized, and processed immediately in a supportive atmosphere.

5. Academic majors can be explored in a comprehensive and personal way. Overviews of majors and specific information may be provided in a classroom setting. Assignments may be given to add to the depth of students' knowledge.

6. Educational and occupational relationships may be explored and students may test these relationships through the information gathered in the class.

7. Perhaps one of the most valuable aspects of a class for undecided students is that students learn that there is a career decision-making process involving specific skills. Once they understand how to make decisions effectively and identify their own personal styles or strategies for approaching the choice process, these skills can be applied at any time during their college experience.

Conclusion

As enrollments of traditional students continue to decline, the retention of matriculated students becomes ever more critical. Many very capable students leave college because they possess an underdeveloped vocational identity, cannot formulate clear career goals, lack vital information, or lack the skills to work through the decision-making process in an orderly way. Undecided students thus constitute a large, complex population that should be targeted for retention efforts. Efforts designed for students who are uncommitted to an academic or vocational direction should focus on providing an organized plan for exploration the minute they set foot on campus. Academic and career advising services must be comprehensive in nature yet flexible enough to work with individual students who are at various levels of the choice process.

Another group of students who are dropout prone are those whose initial choices are thwarted by selective admissions standards or who decide to change majors but have no clear alternative direction in mind. Students going through such transitions can make good use of the services developed for entering undecided students.

Probably the most important component of a program for retaining the undecided student is the availability of specially trained advisers who are knowledgeable about the academic programs on campus, understand how educational and occupational decisions are integrated, and can help students assess their personal characteristics in relation to alternatives. This suggests that a full-time professionally trained staff is needed to serve this group if there is a real commitment to retaining them.

Institutions of higher education have an obligation to help all students learn and proceed through the career decision-making process as smoothly and effectively as possible. When undecided students select a stable, satisfying academic direction and then progress through graduation, this commitment has been fulfilled.

References

Abel, W. H. "Attrition and the Student Who Is Certain." *Personnel and Guidance Journal*, 1966, *44*, 1042–1045.

Ashby, J. D., Wall, H. W., and Osipow, S. H. "Vocational Certainty and Indecision in College Freshmen." *Personnel and Guidance Journal*, 1966, *44*, 1037–1041.

Astin, A. W. *Predicting Academic Performance in College*. New York: Free Press, 1971.

Astin, A. W. *Preventing Students from Dropping Out*. San Francisco: Jossey-Bass, 1975.

Baird, L. L. *The Undecided Student—How Different Is He?* American College Testing Program Research Report, no. 22. Iowa City, Iowa: American College Testing Program, 1967.

Baldridge, J. V., Kemerer, F. R., and Green, K. C. *Enrollments in the Eighties: Factors, Actors, and Impacts*. American Association for Higher Education—Educational Resources Information Center/Higher Education Research Report, no. 3, Washington, D.C.: American Association for Higher Education, 1982. (ED 222 158)

Beal, P. E., and Noel, L. *What Works in Student Retention.* Iowa City, Iowa: American College Testing Program and National Center for Higher Education Management Systems, 1980 (ED 197 635)

Carney, C. "Psychological Dimensions of Career Development: An Overview and Application." Paper presented at a training conference for Ohio Department of Education, Columbus, April 1975.

Chickering, A. W. *Education and Identity.* San Francisco: Jossey-Bass, 1969.

Cope, R. G., and Hannah, W. *Revolving College Doors: The Causes and Consequences of Dropping Out, Stopping Out, and Transferring.* New York: Wiley, 1975.

Crites, J. O. *Vocational Psychology.* New York: McGraw-Hill, 1969.

Crites, J. O. *Career Counseling: Models, Methods, and Materials.* New York: McGraw-Hill, 1981.

Crookston, B. B. "A Developmental View of Academic Advising as Teaching." *Journal of College Student Personnel,* 1972, *13,* 12-17.

Elton, C. F., and Rose, H. A. "A Longitudinal Study of the Vocationally Undecided Male Student." *Journal of Vocational Behavior,* 1971, *1,* 85-92.

Foote, B. "Determined- and Undetermined-Major Students: How Different Are They?" *Journal of College Student Personnel,* 1980, *21,* 29-34.

Goodstein, L. "Behavioral Theoretical View of Counseling." In B. Stefflre (ed.), *Theories of Counseling.* New York: McGraw-Hill, 1965.

Gordon, V. N. "The Undecided Student: A Developmental Perspective." *Personnel and Guidance Journal,* 1981, *59,* 433-439.

Gottfredson, G. D., Holland, J. L., and Ogawa, D. K. *Dictionary of Holland Occupational Codes.* Palo Alto, Calif.: Consulting Psychologists Press, 1982.

Hartman, B. W., and Fuqua, D. R. "The Construct Validity of the Career Decision Scale Adapted for Graduate Students." *Vocational Guidance Quarterly,* 1982, *31,* 69-77.

Holland, J. L., and Holland, J. E. "Vocational Indecision:

More Evidence and Speculation." *Journal of Counseling Psychology*, 1977, *24*, 404–414.

Jones, L. K., and Chenery, M. F. "Multiple Subtypes Among Vocationally Undecided College Students: A Model and Assessment Instrument." *Journal of Counseling Psychology*, 1980, *27*, 469–477.

Kojaku, L. K. *Major Field Transfer: The Self-Matching of University Undergraduates to Student Characteristics.* Los Angeles: University of California, 1972. (ED 062 933)

Lenning, O. T., Beal, P. E., and Sauer, K. *Retention and Attrition: Evidence for Action and Research.* Boulder, Colo.: National Center for Higher Education Mangement Systems, 1980.

Lowe, B. "The Relationship Between Vocational Interest Differentiation and Career Undecidedness." *Journal of Vocational Behavior*, 1981, *19*, 346–349.

McGowan, A. S. "Vocational Maturity and Anxiety Among Vocationally Undecided and Indecisive Students." *Journal of Vocational Behavior*, 1977, *10*, 196–204.

Maier, D., and Herman, A. "The Relationship of Vocational Decidedness and Satisfaction with Dogmatism and Self-Esteem." *Journal of Vocational Behavior*, 1974, *5*, 95–102.

Miller, T. E., and Brickman, S. B. "Faculty and Staff Mentoring: A Model for Improving Student Retention and Service." *National Association of Student Personnel Administrators Journal*, 1982, *19* (3), 23–27.

Osipow, S. H., Carney, C. G., and Barak, A. "A Scale of Educational-Vocational Undecidedness: A Typological Approach." *Journal of Vocational Behavior*, 1976, *9*, 233–243.

Pantages, T. J., and Creedon, C. F. "Studies of College Attrition: 1950–1975." *Review of Educational Research*, 1978, *48* (1), 49–101.

Pascarella, E. T., and Terenzini, P. T. "Predicting Freshman Persistence and Voluntary Dropout Decisions from a Theoretical Model." *Journal of Higher Education*, 1980, *51*, 60–75.

Perry, W. G. *Forms of Intellectual and Ethical Development in the College Years.* New York: Holt, Rinehart & Winston, 1970.

Resnick, H., Fauble, M. L., and Osipow, S. H. "Vocational Crystallization and Self-Esteem in College Students." *Journal of Counseling Psychology*, 1970, *17*, 465–467.

Rose, H. A., and Elton, C. F. "Attrition and the Vocationally Undecided Student." *Journal of Vocational Behavior*, 1971, *1*, 99–103.

Sheffield, W., and Meskill, V. P. "What Can Colleges Do About Student Attrition?" *College Student Journal*, 1974, *8* (1), 37–45.

Slaney, R. B. "Expressed Vocational Choice and Vocational Indecision." *Journal of Counseling Psychology*, 1980, *27*, 122–129.

Spady, W. G., Jr. "Dropouts from Higher Education: Toward an Empirical Model." *Interchange*, 1971, *2* (3), 38–62.

Super, D. E. *The Psychology of Careers*. New York: Harper & Row, 1957.

Tinto, V. "Dropout from Higher Education: A Theoretical Synthesis of Recent Research." *Review of Educational Research*, 1975, *45*, 89–125.

Tinto, V. "Limits of Theory and Practice in Student Attrition." *Journal of Higher Education*, 1982, *53*, 687–700.

Titley, R. W., Titley, B., and Wolff, W. M. "The Major Changers: Continuity or Discontinuity in the Career Decision Process?" *Journal of Vocational Behavior*, 1976, *8*, 105–111.

8

Returning Learners

꒰ꕤ꒱꒰ꕤ꒱꒰ꕤ꒱

James P. Pappas
Rosalind K. Loring

Adults have appeared on campuses in ever-growing numbers during the last decade as a result of sociocultural trends. Their presence (or at least the recognition of their existence) has left faculty and administrators acting like a group of educational Mad Hatters, frantically trying to find the economic tea party that their increasing enrollments promise. Previously ignored administrators of continuing and adult education are now asked to give direction on how to deal with the new adult in the student body. Like Carroll's confused Alice, they are trying to make sense of atypical, and often unrelated, service demands that are generated by the arrival of these students. These demands, to continue the literary analogy, make it seem that "it takes all the running you can do, to keep in the same place."

For a variety of reasons, ranging from enrollment management to a concern for their community missions, colleges and universities now seem willing to educate the adult; but they are at the same time unsure of how to respond to the adult student's needs. They are often naive about how to treat older adults who do not accept the apprentice role, who insist on sharing experiences, who ask for classes on weekends, who complain about the lack of child care, and who threaten to leave before the liberal arts education sequence is finished—taking their tuition with them. As Marienau and Chickering (1982) note, "Relatively few colleges and universities are fully responsive to diverse adult learners." Even in the institutions that have attempted to serve adults, "there have been few thoughtful and systematic applications of current theoretical knowledge about adults" (Weathersby and Tarule, 1980, p. 42).

Accepting the fact that more adults of all types will be involved in postsecondary education (Cross, 1979), we are concerned how they will get along once on campus. Of particular concern to this volume and chapter are their tendencies relative to retention or persistence. An examination of the issue of adult persistence reveals several significant problems. Because the adult student population is quite varied in its characteristics, typical parameters such as chronological age or amount of college credits earned have not been useful in defining subgroups within that population. Still we must seek out common traits in order to establish coherent policies or practices. We must also get beyond defining retention in traditional terms if we are to recognize the unique nature of adult students' educational patterns and goals.

In short, the concept of persistence or retention must be thought of differently for adults. Adults, being problem centered, role bound, "part-time," and self-directed, will have unique patterns of attendance depending on life circumstances. Rather than thinking of factors for retention, with adults we must consider how to reduce barriers that facilitate attrition. In her exceptional text *Adults as Learners*, Cross (1981) documents well the nature of these barriers. Chickering (1981), in his review of her text, summarizes these barriers as follows: (1) situational barriers flowing from the real life conditions of adults, (2) institutional barriers arising from typical administrative organizational and educational practices, and (3) dispositional barriers flowing from the prior experiences and self-perceptions of the learner.

Colleges have attempted to reduce these barriers in many different ways: curriculum and scheduling changes, modified recruitment strategies, and entirely new degree programs. Many have introduced a special division devoted to adult students. Many of these changes are merely cosmetic, while others require substantive revisions of current practices.

In this chapter we will attempt to define some of the variables involved in adult persistence in order to establish guidelines that institutions can use in helping their adult students overcome the barriers described earlier. We will first look at the forces that are pushing mature adults to return to school. We will then consider the problems involved in defining the adult student and delineate three categories of adult learners. We will review the variables that can be drawn from the current literature and consider recommendations for action in adult programs. We then will describe a few exemplary adult education programs and discuss tactics for bringing about change on campus. This chapter will address these issues in hopes of encouraging the kind of institutional planning necessary to assist nontraditional students in persisting until they achieve their self-defined educational goals.

Forces Facilitating Adult Enrollments

Aging Population. Hodgkinson (1983) suggests that colleges will have to plan for a decline in the numbers of traditional students during the 1980s and 1990s. The decline, predicted to last until 2000, is caused by a demographic downturn in births following the baby boom years after World War II. Hodgkinson further points out that we must now think of enrollment in terms of waves. "In 1982, we are looking not at an increase or decrease alone, but at a wave. At the crest of the wave is the baby boom generation," now in and approaching its forties. During the 1980s, the thirty-five to forty-four age group increases in size by 42 percent (p. 2). More adults will be returning to college because there are more of them.

Equal Opportunity. Another major social trend that has put more adults on campuses is the demand for more educational opportunities for women and minorities. These new students have come in the aftermath of the civil rights and feminist movements, strongly believing that they, too, have a right to a college education. Local educators reinforced these growing trends by modifying their programs and services to accommodate these special students.

Competitive Influences. Another trend that has sensitized colleges to respond to adults is the emergence of nontraditional educational experiences offered by industry or professional societies. Today almost four times as many adults are being educated outside college classrooms as in them. American Telephone & Telegraph Company alone is reported to spend $1.7 billion annually on in-house education and training. "If one quarter of these forty-six million adults now being educated had decided to take their education programs at a college or university, there would be no decline in enrollments in higher education" (Hodgkinson, 1983, p. 10).

In addition, many professional associations have become powerful enough to convince state legislators to promote certification for professionals. These forms of certification encourage an array of educational programs by requiring state examinations (often necessitating postgraduation cram courses); accreditation by an association (usually affecting the curriculum and the selection of faculty); and satisfactory completion of designated continuing education courses.

Defining the Adult Student

Colleges typically have defined the adult student within the traditional chronological age framework. At times this has corresponded with the age of majority used by a state for voting or drinking alcohol and at other times it has been based on some sort of idiosyncratic definition stemming from institutional dynamics or policy, for example, the period of time necessary to complete some arbitrary sequence of consecutively accumulated credits. An especially useful compilation and description of chronological age definitions is presented by Levitz and Noel (1980) in *Attracting and Retaining Adult Learners.*

Marienau and Chickering (1982) argue that defining the adult student is particularly difficult because there have not been many thoughtful and systematic attempts to combine theoretical knowledge of adult development and institutional practices. A second definitional problem rests with the fact that there are multiple models of what constitutes an adult, depending upon what aspect the educator or theorist is examining.

It is, however, critical that adult students be defined for this discussion in ways that differentiate them from the more traditional students for whom institutional retention practices are typically designed. We find that we can isolate certain characteristics of adult students that are of particular importance in developing services and instructional practices.

In defining the adult student we must view the terms "adult" and "adulthood" as implying a dynamic and changing process. We must not use the term "adult" in its static sense, which is age-bounded or stage-linked. The static concept might limit the definition of an adult to anyone over twenty-one and would not represent the broad needs of our hypothetical student. Rather, a definition of adult which includes social roles or developmental processes would place an eighteen-year-old single parent with two children, working full-time, in the adult category. Hereafter in this chapter, the terms "adult" and "adulthood" will be used synonymously and will embody this broader, process-oriented definition.

As a corollary, we must recognize that for the adult, the student role is almost always secondary. Even when extensively engaged in education, adults see themselves first in occupational and/or family roles. They are first workers (or potential workers) or parents, and after that students. They are more likely to describe themselves as managers, teachers, mothers and so on, than as students. As Marienau and Chickering (1982, p. 5) note, "The student role remains secondary . . . sandwiched in between other demands."

Another important characteristic of adults is that they are typically voluntary or self-directed learners. Generally, the decision to go to college is totally theirs and is neither the function of some authority figure's recommendation nor the result of societal expectations that they play the student role. Knowles (1970) points out that adult students are mature and that their self-concept moves from one of dependency to self-direction.

Thus, unlike traditional students who generally go on to college because it is the thing to do, or because there is nothing better going on, the adult has made a conscious decision to pursue further education in spite of competing role or time demands. And this positive action implies a different and special set of motivations and expectations.

As a general statement, we can say that adults are part-time students. They are attending school in the evening, on the weekends, via distance learning methods, or in some configuration that allows them to maintain their other social roles of workers and/or family members. Even when they attend school full-time, they try to graduate in as few years as possible and see attendance as a means, not an end. As Marienau and Chickering (1982, p. 10) note, "Adults should be viewed as part-time learners regardless of their credit loads."

Many adults attend college as a function of some specific trigger (Aslanian and Brickell, 1980), marker event (Levinson and others, 1978), milestone (Loevinger, 1976), transition (Gould, 1978; and Levinson, 1978), or task demand (Pappas, 1983), depending on the theorist's semantics, related to their nonstudent roles. Even the adult who is involved in cultural enrichment, leisure, or liberal arts classes is motivated by wanting to be happier or better in one of those other roles, for example, accountant, programmer, gardener, or amateur artist. Adult students' readiness for instruction comes from the developmental aspects of their nonschool life (Knowles, 1970). Related to this characteristic is the fact that adult students often experience disequilibrium because of these marker events. Having a problem to be solved, they seek educational experiences that are problem centered rather than discipline or subject centered. They are also interested in the immediacy of the application of their learning; they do not perceive themselves as repositories of information that is to be stored for later application but as persons seeking current answers.

There are certainly other ways that adult students can be defined, such as on the basis of life cycle (Cross, 1981), life structure (Gould, 1978), and ego stages (Erikson, 1968). These alternatives are, however, not as appropriate for our purposes since they are less relevant to instructional or retention practices.

Three Categories. Despite the diversity of adult students, we can divide them into three broad categories: degree seekers, problem solvers, and cultural enrichment seekers. Much of the literature related to student persistence views students longitudinally. On our campuses we seek to create a curriculum, series of services, and an atmosphere in which students persist longitudinally, over time, in a sequence of courses until they earn a specific degree. The importance of such a view of persistence is obvious in that it maintains enrollment at a set level for academic or funding purposes. In actuality, however, when we take enrollment counts we are looking at students in a cross-sectional way. We essentially tally students at some designated period of time, for example, autumn quarter, and base our calculations on that cross section.

In dealing with nontraditional student groups, it is important that we view them from both a longitudinal and cross-sectional perspective. For the degree-seeking adult we will want to facilitate degree attainment in a timely fashion and reduce barriers that inhibit attainment. For the two other categories of adult students, however, enrollment may be better thought about cross-sectionally. One category is made up of students taking a class or a series of classes to solve a problem. These adult students may simply want to know how to work a computer, prepare for a European trip, or learn accounting to achieve a job promotion. In such cases persistence is an important concept only in so far as students achieve the problem-related goals that they have set for themselves. It behooves us to provide excellent problem-centered courses, course sequences, curricula, and counseling services so that these students will turn to our institutions again when they face another problem. For example, if a student feels good about having learned the accounting necessary for his job, then he may want to come back at some future time to learn more about computers. We must also think in a cross-sectional fashion about those students who are attending classes for cultural enrichment. These students may be coming back to class because of curiosity or interest in a course topic and have their own special needs; institutions must meet those needs if they want these part-time learners to reenroll.

When we think of the first category of students, degree-seeking, we want to allocate our recruitment costs and instructional efforts so as to best serve a longitudinal model. For the latter categories of students, the problem-centered and those seeking cultural enrichment, we want to allocate our resources in a way that will continue to bring a large number of adult students into our system, but recognize that a significant number of them, say one-half to one-third (Gordon, 1983), would be turning over each registration period. We also want to remove or reduce any type of institutional barriers that might inhibit short-term study. In all cases, we want adult students to know that the institution is willing to meet their educational needs, whether these needs are as dramatic as requiring a new degree for a job change or as simple as wanting to be a better flower arranger.

It is important to recognize which group of adult students we are seeking and decide whether we want to offer our adult curricula in a way that attracts the degree seeker, the problem solver, or the culture seeker. At the same time, we must recognize that these categories are not mutually exclusive. Colleges that have sufficient resources may want to present a smorgasbord of classes for the full range of adult students.

Variables Related to Participation and Persistence

The percentage of withdrawals, the reasons given for dropping out, and the variables considered by researchers as probable factors constant in one or more subgroups within the adult population have been surveyed and analyzed for the past forty years. After a review of the literature, we concur with the conclusion reached by Darkenwald (1981), Verner and Davis (1964), and Irish (1980), that it is difficult to isolate single variables or characteristics that predispose participation and persistence and that are consistent across adult populations. In a comprehensive review of thirty studies, Verner and Davis find that almost all produced only limited generalizations because of poor methodologies or sampling.

As earlier researchers suggest, in seeking to isolate critical variables that predict persistence or attrition we may be setting an unrealistic goal. Persistence is a function of an interaction of a variety of student characteristics, situational variables, and the educational environment. At this stage of research in student retention (whether adults or traditional students) it does not appear that we can isolate one or two causes for students staying in school until they have completed a degree or reached their personal goals.

However, a number of studies suggest variables that we should examine if we are to approach the task of designing programs or educational experiences that facilitate the participation of adult learners. Fortunately or unfortunately (depending on one's perspective), with the current wave of adult students approaching our institutions, we do not have the luxury of waiting until conclusive results are established to take action. Even with this limitation, we can still begin to identify variables and student characteristics that seem to predispose either participation or persistence. The practical implications of the current studies would suggest that the following variables are important ones.

Communication. A self-evident variable that controls student persistence is their initial entry into some type of adult education program. In this space, we cannot fully explore all the variables related to promoting participation in educational programs for adults; readers may want to consider Lenz (1980), and Pappas and Foster (1983). Those who advise adult educators on how to attract adults conclude that effective promotion of adult or continuing education programs is crucial. An important factor in a student's entering and persisting in a program of adult education is the ability of the institution to effectively communicate what that program is about and how it will benefit the potential adult student. As Kotler (1975) so effectively outlines in his classic text on marketing for non-profit organizations, there must always be an understanding and articulation of an exchange of values between the participant (adult student) and the service rendered by the organization (educational institution). Research data (Pappas and Foster, 1983) suggest that if adult students have not been informed of an anticipated personal gain, then they are much more likely to drop out of their adult education classes.

We must, however, be sure that our marketing reflects an accurate picture of what we can offer our students. Indeed, the heavy emphasis on marketing education has resulted in far too many promises for products that are not delivered; for example, skill achievement in a short time or personal access to a famous expert whether professor or practitioner. Furthermore, adults are never too old to resist projecting their own fantasies of what might be accomplished in an educational program. Clear communication by the institution can counter this tendency.

Sociological Variables. A second set of variables that relates to persistence in adult learning has been labeled as either sociodemographic or socioeconomic. Included under this category are characteristics such as age, gender, place of residence, parents' occupations, religious affiliation, educational attainment, marital status, parental status, race, family income, and occupation. Only two of these sociodemographic variables seem to us to be of any consequence: age and educational attainment.

Interestingly, in relation to the first of these—age—major research findings have produced strong but contradictory results. Anderson and Darkenwald (1979) confirm earlier findings (Boshier, 1973) that older adults are less likely to drop out than other students. (Older in this instance is taken to mean mature, for example, thirty to fifty, rather than elderly.) However, using a very large sample, Aslanian and Brickell (1980) suggest that adult learners and persisters tend to be at the younger end of the adult age scale. Because of the conflicting results of these two studies, performed according to accepted standards, the reader is encouraged to read these reports to assess their utility for a particular institution.

One finding seems to be consistent for all studies and was confirmed by survey data obtained at the two institutions we represent. If all variables are controlled, either statistically or by sample selection, the most potent correlation between a demographic variable and persistence at any level is previous educational attainment. Basically, if adult students have achieved some level of educational success, then there is a high probability that they will return to an adult education program, either for a degree or a class, and stay in that program or class to completion irrespective of what other variables are involved.

Psychological Variables. A third set of variables relates to psychological qualities of adults and their relationship to persistence. A major body of research (Darkenwald, 1981; and Long, 1982) is centered on examining the relationship of intelligence, academic aptitude or ability, and dropout behavior. Although the results are inconclusive, a consistent finding is that low-ability students are not often successful or do not persist to completion. However, while the low-ability students are significantly less likely to persist in credit courses, there is no difference in persistence between low- and high-ability students in non-credit offerings. The strongest statement that can be made in this area is that low-ability students are at greater risk of dropping out of credit or degree programs.

Studies have also been performed on personality or personal adjustment variables and persistence (Cross, 1979, 1981; and Knox, 1977). The approach in these studies is to administer a personality test, for example, the Minnesota Multiphasic Personality Inventory, and to then correlate scores with persistence or grade performance. One consistent finding is that the presence of anxiety, whether related to feelings of inadequacy, fear of class content (for example, mathematics), fear of failure, or to external factors, predisposes a student to drop out.

It would seem that the generalizations that can be made from psychologically oriented research are that low ability and anxiety increase the risk of dropping out. There are also a number of other personal factors which may influence persistence.

For example, dropout often occurs with the unexpected recognition of students that they have misjudged their capacity to learn an entirely new field, especially in the areas of science and technology, or that they have not allocated the time required to catch up on basic knowledge. Darkenwald (1981, p. 10) covers this briefly: "A course may be highly valued, but if one encounters difficulties with [expectancy factors, such as] learning or regular attendance, then persistence becomes problematical."

A similar process occurs with students' realization that their personal energy is not as great as anticipated and that travel time to class plus concentrated study time are very difficult to manage. Equally unexpected is the discovery that education is still a long and arduous process, that definite solutions or answers are not available immediately, if ever, and that the goal exceeds the grasp.

Program and Classroom Variables. A fourth important set of variables related to adult student persistence is the content and nature of the educational programs and classroom situations, including faculty instructional style. A series of studies discuss the negative effect of such factors as unrealistic admissions requirements; restrictive residency requirements; unnecessary lockstep curriculum sequences; non-relevant degree requirements, for example, three hours of physical education credits; inconvenient schedules; lack of credit by examination or credit for experience options; course sequences that are advertised but not taught; unnecessary prerequisites and generic non-relevant degree programs (Knox, 1977; Darkenwald, 1981; Spratt, 1981).

Two of the most important findings that seem most generalizable to all institutions include the desirability of tailoring adult programs and compressing the time required to complete the programs. Lenz (1980) emphasizes the importance of developing programs for special audiences and custom tailoring the curriculum in meaningful ways. She maintains that successful special-audience programs are self-contained, have a clear focus and definable goals, and are supported by the institution. Lucke, (1981) finds that adult degree programs especially tailored to unique adult audiences have a significantly greater completion rate than comparable programs not so customized. Special programs for women, the elderly, minorities, and professional groups designed to meet marketplace job requirements are the most successful.

Darkenwald (1981) and his colleague (Anderson and Darkenwald, 1979) find a significant negative association between the time required to complete a program and persistence. Even with twenty other variables statistically controlled in a statewide study in Wisconsin, the dropout rates were dramatically lower in courses meeting for fewer than twenty sessions. Less frequent meetings, for example, once a week or biweekly, are also associated with higher persistence rates. Programs developed at our institutions, the University of Southern California in Los Angeles and the University of Utah in Salt Lake City, indicate that persistence is higher in programs that compress the work into three hours one day a week than in those programs that meet three days a week.

Faculty Behavior. Another important variable is faculty-student interaction. While the results are equivocal, if one looks across a number of studies, it appears that adults are more likely to persist in classes where the teacher provides concrete tasks, where class goals are related to the expectations of the class, where the class is relevant to life, and where the advertised program description is followed. This aspect of relevance is found by Sanders (1980) to be the variable most related to persistence and success. This is particularly true in the case of homemakers who are coming back to school after their children have grown or who wish to return to the marketplace.

Another new group of adult learners who require a special teaching approach are professionals returning to school to upgrade their skills. Palmer (1983, p. 25) points out that until recently, teaching adults has meant offering night courses to students eager for personal enrichment and responsive to anything the instructor might provide. "But now, as many colleges and universities seek a growing share of an estimated $30-billion-a-year education market in business and industry, many faculty members are meeting up with a new kind of adult audience: experienced professionals who insist on practical ideas for upgrading their skills." These demands can have an invigorating effect on instructors. It can be more challenging teaching people who are committed to learning how to do their jobs better than teaching people who are striving for grades. In any case, because the demands of teaching adult learners are unique, institutions should provide faculty members with a comprehensive understanding of the learning styles and needs of adults.

While there have been a number of claims that teacher behavior is important, little of the research to date addresses

differences in what traditional and nontraditional students look
for in such behavior. When other factors such as schedules
and program content are held constant, satisfaction with a teacher's performance seems to be less relevant for program completion. As Darkenwald (1981) notes, "Satisfaction with the
teacher-learner process seems to be interrelated with a number
of other variables such as scheduling, learner ability, marketplace demands."

Situational Factors. Other research relates to situational factors in the adult's life or in the educational environment. Unfortunately, factors such as illness, changing jobs, overtime work,
poor public transportation, and lack of child care are so student specific that it is difficult to generalize from one institutional or geographic environment to another. We must assume
that these variables are indeed important even though no research finding can be isolated. Some students seem to persist
in spite of the existence of these factors, while others use them
as the basis for dropping out.

The educational or institutional environment itself seems
to be a significant factor in determining which direction the student will take (Boshier, 1973). Where institutions have provided
strong adult support services relative to these environmental
variables, the persistence rate has gone up. A number of authors
suggest that student services are among the most important in
enhancing retention (Levitz and Noel, 1980; and Beaudin, 1982).
If an institution provides effective advising and counseling, if
it provides for child care, if it makes bureaucratic offices easily
accessible with flexible time schedules, if it provides adult student lounges and opportunities for academic and social support
groups to meet, and if it provides some type of mentoring from
senior student or faculty, persistence rates go up.

The student service that adults seem to have the greatest
difficulty with is financial aid. Institutions that have been able
to create adult scholarships or effectively qualify adult students
for Pell Grants seem to be much more successful in retaining
adult students. Tuition reimbursement from employers also appears to result in a very high persistence rate. This effect increases as one moves up the occupational ladder. Among the

most persistent and successful-to-completion adult students are those who are pursuing M.B.A. programs with the costs being paid for by their companies.

In summary, the variables that have been found to be the most effective for enhancing adult students' participation and persistence follow.

- Clear communication about the availability and nature of adult education programs tends to increase persistence.
- Students who have had previous educational success or attainment, for example, degrees or certificates, will tend to persist.
- Low ability predisposes attrition in credit classes or programs, but not in noncredit work.
- High anxiety predisposes dropping out.
- Participation and persistence increase in tailor-made and time-compressed adult programs.
- Instruction that is life relevant and addresses student needs and expectations increases persistence.
- Adult programs that have strong student support services, particularly in the area of financial aid, tend to be more successful than those that do not.

Exemplary Programs and Practices

Across the nation there are dozens of excellent programs which take creative approaches to many of the issues involved in adult retention. A thorough compendium of such programs may be found in *Attracting and Retaining Adult Learners* by Levitz and Noel (1980). Space permits us to mention only a few representative programs.

University of Utah, Salt Lake City. The Division of Continuing Education hired an outside marketing research firm to assess student needs. A promotional plan was developed that included a newspaper insert, a series of radio and television spots designed for various audience segments, and an extensive billboard campaign. A different thematic approach—such as "Add a Little Class" or "Chart Your Course"—is used each quarter. In the ten-year period since the establishment of the promotional program it seems to have been a significant factor in steadily increasing enrollment.

University of Southern California, Los Angeles. Instructional Television Network is for part-time working professionals in the high technology industrial community. It is beamed via four channels to plant sites at scheduled times from 9:00 A.M. to 9:30 P.M.; its range capability is eighty miles from campus. Approximately fifty-five courses per semester are available in engineering, computer science, and mathematics. Students in work sites participate with students in the classroom via FM radio links or telephones. Twenty to twenty-five noncredit courses are available during lunch hour. The program also makes use of teleconferencing and occasional seminars. A consortium has been formed with twenty-four schools of engineering.

University of Oklahoma, Norman. Nine accelerated master's degrees are offered with intensive, primarily off-campus classroom instruction which includes a thirty-hour week of lecture, discussion and independent study, and readings and papers. A study guide mailed prior to the first class meeting includes preparatory materials, goals statement, and syllabus. Admissions requirements, evaluation of performance, and degree requirements are similar to those for traditional on-campus programs.

Saint Louis Community College, Florissant Valley, Missouri. A self-governing peer group for women age twenty-one to sixty-five, Women in New Goals meets monthly for informational speeches and discussions. A counselor is always present at the meetings; average attendance is fifty. Experienced students serve as mentors to new students. Only rarely does a member drop out of the support group.

Western Oregon State College, Monmouth. The Academic Reentry Program, begun in the fall of 1973 to assist older undergraduate students, consists of three elements: a one-credit seminar, team taught by the dean of students and a student coordinator; a chartered student organization; and a once-a-week brown-bag luncheon at which faculty and administrators discuss the work demands of returning adults, their fears and anxieties, and provide information for effective student participation. Student responses have been positive and the academic level of participants averages one-third to one-half of a grade point higher than that of other undergraduates on campus.

Coe College, Cedar Rapids, Iowa. Traditional barriers such as long application forms, standardized test scores, and probationary status for those with incomplete past records have been removed. A special coordinator in the admissions office works specifically with older students, taking extra time to review admissions procedures and support services available. A training program is provided to sensitize office personnel to the needs of adults who may have been away from campus for many years. Follow-up telephone calls are made one week after the initial visit to offer support and encouragement.

Fostering Campus Change to Accommodate Adults

As the preceding material indicates, by the 1990s most colleges and universities will be facing the issue of how to fully integrate adult students into the mainstream of their activities. The concept of integration is especially important here. Most institutions argue that they have long attended to and attempted to serve the adult learner; as evidence, they point to their divisions of continuing education or to extension service programs where adults are supposedly welcome. However, writings in the field continue to note that these divisions, and the adult students themselves, are often viewed as second-class citizens (Alford, 1980; and Stern, 1983). Miller (1981) states it well: "Surely one of the recurrent and remarkable episodes in educational history is the valiant struggle by continuing educators to have their field accepted on a par with others in the parent organization."

It is difficult to believe that the presence of ever-increasing numbers of adult students will, in and of itself, predispose institutions to effectively integrate adults into the mainstream of their programs. Rather, it is assumed that caring administrators and faculty (such as those who have developed the exemplary programs described earlier) will have to be particularly assertive in changing campus attitudes about adult students and developing honest and realistic curricula and student services which attract and retain adults as fully integrated students.

Three Stages. Ackell (1981) suggests that institutional change to accommodate adults goes through developmental phases. He conceptualizes this evolutionary adaptation to serving adult students in three stages or steps, ranging from a relatively primitive organizational stage through a more specialized kind of adaptation, to the final or ideal stage.

The first stage Ackell labels "laissez-faire." During this stage, adult students are allowed to be as entrepreneurial and aggressive as they choose to be in dealing with the university, but there is no official or organized administrative intervention. Although barriers are reduced, the college or university expects the adults to create their own programs from existing courses and services.

During the second stage, which Ackell labels the "apartheid" stage, adults are essentially segregated from the rest of the student body and given separate, specially developed programs. These programs are better than none; however, they are given lower priority than traditional programs, are often required to be self-supporting, and administrators and faculty who participate in them are generally viewed as being low in status.

The third stage, and the one that Ackell suggests must occur in the future if we are to meet the anticipated lifelong learning needs of the nation, is the stage he labels "equity." In this stage, the institution moves beyond the apartheid approach and adopts principles of justice and fairness to correct inequities in the system that discriminate against adults in favor of more traditional student groups. In this type of model institution there is active recruitment of students, adult-oriented instruction, fully integrated curricula; regular and adult courses are treated the same on transcripts; integrated faculty receive credit in promotional tracks for adult work; administrators deal daily with adult students; and specialized adult program administrators have equal access to decision and policy making on campus.

Tactics for Change. Ackell's three stages suggest that institutional change of this type is never easy and that growth must be incremental in the movement to provide equal opportunity for adults. To achieve this growth, those interested in adapting their institution, department, or agency to create an "equity" position for adults will have to become agents for campus change. One of the authors of this chapter, Pappas, has adapted the work of Baldridge (1975) and Bennis (1975) who consider the rules for being a "Machiavellian change agent" when trying to alter an entrenched professional organization. He has reformulated their concepts to suggest tactics for creating equal opportunity adult education in traditional colleges and universities. These reformulations, originally presented in a series of planning sessions for continuing education administrators (1982), are summarized here.

The first tactic is to focus efforts on the issues of adult learners. Generally, because the adult program fits into an existing administrative unit on campus, it is easy to squander energies in trying to protect current "territory," expand staff, or seek additional resources for other activities unrelated to adult services. Indicating to colleagues and upper-level administrators that one is indeed willing to help the adult student at the exclusion of personal or departmental gain will establish credibility for new adult programs.

As adult programs are created, involved faculty and administrators should look at each program from a total organizational perspective. The question must always be asked: Why is this program good for the institution? Too often the question asked is: Why is this program good for my department or division? Some rather crass, but necessary, secondary questions may be: How will the development of good adult services help my vice president in dealing with the president? How will this program help the president in dealing with our board of trustees?

We should involve all of the power elements in the institution—administrative, governing, and professional. Resistance to changing traditional programs or adapting them for the adult learner can come from a variety of sources. If one has not built a coalition of like-minded people from the various segments of the campus, the new programming is likely to falter. Who will be the key administrators who support the new activities for the adult student? What campus committees relate to new programming? Are you involved with them in a way that will enhance your curricular or program goals? Are there experts in particular disciplines who would find the addition of adult students useful and helpful to their programs? Where possible, a task force for change should be established to include all segments of the campus, including top administrators, adult education professors, and others.

Administrative personnel developing adult courses or services must effectively follow and push the decision-making process through the formal system. Assuming that a well-written adult program proposal sent to a department head or vice president will be implemented immediately is naive. Assuming that an ad hoc task force appointed to study the adults will take line responsibility for program implementation is likewise unrealistic. If possible, identify the faculty member or administrator who must answer for the program, get approval for exploratory services or courses in existing units, and develop these in a high-quality fashion. Such services can then become the basis for success stories and provide data for expanding the adult offerings. There are very few institutions that have not been featured in a local newspaper story about the sixty-five-year-old grandmother who finally received her bachelor's degree through persistence and grit. The sense of pride that institutions feel in the appearance of these stories can be built upon to expand programs for the adult learner.

Identify external constituency groups that can influence the internal process. In addition to on-campus coalitions, outside groups such as local industries seeking more trained technical employees, adult professional organizations, and alumni groups can all be potent forces to convince administrators that adults are an important student segment. Identification and feedback from these groups are essential to creating a responsive institutional climate.

It is also necessary to plan for effective and objective evaluation as part of the program development. Once the class or service has been initiated, use evaluation data honestly to alter the program for the better. Adult educators should be careful to develop programs based on reasonable programmatic research and should avoid becoming as possessive of the new adult programs as many people are of traditional younger student programs. Too many times in higher education, we retain programs because they are good for faculty or administrators, not because they are helpful for students. To repeat this tendency with emerging adult programs may jeopardize the future of adult programs at many institutions.

Each institution and geographic area is different and local adaptations are essential. Create programs for your adults—don't just follow fads. For example, in the Los Angeles area a weekend college is appropriate, but evening classes are difficult because people must drive long distances from their suburban homes to the metropolitan campuses. In Salt Lake City, weekend colleges are not as effective because so many people are involved with family activities (Utah has the highest number of children per family in the nation), but evening classes are well received since the drive to campus is relatively short and the other spouse can stay with the children.

What the need for these tactics suggests is that most colleges and universities are essentially divided into separate—and often warring—fiefs, each making its own decisions. If we are to be successful in developing programs for adult students and in retaining them in the system, then we must base our programming on honestly trying to relate to their needs while still recognizing the restraints and context of the institution.

The exciting thing about having the adult return to campus is that it resensitizes us to the need for better understanding of student segments. The planning of retention activities that will effectively respond to adult needs will, it is hoped, reaffirm the fact that students are not merely academic slaves or sycophants who owe us their tuition income. We must recognize that students are colleagues in learning. As we focus on adult learners, we are reminded that they bring with them a set of life experiences, attitudes, and problems to be solved that will enhance the teaching and learning process. As we seek to better serve the older student, we will also be better attending to all of our students. Can we, after all, continue to say that a student eighteen to twenty-two years old is not also an adult?

References

Ackell, E. F. "Adapting the University to Adult Students." Unpublished manuscript presented to Council for Advancement of Experiential Learning, Columbia, Md., May 1981.

Alford, H. J. *Power and Conflict in Continuing Education.* Belmont, Calif.: Wadsworth, 1980.

Anderson, R., and Darkenwald, G. G. *Participation and Persistence in American Adult Education.* New York: College Entrance Examination Board, 1979.

Aslanian, C. B., and Brickell, H. M. *Americans in Transition: Life Changes as Reasons for Adult Learning.* New York: College Entrance Examination Board, 1980.

Baldridge, J. V. "Rules for a Machiavellian Change Agent: Transforming the Entrenched Professional Organization." In J. V. Baldridge and T. E. Deal (eds.), *Managing Change in Educational Organizations.* Berkeley, Calif.: McCutchan, 1975.

Beaudin, B. "Retaining Adult Students." Information Fact Sheet, no. 12. Columbus, Ohio: Educational Resources Information Center Clearinghouse on Adult, Career, and Vocational Education, 1982.

Bennis, W. G. "Who Sank the Yellow Submarine?" In J. V. Baldridge and T. E. Deal (eds.), *Managing Change in Educational Organizations.* Berkeley, Calif.: McCutchan, 1975.

Boshier, R. W. "Educational Participation and Dropout: A Theoretical Model." *Adult Education,* 1973, *23* (4), 255–282.

Chickering, A. W. "Characteristics of a Healthy Person— Healthy Environment and Educational Responses." Unpublished presentation to the Higher Education for Adult Mental Health Summer Institute, Memphis, Tenn: Memphis State University, May 1981.

Cross, K. P. "Adult Learners: Characteristics, Needs, and Interests." In R. E. Peterson, and Associates, *Lifelong Learning in America: An Overview of Current Practices, Available Resources, and Future Prospects.* San Francisco: Jossey-Bass, 1979.

Cross, K. P. *Adults as Learners: Increasing Participation and Facilitating Learning.* San Francisco: Jossey-Bass, 1981.

Darkenwald, G. G. *Retaining Adult Students.* Information Series, no. 225. Columbus, Ohio: Educational Resources Information Center Clearinghouse on Adult, Career, and Vocational Education, 1981. (ED 205 773)

Erikson, E. *Identity: Youth and Crisis.* New York: Norton, 1968.

Gordon, O. J. "Analysis of Student Enrollments in Continuing Education." Unpublished report to Division of Continuing Education staff, Salt Lake City: University of Utah, 1983.

Gould, R. L. *Transformations: Growth and Change in Adult Life.* New York: Simon & Schuster, 1978.

Hodgkinson, H. L. "Guess Who's Coming to College: A Demographic Portrait of Students in the 1990s." *Academe*, 1983, *69* (2), 13–20.

Irish, G. H. "Reaching the Least Educated Adult." In G. G. Darkenwald and G. A. Larson (eds.), *Reaching Hard-to-Reach Adults.* New Directions for Continuing Education, no. 8. San Francisco: Jossey-Bass, 1980.

Knowles, M. S. *The Modern Practice of Adult Education: Andragogy Versus Pedagogy.* New York: Association Press, 1970.

Knox, A. B. *Adult Development and Learning: A Handbook on Individual Growth and Competence in the Adult Years.* San Francisco: Jossey-Bass, 1977.

Kotler, P. *Marketing for Nonprofit Organizations.* Englewood Cliffs, N.J.: Prentice-Hall, 1975.

Lenz, E. *Creating and Marketing Programs in Continuing Education.* New York: McGraw-Hill, 1980.

Levinson, D. J., and others. *The Seasons of a Man's Life.* New York: Knopf, 1978.

Levitz, R., and Noel, L. *Attracting and Retaining Adult Learners: Summary Report and Program Descriptions.* Iowa City, Iowa: American College Testing Program National Center for Advancement of Educational Practices, 1980.

Loevinger, J. *Ego Development: Conceptions and Theories.* San Francisco: Jossey-Bass, 1976.

Long, H. B. *Theoretical Foundations of Adult Education: Borrowing from Other Disciplines.* Tallahassee: International Institute of Andragogy, Florida State University, 1982.

Lucke, D. B. "Adult Degree Program: Design and Implementation." Grant report to Fund for Improvement of Postsecondary Education. Staunton, Va.: Mary Baldwin College, 1981.

Marienau, C., and Chickering, A. W. "Adult Development and Learning." In B. Menson (ed.), *Building on Experiences in Adult Development*. New Directions for Experimental Learning, no. 16. San Francisco: Jossey-Bass, 1982.

Miller, P. A. "Strengthening the University Continuing Education Mission." In J. C. Votruba (ed.), *Strengthening Internal Support for Continuing Education*. New Directions for Continuing Education, no. 9. San Francisco: Jossey-Bass, 1981.

Palmer, S. E. "Teaching Corporate Students: There's More to It than a Variation on 'Business 101.'" *Chronicle of Higher Education*, 1983, *27* (8), 25–27.

Pappas, J. P. "Adults in Transition: Notes on Institutional Marketing." Unpublished paper presented at Daytona Beach Community College's fall faculty retreat, Daytona Beach, Fla., 1982.

Pappas, J. P., and Foster, K. S. *Promotional Techniques and Practices for Recruiting Adults*. Iowa City, Iowa: American College Testing Program National Center for Advancement of Educational Practices, 1983.

Sanders, M. D. "Educational Opportunities for the Night People, the Drop-Ins, the Young Adults, the Diaper Crowd, the Midlifers." Prepared for the House Subcommittee on Elementary, Secondary, and Vocational Education (96th Congress, 2nd session), 1980.

Spratt, P. "Attracting and Retaining Adults Begins with Assessing Their Needs." Paper presented at Campus Program to Attract and Retain Adult Learners, Chicago, Dec. 1981.

Stern, M. R. *Power and Conflict in Continuing Professional Education*. Belmont, Calif.: Wadsworth, 1983.

Verner, C., and Davis, G. S., Jr. "Completions and Dropouts: A Review of Research." *Adult Education*, 1964, *14*, 157–176.

Weathersby, R. P., and Tarule, J. M. *Adult Development: Implications for Higher Education*. American Association for Higher Education-Educational Resources Information Center/Higher Education Research Report, no. 4. Washington, D.C.: American Association for Higher Education, 1980. (ED 191 382)

9

Students Who Commute

Sylvia S. Stewart
Martha C. Merrill
Diana Saluri

In evaluating an adjunct faculty member, a commuting student might write, "This course is the first one I've taken since I left high school fifteen years ago, and it has been an excellent reintroduction to school. I'm considering going for a degree." The statements are related. Because the commitments made are fewer, commuting students are more likely than residential students to be trying out college. Colleges can do much to make that tryout a success.

Three major studies have identified commuting students as being particularly high attrition risks (Chickering, 1974; Astin, 1980; and Beal and Noel, 1980). This is because these students have, in many cases and for many reasons, made less of a commitment to attending and to continuing to attend college than residential students. For a residential student, not reenrolling means packing up, moving, getting out of a lease, leaving friends, and changing a style of life. For a commuting student, not reenrolling is likely to be much less disruptive, and the choice not to reenroll may be made for relatively minor reasons. For this reason, and the fact that 80 percent of undergraduates nationally are commuting students (Stewart and Rue, 1983), institutions that wish to improve their retention rates are well advised to take a serious look at the needs of commuter students.

In this chapter we will first consider four cycles in the development of interest in and research on commuter students and the factors that have slowed that development. We will then go on to consider how, given the diversity of commuter students, institutions can establish a local definition of commuters and become better acquainted with the characteristics and needs of the commuters on their own campuses. The chapter concludes with a description of specific programs for commuter students at a number of institutions designed to meet the diverse needs of a diverse population of students.

Four Historical Cycles

At least four historical cycles of understanding about commuter students can be delineated. Cycle one was characterized by mostly descriptive studies in the 1950s which focused on fixed variables involving commuter student characteristics. During this period the term commuter was used to describe what was then viewed as a homogeneous group of students; most of the research focused on full-time, traditional-age students.

Cycle two in understanding the commuter student was characterized by research led by Chickering (1974) and Astin (1975). Again the emphasis was on fixed variables with some limited discussion of students' interaction with the campus environment. The focus continued to be on describing full-time, traditional-age, first-time-enrolled students. Commuting students still were considered anomalies; residential students were the norm (Knefelkamp and Stewart, 1983).

Later, in the 1970s, cycle three was characterized by interest in the adult learner and/or Cross's "new student' (1971). With the increasing introduction of this part-time, nontraditional-age population into the higher education pool, discussions about commuter populations became even more complex and confused. It is important to note, for example, that although most older students are commuters, most commuters are not older students.

We are now entering the fourth cycle of our understanding of the commuter student in higher education. In the 1980s, the commuting student has become the norm and institutions must find a way to respond. Just as the focus of retention activity and research has shifted from an emphasis on profiling the characteristics of dropouts to an emphasis on the institutional characteristics which affect persistence, so has the study of commuter students begun to focus more on what institutions can do to adjust to the needs of a changing student population.

Factors Inhibiting Research

Despite this growing interest in the needs of commuter students, several major factors have acted to slow the pace of research in this current cycle. First, the history and tradition of higher education is residential. In many institutions this image is perpetuated by the memories and experiences of faculty, staff, graduates, and others long after a shift to a predominately commuter student population has taken place. Indeed, this shift nationwide has been quite dramatic. The perception that commuter students are concentrated in community colleges and certain urban institutions was challenged in the fall of 1980 when the American Council on Education studied student housing in the nation's 3,037 higher education institutions. More than one-third of all institutions had no student housing and could be considered 100 percent commuter campuses (Andersen and Atelsek, 1982).

An extrapolation from the results of this study shows a distribution of full-time commuter students across different types of institutions as follows: all institutions, 61 percent commuters; public universities, 68 percent; public four-year colleges, 66 percent; public two-year colleges, 76 percent; private universities, 58 percent; private four-year colleges, 41 percent; and private two-year colleges, 50 percent. While these percentages involve full-time students, 41 percent of all undergraduates are part-time students (National Center for Education Statistics, 1981).

Thus, if part-time enrollments had been included in the study, the percentages would be even higher. There would be no type of institution that could not be described as having a majority of undergraduates as commuter students.

Problems with Defining Commuters. A second factor that has slowed institutional change in relationship to commuter students is that the definition of the commuter student population is multidimensional. To date, college personnel have had limited understanding of these subgroups as they are defined in the research. Much of the activity involving commuter students has centered on debating not only how to define commuter students, but whether or not these students need special efforts and attention.

Competition for Resources. A third factor that has slowed campus action for commuters is that much of the awareness and study of the commuter student phenomenon began at a time when most institutions were faced with shrinking resources. In many cases, adding a new group to the long list of subpopulations who already need faculty and administrative resources has met with resistance. And, in those institutions where action for commuters has been implemented, the staff members assigned to such programs have been, for the most part, located in relatively low levels of the organizational hierarchy, usually within student services. Little impact has been made on the faculty or in the classroom where commuters have their most intense interactions with a campus.

Students' Lack of Interest. Finally, the general challenge of accommodating commuter students has met with a seeming lack of interest on the part of these students themselves. Low group identity and limited affiliation with the institution has made it difficult to organize commuter students as a strong constituency group on campus.

Establishing a Local Definition of Commuting Students

The first step to overcoming these obstacles and increasing the retention of commuter students is to understand who they are on a particular campus. The thirty-year-old taking two business classes at night; the eighteen-year-old living with her parents and attending full-time; the unemployed steelworker, back for a semester, desperate to learn a new skill; the homemaker with children in school who will not take a class that gets out after 2:00 P.M.: all of these and more are commuting students. The commuter student population thus includes a number of subgroups and not all these groups are represented on each campus. Discussing commuter students, like discussing retention itself, can become confusing if terms are not defined.

Nature of the Campus. The first issue which needs to be clarified is the nature of the campus. Is it a community college with no residential students? Is it a small, traditional liberal arts college with a handful of returning women enrolled full-time? Is it an urban university which has had a mix of commuting and residential students ever since its founding? Many educators think of commuter students as attending primarily community colleges, but commuting students are an important component of the student body at all types of institutions. Nationwide, 59 percent of all full-time undergraduates are commuters; understanding the needs of commuter students is thus important for all kinds of institutions.

Nature of the Students. The second issue which needs to be clarified is the nature of the students. Commuting students may be traditional-age or adults; they may be full- or part-time; they may be financially independent, or they may be dependent upon parents or others; they may have goals which are similar to those of residential students or they may have goals which are different. Commuting students may be remedial students who aren't willing to make the kind of commitment to further education that moving away from home implies, or they may be honor students who were accepted at colleges hundreds of miles from home but who decided not to place that kind of financial burden on their families. They may be students living at home or in an apartment for whom college is first priority, or they may have jobs, spouses, and children (or, increasingly, elderly parents) whose needs make attending college a third- or fourth-place priority.

We have focused on some of these variables to establish a profile of undergraduate commuter students. Those under twenty-five years of age constitute 65 percent of the under-graduate commuter students; those twenty-five and older con-stitute the remaining 35 percent. Of the students, 59 percent attend full-time; 41 percent, part-time. Financially dependent undergraduate commuter students constitute 31 percent of the group; financially independent, 69 percent (Astin, 1980; Car-negie Council on Policy Studies in Higher Education, 1981; National Center for Education Statistics, 1981; and U.S. Bureau of the Census, 1979).

What Campuses Need to Know About Their Commuting Students

Faced with this diversity in the commuter student popula-tion, how should the concerned staff of a college react? The first and most essential step is simple. College personnel should know the answers to the following questions.

- How many commuting students attend the college?
- Of these, how many are full-time and how many are part-time?
- How many are of traditional college age and how many are adults?
- How many are financially dependent? Financially indepen-dent? A mixture? On financial aid?
- Why did the students choose to attend this college?
- What majors do commuting students have?
- Where do the commuting students live?
- What are the goals of the commuting students?
- Is there a difference in the proportion of commuting students who drop out versus the proportion of residential students who do so?

Knowing this information is essential. Without it an institution may spend time and effort solving the wrong problem. For ex-ample, if a large number of commuting students are majoring in business, and a large percentage of that group leaves without completing a degree, the institution may want to take a look at the business department rather than look solely at the commuting students.

Knowing how many commuting students attend the college is essential for program design. Thirty students on a small campus can be individually known to faculty members, can use a small room for a lounge, can be paired with residential students as "buddies," or can be "adopted" by dormitories. A thousand students at an urban university will require a very different approach.

Attendance Status. Knowing how many students are full-time and how many are part-time is also important. Full-time students may desire to be active on campus: for example, work on the yearbook, participate in the Spanish Club, or join the chorus. Part-time students, on the other hand, often are part-time precisely because they have so many competing demands on their time: work, family responsibilities, community commitments, and the like. These students may want to take their classes and go home and will be pleased with a college that allows them to do so. In an evening class of predominantly part-time, commuting students taught by one of the authors, for example, an assignment which involved going to a play, a poetry reading, an operetta, an art gallery, or a choral performance at any time during a six-week period was vigorously protested: "I live half an hour from here, I can't come back." "My husband thinks it's a big deal to stay with our three-year-old while I'm in class. He'd never do it for me to go to a play." "I share a car with my brother and I don't think he'll let me have it."

Age. Similarly, knowing how many students are of traditional college age and how many are older is important. Younger students, like full-time students, may identify strongly with being a college student; for older students, attending college may be one more responsibility to juggle. Younger students may want to try out being responsible by running a student government meeting or holding a bake sale to raise money for the ski club; older students may run meetings for their companies or for community organizations and may earn money to buy groceries. Such students do not need the college to provide these opportunities for them.

Financial Status. The financial status of students is important, too. A financially independent student may not be a financially stable student and college attendance may be on a stop in/stop out basis, depending upon factors unrelated to the college and its quality: "My wife's mother is coming to live with us and I have to remodel the back room." "They put me on second shift, so I have to drop out of this class." Financially dependent commuting students may be commuting because they come from families without sufficient financial resources to send them away to college. Perhaps more importantly, families may not have sufficient confidence in the students' ability to be successful, sufficient conviction of the importance of the residential experience, or sufficient evidence of the students' interest in college to warrant support at a residential college. Although the financial aid available to part-time students may be very limited, such aid opportunities need to be publicized to commuting students whose financial situations are precarious.

College Choice. Knowing why students choose a particular college is important, too. A young man accepted by an Ivy League college and a local university who chooses to live at home and attend the local university because his scholarships cover 100 percent of the tuition—versus half the tuition at the Ivy League college—will be likely to remain at the local university *if* he finds high caliber academics, stimulating friends, and faculty who show an interest in him. A twenty-year-old woman with a two-year-old child may choose a college because it is the only one in the area with a day care center. Working adults have been known to choose colleges because they offer twilight hour courses at convenient places along commuter routes. If a college does not know why commuting students—or any kind of students—first decide to attend, the college will have trouble figuring out how to keep those students attending.

Major. Looking at the majors commuting students choose can also be revealing. Commuting students may concentrate in one or two majors simply because of scheduling convenience: "I only have to come up here two days a week to get my psych courses." "English is the only major you can finish entirely in the evening and on weekends." "I can't take biology because the labs are all in the afternoon and I have to be back home by the time the kids are out of school." Students who choose majors because the schedule is convenient rather than because the subject matter is interesting to them would seem to have a good chance of becoming dropouts.

Location. Where commuting students live can make a difference in their persistence. Some students sign up for 8:00 A.M. classes and then discover that the first bus they can catch in the morning arrives on campus at 8:20 A.M. They miss work, begin not to do well, consider skipping class, and then may consider dropping the class altogether. Other students have unreliable cars or share cars with spouses or siblings. Some depend on other people to drive them. Some may miss class because heavy snows, which mean snowball fights for residential students, mean treacherous driving for them. Organizing a ride-sharing program, negotiating with the local bus company, or improving the availability of information about snow closings may be worthwhile responses.

Looking at where commuter students live may reveal other important facts. Are students from a certain zip code area more likely to drop out than others? What are the characteristics of that area? Is it an area where minority students live? If so, perhaps college staff should look at the climate for minority students on campus. Has another college opened an outreach center in that town that is drawing away students? Do students from the wealthy areas come for a semester and then leave? Perhaps it would be worthwhile to look at the laboratories, computer equipment, or other resources of the high schools in that area. Would students be disappointed with what the college has by contrast? Has a train added a stop or a bus changed a route? Perhaps that is making it easier for students to attend other colleges. Has a major factory in the area closed? Perhaps students from that area now need more information about financial aid.

Goals. Knowing the goals of commuting students is extremely important and frequently overlooked. The very fact that commuting students are commuting students suggests that they may have financial situations or priorities which will influence their reasons for attending college. In a study of commuting community college students, Merrill (1982) discovered that 50 percent of the students in technical programs and 65 percent of those in transfer programs did not intend to earn degrees at the college at which they were enrolled. Their reasons for enrolling included trying out college to see if they could do it, obtaining some skills needed for a job, taking some courses that were of interest, and taking courses which would transfer to another college when extenuating circumstances change. One inventive engineering student at a Big Ten university told one of the authors that he took all of his humanities and social science electives at the local community college because he found these subjects difficult. If he did well, he transferred the courses to the university. If he did badly, he had not lost much in tuition and he had not ruined his grade point average.

Knowing student goals is important when a college considers its attrition problem. If the engineering student does not complete a degree at the community college, or if he does not come back for another semester, has the college failed in any way? Certainly some commuter students who intend to earn degrees do not earn them for reasons which the college could prevent. On the other hand, students may have self-designed goals, and institutional practices may either help or hinder them in the achievement of those goals.

This became clear in another portion of Merrill's study (1982). At one college, black students and white students persisted in relatively similar proportions. It appeared, therefore, that the college was meeting the needs of black students as well as it was meeting the needs of whites. However, when students' goals were studied, it was discovered that a higher proportion of black students than whites originally had intended to earn degrees. For the white students, then, not completing a degree was intentional; for the black students, it was a sign that something had gone wrong.

Comparing Commuter and Residential Attrition. Similarly, it is important for a college to know the retention rate (however defined) of commuter students and that of residential students. If the rates are drastically different, with the rates of commuting students considerably lower, then a program to meet the needs of commuter students is in order. If the rates are similar, college staff might better look at factors which affect the retention of all students.

Specific Programs for Commuter Students

Knowing the specific characteristics and needs of commuting students on one's own campus is an essential step in designing a campuswide retention plan. However, there are basic considerations which are important for the retention of almost any kind of commuting student and these are reflected in programs implemented at several campuses nationwide.

Creating Awareness. The first step is simply a campuswide awareness of the existence of and needs of commuting students. Student activities directors, full-time and adjunct faculty, counselors, institutional planners, security guards, publications editors, food service managers, and others all need to be aware that commuting students are on campus and that they have special needs.

One source of information about commuter students is the National Clearinghouse for Commuter Programs centered at the University of Maryland in College Park. The clearinghouse was created to share data about the characteristics and needs of commuter students and to establish channels of communication among schools that serve commuter students. In addition to a quarterly newsletter, *The Commuter*, the clearinghouse biennially publishes *Commuter Students: References and Resources*, a comprehensive, cross-referenced listing of literature on commuter students and the associations and organizations concerned with their needs, and an annual *Commuter Institution Index* which surveys current programs for commuter students nationwide. The clearinghouse also conducts and promotes research about issues related to commuter students and sponsors a referral service for sharing information about specific programs.

Promoting Affiliation. A campuswide awareness of the needs of commuter students should lead to efforts to promote their affiliation with the institution. This sense of affiliation is important for a commuter student. If, for example, not reenrolling means losing the chance to have a lead in a play, losing a part-time job, losing contact with friends, or losing touch with a faculty member who is interested in the student and the student's future, the decision not to reenroll becomes more difficult. Although some students, particularly older, part-time working students, may want to attend their classes and go home, others want the feeling of belonging that campus activities offer.

Linda Faaborg, vice-provost for student affairs at the University of Cincinnati in Ohio, pointed out in a telephone conversation with one of the authors (Mar. 1984) that organizations for commuter students per se do not always go over well because "commuters don't think of themselves primarily as commuters. They would rather belong to a content area organization in which they can pursue a particular interest."

Many campuses have found that the key to getting commuter students involved in such activities is flexible scheduling. The University of Central Florida in Orlando offers early morning and late afternoon noncredit courses in such activities as dance exercise, scuba diving, and yoga. Students can drop by these courses before and after their regular classes. Outdoor popular music concerts are scheduled over the noon hour. The film society of Cleveland State University in Ohio has begun showing free films not only on weekends, but on weekday afternoons in lounges and is getting a good response. Indiana University-Purdue University at Indianapolis schedules special activities such as its spring festival before and after lunch instead of in the evenings. Chicago State University schedules two showings—one in the afternoon and one in the evening—of campus events such as lectures, films, or special events whenever possible. This double scheduling works particularly well for special programs such as black history month.

Many colleges have found that having a part-time job on campus increases commuter students' affiliation with the institution. At the University of South Florida in Tampa, orientation sessions feature a panel of representatives from offices on campus which employ students as well as a representative from the office of financial aid and student employment. The message is: If you have to work, work on campus.

In addition to acquainting commuter students with on-campus work opportunities, colleges need to consider other factors. Is there equal access to part-time student employment for all students? Are there financial aid policies or procedures that penalize students who work on campus and therefore encourage off-campus employment? Are there new part-time work opportunities that can be created on campus?

Special approaches to orientation, advising, and support services can also help integrate commuter students into the life of the campus and increase their sense of affiliation with the institution. Oakland University in Rochester, Michigan, requires all freshmen to enroll in a two-day orientation program involving an overnight stay on campus. This extended experience on campus provides students with an opportunity to meet resource personnel and student leaders and to make friends.

To counter the isolation and confusion experienced by many new students, Wayne State University in Detroit, Michigan has established a Faculty Friends Program. Freshmen and transfer students are matched with faculty and staff who volunteer to offer support during the first weeks on campus and throughout the term. Matching students with persons who are working outside the students' intended field of study "broadens the student's contact with the campus and emphasizes the personal nature of the student-faculty-staff relationship" (Taylor, 1984, p. 2).

In 1979, in response to a rising attrition rate, Indiana University at South Bend implemented three programs to serve beginning commuter students. In the Mentor Program, faculty and advisers are assigned incoming freshmen to meet with individually during fall orientation. The students also meet in small groups and programmed social events encourage informal interaction among students, staff, and faculty. University Life Seminar, an eight-week, one-credit-hour course focusing on developing an awareness of co-curricular activities and university policies, developing study skills, and identifying career goals, is required for all high-risk students and encouraged for all freshmen. Under the Beginning Student Early Warning System, a brief student report form is sent to instructors during the fourth week of classes to identify students in need of assistance.

The College of St. Catherine in St. Paul, Minnesota recently instituted a peer-advising system for commuters. Upperclass commuter students serve as advisers to a group of ten to fifteen new commuting students. During the fall semester the groups meet every two weeks, often at a member's home. Groups are organized according to area of residence to facilitate carpooling and home meetings. Groups also attend area theaters and restaurants. As Student Activities Coordinator Ann Garvey stated in a telephone conversation with one of the authors, "the groups help set up the kind of informational network students living on campus have when they say 'I've had Professor Harris' or 'I've used that book.' They mainly focus on how to get access to information, how to figure out the college as a system, and provide the kind of informal referral network that exists in the residence halls." Second semester the group sessions tend to give way to individual follow-up meetings with advisers who are available two hours a week on a drop-in basis.

At the University of Cincinnati, a Central University Tutorial Service which serves students on a drop-in basis between classes has helped retain high-risk commuter students. Students classified as high-risk (freshmen, transfer students, and those on probation) receive tutoring for one dollar an hour, using a subsidized ticket system. (Others pay five dollars an hour.) The service acts as a clearinghouse for commuters, bringing together tutors and students. Since most students leave the campus by 3 P.M., this drop-in arrangement works better than the kind of peer study groups often found on residential campuses.

At the University of Iowa in Iowa City, commuters have access to computer-assisted instruction laboratories and special study skills sessions in the residence halls and can purchase board contracts.

At Western Michigan University in Kalamazoo, the office of commuter services offers a number of services related to off-campus housing. The housing locator service provides a listing of apartments and roommates as well as a housing locator room with a telephone and wall maps for apartment searchers. The office also offers a tenant-landlord mediation service, a rent escrow program, a library of twelve audiotapes covering such topics as subletting and security deposits, and brochures aimed at helping first-time housekeepers.

Child Care. Providing child care on a flexible basis is another way of working around commuter students' schedules and responsibilities. Indiana University-Purdue University at Indianapolis's widely used child care center offers full educational programs for a minimal fee of thirty-five cents an hour. The University of Cincinnati Child Care Center offers full-fledged day care and also accepts children on a drop-in basis, allowing the part-time student to commit for day care for as few as three hours a week.

Central Missouri State University in Warrensburg finds that its child care programs function as a recruitment tool for the school since word is getting around that parents do not necessarily have to give up a college education because they have small children. In addition to a traditional day care facility, Central Missouri offers a centrally located alternative drop-in service where parents can leave their children for an hour or two while they attend class ("Child Care—A Retention Tool," 1984).

Enlisting Support of Students' Family and Friends

Another consideration in dealing with commuter students is gaining the support of the significant others—parents, spouses, or children—in the students' lives. Expecting the parents of commuting students to be as interested in the students' education as are the parents of residential students is sometimes unrealistic; as mentioned earlier, students may be commuting students precisely because their parents do not support or understand their desire for further education. Spouses and children, too, may waver in their support; classes and homework may mean household repairs left undone and store-bought cookies instead of homemade ones.

What can the college do to encourage support from these significant others? It should encourage advance planning so that households will not be disrupted. Field trips, for example, should not be scheduled on the spur of the moment if they mean a change in schedule or an unplanned need for a car. Students

may have responsibilities at home such as babysitting or chauf-
feuring a brother to work which may be disrupted by sudden
schedule changes. If the college is a source of family disruptions,
attendance is unlikely to be encouraged.

Similarly, examination and term paper due dates should
be announced well in advance so that commuting students can
make arrangements to lighten other responsibilities at home.
Involving family members in campus life by offering family
memberships for the gym, encouraging spouses to come to
French Club dinners, or holding "bring a guest to class" days
may help elicit a feeling of belonging to the college that will make
family members more supportive of the commuting student's
college going. Fairleigh Dickinson University in Rutherford,
New Jersey offers weekend family programs such as Halloween
Carnival and Easter egg hunts.

Communicating with Commuter Students. Communicating with
commuter students is yet another challenge. How do students
find out what's going on on campus? Do residential students
use dormitory and dining hall bulletin boards or have notices
distributed directly to their mailboxes? if so, other means of communicating with commuter students should be devised. A lack
of information about registration deadlines, for example, might
cause a wavering commuting student not to reenroll.

Many predominately commuter campuses report that
their best source of communication with commuter students is
the campus newspaper. Others reach commuters through special
newsletters. At Oakland University in Rochester, Michigan,
calendar information is disseminated through the university's
mainframe computer. When a student logs on to the computer,
a variety of "Help" messages appear first. If the student types
in "Help Events," the campus calendar with the coming week's
events appears on the screen. It is estimated that during any
given semester well over 50 percent of the student body has access to computer time through a class and the file has become
an important complement to the more traditional communication channels of the student newspaper and the campus radio
station (Euculano and Andreas, 1982).

Physical Environment. A final item to be addressed—and

a difficult one in time of tight budgets—is the physical environment of the campus. Sufficient parking near classroom buildings rather than near dormitories is an obvious requirement. Cafeterias not connected to dormitories are another. Lounges and lockers may be desirable. College staff may want to think of times they have attended conferences while not staying at the conference hotel. What would have made the experience more pleasant? A quiet spot for coffee, a convenient place to buy an extra pad of paper, a public telephone with a little privacy, a place to leave a wet raincoat and an umbrella: commuting students would appreciate the same kinds of amenities.

Campuses also might think of new ways to use space on campus as their percentage of commuter students increases. A traditionally residential college which now has empty residence hall rooms might keep one residential hall two-thirds full and rent out the remaining rooms on a daily basis (H. Berry, personal communication to authors, Feb. 1984). Young, full-time commuters would find having an on-campus room available the night before a test or during final examinations to be a luxury and an incentive to achievement; they also would be encouraged to participate in plays, musical groups, and other activities which involve evening rehearsals or meeting times. Such involvement could lead to a greater sense of belonging to the college, which in turn makes retention more likely. Through occasionally staying in a residence hall, the commuting student is also likely to make new friends; these friendships may encourage remaining at the college. For as Spady (1971) and others note, both social and academic integration into college life are necessary if a student is to remain at an institution.

The commuting student also would have an opportunity to try out living away from home for a day or two. This might satisfy the impulse to sample independence and make a quiet room with homecooked meals look good, thereby strengthening the student's resolve to stay at home and commute rather than to incur the expense of a residential college elsewhere.

If faculty, too, could rent dormitory rooms in a separate wing or perhaps a resident adviser's apartment after an evening class or a late play rehearsal, opportunities for faculty-student interaction outside of class could be increased. This interaction, which assures the student that someone is personally interested in him or her, also has been linked to increased student retention.

A Comprehensive Program

At Marist College, a private liberal arts college in Poughkeepsie, New York, retention of commuter students (defined as the rate at which freshmen return as sophomores) increased from 59.3 percent in 1980–81 to 92 percent in 1981–82. A major reason for this increase is the comprehensive program for commuters which the college has initiated. One important part of this program is the Mentor Program; others include a computerized early warning survey, learning skills workshops, an orientation program, and a student group called the Commuter Union.

The Mentor Program, in which full-time mentors living in the residence halls serve as advocates for students, was initiated in 1979 for residential students. In 1981 commuter student mentors were added to meet the needs of the 700 commuter students, who make up one-third of the student population. Any kind of problem can be brought to the mentors, who either deal with the situation, or make appropriate referrals.

Students must share their academic situations with their mentors. Midterm grades are not mailed to students' homes until the students have seen them, and the only way they can do so is to see their mentor. Students whose grade point averages are 1.7 or lower at midterm or at the end of the semester are required to sign a learning contract which sets academic goals for the remainder of the semester or for the following semester. It is worth noting that not only has the retention rate for both residential and commuter students increased since the Mentor Program was initiated, but the number of students qualifying for the dean's list has also increased. Improved academic quality and an improved retention rate seem to be going hand in hand.

Other components of Marist's comprehensive retention program include a computerized survey which provides information to help staff identify dropout-prone students. The survey determines if Marist was the student's first, second, or third

choice of college; if the student has used health services; if the
student is employed; what grade point average the student expects; what the highest degree is that the student is seeking; if
either of the student's parents is deceased; if the student wishes
to be tutored in any subject; and so on.

The orientation program involves group sessions both
in the summer before enrollment and during the opening days
of school as well as individual appointments with mentors. Learning skills workshops on subjects such as time management are
offered throughout the semester. The Commuter Union, a group
coadvised by commuter mentors but run by students to meet
students' needs, publishes a newsletter for commuters, cospon-
sors mixers with residence halls, and sets up teams to participate
in intramurals.

The components of Marist's program for freshmen—
mentors, a survey to identify students in trouble, learning skills
workshops, an orientation program, and a Commuter Union—
have proved to be both comprehensive and effective in making
commuter students feel at home on campus.

Conclusion

Commuting students are a majority of the undergraduates
in this country, and their numbers are likely to grow as residential costs rise and as the rapidity of change in our society forces
us all to become lifelong learners. However, in many cases and
for many reasons, commuting students have made less of a commitment to attending and to continuing to attend college than
have residential students and are therefore more likely to drop
out. If colleges wish to better serve commuter students and to
help them succeed in achieving their diverse goals, they are advised to know their commuting students well and to attend
carefully to their needs.

References

Andersen, C. J., and Atelsek, F. J. *An Assessment of College Student Housing and Physical Plant.* Higher Education Panel Report,

no. 55. Washington, D.C.: American Council on Education, 1982. (ED 222 161)

Astin, A. W. *Preventing Students from Dropping Out.* San Francisco: Jossey-Bass, 1975.

Astin, A. W. *The American Freshman: National Norms for Fall 1980.* Washington, D.C.: American Council on Education and University of California at Los Angeles, 1980.

Beal, P. E., and Noel, L. *What Works in Student Retention.* Iowa City, Iowa: American College Testing Program and National Center for Higher Education Management Systems, 1980. (ED 197 635)

Carnegie Council on Policy Studies in Higher Education. Staff Consultation Report, Washington, D.C.: Nov. 1981.

Chickering, A. W. *Commuting Versus Resident Students: Overcoming the Educational Inequities of Living Off Campus.* San Francisco: Jossey-Bass, 1974.

"Child Care—A Retention Tool." *The Commuter,* 1984, *9* (2), 5.

Cross, K. P. *Beyond the Open Door: New Students to Higher Education.* San Francisco: Jossey-Bass, 1971.

Euculano, J. M., and Andreas, R. "Adapting Technology for Management in Commuter Affairs." *The Commuter,* 1982, *8* (1), 3-4.

Knefelkamp, L. L., and Stewart, S. S. "Toward a New Conceptualization of Commuter Students: The Developmental Perspective." In S. S. Stewart (ed.), *Commuter Students: Enhancing Their Educational Experiences.* New Directions for Student Services, no. 24. San Francisco: Jossey-Bass, 1983.

Merrill, M. C. "The Educational Goals and Degree Objectives of Community College Students: Implications for Planning Instructional Programs and Student Services." *Dissertation Abstracts International,* 1982, *43,* 1806A. (University Microfilms order no. DA8225010)

National Center for Education Statistics. Staff Consultation Report, Washington, D.C.: Nov. 1981.

Spady, W. G., Jr. "Dropouts from Higher Education: Toward an Empirical Model." *Interchange,* 1971, *2* (3), 38-62.

Stewart, S. S., and Rue, P. "Commuter Students: Definition and Distribution." In S. S. Stewart (ed.), *Commuter Students:*

Enhancing Their Educational Experiences. New Directions for Student Services, no. 24. San Francisco: Jossey-Bass, 1983.

Taylor, S. L. "High-Risk Student Retention at Commuter Colleges." *The Commuter*, 1984, 9 (2), 1–2.

U.S. Bureau of the Census. "Living Arrangements of College Students: October 1976." Current Population Reports, series P-20, no. 348, Washington, D.C.: U.S. Government Printing Office, 1979.

10

Admissions

William Ihlanfeldt

The college choice process—who goes where to college and why—is substantially different today than it was in the early 1960s. The college population is pluralistic, many more students enroll than in the 1960s, and a far greater number of institutions serve their divergent needs.

There is considerable research addressing the question of who remains and why (Astin, 1975; and Noel, 1978). Yet individual colleges and universities have made little effort to relate this information to who is recruited and why. The purpose of this chapter is to assist institutions in developing admissions marketing plans that achieve the objective of recruiting students who are likely to remain once enrolled.

To achieve such congruence, prospective students should have a good understanding of the product the institution has to offer, including opportunities that the college experience will create; financing alternatives; skill development; and the social, psychological, and religious values inherent in the institution's mission. These are the factors that affect demand and that each institution must address if it is to successfully achieve or maintain its enrollment objectives.

What are the desired outcomes of a specific college experience? Few, if any, institutions attempt to answer this question for prospective students. Most colleges and universities offer a value-added or developmental experience but lack the empirical data to support their perceptions (Ihlanfeldt and Davis, 1982). The college that can clearly identify student growth in terms of outcomes should have a decided advantage in developing consumer interest. As prospective students become better shoppers, they will force institutions to support their developmental claims. Thus, measuring outcomes through institutional assessment is one way for a college to reposition itself in relation to competing institutions.

After first analyzing the problem of enrollment decline, I will consider the question of prospective enrollments and tuition revenues. Next I will consider how to conduct a marketing analysis in order to find the group of students that best fits an institution. Finally, I will look at ways to achieve market penetration by communicating with this best-fit group.

Analyzing the Problem of Enrollment Decline

Numerous institutions, both public and private, graduate fewer than 50 percent of their entering freshmen, and an even larger number of colleges and universities graduate no more than one-third (Holstrom and Knepper, 1976). Such schools may be severely threatened by demographic trends in the 1980s and 1990s if they continue to count on their admissions departments to solve their enrollment and revenue problems. However, if they address the reasons for the retention problem by analyzing their current and prospective markets and by implementing a strategic admissions plan, that threat will be greatly reduced or eliminated. Not infrequently, a given college has succeeded in recruiting more freshmen but still has not achieved its enrollment objectives. We tend not to translate such a statement to our own institutions unless forced to examine such ratios as the number of new students to total enrollment or the distribution of new student enrollments across departments or schools.

Each year colleges across the country close their doors because they have been unable to stop attrition. Shortly before closing, one small, four-year college in Missouri found that although its total enrollment was stable, each year 50 percent of its student body consisted of new enrollments. This situation is similar to that of a two-year women's college which hired me for my first position as an admissions officer. Each year freshmen made up two-thirds of the entire student body. Fifty percent of the previous freshman class failed to reenroll. Yet few members of the campus community appeared to be concerned. Few asked if the environment could be improved or if a different type of student could be recruited, a student who would be more satisfied with the experiences offered by the college and thus more likely to return and to graduate. This school, too, eventually closed its doors, partly because it no longer had a marketable mission, and partly because it did not have an institutional strategy to address its overall enrollment objectives other than spending more money on student recruitment.

Neither of these institutions was able to improve its attractiveness by first improving its environment and then by successfully conveying this change to the marketplace. The challenge they both faced was to improve the match between what enrolled students expected and what they experienced. They failed at a time when ample numbers of prospective students were in the marketplace. They failed because their administrators and faculty did not understand or accommodate the needs of their markets.

Advantage to Enrollment Decline. There is at least one advantage to the current fear of enrollment shortfalls and the increasing budgetary dependency on tuition revenues: the attendant problems related to attrition are now receiving attention from administrators and faculty. Such concern often results in an improved product that increases the attractiveness of the institution. New and modified programs, better defined standards of performance, a greater array of support services, and a growing student perception that the faculty and staff do care—all of these factors can help improve the level of student satisfaction and redefine the image of the institution in the marketplace. Note that these factors *can* help, rather than *will* help. To influence recruitment, changes in programs and/or the existence of new programs have to be communicated to prospective students within various market segments. The difficulty of doing so is evidenced by the fact that many institutions have improved programming within the past decade, but have been unable to change their relative market positions. As admissions officers explain the changes that their institutions have made in certain programs, they are often confronted with prospective students whose response is: "So what else is new? Every college representative says the same thing."

The Current Challenge. How can an institution identify, penetrate, and gain the attention of the market segment it can best serve? This objective cannot be achieved by employing the same old techniques used by hundreds of other admissions offices. Once the product has been transformed to better serve students, the institution must be able to package its promotional effort in a way that will differentiate it from other institutions with which it competes. The usual approach is what I define as an attempt at a quick fix, a shotgun effort which involves spending more for flashier promotional brochures, more on merit scholarships, and more on additional personnel for the admissions department. Seldom is the question asked: "Are there other management styles and methods of communication that could transmit the message in a more effective and timely manner?"

The strategic planning objective should be to create a better fit between the institution's total environment and various market segments and to communicate this fit to students. The primary need is then for an admissions department that views itself as managing a communication process rather than as a sales force to recruit students. Such an approach should result in a higher retention rate and decreasing dependency on new enrollments to balance the institutional budget.

Prospective Enrollments and Tuition Revenues

As institutional budgets become increasingly tuition dependent, it is common for faculty and staff who do not have the primary responsibility for student recruitment to quantify various enrollment objectives without the benefit of prior market research. The faculty, trustees, and administrative staff are often quick to agree that enrollment must either be stabilized or increased, and to make the related requests that quality be improved and racial, ethnic, gender, and class diversity be expanded. It is presumed that these objectives can be attained without any change in the distribution of enrollments across the institution or any real increase in the financial aid budget. Each of these variables—enrollment, quality, diversity, and student aid—is viewed as a discrete entity with little or no interdependency.

In fact, in pondering the problem of attempting to maintain or increase enrollment, we must consider many interdependent factors: the demographic trends by geographical region, changes in participation rates of various age groups, the present market position of the institution as a whole and of the programs within the institution, the opportunities for program development, the flexibility of programs in meeting changing demands, the price and the cost of price discounting, and the prospective student's perceptions of the value of the education offered by the institution.

Demographic Trends. Demographic trends and interests in particular programs are well documented, particularly among the eighteen- to twenty-four-year-old population. The 30 to 40 percent decrease in this population over the next ten years is already being offset by increasing participation rates among an older student population. Many smaller institutions have proved their resiliency by creating programs that meet the needs of the older, part-time student. Evening programs have emerged, off-campus offerings have become common, and the weekend college is now the dominant educational curriculum at some institutions. Mundelein College in Chicago and Hiram College in Ohio, among others, have initiated efforts to provide special services and areas on campus for adult students.

As we assess current and future market demand, the "survival curriculum" appears to include some or all of the following: programs in the health and managerial sciences, in information systems and computer science, and in the fine and applied arts. The availability of these curricular offerings coupled with opportunities for field internships, work-study arrangements, and foreign study provide an attractive educational package. When such educational opportunities are offered to older students interested in part-time study in the evenings or during weekends on campus or at off-campus sites, both demand and the financial viability of the institution are enhanced.

Price. Once the program is defined and made accessible to students and the market is sensitized to the offerings of the institution, the interest of the market turns to price, both in the out-of-pocket sense (market price) and, increasingly, in the rate-of-return sense (future earnings). Potential students, however, are less concerned with price if career opportunities and related salaries are substantial. Moreover, because of the variety of student aid programs, price can be marketed in such a way as to reduce the drain on family resources. Thus, perceived value is more important than gross price, and price is even less of a factor when it can be prorated over an extended period of time. One thing for certain is that the American public is well sensitized to the use of and advantages of installment credit options.

If, as is usually the case, the economics of the institution is the determining factor in projecting desired enrollments, how can the number of full-paying tuition equivalents, rather than just the number of full-paying students, be increased? The financial objective is to increase the net-to-budget tuition figure. Whether the student aid budget should increase is determined by the quality and the quantity of full-pay students in the applicant pool. However, raw numbers suggest that, in most cases, it is almost impossible to increase the number of full-pay students. Annually, no more than 200,000 graduating secondary school seniors and their families can afford the average cost of attendance at public institutions; of these, fewer than 100,000 can afford the cost at private institutions. The average annual cost of public higher education in 1983 including tuition, fees, room, board, and books was estimated to be between $4,500 and $5,000, and the average cost for private higher education to be between $7,500 and $8,000. Thus, if enrollment goals are to be achieved, it is necessary to discount the cost of attendance.

In assessing the student aid costs related to achieving enrollment objectives, I find that the pool of paying customers at high-ability levels is quite small indeed (Table 1). For example, in 1982 there were only 27,990 high school graduates who

Table 1. National College-Bound High School Students:
Upper Income Group (> $50,000).

Characteristics	1982	1984	1987
SAT Verbal and Math ≥1100 or class rank top 20 percent	27,990	25,247	24,515
SAT Verbal and Math *each* above 550 or class rank top 20 percent	16,959	15,297	14,853
SAT Verbal and Math ≥1200 or class rank top 20 percent	15,608	14,078	13,670
SAT Verbal and Math ≥1200 or class rank top 10 percent	11,758	10,606	10,298

Source: Adapted from Koester, 1983.

fell in the top 20 percent of their class, achieved a composite
Scholastic Aptitude Test (SAT) score of 1100 or higher, and
whose family income was in excess of $50,000. By 1987, that
number will drop to 24,515. If the composite score is 1200 or
higher and the other variables remain constant, the number of
students meeting these criteria in 1982 was only 15,608. By 1987,
this number will decrease to 13,670.

If family income is not considered, with Verbal and Math
scores above 550 and top 20 percent of class as parameters, the
potential pool in 1982 was 76,662; by 1987 the pool will have
decreased to 67,144 (Table 2). Thus, even independent of family

Table 2. National College-Bound High School Students by Income Level:
SAT Verbal and Math above 550, class rank top 20 percent.

Family Income	1982	1984	1987
$ 0 – 3,000	312	281	273
$ 3,001 – 12,000	4,888	4,409	4,281
$12,001 – 21,000	11,857	10,695	10,385
$21,001 – 30,000	14,769	13,322	12,936
$30,001 – 40,000	17,476	15,763	15,306
$40,001 – 50,000	10,401	9,382	9,110
Over $50,000	16,959	15,297	14,853
Total	76,662	69,149	67,144

Note: These projections are understated because they do not include
college-bound students who have taken only the American College Test Program (ACT).

Source: Adapted from Koester, 1983.

income, the size of the high-ability pool is a small fraction of the total market.

We estimate that independent of income, in 1984 no more than 2.8 percent of the total high school graduate population of 69,149 could meet the admission criteria for Northwestern University in Evanston, Illinois. These criteria are defined as 1100 on the SAT and a *B* average in high school. Such an analysis suggests but one alternative: if an institution wishes to maintain its enrollment as well as some semblance of quality, it must have a substantial financial aid program. Thus, as we attempt to manage our enrollments to achieve both our revenue goals and maintain our academic standards, greater retention of enrolled students becomes one primary objective of our enrollment management plan, while the other is to attract those students most likely to be satisfied with the educational offerings of the institution. Each of these objectives has a cost factor, one in terms of improved programs and services and the other in terms of student aid, neither of which can be overlooked.

As college and university budgets become more tuition intensive, the dollars that flow to the financial aid program are of increasing concern. Many view student aid dollars as a loss in income rather than as a necessary investment. As the preceding suggests, the real challenge is to increase the dollars that flow to the budget from tuition revenue. Reducing student aid costs is but one way to achieve this objective, and because a shortfall in enrollments is likely to be the outcome, decreasing student aid may not be a viable alternative for most institutions. Commonly, institutions will increase their financial aid budget by the same percentage that tuition is increased. This approach assumes that family income and student self-help will increase at the same rate as the increase in tuition and that there have been no changes in government aid programs. What I am suggesting is that any enrollment goal has a cost factor and that the more refined the enrollment goal is in terms of a distribution of interests, quality, and diversity, the higher the student aid cost.

Tuition Analysis. In analyzing revenues from enrollments, the critical variable is the net-to-budget tuition figure which represents gross tuition revenues minus institutional grant aid. Once the desired increase in the net-to-budget tuition revenue figure is determined, various options are available to the institution. The announced tuition increase may have to be more than desired to compensate for required increases in the student aid budget, or it may be possible to increase substantially student aid and enrollment at the same time. In the latter case, the typical student would be paying less in terms of out-of-pocket cost, yet the net-to-budget tuition figure would increase because of marginal growth in enrollment. Alternately, enrollment could decrease as long as the net-to-budget figure was achieved. Under this scenario, there would be fewer dollars available for student aid. This would presume either a sufficient number of paying customers in the applicant pool to make up for the decreases in institutional aid or increases in external student assistance.

Such a net-to-budget analysis requires that the director of admissions, or the appropriate committee concerned about enrollment assume responsibility for delineating various options. The problem is that the skills necessary to assess the various options available to most institutions are often not available. Thus, the standard procedure is to increase tuition by a given percentage and to increase the student aid budget by a corresponding amount. Additionally, it may be possible to increase tuition without expanding the student aid budget substantially if the expected self-help component is not excessive and can be increased.

Options. To review, realistic options related to a desired increase in tuition revenue are (1) increase tuition, increase grant aid, and maintain current enrollments; (2) increase tuition, maintain or decrease grant aid, and maintain or decrease enrollments; (3) stabilize or decrease tuition, decrease student grant aid, and maintain or increase enrollments; and (4) increase tuition, decrease grant aid (increase self-help), and maintain or decrease enrollments. Each of these permutations must be considered, for each can result in a substantial net increase in tuition revenue. The most appropriate combination depends upon the market position of the institution at various prices and the size of the present grant aid budget. It is quite possible that an institution may have a much stronger market position at its market price than at its list price. This situation would suggest that a college could keep its list price constant but increase its market price, thereby decreasing institutional grant aid and thus increasing net tuition revenues.

The details of such options matter little to students and their families. What *is* critical is the out-of-pocket cost or market price at any given time. Since most families pay a discounted rate (an amount much less than the actual cost of attendance), each family pays a separate market price based upon its financial resources, the amount of expected student self-help, and the financial capability of the institution to vary the market price in relation to individual family needs. The market price, the perceived value of the desired program as defined by market position, and the potential future earning of graduates in the program must be conveyed to prospective students and their families. What needs to be watched is the behavior of competing institutions.

Market Analysis: Is There a Best-Fit Group?

The college admission selection process matches certain types of potential students with specific institutions and with specific programs within our colleges and universities. To a great extent, it is also a subtle self-selection process. To recognize that such a selection process exists is to begin to ask a variety of other questions that will assist the admissions department in its efforts to achieve institutional enrollment goals. "Who enrolls and why? Who does not and why? Who persists to graduation and why? Who leaves and why?" represent a few of the types of questions that each institution must answer in order to address problems of retention and market identification. Once such questions are answered, we can turn our energies to identifying potential markets that provide the best fit for the institution.

Exogenous Influences. Levels of ability, geographical distribution, variation in high school preparation, and socioeconomic class of the student body are examples of exogenous factors that often affect retention. Students of high-ability levels may be transferring or dropping out simply because they are bored or find few people like themselves within the institution. The residential institution may find that students from distant markets are far more likely to transfer than students from local or regional markets. A not uncommon finding is that students who have a good background in mathematics and science are more likely to complete their education because they are more task oriented than other students. Social and economic class can be a cause of attrition if students simply no longer feel that the perceived value of the education they are receiving is worth the price or if they fail to find the proper subculture which reinforces their values.

Appropriate subculture identification, however, is a double-edged sword. The greater the variety of subgroups within an institution, the greater the likelihood that different students will find groups with which to identify. This greater opportunity for identification is likely to have a positive effect on retention. At the same time, having a large number of subgroups tends to cause stereotypical communication problems: blacks and whites often do not talk, intrafraternity groups may fight with one another, theater majors tend not to get along with engineers, and so on. A great variety of students requires additional support services as well as far-reaching recruitment efforts, all of which translate into a need for more dollars. The least expensive student body to recruit and maintain is one that is fairly homogeneous and regional, given the fact that an institution has a strong position in its primary market.

Once the character of the student body is analytically quantified, an institution has the opportunity not only to address its environment but also to seek enrollments from markets made up of students who are most likely to persist. Given the nature of the institution, is there one group that fits best? There certainly is for many institutions with respect to such factors as religious values and the nature of their student bodies. To cite one obvious example, there is not likely to be a high percentage of Jewish students at a Southern Baptist institution. Less obvious, yet distinct, are the types of students that would be attracted to Columbia University versus the University of Southern California. Often the best fit is not as clear as in these examples. Nonetheless, recruitment plans can be targeted to reduce costs, increase efficiency, and improve yield. (Yield is defined as the conversion ratios of prospects to matriculants, applicants to matriculants, and admitted to matriculants.)

A process of classification and quantification by type provides administrators at each institution with the capability to optimize recruitment efforts to penetrate the largest possible market in the most efficient and personalized way. Such an objective cannot be realized simply by expanding staff and visiting more secondary schools, yet that remains the principal tactic when an institution becomes concerned about its enrollment.

Three Principal Markets. Where are the markets? I have previously identified three principal markets: the primary, the secondary, and the tertiary, as well as specific subgroups within each market (Ihlanfeldt, 1980). The primary market is one with a high yield. Generally, a high-yield market has some geographical or economic constraints: geographical, in that the market probably exists within a specific radius of the institution; economic, in that the students from given socioeconomic backgrounds are more or less attracted to given types of institutions. The secondary market produces applications for admission but fewer student enrollments. Secondary markets are larger than the primary market and far more random in production. They usually exist beyond a radius of 300 miles from the institution, although many high schools within a radius of 300 miles would be identified as low-yield secondary markets. Thus, yield, not location, is the determining factor. A tertiary market is not only unpredictable but also often unknown. For some colleges an unknown market may be identified as older, ethnic, religious— one whose participants have demonstrated little interest in the institution previously.

Traditional students, particularly those from major metropolitan areas, can generally be further classified according to type of secondary school attended—national, regional, or local. Colleges and universities can similarly be classified by the types of secondary schools represented in their student bodies. A national secondary school is one that will send as many as 90 to

95 percent of its students on to college. These students, because of their previous experiences, are not inhibited in their college choice by psychological or geographical boundaries and clearly differentiate between and among the most distinguished colleges and universities in the country. The background of these students is generally upper-middle to upper class and they attend public secondary schools such as Beverly Hills, New Trier, Shaker Heights, Scarsdale, and Newton, as well as New England and Mid-Atlantic area private preparatory schools.

A regional secondary school sends 40 to 60 percent on to college, but seldom sends a student beyond a radius of 200 to 300 miles from the student's home. A local secondary school sends no more than 20 to 30 percent on to some type of post-secondary education at the time of graduation. Such students are likely to commute and generally come from a lower socio-economic background. Students attending local and regional secondary schools generally do not differentiate very well between the reputations of various colleges beyond their immediate area. To such students, most colleges tend to look alike, and the flagship public university is often considered to be "The University."

A college classified as national mainly attracts students from national secondary schools and from regional and local schools within the geographical radius of the college's primary market area. Such a college would not likely attract students from local and regional high schools outside its primary area. A regional college is more likely to attract students from regional and local secondary schools within its primary market and less likely to enroll students from national secondary schools. It would be rare for a regional institution to attract students from any national school in a secondary market on a regular basis. Students who elect to attend a regional institution and who live outside its primary market usually do so either because of emotional ties such as being the son or daughter of an alumna or alumnus, or to pursue a specific program opportunity. Occasionally, certain programs within a regional institution may have a national market. This type of quantitative analysis permits the admissions office to define various markets and to determine the market position of the institution's programs in terms of their ability to draw from certain types of secondary schools.

Quantification of the types of secondary schools represented in the student body permits the development of a plan concentrating resources on those types of secondary schools that have been the most productive in the past. At Northwestern University, we find a correlation between retention and the distance between a student's home, the type of secondary school attended, and the institution. For example, students who enter the university from geographical secondary markets, and who attended a regional or local secondary school are more likely to transfer than students who live within a 500-mile radius of Northwestern. Clearly, there are other factors such as social class and available group identification that affect retention, but geographical distance and type of secondary school attended are distinguishing variables. A student who attended a national secondary school outside of Northwestern's primary geographical market is more likely to graduate from Northwestern than a student who attended a regional secondary school in a remote market. Thus, the number of students who enroll from secondary markets is a factor that should be considered in projecting recruitment costs and enrollment yields.

The working adult market can be segmented into part-time students whose interests are restricted to single courses and those interested in seeking a degree. Further subdivision can be made by day, evening, weekend, on-campus and off-campus attendance, zip code, employment status, reading and listening habits, hobbies, and so on. The more that is known about the characteristics of the working adult, the easier it is to direct specific promotional efforts toward a primary market or to redefine and expand the primary market through general or direct mail advertising.

A recruitment plan for a college classified as national should involve attempting to penetrate thoroughly a geographical area within 300 to 500 miles of the institution. Additional resources should be focused on students attending national secondary schools outside of the geographical area of the college's primary market. A regional institution should focus nearly all of its efforts within its primary market area except for a limited direct mail effort in secondary markets contiguous to the primary market. Alumni should be used to follow up on a personal basis in the secondary markets, but high school visits by professional staff in secondary markets are not efficient. A local institution is probably local because it is a commuter college. Such an institution will be able to attract students from secondary schools that are classified as local, regional, and national within a five- to ten-mile area; the greatest concentration of prospective students will come from local and regional secondary schools.

Market Penetration: Communicating with Best-Fit Students

Once an institution has identified its mission, assessed the market position of its programs, and determined the type of student who is most likely to benefit from the experiences offered, the objective is to develop a strategic recruitment plan that will enable the institution to achieve its enrollment objectives. Although the development and implementation of this plan is the responsibility of the department of admissions, faculty and other administrators should be involved. Too often the admissions staff is isolated from the rest of the campus community, frequently as a result of their own choosing. A director of admissions must recognize that the risks of isolation are far greater than the risks of involvement.

Sales-Oriented Versus Management-Oriented Approach. As a first step, the director must rethink the mode of operation of the admissions office and consider a transfer from a sales-oriented to a management-oriented operation. The sales model whereby admissions officers travel extensively, visiting secondary schools generally outside of the primary market, is no longer appropriate and is quite costly. The management model involves not only research and planning, but also a communication process employing a substantial number of volunteers. These volunteers would be principally graduates and enrolled students who are loyal to the institution and willing to commit the time necessary to encourage students and their parents to take a closer look at the college.

A good source of potential volunteers are graduates who were involved in campus activities when they were students. Such an approach would involve up to 100 volunteers for a small college and as many as 1,000 for a large university. Volunteers should be carefully identified and required to attend workshops on a regular basis. Their activities must be monitored by the admissions offices, and they should receive frequent reports on the status of potential students within their geographical areas.

Enrolled students should be organized to facilitate campus visits, to contact students during vacation periods, and to follow up inquiries through telephone contact. Enrolled students remain the best representatives of the institution. Faculty should be involved only in presenting information related to their subjects and not required to contact prospective students to discuss the institution in general. Faculty time is best spent working with students who are already on campus.

To penetrate old as well as new markets more effectively, the student recruitment cycle needs to be accelerated by at least six months. The components of the marketing plan should include: (1) identification of a larger pool of prospective students with characteristics similar to students currently attending the institution; (2) a variety of direct mail activities; (3) on- and off-campus programs, including visits to secondary schools that have produced students in the past; (4) home visits directed at the most talented students in the applicant pool; and (5) telephone contact between graduates and the parents of prospective students, as well as between enrolled and prospective students.

Components of a Management-Oriented Approach. All the components of a marketing plan as outlined in this section may not apply to all colleges in all situations. Each college must adopt those strategies that it can best implement at a given time.

- Focus upon, or create if one does not exist, a primary market within a 300-mile radius of the institution.
- Develop an early contact program to increase the name recognition and visibility of the institution
- Develop a data base which includes: (1) the names and addresses of freshmen and sophomores by market area and

feeder secondary schools, (2) students with appropriately defined characteristics provided through the Student Search Service and/or the Education Opportunity Service, and (3) those who make self-initiated inquiries.

- Use direct mail as frequently as necessary to stimulate additional demand. Direct mail should provide an easy response capability and permit identification of interests. Once interests have been identified, information should be targeted toward such interests.

- Develop an alumni admissions program in five to ten cities. Begin with at least two graduates in each city and conduct a workshop on campus for these volunteers in the early fall. Secondary market cities contiguous to primary market areas are good places to begin involving graduates.

- Make a limited number of well-targeted secondary school visits in the spring. Such visits should be directed toward sophomores and juniors who have previously received notification from the college that a representative will be visiting their school. The visits should be targeted toward secondary schools identified in ACT assessments and Admission Testing Program profile reports.

- Except for a limited number of well-targeted secondary school visits, reduce the number of such visits. National secondary schools and college fairs outside the primary market can be visited by graduates. Local and regional high schools that are outside the primary market area should not be visited by college representatives or graduates.

- Offer on-campus Sunday programs in the fall and spring for prospective students and their parents who live within the immediate area, and on a Sunday to Monday overnight basis for prospective students who live outside the immediate area. The principal model should be a kind of reverse college night in which students come to campus instead of campus representatives coming to students. The faculty should be very much involved in presenting various programs. A similar program should be offered in the spring for applicants, accepted students, and transfer candidates. An overnight stay on campus is the most effective recruitment tool and will also facilitate retention because students who find the match to be a bad fit after a campus visit are not likely to enroll.

- Use enrolled students and graduates to contact prospective students locally after they have indicated an interest in the college. Attempt to match enrolled students with prospective students on the basis of geography and academic or extracurricular interest.

- Host off-campus programs in a neutral environment, preferably at a conveniently located hotel or civic facility. Graduates should be present. The program should be conducted by a member of the admissions staff and, if possible, a member of the faculty.

- Host on-campus workshops for high school teachers and counselors and for transfer counselors from community colleges.

- Visit the homes, on a selective basis, of the most talented prospects in the active file.

- Establish a hometown news release program that sends mailings on a timely basis. These releases should be personalized, not canned.

- Be aware that every visitor to the campus may be either a potential student or ambassador of goodwill. Summer camp programs and corporate workshops on the campus offer ideal opportunities to promote the institution.

Consider the preceding steps as objectives to be achieved over time. Although all of these suggestions cannot be implemented immediately, the entire system should be operational within a three-year time frame. The successful adoption of such a plan will require a well-organized admissions department with a management rather than a sales orientation that is attentive to detail. In such an office, individual members of the staff should be assigned specific projects. Once a principal project assignment is made, all other members of the staff should, in varying degrees, play supporting roles. For example, the project director of the alumni admissions program should view other members of the staff as assisting him or her in achieving the defined objectives. The same could be said for any other component of the plan. The role of the director of admissions is to establish priorities and to manage the activities and monitor the competing interests of the various project directors. The basic management objective is to develop a staff that views its individual responsibilities as complementary in achieving enrollment goals.

Conclusion

What has been presented here is a methodology by which colleges and universities can improve their enrollment and revenue base through more sophisticated market research and price and student aid analyses. Strategies to achieve greater market penetration were presented and an outline provided to assist more enlightened admissions officers in developing an admission marketing plan specific to their institutions. The challenge to the admissions staff at most institutions is to reorient their thinking from that of a sales force to that of a management team—a management team made up of individuals with complementary skills working in concert to achieve more effective market penetration through the implementation of a sophisticated communication plan. Such an approach will benefit the institution and ensure that students are choosing to attend institutions at which they are most likely to flourish and succeed.

References

Astin, A. W. *Preventing Students from Dropping Out.* San Francisco: Jossey-Bass, 1975.

Holstrom, I., and Knepper, P. "Four-Year Baccalaureate Completion Rates: A Limited Comparison of Student Success in Private and Public Four-Year Colleges and Universities." Washington, D.C.: Policy Analysis Service, American Council on Education, 1976, p. 45.

Ihlanfeldt, W. *Achieving Optimal Enrollments and Tuition Revenues.* San Francisco: Jossey-Bass, 1980.

Ihlanfeldt, W., and Davis, C. G. "The Restoration of Quality and the Private Sector.'' In P. Conran (ed.), *The Ninth-Decade Kappans: Precursors of the Future.* Evanston, Ill.: Phi Delta Kappa-Northwestern University Mini-Grant Project, 1982.

Koester, R. "Analysis of Volume Projection System, College Entrance Examination Board, Western Interstate Commission on Higher Education, 1979.'' Unpublished paper, Northwestern University, 1983.

Noel, L. (ed.). *Reducing the Dropout Rate.* New Directions for Student Services, no. 3. San Francisco: Jossey-Bass, 1978.

11

Financial Aid

A. Dallas Martin, Jr.

College administrators have long known that having adequate financial aid resources available at their schools is an important factor in attracting and enrolling students. This knowledge has encouraged institutions to conduct additional fund-raising initiatives in hopes of increasing their scholarship funds and using more of their endowment earnings to supplement their financial aid programs. Elected officials also have substantially increased the pool of federal and state financial aid in the past twenty years, indicating that they too recognize the impact such dollars have on providing students with greater access to postsecondary education. And considering the financial investment that must be made by students or their parents to obtain a degree in today's economic environment, it is certainly understandable that selection of a college may be influenced by the availability of financial aid.

However, the impact that financial aid has on preserving enrollment has received far less attention than it should at most institutions, in spite of the fact that one of the most frequent reasons cited by students for dropping out of school is purported financial difficulties. All too many schools have concentrated far more on their admissions and recruitment efforts than they have on trying to implement an overall institutional program to reduce attrition rates.

As Ihlanfeldt notes in his chapter on admissions, faced with a decreasing pool of traditional age college students and increasing competition among schools to attract these students, administrators today are searching for better ways to maximize their full-time enrollment equivalents. This process usually begins with a careful review of what is known about retention. Research in this area has identified a number of personal and environmental factors that most frequently contribute to a student's decision to withdraw from school.

The link between admissions and financial aid is clear in that students often make their college choice on the basis of the financial aid offered to them and the manner in which financial aid officers present aid options. Unfortunately, many of the studies conducted on student retention during the past fifty years have tended to ignore the influence of financial aid. This may be partly because increased reliance upon student aid as a significant means of helping to finance postsecondary education is a relatively recent phenomenon that has grown substantially only since the mid-seventies.

This chapter will look first at the research on factors relevant to the impact on retention such as students' socioeconomic backgrounds, student employment, and the impact of student loans. It then will consider how, taking these factors into account, an effective institutional packaging policy can be developed. Such a policy should take the institution's mission, as well as manageable debt and unmet need into consideration and should be equitable yet flexible in its distribution of resources. The chapter concludes with a consideration of appropriate support services such as money management training, job placement, and a discussion of how the financial aid office can intervene in the withdrawal process.

Financial Aid and Retention

Today student financial aid has a major effect upon students' choices and upon their ability to persist. As noted, a lack of adequate financial resources is frequently cited by students as a reason for dropping out of school, although whether or not such is actually the case can certainly be debated. Many aid administrators have found that offering to increase the amount of financial assistance to a student who is leaving school supposedly because of inadequate resources will not necessarily deter the student from dropping out. Therefore, it is believed that many students simply cite financial difficulties as their reason for dropping out because this seems more socially acceptable than openly admitting the underlying causes for their withdrawal.

Socioeconomic Background. Research shows that financial aid is an important factor in college choice and persistence, particularly when the student's socioeconomic background is taken into consideration. Baird (1967) and Eichhorn and Kallas (1962) find, not surprisingly, that students from lower economic backgrounds tend to be more concerned with tuition costs, location of the school, and other practical considerations than students from more affluent economic backgrounds. Their research and that of Astin (1975), Slater (1960), Spady (1967), and Wegner (1967) also indicate that there is less likelihood that students will withdraw if they come from more affluent rather than lower socioeconomic backgrounds.

For the past several years, institutions themselves, particularly private colleges and universities, have also demonstrated their belief that financial aid is important—at least in increasing access and diversity—by using more of their unrestricted general funds to provide need-based grant aid to qualified but needy students (Gomberg and Atelsek, 1979). Although it can certainly be argued that budgeting increasing amounts of unrestricted institutional funds for student aid may substantially decrease funds that should have been spent on improving the educational programs and facilities of the school, as Bacchetti (1980) notes, the practice is likely to continue until there are more adequate and structurally appropriate state and federal aid programs.

Most institutional administrators readily admit that it is important to amass adequate financial aid resources to attract potential students. Further, most of them operate under the premise that continuing to make such aid available to students from year to year will be a positive factor contributing to completion of the students' degrees.

Scholarships. Research by Bergen, Upham, and Bergen (1970) and Astin (1975) indicates that students who receive grants or scholarships are slightly more likely to persist toward graduation than are nonrecipients; Fields and Le May (1973) note that such aid is helpful to particular schools in attracting students with desirable qualities or skills. However, Astin points out one anomaly regarding the impact of scholarships upon persistence. His analysis of differing kinds of scholarships and grants indicates that scholarships associated with a business or industrial firm have a negative impact upon college persistence. Astin suspects the reason may be that such awards often require alternate periods of enrollment and employment, an arrangement which generally seems to increase the likelihood of a student dropping out. Astin also notes that scholarships or grants awarded on the basis of merit are more likely to increase a student's chances of persistence than those awarded on the basis of financial need. This is not surprising: in most cases students who are selected for merit awards generally have attained a higher scholastic record than students receiving need-based aid.

Employment. College work-study awards and student employment also contribute positively to student retention. Astin (1975) notes that having a job for fewer than twenty-five hours per week substantially increases a student's chances of finishing college. In fact, his study indicates that a student's dropout probabilities are reduced by as much as 15 percent by such employment. Astin also finds that on-campus employment, either in academic or nonacademic areas, has a more positive impact on persistence than off-campus employment. On-campus employment during a student's freshman year in particular seems to enhance the student's chances of completing school. Several additional studies show that student employment does not have a negative impact on a student's grade point average, provided that such work does not exceed twenty hours per week (Apostal and Doherty, 1972; Henry, 1967; and Merritt, 1970). Noel (1976) reports that a study by Wieger at Nebraska Wesleyan University in Lincoln which examines persisters and dropouts finds that almost twice as many students who remained in school had a part-time job than did those who left. It is not known why student employment correlates so significantly with persistence, but it is believed that a job helps to develop a strong sense of being needed and of belonging to the community in addition to providing financial support.

Student Loans and Persistence. The impact of student loans upon a student's persistence is less clear. Trent and Medsker (1968) find that students who secure loans are more likely to stay in school than those who do not. Such a finding might be questioned, however, since overall, more upperclass students borrow money than do freshmen. Astin (1975) finds that dependency upon loans adversely affects the persistence rate for men, particularly if the student was forced to borrow during his freshman year. The impact upon women seems to vary depending upon how much they had to borrow and how much their parents contributed to their educational expenses. Small loans to undergraduate women, particularly at public institutions, seem to be of benefit in promoting retention, but large loans are a detriment at all schools.

Astin's findings also seem to suggest that students from lower income families (below $20,000) are far more likely to view loans as a negative factor associated with completing their degrees than are students from higher income families. A student's after-college satisfaction with borrowing also seems directly related to whether the student subsequently enters a profession or a blue-collar or clerical position. Tombaugh and Troutman (1972) find that National Direct Student Loan borrowers who borrow later in their college careers feel more positive about such borrowing than students who borrow during their freshman year. They also found that continued favorable attitudes about borrowing were more prevalent among persons who entered a profession after graduation than those who worked in factories, or in construction, or in clerical jobs.

These studies may not tell us everything that we would like to know, but data from the research that has been done clearly suggest that the type and mix of financial aid provided to a student can have either a positive or negative influence upon that student, depending upon the student's circumstances and background. Therefore, an institution concerned about creating a staying environment for its students must make sure that careful consideration is given to the practices and policies of its financial aid office. Likewise, financial aid administrators must be aware that many of their decisions and actions can have profound effects upon the institution's retention patterns.

Developing an Institutional Packaging Policy

Packaging of student aid resources is one of the most fundamental yet essential tasks performed by the financial aid administrator at any school concerned with improving retention. Charged with the significant task of pooling resources and making professionally informed judgments about a family's ability to contribute to the education of its children, the financial aid administrator is literally at the center of all the programs and operations involved in the student meeting his or her educational goals or objectives.

Not only is the student's calculated financial need at the institution a factor to be reviewed, but in many cases his or her academic potential, prior educational debt, course load, and career objective also have to be considered before a proper aid package can be constructed. This task is further complicated by the fact that the institution's available financial aid resources are almost always insufficient to meet the needs of its pool of eligible students. Therefore, it is essential for institutions to develop a plan for retention that will help them to secure needed sources of aid and simultaneously to monitor carefully the resources they have.

Institutional Goals and Basic Standards. Each college or university that administers student aid should have a well-thought-out packaging policy designed to meet the mission and goals of the institution. The policy should be agreed upon by the faculty, administrators, and governing board of the institution and suitable to the primary student clientele being served. The basic standards to be used in developing such an institutional packaging policy should be consistent with the recommended guidelines developed by the National Association of Student Financial Aid Administrators (1983, pp. 9–12). These guidelines are

1. Institutions should adopt equitable and consistent packaging policies that address the types of aid to be awarded, the amounts of each, and the sequence.
2. Need-based aid awards should be determined using an approved need analysis system that measures expected family contribution.
3. These awards should be made to those students determined to have the greatest need for such assistance.
4. Institutions should adopt student expense budgets which reflect direct educational and realistic living costs.
5. Institutions should inform students about application procedures, how financial need is determined, and packaging policies.
6. The Pell Grant is to be used as a foundation program for undergraduate student awards.
7. Institutions should provide adequate support, both administrative and fiscal, to enable the financial aid administrator to coordinate the resources received by each financial aid recipient.
8. Financial aid award packages should be based on documentation considered necessary to verify the data provided in order to assure integrity and equity in all student aid programs.
9. Financial aid administrators have an obligation to provide students with the terms and conditions of their financial aid awards.
10. Students who are not eligible or whose full need has not been met should be informed of the reason(s) for such decisions and referred to alternative sources of funding.

Manageable Debt. As mentioned earlier, several other considerations must also be factored into the development of the institution's aid packaging policy. Manageable debt has only recently begun to receive attention at many institutions. Unfortunately, until recently the question of how much a student should reasonably be expected to borrow given his or her future ability to repay has been virtually ignored, as have the impact that such borrowing may have upon persistence and upon financing of future generations and attitudes toward repayment. However, now that spiraling educational costs coupled with limited growth in grant and work programs have fostered an even greater reliance upon student borrowing, loan debt should be a packaging consideration. Considering the recent increase in parent loans to undergraduate students, schools should also develop debt management models which will effectively help educate students and parents about their future financial obligations.

Students should consider their educational debt in light of their future income potential. Indirect costs, those earnings forfeited because of graduate or professional studies, must be factored into the future financial prospects of each student. Debt management models should also take into consideration inflation rates, amortization schedules, tax reductions for interest payments, marital status, spouse's income and liabilities, investment portfolios, and retirement plans. A desirable repayment scheme allows the student to borrow the funds necessary to meet educational expenses while keeping annual repayments below an established percentage of income. It is generally acceptable to use a standard of 8 percent of first-year gross salary for undergraduates, with amounts increasing to as much as 12 percent to 15 percent for graduate and professional students. Using debt management models coupled with a good loan counseling and future financial planning program for prospective and enrolled students can help an institution offset the negative stimuli to college attrition associated with borrowing.

Students should also be properly advised about loan consolidation alternatives which are available to them upon graduation. Programs such as the options plan currently being administered by the Student Loan Marketing Association provide students with an opportunity to consolidate their outstanding student loans, thus helping them to achieve a more manageable educational debt repayment schedule. Similar loan consolidation programs are almost certain to be established in the future to assist the growing numbers of students forced to finance their education exclusively with student loans.

Unmet Need. Another consideration in developing a packaging policy is the institution's definition and treatment of unmet financial need. Since so few schools have adequate aid resources available to meet the financial needs of their students, unmet need is perhaps the most challenging issue for nearly all types of institutions. The unmet need factor influences how aid administrators construct student expense budgets and how adjustments are made to standardized calculations of expected students' and parents' contributions, as well as the objectives adopted in selecting a particular packaging strategy.

In general, however, the issue of unmet need must be dealt with based upon one of two alternatives. The institution either elects to package awards on the basis of a rationing system to ensure that student needs (even if particularly constructed for rationing purposes) are met, or it takes care to calculate need realistically, even if doing so requires factoring into the packaging formulas certain levels of unmet need for all applicants. Schools also must calculate carefully their own break-point level of unmet need which will still enable the student to attend but above which, even with some financial aid, enrollment would be impossible.

Equitable Yet Flexible Distribution. A packaging policy must also attempt to distribute available funds in an equitable manner. This is not to say that all students must be treated alike, but rather that students with like characteristics should have their financial aid packaged in the same manner. On the other hand, students with different characteristics, or less financial need, may appropriately receive quite different awards. It is important to build consistency and equity into the institution's packaging policy to ensure that students are being treated fairly; it is also appropriate to allow for some flexibility that will provide individual students with an opportunity to appeal their awards and permit the financial administrator to make adjustments or exceptions for a student when circumstances or events warrant such changes.

Proper Balance. A packaging policy that attempts to be responsive to student retention also carefully reduces the amount of loan burden that students are asked to assume over the course of their academic programs and controls the number of hours per week that they are expected to work during the school year. The financial aid administrator, in essence, must attempt to allocate carefully the dollars that are available in a manner that will provide each student with a reasonable balance of grant, work, and loan assistance in amounts appropriate for that individual. Unfortunately, this is not always possible given institutional, state, or federal limitations on funds. Priorities have to be established carefully to ensure that those students who are most affected by variations in the mix of their financial aid packages are having their needs met, thus helping to make certain the financial investment that is being made in each student is one that is appropriate and likely to foster success.

Still, providing a student with an appropriate financial aid package in and of itself is only the first step for the aid administrator who is concerned with ensuring that the student is going to succeed and continue to persist. It is also necessary to reinforce that action with a meaningful support system that will make the individual student feel that he or she is an important part of the institutional environment.

Providing a Support System

In addition to simply presenting the student with an annual award letter, the financial aid office has a legal and moral obligation to make sure that the student understands the kind of financial aid that is being given as well as his or her rights and responsibilities. Federal regulations specify the kinds of information that must be provided to student aid recipients, but the process by which that information is transmitted to the student is generally left entirely up to the institution. Most schools simply send this information to the student either at the time the financial aid letter is tendered or prior to disbursing the actual funds. Although this technique satisfies the statutory requirements, institutions concerned about establishing a caring environment might well consider employing a more personal approach.

We all enjoy feeling that someone cares about us and that we are more than simply a matriculation number or a typed name on an award letter. A personal call or contact from a financial aid counselor or a face-to-face interview in the aid office to review the aid package, or to answer aid questions, or simply to express concern and interest in the individual can help give the student a feeling that someone cares. Such beginnings can be followed up with other contacts, either in person, by telephone, or in writing once or twice throughout the school year to see how the student is doing and to offer to answer other questions that will undoubtedly arise.

Retention studies show that students are much more likely to withdraw during their first year than at any other time in their postsecondary education. Therefore, providing them with an additional support system during this period can be very helpful in reducing unnecessary tension, uncertainty, and doubt about the financing of their education.

Cost-Effective Support Services. While some will argue that the expenses associated with this type of follow-up cannot be justified, the counterargument is that if it is done efficiently, such follow-up will prove to be far more cost effective than trying to find replacements for students who drop out because they feel alienated from or nonaligned with their new environment. Additionally, the cost involved need not be exorbitant if some creativity is used in implementing follow-up procedures. For example, peer counselors can be used, and their salaries financed with college work-study funds. Graduate students enrolled in student personnel, psychology, counseling, and guidance degree programs can participate as a part of their practicums or internships. Graduates, faculty spouses, or community service groups might also assist in helping to follow up with students to see how they are adjusting to their new college life in general and to provide additional positive reinforcement.

Effective Money Management. Another important activity that the financial aid office can perform to assist students in adjusting to their new environment is to offer seminars on money management. All too often when a student enrolls for the academic term, the financial aid or business office simply collects the institution's share of the financial aid award and then turns the balance over to the student, with the naive belief that the student will budget those funds to cover expenses over the next three or four months. Unfortunately this is often not the case, and the student's failure to manage funds wisely can increase the likelihood of encountering financial problems later in the term.

Some banks and lending institutions also disburse the entire yearly loan proceeds to students at the beginning of the academic year, again leaving the responsibility for prudent financial budgeting up to students. Faced with such responsibility, a lack of experience in such matters, and limited knowledge about what should be done to manage such resources properly, it is not surprising that some students exhaust or unwisely spend their available resources before the end of the year. A student who suddenly confronts these problems later in the term—usually when there is increased pressure to complete academic work satisfactorily—is much more likely to consider withdrawing than one who is financially secure.

Certainly the financial aid office cannot prevent all students from getting into such a bind; it can, however, attempt to minimize the chances of it happening by regularly counseling students on money management techniques, either in group settings or on an individual, as-needed basis. Many students arrive at college without ever having had a checking or savings account of their own. Many of them have never had to shop for their own groceries or to be financially responsible for their personal grooming and clothing needs. They are unaware that utility costs can be reduced by careful conservation and that wise shopping can help stretch monthly allocations for food and personal care items. A seminar or series of seminars on personal budgeting and money management techniques can thus prove very helpful to many students. Aid administrators who have developed programs to assist students in these matters are firmly convinced that students benefit immensely and subsequently make better financial decisions. Of course, the manner in which such programs are handled determines their effectiveness.

Retention Data and Support Needs. An effective institutional program should also use the school's past retention study data to profile the types of students who are most likely to withdraw, thereby allowing staff to focus primarily on individuals with these characteristics. Such profiles can be drawn on students' personal, social, academic, and financial characteristics. Specific subsets of students who may need a particular kind of help can be identified.

Even though the financial aid office will not be directly involved in helping students select their courses of study, if kept informed, it might be able to adjust the number of hours that students are expected to work in a given term. If, for instance, a student is enrolled in two or three classes that demand that a lot of time be spent in a laboratory or studio, a lighter work schedule could be established. Likewise, if the financial aid office is an integral part of the institution's academic program, it may very well be able to help finance higher-achieving students who can serve as tutors for lower-achieving students. By doing so, the financial aid office is not only ensuring that students who are in need of academic help are receiving it, but is using its resources in a way which ensures that benefits will also accrue to other students and thus increase overall retention.

Job Placement Services. Still another important task the financial aid office can perform to help reduce student attrition is to establish an effective and personally oriented job placement service for work-study recipients and others. As already mentioned, having a job for fewer than twenty-five hours a week substantially increases a student's chances of finishing college, and an on-campus job during a student's first year in school particularly seems to enhance the chances of completing the course of study. Again, this seems to be because a job satisfies psychological as well as financial needs.

Students, like all other human beings, need to feel that they belong, that they are members of a team, and that someone depends upon them. Part-time jobs in positive working environments can help students feel they are needed and are important to the larger operation. Not only will students' own self-worth be reinforced, but they will develop positive attitudes, work habits, and practical knowledge that will assist them throughout their lifetimes.

Building an effective and personally oriented job placement service requires more than simply providing students with a listing of available jobs and monitoring their monthly time cards. An effective job placement program requires an institutionwide commitment that depends upon administrators, faculty, staff, and in some cases community employers, truly understanding the needs of students and the impact of their working experiences on their total college experiences. Periodic orientation sessions for employers of students should be held to acquaint them with the policies and procedures that must be followed in administering the school's part-time employment program, including what they should expect from students as well as what students should expect from their employers. Additionally, employers should be advised of students' characteristics, their academic responsibilities, and their general psychological needs and problems. Attitudes and values often differ between younger students and their employers: these generational issues need to be raised so that everyone involved has a heightened awareness of potential problems. Employers should make certain that their expectations of what students will be required to do—or not to do, in some cases—are clearly defined in the job listing and that they are explained again before students are hired.

Employers should also be advised to take a personal interest in students and to provide them with positive reinforcement and constructive criticism often. They should likewise be encouraged to involve students in decision making and to seek their advice when possible. They should be reminded that as employers they are important parts of the students' contacts with others and as such can provide either a favorable or unfavorable climate.

The employer has a major role to fulfill in helping the student, but the financial aid office is obligated to establish its own student-oriented placement service to ensure that the right students are placed in the right jobs and that a systematic monitoring system is established to follow up on the students' job performance and satisfaction. The initial placement of students should include, if at all possible, a personal interview at the school with a trained employment counselor who can inform students of what will be expected of them as a part of their employment and what their rights are. Initially, an attempt should be made to find out the kinds of jobs students desire, the skills they have acquired in previous work experiences, their planned courses of study, and their vocational and avocational goals. Such information will assist the counselor in trying to help students find the type of job for which each is best suited. An employment counselor must be firm in explaining what is expected of the student, while also projecting a caring attitude that will encourage the student to come back for additional help if it is needed.

A representative from the financial aid office should also be given the responsibility of coordinating and monitoring the institution's employment program. This person should meet with students to see how they are enjoying their work assignments and should regularly contact employers to evaluate students' job performance and to ensure that program guidelines and policies are being followed. Contacts with employers also provide an excellent opportunity to inquire about students' adjustment and general satisfaction with their school environment. Observant employers will be able to provide insights into how students are doing and what things seem to be bothering them.

These clues can then be used by the financial aid office as an early warning system to indicate whether or not it is necessary to invite a particular student in to reexamine his or her aid package or job placement. Such information may also suggest that the student's dissatisfaction is not with the aid office but with the academic program or with living arrangements. Consequently, the aid administrator may wish to refer the student to someone else on campus who may be of help, or the administrator may contact that person directly, informing him or her of the student's problem so that appropriate action may be taken.

Involvement in Withdrawal Process

A final technique that can be used to help prevent students from dropping out is to involve the financial aid office directly whenever a student is officially withdrawing from school. While many institutions have a formal withdrawal policy for students to follow, such policies are often not structured in a way that can prevent withdrawals. A policy that is based on concern for the student will first attempt to determine the cause or reason for his or her decision and secondly will direct the student to an office that may be able to help solve the problem.

Considering that financial difficulty is often cited by students as one of the primary reasons for withdrawing from college, all institutions should develop and implement a procedure that addresses this problem. A withdrawing student should be encouraged, if not required, to meet with a counselor in the financial aid office during the withdrawal process in order to determine whether additional financial aid or credit arrangements might be provided to ease the financial plight. If financial aid difficulties are at the root of the problem, then the financial aid office may be able to address the issue. If finances are not the real problem, experience suggests that the student may well confide in the financial aid counselor what the actual problem is. The financial aid counselor will then be in an excellent position to discuss the problem with the student or to refer the student to someone else who can be of assistance.

Such action is strongly suggested for all students who are withdrawing, but it is particularly important to establish such a procedure for financial aid recipients. If an aid recipient is withdrawing in mid-year, the financial aid office needs to be aware of this action in order to monitor refunds and repayments properly, to cancel subsequent aid dollars that were earmarked for that student and redirect them to another, and, if applicable, to advise the student of when loan payments will begin.

Conclusion

In a time when financial considerations are becoming even more important to students, it is essential that financial aid programs take an intrusive, active stance in advising students on aid options, part-time employment, and money management. Such an approach will demonstrate concern for the individual student's welfare and, therefore, encourage student satisfaction and persistence.

References

Apostal, R. A., and Doherty, C. P. "Effects of Positive and Routine Job Assignments on Academic Performance." *Journal of College Student Personnel,* 1972, *13,* 270-272.

Astin, A. W. *Preventing Students from Dropping Out.* San Francisco: Jossey-Bass, 1975.

Bacchetti, R. F. "Planning Aid and Aiding Plans." In J. B. Henry (ed.), *The Impact of Student Financial Aid on Institutions.* New Directions for Institutional Research, no. 25. San Francisco: Jossey-Bass, 1980.

Baird, L. L. "Family Income and the Characteristics of College-Bound Students." *American College Testing Program Research Reports,* no. 17. Iowa City, Iowa: American College Testing Program, 1967.

Bergen, G. R., Upham, J. A., and Bergen, M. B. "Do Scholarships Affect Academic Achievement?" *Journal of College Student Personnel,* 1970, *11* (5), 383-384.

Eichhorn, R. L., and Kallas, G. J. "Social Class Background as a Predictor of Academic Success in Engineering." *Journal of Engineering Education,* 1962, *52,* 507-512.

Fields, C. R., and Le May, M. L. "Student Financial Aid: Effects on Educational Decisions and Academic Achievement." *Journal of College Student Personnel,* 1973, *14* (5), 425-429.

Gomberg, I. L., and Atelsek, F. J. *The Institutional Share of Undergraduate Financial Assistance, 1976-77.* Higher Education Panel Report, no. 42. Washington, D.C.: American Council on Education, 1979.

Henry, J. B. "Part-Time Employment and Academic Performance of Freshmen." *Journal of College Student Personnel,* 1967, *8* (4), 257-260.

Merritt, R. "Academic Performance of Work-Study Students." *Journal of College Student Personnel,* 1970, *11* (3), 173-176.

National Association of Student Financial Aid Administrators. *Standards for the Development of Policy Guidelines for Packaging Need-Based Financial Aid.* National Association of Student Financial Aid Administrators Management, no. 2. Washington, D.C.: National Association of Student Aid Administrators, 1983.

Noel, L. "College Student Retention—A Campuswide Responsibility." *Journal of National Association of College Admissions Counselors*, 1976, *21* (1), 33–36.

Slater, J. M. "Influences on Students' Perception and Persistence in the Undergraduate College." *Journal of Educational Research*, 1960, *54*, 3–8.

Spady, W. G., Jr. "Peer Integration and Academic Success: The Dropout Process Among Chicago Freshmen." Unpublished doctoral dissertation, Department of Education, University of Chicago, 1967.

Tombaugh, R., and Troutman, W. "Student Attitudes Toward Borrowing and Working—Results of National Surveys." *College and University*, 1972, *47* (4), 439–441.

Trent, J. W., and Medsker, L. L. *Beyond High School: A Psychosociological Study of 10,000 High School Graduates.* San Francisco: Jossey-Bass, 1968.

Wegner, E. L. "The Relationship of College Characteristics to Graduation." Unpublished doctoral dissertation, Department of Education, University of Wisconsin, 1967.

12

Orientation Programs

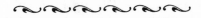

Bonnie S. Titley

Coming as it does at the beginning of the college experience, orientation serves as the transition cushion between past and future learning experiences. Following the recruiting-admissions phase, which relies primarily on written materials to communicate a match between students' expectations and needs and institutional programs, the orientation program may be the first face-to-face meeting of student and institution. As such, it can determine and perhaps even cement the relationship between the two. As we all know, one never has a second chance to make a first impression.

Most orientation programs aim at getting things off to a running start (Mueller, 1961; and Breckenridge, 1967). They try to define the college experience in terms of general information (Snider, 1970), the role of higher education in life preparation (Shaffer, 1962), the services available at the institution (McCann, 1967), and so on. They all strive to make students feel welcome. Early programs most often took the form of a freshman week preceding the fall term; occasionally schools offered academic credit for courses of varying duration (Brubacher and Rudy, 1968). In mid-century, the summer clinic (Drake, 1966) was used more often than the course format. Renewed interest in orientation courses is, however, clearly evident in recent decades (O'Banion, 1969; Snider, 1970; and Felker, 1973).

The variation in the formats of orientation programs makes it difficult to pinpoint their effect on retention; however, they clearly do have an effect. Beal and Noel (1980) find orientation to be the third most effective retention activity overall; a number of institutions in their survey rank it as their most effective retention activity when focused on a special target group. Why it is so important is not immediately clear. Results from the American College Testing Program (ACT) College Outcome Measures Program (COMP) strongly suggest that the existence of formal orientation and advising activities has a positive effect on student persistence to graduation (Forrest, 1982). Other researchers, emphasizing design and content, suggest the basis for impact is a designed focus rather than a one-shot approach to providing general information (Lenning, Sauer, and Beal, 1980). All of these reports view orientation as a significant part of a multifaceted approach to retention.

It is possible, then, to deduce from available research that orientation is a retention activity worthy of significant institutional attention. The primary stated purpose of orientation—to ease the transition to college and to aid students during the initial adjustment period—are mentioned time and again in retention literature as factors that contribute to the staying environment of an institution.

To escape the trap of viewing it only as a beginning, we must look again at our definition of orientation. In this chapter, we will look at the various options involved in the "who, what, where, when, and why" of orientation. We will consider the importance of putting persons who have sufficient information about the institution as well as training in management and evaluation skills in charge of orientation programs. After considering techniques for orienting special populations on campus and research on the effects of orientation programs, we will look at a variety of current approaches to orientation: the "how" of orientation. We will then consider how to transform orientation practices into a continuing process by integrating them with other academic services and programs. Since faculty-student interaction is a prime factor in creating a staying environment and faculty advising is a critical initial orientation activity, as part of this integration process, faculty will need to assume an increasing role in orientation.

Overall, we must look at new ways of achieving traditional goals and additional ways of meeting new goals. We must be cognizant of changes in the milieu of higher education and in our student populations and keep abreast of political factors that affect orientation. If we do not do all these things, we will not be able to sustain the positive and growing impact of orientation on retention in recent decades.

Orientation: Who, What, Where, When, and Why

Everyone knows, and no one knows, what orientation is. Wherever there is an orientation program, everyone knows that orientation is that set of activities designed to ease the transition from high school to college. The activities vary with the institution, but, all in all, making the incoming student comfortable in a new environment is the focus. Toward that end, orientation directors articulate a set of goals and objectives and list expectations and results. They delineate historical and theoretical underpinnings for program activities and point to pragmatic solutions to problems that may develop. In other words, they answer the critical questions: Who? What? Where? When? Why?

Why Orientation? Why does orientation exist? That's easy. It is important for things to get off to a good start. But what things? And a start *from* where *to* where? Dannells and Kuh (1977, p. 103) provide a good summary definition of orientation: "In its purest sense, orientation attempts to provide a balanced introduction to the constraints imposed by, and the opportunities available in, the collegiate environment as well as to enable students to more clearly define their educational purpose."

To this definition, orientation directors nationwide respond: "That's what we do." And they are probably right. They are, no doubt, (1) explaining to students and their parents the general and specific educational requirements for programs offered at their institutions; (2) working with students on how to get the most out of the programs offered to fit their personal needs; (3) helping students to examine their interests, abilities, values, and limitations; (4) encouraging faculty and students to establish good working relationships; and (5) dealing with the myriad other intellectual, cultural, psychological, physical, social, and spiritual adjustments of the freshman year, such as acquiring study skills, coping with challenges to self-concept and personal belief systems, living with a roommate, and adjusting to group interaction.

Dannells and Kuh's next point, however, should encourage all orientation directors to reevaluate their local definition of orientation. They say: "In order to ensure that students periodically reassess their own goals and personal development, the definition of orientation should, perhaps, be expanded to suggest a process which continues during the entire college experience" (p. 103).

Currently, orientation programs employ one of three basic formats—a summer program (one to three days), a fall program (usually a week), or a course (one term). Local constraints usually dictate time frames and limitations for orientation programs and tend to establish local definitions, goals, objectives, and so on. It is possible, however, that the converse is also true: the local definition of orientation dictates the constraints placed on program content. For example, if orientation primarily emphasizes getting off to a good start, its focus will be on a time frame (perhaps the first term); but if this emphasis is expanded and orientation viewed as a process that should continue during the entire college experience, orientation will become only an early facet of retention. Because its focus would go beyond solving first-term problems, it would involve a much longer time frame and could even encompass the senior-level courses taught in some institutions that serve to tie things together, cap the entire educational experience, and prepare students to enter the real world.

Who Benefits From Orientation? Clearly, five groups benefit from orientation. Students gain insights into themselves and the new environment they will be in with all of its educational, personal, and social complexities. Parents are given some understanding of their role in the student's educational pursuits and an introduction to the educational expectations of the institution and the services available to students. (Most programs have a component for parents, though the extent of parental involvement and the attention paid to parents as active participants in the student's education vary.) Faculty benefit by meeting students in the fall who have had some introduction to curricular requirements and scholastic expectations. Once the term has started, student affairs professionals can set about involving students in the co-curriculum with some assurance that they have already been introduced to its educational value. Finally, the institution as a whole benefits from an organized presentation of its programs and personnel and from the initial advising and registration of large numbers of students in a timely, economical fashion.

What Can Orientation Do? What does orientation achieve? What can it? Orientation does serve as the link between high school and college; or, acknowledging the demographic changes in our student populations, between precollege and college experiences. It introduces students to the components of the environment, giving them the information necessary to map it and encouraging them to explore the environment to discover how it can meet their educational needs. It outlines the services available to facilitate survival in the environment. And it usually results in a paper-and-pencil commitment to the environment: registration for classes.

For parents, the primary achievement of orientation is in the area of public relations (Cantor, 1974). They meet some faculty, find out about program requirements, confront value differences that may arise between them and the students, and have the separation anxiety they might be feeling eased. There are those who feel that institutions might do even more to acknowledge the role of parents as participants in the educational process (Gohn, 1975). At least one university, Eastern Michigan University in Ypsilanti, arranges special orientation sessions for parents, separate from sessions for students. The program is based on the premise that parents are important and its execution reflects that premise. Parents are sent separate letters inviting them to the session and are given a manual designed especially for them. Once on campus and in small groups, they discuss common parental concerns and how they can help their students succeed. They receive pertinent information about student performance, career exploration and opportunities, financial aid, and similar topics. They also meet with representatives from the institution's parents' association.

When Should Orientation Occur? When is orientation most effective? This is much more than a rhetorical question. Obviously, orientation comes at the beginning—but the beginning of what? Generic orientation begins the first time a person inquires about the institution as a step in deciding which school to attend. Responding to this request requires effective materials and good information. Though usually called recruiting, this is a kind of orientation. Traditional orientation follows application and acceptance and precedes actual enrollment. This time frame dictates the information and activities included in most orientation programs nationwide. Orientation courses are designed to integrate students more fully into the institutional community by suggesting solutions to problems and needs that may develop as new situations are encountered. They help students to adapt more readily to the roles they must assume in various learning environments by introducing them to the survival skills most useful in those environments. Although these survival needs may vary somewhat from campus to campus, they include overcoming skill deficiencies, managing time, making sound decisions, talking to professors, coping with stress, planning financial matters, improving communication skills with peers, and the like.

More practical answers to the question of when is orientation most effective lie in the goals, budget, and needs of individual institutions. No single approach is adaptable for all institutions and students. Summer programs, of whatever length, have time advantages. Students and parents come away with a better idea of a student's physical needs such as clothing, furniture, transportation, money, and corn poppers. More importantly, they have time to begin the transition involving their mutual dependency-independency needs. The time advantage for institutions lies in getting scheduling information far enough ahead to adjust the class sections offered to meet student requests.

Fall orientation weeks can achieve the same results without the time advantages of summer programs. They seem to work reasonably well for smaller institutions that can give special attention to the information materials sent to students ahead of time. One major problem for any one-shot program is the danger of information overload. New students simply cannot remember everything they are told or read and may not be able to recall or find the answer to a question when it arises later on.

Research literature tells us little about which orientation time format is most effective. Virtually no interinstitutional research has been performed in this area. What little research has been performed seems of little help to institutions of differing types. For example, Atkins (1979) finds that implementation of a one-day advising/orientation session at a technical college followed by regular advising sessions throughout the year did result in a reduction in the attrition rate, but that the reduction was not statistically significant. The multiplicity of factors affecting attrition and retention are difficult to control for in research within one institution, much less across institutions. This factor alone would account for the absence of meaningful research in this area.

While some institutions are promoting student-faculty interaction by improving advising programs during the first year, increasing numbers of institutions are introducing a semester-long class for academic credit. Early in this century, a number of institutions held classes for incoming students, varying from two weeks to a term in length (Drake, 1966; and Mueller, 1961). Faculty objection to giving academic credit for such courses (Caple, 1964) resulted in a drastic reduction in this practice during mid-century, though the recent emphasis on retention has apparently spawned renewed interest in this approach (O'Banion, 1969; Snider, 1970; and Felker, 1973).

The orientation course format reflects the developmental approach to meeting student needs, allowing presentation or reiteration of information as needs arise or as other developmental activities reinforce it. Further, because information is imparted in portions, overload is less likely to occur. Courses allow a more in-depth look at an institution and its personnel and programs as class members become a support group learning survival skills together. Adjustment to the new environment is thus more gradual and integrated and more likely to be lasting.

Orientation courses, in addition to introducing programs and services, deal with library skills, decision-making skills, values clarification, social skills, and strategies for maneuvering through the local procedural maze. Some can and do incorporate content-specific workshops on such topics as sexism and racism—an efficient and workable way to incorporate orientation needs for special target groups and to promote their adjustment to the college environment (Gohn, 1975; Butts, 1971; and Goodale and Sandeen, 1971).

It would be very difficult to argue that the orientation course approach is not the most effective overall for students. However, it cannot produce the same institutional benefits when it comes to registration as do summer programs; it requires ongoing personnel commitment—a luxury some institutions can ill afford under budgetary constraints—and it cannot replace a summer or fall activity entirely. Its greatest benefit, in my opinion, is its lifelong learning enrichment through establishing a positive attitude toward learning of any kind. This is true even for students who do not persist to a baccalaureate degree. No day-long or week-long program can achieve anything close in long-term effect.

Where Should Orientation Lead? Regardless of the time frame, where should orientation lead? Well done, orientation leads students to greater developmental independence, parents to more realistic expectations for offspring and institution and to more effective participation in the educational process. It leads institutions to a greater awareness of the needs of incoming students, enabling them to enhance the learning and staying qualities of the campus environment.

Role of the Orientation Director

It would not be hyperbole to say that the key person in any orientation program is the director. The director develops and sustains the philosophical and conceptual base for a program that, despite commonalities with other orientation programs, reflects the nature of the individual institution. The director designs the programs, selects and trains the staff, and finally plans specific activities to convey the philosophy and character of the institution to participants. If the role of director is to be more than perfunctorily fulfilled, the director must know the institution well enough to understand its mission as well as its commitment to students and their needs. It is, therefore, unfortunate that in many institutions the post of orientation director is considered an entry-level position: often a person who is unfamiliar with the programs, personnel, and politics of an institution is hired to plan a program presenting the institution to the consumer public.

Director's Needs. The orientation director must be familiar with the literature relevant to orientation, obviously, but also with national and local issues in higher education and with local political idiosyncrasies that influence the program. The director must know institutional programs, personnel, policies, procedures, and services, as well as what students have been like and are going to be like in the future. The director must have experience in money and people management plus some insights into methods of program evaluation. Without this knowledge and experience, the director cannot realistically determine what program content will help participants and what might precipitate confusion; whether content is likely to result in information overload or, perhaps worse, information imbalance if the time allotted to various activities is too much or too little to allow meaningful integration of the information presented.

Background Information. Some required background information can be obtained through formal class work or extensive reading; institutional information comes from experience. A little experience often upsets a lot of theory. Thus, any newcomer to an orientation program—even from the same institution—has a lot to do before beginning to work on the program. After completing a great deal of reading (the National Orientation Directors Association has a good bibliography available), the newcomer then must gather, read, and study all available information about the institution (catalogues, brochures, and the like), and finally should visit every college or department to meet key personnel and learn firsthand about expectations, needs,

requirements, programs, procedures, and local idiosyncrasies—
and to become known to those key personnel. The new director
who fails to complete this kind of basic visitation misses valuable
insights into institutional policy. This unintentional signaling
of a negative attitude toward involvement with the institution
could adversely affect the public relations factor for the entire
program. The director is, in fact, a public relations manager
first and foremost, both within the institution and externally,
and is likely to expend more energy in this area than in others,
depending upon the size of the staff.

Staff Selection. Because the selection and training of staff
is an especially important consideration for the director, good
selection criteria including motivation, knowledge of institution, interpersonal skills, and personal view of students must
be established. And because faculty involved in orientation initiate the critical faculty-student contact so important to retention in their academic advising and information giving, they
must be selected carefully and trained fully to achieve maximum
impact at this critical point. Most orientation staffs have a goodly
proportion of student paraprofessionals (Delworth, Sherwood,
and Casaburri, 1974; and Trotter, 1975), providing both personal and financial benefits for the program. However, in the
light of retention research findings indicating that interactions
with faculty are crucial to student persistence (Beal and Noel,
1980; and Pascarella and Terenzini, 1980), programs that are
currently entirely student-staffed or are considering moving in
that direction for budgetary reasons should reconsider the overall impact of such a move for the institution and its retention
efforts. Indeed, increasing faculty involvement, although more
costly, could result in enhanced internal acceptance of the orientation program and its contribution to the achievement of the
institution's goals, above and beyond the positive impact it has
on student retention.

Orientation for Special Groups

Focusing orientation on a special target group is cited by
many institutions as a successful retention activity; such focus

is preferable to a one-shot approach. Though apparently in agreement, these two findings are based on different definitions of what constitutes a special target group. A majority of the orientation action programs noted by Beal and Noel (1980) define the special target group as all freshmen; in the Lenning, Sauer, and Beal study (1980) the target groups are more specifically defined—residential freshmen, marginally qualified entering freshmen, high-risk freshmen, minority students, handicapped students, and so on. To this list one could add veterans, commuters, and foreign students. It can be easily argued that the *basic* necessary orientation information does not differ for these groups, but it is obvious that we must respect the needs of specific categories of students. Academic preparation, cognitive styles, services required, advising and counseling needs, skills development programs, financial aid, tutoring—all are areas requiring differing approaches for each special target group (Kane, 1979). Often the necessary adjustments can be incorporated into a more general program; but more likely they dictate special sessions at a minimum. Training for staff must include sessions focused on various special needs (Troy and others, 1975). It is possible that such special sessions can meet these needs without getting involved in elaborate special programming. It is, unfortunately, highly unlikely that institutions will, at this time, find such entirely separate special programs to be economically justifiable.

Effects of Orientation

Whether an orientation program has achieved its goals can only be determined by systematic evaluation. One review of orientation practices (Van Eaton, 1972) suggests that research findings are primarily institution-specific, and thus often contradictory. Such studies are hampered by inconsistent methodology, making results almost unusable in situations even slightly different from the one under scrutiny. However, in developing a more systematic approach to planning orientation activities, it is useful to look at the kinds of studies that have been done.

A large portion of orientation research looks at effects on

academic performance, with results showing little effect occurs (Griffin and Donnan, 1970; and Weigel and Smith, 1972). There is some evidence that orientation cuts the attrition rate and little evidence that orientation results in a reduction in feelings of alienation (Donk and Hinkle, 1971; and Herron, 1974). Attitudes in other areas have been shown to be affected by orientation programs. For example, orientation programs can develop more positive feelings toward learning (Reiter, 1964); more interest in non-classroom activities (Chandler, 1972); a better understanding of academic expectations (Cole and Ivey, 1967); and a clearer understanding of the role of a student (Rising, 1967). One study clearly suggests that the atmosphere of the orientation sessions colors a student's view of the total college environment (Foxley, 1969). Whether information about an institution is more easily assimilated when presented orally rather than in writing is almost insignificant since research tends to suggest that it is the *quality* of the presentation that makes the impact rather than the *content* (Forrer, 1974; and Packard, 1968).

I am dismayed to find a relative dearth of sound, rigorous, recent, documentary evaluation of orientation efforts, especially in light of the current severe budgetary constraints nationwide (Pappas, 1967; and Butts, 1971). Extensive review of Educational Resource Information Center documents and other abstract collections reveals a collection of articles that might be subtitled "Here's What We Do: It Works for Us," a relatively large number of detailed descriptions of programs and their various activities, and even a few that describe surveys taken of participants on how to improve programs. This kind of evaluation is locally valuable, of course, but serves only as an observational model for other institutions. If orientation programs are to sustain financial support at reasonable levels, more than observational research will have to be done. The literature reviewed suggests that orientation directors in the future will be required to spend significant time designing and executing more sophisticated research and evaluation studies than have appeared to date in the journals even though such research will require expenditure of already dwindling funds.

Current Programs

Anyone wanting to begin an orientation program or make changes in a current one is well advised to request information about programs at similar institutions (most schools have a list of sister institutions). Further, Beal and Noel (1980, pp. 74–87) discuss special retention leaders and programs of special interest in some depth. Although not always identified specifically as orientation activities, many of the programs they describe are clearly directed toward achieving objectives similar to the orientation goals defined earlier in this chapter.

No single approach can serve as a prototype for a new program because local idiosyncrasies must be addressed; it is more likely that parts of several programs should serve as a composite model. It is to that end that the following examples of typical and successful orientation programs are summarized and presented as models. Obviously, the list is very selective, but it is a good beginning.

Generic Entry Points. A number of schools have a generic entry point for new freshmen that encompasses a full academic year. In some cases, all freshmen are involved; in others, only some of them. These programs include orientation, advising, testing, general education requirements, and the like. Two such programs stand out as exemplary: the College of General Registration at South Dakota State University in Brookings and the Freshman Year of Studies at the University of Notre Dame in Indiana. These programs, both described in case studies in Saluri's Chapter Twenty-one, balance structure and flexibility in such a way as to recognize the developmental needs of incoming students and to integrate these needs into an overall educational program balancing academic and nonacademic components.

Orientation Courses. Orientation courses—either semester or year long—have the potential for achieving similar results as well as others. Perhaps the best single example available of such a course is University 101 at the University of South Carolina in Columbia. Designed to help freshmen adjust to the university setting, the course benefits the entire academic community. In classes of twenty to twenty-five members, students are oriented to the institution and to the specific programs it offers, consider solutions to common problems in a peer support group atmosphere, and gain skills required to survive as college students.

Faculty and administrative staff who volunteer to teach University 101 are given training specific to the course and are exposed to new ways to communicate subject matter to undergraduates. An added benefit is that academic and student affairs personnel are involved in an activity that reinforces their mutual educational philosophies and goals. As an overall result of the program, the institution has maximized cost effectiveness in a number of overlapping areas. As John N. Gardner, the director of the course, notes: "Postsecondary education must take into account the steady state, declining enrollments, and the need for faculty and student development. In that spirit, University 101 is offered as a tested, replicable model for humanistically oriented student and faculty growth, with numerous additional institutional benefits" (unpublished report).

Programs such as University 101 or the Freshman Seminar at Hunter College in New York City (Cohen and Jody, 1978) represent the multifaceted approach to orienting new students so highly acclaimed in 1980. For a general review of orientation course content, see Sagaria (1979).

Summer Programs. Summer programs one to three days in length might be represented by any one of a number of programs; I will highlight Preview CSU of Colorado State University in Fort Collins. Essentially one day long, this twenty-year-old program is streamlined and efficient, with parallel schedules for parents and students. From the seven-minute, 450-slide, multimedia presentation at 8:15 A.M. to the "This Is Your Life, Fritz Freshman" presentation by student staff at 4:15 P.M., the participants are greeted by university personnel and immersed in the campus, its services, and its programs. Parents and students have separate opportunities to meet with faculty advisers, administrators, and student staff and to tour campus facilities. In addition, students have an opportunity to examine their initial major choice, change it if desired, and get preregistered for fall semester classes. The program staff is made up of faculty members, students, and administrators, all working closely together to give an honest and straightforward view of the campus community. "There's no such thing as an inappropriate question" is the prevailing attitude, and "It's okay if you change your mind" is the vocational approach taken. As a matter of fact, these very phrases are heard repeatedly during every session of the program. Placement tests are administered in composition, mathematics, and foreign languages the afternoon and evening before program participation; results are available the next morning for use in individual advising sessions. A registration packet and browsing tables provide printed materials about programs and services and often stimulate additional questions. All in all, educational, personal, social, and public relations goals are met and the program positively evaluated by attendees, who include 75 to 80 percent of all new freshmen and their parents.

Three-day programs, often held throughout the summer, have the flexibility to include more activities while achieving similar goals. Communications and decision-making workshops, extensive tours of campus facilities, discussions with faculty, staff, and students, and various kinds of social events are common.

In recent years, a combination of the one-day and three-day approach was instituted at the University of Maine at Orono (Krall, 1981). As a supplement to the regular one-day program, three days of activities (called New Student Welcome Days) are planned to help channel new student enthusiasm and energy into better performance as students. The activities are designed to emphasize the importance of the freshman year and to aid freshmen in establishing a campus identity. They also help students establish a positive peer association and identify adult role models while emphasizing the importance of the residence hall environment. Included are talks by administrators, information about the history of the institution and its programs, banquets, small group meetings, tours of campus, meetings with student leaders and upperclass students, lectures by distinguished faculty, placement examinations, exhibits of equipment available for rental, and lots of interaction activities. All activities are designed to alleviate anxiety and ease the transition to a college setting.

Students' Concerns. The admissions and orientation center
at State University of New York Empire State College in Saratoga Springs serves as a vital link between recruitment and
matriculation by using faculty and students, slide-tape presentations, group meetings, and orientation workshops to ease adjustment to the academic environment and begin the orientation process which continues throughout an individual's career
(Chickering, 1973). Beginning with an application form which
asks such questions as "What kind of life do you want to be
leading five or ten years from now? What are your long-range
vocational or professional plans or aspirations? What resources
might you use [at Empire State]?", students are placed in the
position of examining their varied needs on an ongoing basis.
During preadmissions meetings, professional and peer counselors—in individual and group settings—discuss program alternatives, the interests and background of faculty, activities on
campus, and work alternatives. If admitted, students then attend a two and one-half day orientation workshop to outline
their educational goals, learn about campus resources, meet
other students, and begin to acclimatize themselves to the campus community. During the workshops, students may discover
ways to remedy personal weaknesses, to combine several interests
and abilities, and to deal with their own learning styles. Institutional staff can identify those who need specific follow-up after
matriculation. For everyone it is the beginning of a continuing
orientation process that links recruitment, admissions, orientation, and academic advising.

An Approach to Academic Advising. As indicated earlier, program evaluation is difficult to accomplish meaningfully, but
Weber State College in Odgen, Utah, has an approach to designing an evaluation that can be useful for many institutions (Stephenson, Blake, and Casper, 1975). Following the development
of a basic intervention philosophy, the counseling center, using
the ACT Institutional Self-Study instrument plus a student steering committee, completed an institutional preassessment that
identified local areas of concern for their campus. After establishing a two-goal program, they established both experimental and control groups from the incoming freshman class. An

orientation program was built around eighteen behavioral goals for the experimental group, and a traditional large-group orientation for all other students, including the identified but anonymous control group. A survey of the groups after two quarters allowed orientation staff to draw conclusions about the content of orientation, the main finding being that decision making about career selection is probably what orientation programs should emphasize.

Orientation Activities. Highlights of several other programs will emphasize the scope of orientation activities across the country that have potential impact on retention. The Peer Orientation Center at the University of South Carolina is a very recent example of the use of peers to meet student needs (Simpson and Strumpf, 1979). Selected and trained students are available in a central office to answer questions of all kinds. Referrals to specific agencies or personnel are made to meet individual needs.

Making use of a popular means of communicating efficiently, the University of Kansas in Lawrence stimulates learning along with communication of information in two slide-tape presentations on career planning and sex-role socialization (O'Neil and Van Loon, 1977; and O'Neil, Meeker, and Borgers, 1978).

Many other activities may be included in orientation programs, including retreats, values clarification exercises, vocational testing, seminars, workshops, camping trips, and so on. Their appropriateness must be determined by local needs, facilities, personnel, and financial constraints.

Integrating Services

As mentioned earlier, there is yet another kind of orientation that college students receive, although it is not often considered a responsibility of orientation personnel: lifelong orientation. One of the missions of postsecondary education is to prepare students for the role of contributing citizens. This includes general education in basic skills and disciplines as well as specific training in the development of more pragmatic, marketable skills. It would be correct, of course, to assume that on most campuses this last kind of orientation is called advising. The point at issue, however, is that what we call advising we could also call orientation and vice versa; perhaps our whole approach to orientation would be a bit different if we did. The role of orientation programs and courses in retention might be easier to define and support if we viewed orientation as an activity continuum with recruitment on one end and commencement on the other. As Beal and Noel (1980) point out, it is not easy to understand all of the variables involved in retention; it is, however, easy to include any program or activity that contributes to the staying environment as one of those variables. This kind of integration requires two main ingredients: increased faculty involvement and enhanced service delivery.

Too often, faculty, caught up in the chaos of teaching, research, and service, are not included in many of the student-oriented activities planned by student affairs staff. Faculty may tend to see these activities as extracurricular—not beneath their attention, but certainly not an integral part of their jobs. They thus fail to see that integrating student development efforts with traditional learning experiences enhances both activities and makes the entire educational endeavor more valuable and meaningful for all participants. Introducing faculty to this co-curricular concept will require more assertive efforts on the part of student affairs personnel. The more faculty become involved in and recognize the educational results of the co-curriculum, the more supportive they will be of it, the more unified and consistent will be the college experience for students, and the more likely it will be that the institutional environment will develop and sustain the staying qualities critical to retention. Finally, when both academic and student affairs personnel are cooperating to maximize the students' educational experiences, the more complete will be the students' orientation to lifelong learning.

Beyond 1985

Oh, for a crystal ball! With dwindling applicant pools, changing student populations, vacillating public opinion regarding higher education, and increasing limits on financial support, it is challenging to speculate on the future of orientation.

The need for orientation will not diminish. As the maze of academe continually becomes more complex and curricular choices more diverse, students will need additional help in making ever more complex decisions. Gone are the days when students chose one of a dozen areas of study; at Colorado State University, for example, freshmen have ninety-six specific points of entry and many subspecializations from which to choose.

As our student population and our curricula change, we must be alert to the modifications required to serve new groups of students. We must continuously assess and reassess what business we are really in, what we want to achieve, what we want our students to be and become, and what we must become in the future in order to help them. We cannot rely solely on old approaches and materials, although we may find some traditional techniques and indicators—length and timing of program, media presentations, and so on—reliable.

We are an information society with high technology capabilities. We should not fear the intrusion of computers into our comfortable lives; we should seek to harness them with our human resources and thus maximize their usefulness. This is not to say that orientation should become an academic video game, but to suggest that creative use of software can leave more time for staff to discuss personal individual issues during orientation and advising sessions. We already capitalize on software for scheduling and related registration processing. We should make it do even more for us, so we can spend more meaningful time with future students.

Perhaps most important for the future is the look we take at ourselves. The orientation programs we plan will not change unless we do. We must be risk takers—realistic about consequences and willing to break old molds. Just because something has worked several times before does not mean we must use it again. Of course, it is easier to repeat what has worked, but this, I submit, is a head-in-the-sand approach. Our students are different; many of them are more sophisticated and proficient technologically than we are. To retain them, we must speak to their needs; to meet their needs, we must first catch up with them.

References

Atkins, K. B. "The Effect of an Orientation-Advising Program on Attrition Rates of the Allied Health Division at Spartanburg Technical College." Ft. Lauderdale, Fla.: Nova University, 1979. (ED 174 272)

Beal, P. E., and Noel, L. *What Works in Student Retention*. Iowa City, Iowa: American College Testing Program and National Center for Higher Education Management Systems, 1980. (ED 197 635)

Breckenridge, J. W. "New Student Testing and Orientation." *National Association of Student Personnel Administrators Journal*, 1967, *5*, 210–212.

Brubacher, J. S., and Rudy, W. *Higher Education in Transition*. New York: Harper & Row, 1968.

Butts, T. A. *Personnel Services Review: New Practices in Student Orientation*. Ann Arbor: University of Michigan, 1971. (ED 057 416)

Cantor, S. J. *Issues in Orientation: Programs and Goals*. Unpublished manuscript, University of Iowa, 1974.

Caple, R. B. "A Rationale for the Orientation Course." *Journal of College Student Personnel*, 1964, *6*, 42–46.

Chandler, E. M. "Freshman Orientation—Is It Worthwhile?" *National Association of Student Personnel Administrators Journal*, 1972, *10*, 55–61.

Chickering, A. W. "College Advising for the 1970s." In J. Katz (ed.), *Services for Students*. New Directions for Higher Education, no. 3, San Francisco: Jossey-Bass, 1973.

Cohen, R. D., and Jody, R. *Freshman Seminar: A New Orientation*. Boulder, Colo.: Westview, 1978.

Cole, C. W., and Ivey, A. E. "Differences Between Students Attending and Not Attending a Precollege Orientation." *Journal of College Student Personnel*, 1967, *8*, 16–21.

Dannells, M., and Kuh, G. D. "Orientation." In W. T. Packwood (ed.), *College Student Personnel Services.* Springfield, Ill.: Thomas, 1977.

Delworth, U., Sherwood, G., and Casaburri, N. *Student Paraprofessionals: A Model for Higher Education.* Student Personnel Monograph, no. 17. Washington, D. C.: American College Personnel Association, 1974.

Donk, L. J., and Hinkle, J. E. "Precollege Orientation and Longitudinal Changes in Student Attitudes." *National Association of Student Personnel Administrators Journal,* 1971, *8,* 264–269.

Drake, R. W. *Review of the Literature for Freshman Orientation Practices in the United States.* Fort Collins: Colorado State University, 1966. (ED 030 920)

Felker, K. R. "GROW: An Experience for College Freshmen." *Personnel and Guidance Journal,* 1973, *51,* 558–561.

Forrer, S. E. "Dissemination Systems in University Orientation: An Experimental Comparison." *Journal of College Student Personnel,* 1974, *15,* 394–399.

Forrest, A. *Increasing Student Competence and Persistence: The Best Case for General Education.* Iowa City, Iowa: American College Testing Program National Center for Advancement of Educational Practices, 1982.

Foxley, C. H. "Orientation or Dis-orientation?" *Personnel and Guidance Journal,* 1969, *48,* 218–221.

Gohn, L. "Program Development." In A. G. Matthews (ed.), *Handbook for Orientation Directors.* Iowa City, Iowa: National Orientation Directors Association, 1975.

Goodale, T., and Sandeen, A. "The Transfer Student: A Research Report." *National Association of Student Personnel Administrators Journal,* 1971, *8,* 248–263.

Griffin, M. H., and Donnan, H. "Effect of a Summer Precollege Counseling Program." *Journal of College Student Personnel,* 1970, *11,* 71–72.

Herron, D. G. "Orientation Effects on Student Alienation." *Journal of the National Association of Women Deans and Counselors,* 1974, *37,* 107–111.

Kane, J. A. "Peer Counseling: An Experience." *Journal of Non-White Concerns in Personnel and Guidance,* 1979, *7,* 59–61.

Krall, J. K. "New Student Welcome Program." *Journal of College and University Student Housing*, 1981, *11* (2), 30–33.

Lenning, O. T., Sauer, K., and Beal, P. E. *Student Retention Strategies*. American Association for Higher Education—Educational Resources Information Center/Higher Education Research Report, no. 80. Washington, D.C.: American Association for Higher Education, 1980.

McCann, C. J. "Trends in Orienting College Students." *Journal of the National Association of Women Deans and Counselors*, 1967, *30*, 85–90.

Mayhew, L. B. *The Carnegie Commission on Higher Education: A Critical Analysis of the Reports and Recommendations*. San Francisco: Jossey-Bass, 1973.

Mueller, K. H. *Student Personnel Work in Higher Education*. Boston: Houghton Mifflin, 1961.

O'Banion, T. "Experiment in Orientation of Junior College Students." *Journal of College Student Personnel*, 1969, *10*, 12–15.

O'Neil, J. M., Meeker, C. H., and Borgers, S. B. "A Developmental, Preventive, and Consultative Model to Reduce Sexism in the Career Planning of Women." *Catalogue of Selected Documents in Psychology*, 1978, *8*, 39.

O'Neil, J. M., and Van Loon, K. C. "Career Planning Sensitization (Slide-Tape Show) with Needs Assessment During Freshman Orientation." Paper presented at American Personnel and Guidance Association, Dallas, Texas, March 1977.

Packard, R. E. "Programmed-Instruction Technique in New Student Orientation." *Journal of College Student Personnel*, 1968, *9*, 246–252.

Pappas, J. P. "Student Reactions to a Small-Group Orientation Approach." *College and University*, 1967, *43*, 84–89.

Pascarella, E. T., and Terenzini, P. T. "Predicting Freshman Persistence and Voluntary Dropout Decisions from a Theoretical Model." *Journal of Higher Education*, 1980, *51*, 60–75.

Perry, W. G. *Forms of Intellectual and Ethical Development in the College Years*. New York: Holt, Rinehart & Winston, 1970.

Reiter, H. H. "The Effect of Orientation Through Small-Group Discussion on Modification of Certain Attitudes." *Journal of Educational Research*, 1964, *58*, 65–68.

Rising, E. J. *The Effects of a Prefreshman Orientation Program on Academic Progress.* Amherst: University of Massachusetts, 1967. (ED 022 413)

Sagaria, M. A. D. "Freshman Orientation Courses: A Framework." *Journal of the National Association of Women Deans and Counselors*, 1979, *43*, 3–7.

Shaffer, R. H. "A New Look at Orientation." *College and University*, 1962, *37*, 272–279.

Simpson, J. C., and Strumpf, G. B. "Ongoing Personal Orientation Program—What's It All About." *The Orientation Review*, Oct. 1979, p. 11.

Snider, P. A. "A Student Comes to Us." *Journal of the National Association of Women Deans and Counselors*, 1970, *33*, 138–141.

Stephenson, B. W., Blake, L. H., and Casper, G. G. "Freshman Orientation and Career Articulation." In W. H. Morrill, E. R. Oetting, and J. C. Hurst, *Nine Outreach Programs.* Fort Collins, Colo.: Colorado State University Press, 1975.

Trotter, M. "Selection and Training of Student Paraprofessionals Who Serve as Orientation Leaders." In A. G. Matthews (ed.), *Handbook for Orientation Directors.* Iowa City, Iowa: National Orientation Directors Association, 1975.

Troy, W. G., and others. "An Evaluation of Three Methods of Racism-Sexism Training in a University Student Orientation Program." Research report no. 1–75, Cultural Study Center, University of Maryland at College Park, 1975.

Van Eaton, E. N. "National Study of Trends in Orientation." *The National Orientation Bulletin*, 1972, *2* (4), 3.

Weigel, R. G., and Smith, T. T. "The Effects of Preorientation Information Dissemination on Academic Choices and Performance." *Journal of College Student Personnel*, 1972, *13*, 452–455.

13

Academic Advising

~~~~~~~~~

David S. Crockett

Academic advising, effectively delivered, can be a powerful influence on student development and learning and as such, can be a potent retention force on the campus. The literature in recent years is replete with references to the relationship between advising and student retention. The importance of academic advising in increasing student persistence is well documented. Habley (1981) presents a particularly convincing case for an advisement-retention model which underscores the critical link between academic advisement and student retention. Based on the assumption that retention programs should focus on services which enable students to clarify their educational and career goals and relate those goals to academic offerings, quality advising provides the most significant mechanism through which this can be accomplished. Habley concludes that the adviser is the key in assisting students to explore goals and choose appropriate educational offerings consistent with those goals.

To gain a better understanding of the role of advising in fostering student retention, we might first examine the importance college officials attach to advising as a retention strategy. Beal and Noel (1980) speak directly to the perceived importance of academic advising. The purpose of their study of over 944 institutions was to compile and analyze information about campus action programs or efforts designed to improve student retention.

College administrators in this comprehensive study identify inadequate academic advising as the major characteristic linked to attrition at their institutions. Other negative characteristics related to the advising function and frequently cited are inadequate counseling systems, academic support services, career planning services, as well as a lack of student-faculty contact.

These same administrators rate a caring attitude of faculty and staff as the single most potent retention agent on campus. Obviously, advising is not the only context in which a caring attitude toward students can be demonstrated; it does, however, represent an opportunity for a significant one-on-one relationship between faculty/staff and students to develop. It is not surprising, therefore, that improvement of academic advising services was also the most common retention strategy being employed by the institutions surveyed. Baldridge, Kemerer, and Green (1982) identify orientation, counseling, and advising as the activities colleges report as having the second greatest impact on student retention. In their study, only learning centers/academic support services are mentioned by a higher percentage of respondents.

In Chapter Four, Forrest presents compelling evidence of the relationship between advising and the achievement of general education objectives, as well as increased student persistence. As a result of an earlier study, Forrest (1982, p. 44) states that "probably the single most important move an institution can make to increase student persistence to graduation is to ensure that students receive the guidance they need at the beginning of the journey through college to graduation."

It is clear that an increasing number of institutions now see effective advising as clearly linked to improved student retention. These institutions recognize that good advising is vital to students as they develop their educational and career goals. They also know that good advising does not just happen; it is the result of a carefully developed institutional plan and a commitment to excellence in advising.

However, despite this recognition of the importance of advising, advising on many college campuses today is not as effective as it might be. Substantiating this observation are the results of the second nationwide survey of academic advising (Crockett and Levitz, 1984). Some of the more disappointing findings from this study of 754 institutions follow.

- The majority of institutions have no formal recognition/reward system for individuals engaged in advising.
- Three-fourths do not consider advising effectiveness in promotion or tenure decisions.
- Most institutions provide only a minimum of training for advisers.
- The vast majority of institutions have no systematic appraisal of either their advising programs or individual adviser's performance.

In the light of these findings, this chapter will examine the basic elements necessary in the development of an effective advising program. After proposing a developmental definition of advising, I will present an overview of proven strategies for the organization and delivery of advising services, ending with a model for a dual approach to delivery systems to meet differing student needs. Next, I will discuss ways of providing administrative support, particularly through in-service programs, an effective evaluation and recognition/reward system, and through providing information on advisees and other adviser resources. Finally, the chapter concludes with a checklist of elements to consider in designing an effective academic advising program.

A Developmental Approach

The growing evidence of the link between advising and improved student retention is not surprising if advising is viewed developmentally. And indeed academic advising is evolving on many campuses from a simplistic, perfunctory course scheduling activity performed primarily by teaching faculty to a more integrated and complex process designed to facilitate student growth and development.

O'Banion's (1972) five-step advising model is now generally recognized as the origin of the developmental model of academic advising which recognizes that there is a logical and sequential set of steps to the advising process. O'Banion's five steps are (1) exploration of life goals, (2) exploration of career goals, (3) selection of a major or program of study, (4) selection of courses, and (5) scheduling of courses. O'Banion's model thus assumes that a developmental approach to academic advising must involve more than course selection and scheduling. Rather, these necessary, but mechanical activities must be accomplished within a broader context that needs to be discussed and developed by the advisee and the adviser. The quality of academic advising on college and university campuses could be greatly enhanced by placing more emphasis on and devoting more time to steps one and two of the O'Banion model. Walsh (1979) presents a convincing case for redefining advising so that these developmental functions—exploring, integrating, and synthesizing a student's life, career, and academic goals—are central to the process.

However, a developmental approach to advising is sometimes resisted by advisers who may feel they lack the necessary background and training to engage in what they see as basically a counseling or life/career planning function. Walsh (1979, p. 447) addresses this concern, saying that the developmental function of advisement "should not be confused with either psychotherapy or personal counseling. The focus of advisement remains a student's academic self, not simply in the narrow sense of one who absorbs knowledge, takes courses, and completes requirements, but in the broader sense, which includes the integration of the academic self with one's other selves." Viewed thus, developmental advising is a person-centered approach that integrates the activities of career/life planning and academic advising to assist students in developing a personally relevant educational and career plan.

A major goal of developmental advising then should be student growth (Thomas and Chickering, 1984). Accordingly, developmental advising should include the following:

- Assessment activities for the formation and clarification of the advisee's values, interests, abilities, and goals

- Activities which help students to relate self-information to career and educational information
- Activities which encourage broad exploration of career and educational options
- Activites which teach decision-making skills and assist with the implementation of choices

It is important to recognize that individual student readiness for developmental advising may vary considerably. Students are likely, at first, to view advisers in their informational role. Advisers need to help them go beyond this stage to reach the relational and developmental components of the advising function. As Walsh (1979, p. 48) emphasizes, "Advisers must learn how to translate a question about course selection (an informational question) into a question of goals—career, academic, and life goals—by exploring the implications. They need to know how to ask cue questions to start the student along the developmental path."

A developmental adviser must serve a variety of roles, including facilitator of communication, coordinator of a student's educational experience, frontline interpreter of the value and benefit of higher education, caring and concerned individual, and referral agent. The role of referral agent is particularly important since a truly developmental approach to advising will require a cooperative and integrated effort among all constituents and program areas of the institution in order to make the best use of all resources to address the individual student's special educational and career plans.

Overall, a developmental approach to advising suggests the following definition of academic advising. Academic advising is a developmental process which assists students in the clarification of their life/career goals and in the development of educational plans for the realization of these goals. It is a decision-making process by which students realize their maximum educational potential through communication and information exchanges with an adviser; it is ongoing, multifaceted, and the responsibility of both student and adviser. The adviser serves as a facilitator of communication, a coordinator of learning experiences through course and career planning and academic progress review, and an agent of referral to other campus agencies as necessary.

Delivery Models

Given this developmental definition of advising, each institution must select the delivery system or combination of systems most appropriate for its situation and student body. For when everyone is responsible for advising, no one is accountable. Managing the advising program typically consists of planning, organizing, staffing, directing, and evaluating. Grites (1979) and I (1982) discuss in some detail the more common advising delivery systems employed by colleges and universities: for example, faculty professional, peer, and paraprofessional advisers; and advisement centers. Habley (1983) takes a different approach, viewing delivery from an organizational perspective and distinguishing between those who deliver advising and the organizational structure in which advising takes place.

It is important to note that there is probably no one best administrative structure appropriate to all institutions. Totally decentralized administration for advising often suffers from the problem of inconsistency in delivery. Some departments may do an excellent job of delivering advising services to their students, while other academic units provide less than satisfactory service. Totally centralized systems provide for consistency, but may fail to involve those best equipped to deliver certain aspects of the advising process: for example, faculty. A combination of administrative structures probably incorporates most of the advantages and few of the disadvantages associated with the other models.

I (1982) suggest six factors to consider in deciding upon an appropriate delivery system for advising. These are (1) advising needs of student, (2) organizational structure of the institution, (3) desired outcomes, (4) available resources, (5) collective bargaining or faculty contract agreements, and (6) adviser load.

The most common delivery systems for academic advising are discussed briefly in the next sections.

Faculty Advisers. Institutions have traditionally relied heavily on faculty as the major providers of advising services. This is easily understood from a historical perspective since student-faculty relationships have always been viewed as an integral part of the higher education process.

Faculty advising systems have emerged primarily because many institutions have assumed, correctly or incorrectly, that faculty are interested in advising and perceive advising as an important faculty role. Administrators often feel that faculty are the most knowledgeable individuals when it comes to providing academic information; that the students want advice from faculty; and that this form of delivery represents the most financially feasible way to deliver advising services. Further, the advising process facilitates the development of mutually beneficial relationships between student and teacher. However, in considering a faculty advising delivery system, the institution should thoroughly test these assumptions. Faculty advisers are experts in their disciplines and knowledgeable about specific courses in their departments and about educational and career opportunities in their fields. But faculty may have a bias toward their own departments or may feel that their advising duties conflict with other responsibilities.

Professional Advisers. Second to faculty advising, the most frequently used advising delivery system is the employment of persons whose full-time jobs are devoted to advising. Obvious advantages to this practice include the fact that they are free from academic department biases which may plague faculty advising systems and, more importantly, they can be selected on the basis of their ability to serve as effective advisers.

The use of professional counselors as advisers has several limitations. Professional counselors may often be more interested in psychological and therapeutic counseling than in academic advising. Advisee load also becomes a real problem for many institutions using only counselors for academic advising. Finally, counselors may not have the time to become as knowledgeable about specific course content, requirements, and graduate and career opportunities, as faculty members who are experts in their fields. Professional advisers, on the other hand, may or may not have been trained as counselors but are selected on the basis of their skill, ability, and intent to assist students in the advising process.

Peer Advisers. The concept of using upperclass students as peer helpers in orientation programs, as residence hall assistants, and as tutors has a long tradition in higher education. In more recent years, institutions have turned increasingly to this group as a means of supplementing their academic advising delivery systems.

The major disadvantage associated with peer advising is that the typical undergraduate peer adviser simply does not have the background or skill to deal effectively with some of the more complex aspects of the advising process. However, as with faculty advising programs, many potential disadvantages of peer advising can be overcome by proper selection, training, and management of advisers.

Perhaps the single most persuasive argument for peer advising is that it works. The literature on this delivery mechanism strongly supports the assumption that peer advisers can be as effective as professionals and faculty in many advising situations (Murry, 1972; and Zunker and Brown, 1966). Because peer advisers can best provide subjective and experiential information, good peer advising programs should rely heavily on referrals to professional staff on campus who are more experienced and better equipped for such advising functions as determining career goals and selecting majors. Peer advising can be an economical way of delivering academic advising, especially in colleges and departments with large numbers of advisees, but in all cases, careful training of peer advisers is essential.

Paraprofessional Advisers. A relatively small number of institutions use paraprofessionals or volunteers as adjuncts to the advising delivery system. Anyone familiar with campus life recognizes the valuable informal advising which often occurs through departmental secretaries, clerks in the registrar's office, and others. These systems are generally not formally recognized as delivery systems and, often as not, individuals in these positions receive no specialized training for their advising responsibilities.

The advantages of an organized program of paraprofessional advisers are continuity, freeing professional staff for more substantive work with students, sense of worth and contribution for the paraprofessional, and cost. Paraprofessionals can be adequately trained to provide accurate and specific information to students on routine matters related to the advising process. Unfortunately, they do not generally possess the background, depth, and experience to deliver the full range of developmental advising services cited earlier in this chapter. However, as a supplement to other delivery systems, the use of paraprofessionals as advisers has merit.

Advisement Centers. A more recent development in delivery systems for advising has been the advising center. In general, these centers are student service agencies designed to make information easily accessible and to assist students in their academic decision-making process on an as-needed basis. They are most frequently staffed by full-time professional advisers, but are often augmented by using faculty on release time or peer advisers and paraprofessionals. They may be established campuswide or in specific colleges or academic units and can assume responsibility for a wide range of advising-related functions, thus providing campuswide coordination for the advising program.

Some advantages of a centralized advising center include a centralized location easily accessible to students, a corps of well-trained advisers who can establish continuity of contact, a wide range of advising services, student-centered rather than department-centered advising, more complete record-keeping and monitoring capability, greater accuracy of information, and ease of administration, training, supervision, and evaluation. A major disadvantage is often the direct cost of such a center.

Of the various delivery models for advising institutions, no single model has proven universally successful. Each institution should select the delivery system or combination of systems most appropriate for its situation and student body. Generally, successful advising programs use a combination of delivery systems to ensure that students are provided with several options in obtaining advising services.

In the final analysis, a key consideration in the selection of any delivery system is meeting the diversity of student advising needs that exist on college and university campuses. Table 1 sets forth Noel's model depicting the difference in student

Table 1. An Advising Model to Meet Diverse Student Advising Needs.

Phase	Student Needs	Primary Delivery Mode
Intake (decision making)	Transition advising	Advisement Center/ Professional Advisers
	Self-information	
	Academic information	
	Career information	
	Monitoring adjustment to college and academic progress	
	Selection of core/general education course	
	Developing an academic plan	
	Referral where appropriate	
Academic Mentoring (post-selection of major)	Course selection and scheduling	Faculty Advisers
	Monitoring academic progress and graduation requirements	
	Encouraging good academic performance	
	Linking program of study with opportunities and uses beyond graduation	
	Consideration of graduate school where appropriate	
	Selection of minor or double major	
	Referral where appropriate	

Source: Adapted from Noel, 1983.

advising needs at different point of their progress through the institution and suggests a dual approach to the delivery of academic advising services. The approach is developmental in that students in the intake or decision-making stage are assigned to professional advisers in an advisement center, while those who have selected a major and are in the academic mentoring stage are assigned to faculty advisers.

Administrative Support for Advising

Respondents to Crockett and Levitz (1984) indicate that administrative recognition of the importance of advising takes precedence over all other concerns in the delivery of advising services. Good advising programs are not inexpensive; they require allocation of human, financial, and physical resources. Unless administrators believe that advising is an important and necessary educational service and support that commitment both fiscally and psychologically, advising is likely to be neglected.

Increased administrative support for academic advising can be gained through making recommendations for improvement of the advising program as specific as possible, adding them to the data base, linking recommendations to issues of high interest to administrators (for example, increased student persistence), and making sure that recommendations are supported by those who will be affected by the changes. In addition, resource needs should be quantified and the outcomes and benefits of proposed actions highlighted.

Administrative support of the institutional advising program may be demonstrated through development and support of a comprehensive policy statement on advising, allocation of appropriate resources—fiscal, human, informational, and physical—to ensure the success of the advising program, and explicit assignment of responsibility and authority for the advising program. And perhaps most importantly, administrators can also support an evaluation system for individual advisers and provide a reward system for those involved in advising.

Effective In-Service Training. Expanded adviser training programs and activities are cited as the second most important need in academic advising (Crockett and Levitz, 1984). By and large, institutions have done an inadequate job of training advisers. Yet, because most advisers are receptive to improving their advising skills and techniques, well-planned and properly presented in-service training sessions can be very effective in improving the quality of advising.

A number of authors present strategies for developing training programs for academic advisers (Bonar, 1976; Bostaph and Moore, 1980; Gordon, 1984; and Ender and Winston, 1982). Grites (1978) suggests some general objectives of an adviser training program: (1) to provide advisers with accurate and timely information about the policies, procedures, and processes which affect the advising relationship, (2) to provide advisers with additional skills often required in their advising responsibilities, (3) to increase student satisfaction with advising, (4) to increase adviser satisfaction with advising, and (5) to develop a comprehensive approach to academic planning as a part of the total advising process.

Training sessions and support materials can correct some common obstacles to effective academic advising: lack of familiarity with curricular offerings, core requirements, referral sources, job opportunities, available data sources, and administrative forms and procedures used in the advising process; inadequate understanding of the role of adviser; and lack of basic advising and counseling skills. The training sessions can be structured around the needs perceived as most important to advisers and can be made more meaningful and interesting by use of appropriate handout materials, presentations by campus experts (for example, the director of counseling could speak on basic counseling skills and techniques), videotapes, and simulation and role playing.

Those with responsibility for the design of the training program should also develop evaluation procedures to determine the program's effectiveness. And since effective training is an ongoing activity, appropriate follow-up activities should be designed as well.

Evaluation of Advisers. The vast majority of institutions have not implemented a systematic appraisal of either their advising program or individual adviser performance (Crockett and Levitz, 1984). There is a clear need for institutions to develop more formal methods of assessing the effectiveness of their advising programs.

A well-designed evaluation program should (1) determine how well the advising system is working, (2) obtain information on individual adviser performance for the purpose of self-improvement, (3) gain information on areas of weakness in order to better develop in-service training strategies, (4) provide data for use in administering a recognition/reward system for individual advisers, and (5) gather data to support requests for funding or gain improved administrative support of the advising process.

Generally, evaluation can be thought of as either formative or summative. Formative evaluation is designed to foster individual self-development or improvement of the overall advising program. Formative evaluation is, for obvious reasons, more readily accepted by advisers and therefore easier to implement. Summative evaluation, on the other hand, is more threatening to many advisers. This type of evaluation, represented by objective four earlier, is designed to provide specific information on individual adviser performance for the purpose of making judgments or decisions regarding effectiveness. A good comprehensive evaluation program should feature both formative and summative components.

A number of important factors should be considered when developing and implementing an evaluation program. First, there is no substitute for strong administratve commitment and support. The support of the person or persons to whom advisers are responsible (for example, the chief academic officer, deans, or department heads) should be obtained at the outset. Once such a commitment has been made and communicated, the next step is to seek the involvement of the advisers themselves in the formulation of the evaluations. A committee of advisers should be appointed to develop the specifics. By involving advisers and developing a feeling of "ownership" early, many potential problems and concerns can be avoided.

Another critical initial step is to obtain consensus on the criteria that will be used to determine program and adviser effectiveness. Institutional policy statements on advising can be helpful in identifying desired outcomes, adviser behavior, and functions. Some common criteria include demonstration of a caring attitude toward advisees, effective interpersonal skills, availability and frequency of formal and informal contacts, intrusive behavior designed to build a strong relationship with advisees, and monitoring of students' progress toward academic and career goals.

It should be noted that it is often much easier to determine criteria than to develop satisfactory measures to assess the criteria selected. The method of evaluation needs to be determined early in the planning process. Whether evaluating the overall advising program, individual adviser performance, or both, three possibilities exist: (1) advisee evaluation, (2) adviser evaluation, or (3) administrative evaluation of advising. Although all can contribute, advisee evaluation is probably the most direct and useful, since it is students who are the recipients of the service.

Institutions may choose to develop their own evaluative instruments, borrow from other institutions, or use the *Academic Advising Survey* developed by the Center for Faculty Evaluation and Development, Box 3000, Manhattan, Kansas, 66502. Each approach has certain advantages. Self-developed instruments ensure "ownership" and often assess local objectives and desired outcomes more completely. The *Academic Advising Survey* has broad institutional use and is supported by a research base.

In order to ensure that the results of any evaluation are as valid as possible, consideration must be given to how and when the data will be collected. When evaluating the overall advising program, a sampling of advisee, adviser, and administrative input will probably suffice. However, when evaluating individual adviser performance, it is obviously desirable to have results that are as complete as possible. Building advising evaluation into the registration process or a common class period will often result in the most complete data collection.

A final, and sensitive consideration in the development of an advising evaluation program is the matter of providing advisers with appropriate feedback of the results. Confidentiality should, of course, be observed for both advisers and advisees. Advisers should be provided with their own results and, if possible, a mean or average score for each item for the total adviser group. This lets each adviser determine areas of strength and those which need to be strengthened and allows for comparative performance data for all advisers on the campus. For in the final analysis, advisers who achieve competence do so as a result of genuine interest and dedication.

To assist institutions in evaluating the current status of their advising programs, the American College Testing (ACT) Program has recently developed an academic advising audit (Crockett, 1983). The audit is a four-step process—information gathering, evaluation, analysis, and action planning—very similar to that which an external consultant might follow if called upon to review an institution's advising program. The elements identified in the audit are those that are discussed in this chapter and those identified in the research on academic advising as being key characteristics in the delivery of effective advising services.

Those seeking to improve their advising programs will also find it helpful to review the National Academic Advising Association's (NACADA) standards for academic advising. This excellent statement provides guidelines for institutions in the development of their advising programs (*Standards* . . . , forthcoming).

Recognition/Reward. The majority of institutions have no formal reward system for those engaged in advising students (Crockett and Levitz, 1984). A number of authors (Polson and Cashin, 1981; Teague and Grites, 1980; and Kramer, 1981) have stressed the importance of such a reward system.

The type of reward system employed for advising at a given institution is closely related to the importance placed on advising at that institution. Although it is important not to overlook the intrinsic rewards an adviser may find in helping students, lack of some type of tangible reward can impede effective advising. Administrators may reinforce good advising by a variety of means, including extra compensation, reduction in work load, paid in-service training, consideration of advising effectiveness in promotion and tenure decisions, and awards or other forms of public recognition. If advising is an agreed-upon responsibility, then it should be a factor in evaluation of the individual and recognized in decisions concerning salary, promotion, and tenure, for example.

To address the lack of tangible recognition and reward systems for advising, in academic year 1983–84, ACT and

NACADA introduced the National Recognition Program for Academic Advising. The awards in this program are designed to honor individuals and institutions who are making significant contributions to the improvement of academic advising and to disseminate information about these contributions to others in the field. The goal is to encourage wider institutional support and recognition of the importance of academic advising. Larsen and Brown (1983) suggest that reward systems include a reduction of teaching and research responsibilities, merit salary increases, and recognition of advising efforts in promotion and tenure evaluations.

Information on Advisees and Other Adviser Resources. Quality advising is based on the premise that advisers can never know too much about their advisees. Institutions need to give careful thought to the type of information sources they wish to provide on a routine basis to advisers and advisees. At a minimum, the typical advising folder should include such items as a secondary school transcript, ACT Assessment College Report, college transcript or grade report, locally administered placement tests, academic planning work sheets, and anecdotal records of significant discussions.

The ACT Assessment College Report provides one of the most comprehensive information sources about students entering postsecondary institutions currently available. This report has been designed to assist advisers and advisees by providing relevant information useful in a wide range of decisions (Crockett and Silberhorn, 1982).

Because most students providing ACT information to colleges and universities do so in advance of their enrollment, advisers have the opportunity to familiarize themselves with advisees through this information prior to their first interview with freshman advisees. They can identify patterns of needs, goals, interest, and abilities, and formulate questions they need to discuss with the student. This preinterview technique can do much to make the face-to-face advising session more valuable to the student.

Clearly, the availability of accurate and timely resources contributes significantly to good advising. To this end, in several institutional settings, computer-assisted advising has proven to be an effective and efficient support service for academic advisers. The obvious advantage to this technique is its ability to provide current information on advisees. For example, an adviser can receive a printout each term for his or her advisees showing courses completed to date, grades earned, courses or hours needed to complete major or minor requirements, and so on. Such a system can provide relief from repetitious record keeping, allowing the adviser more time to spend with the advisee on the substance of the advising process. Institutions with effective computer-assisted advising systems include: Brigham Young University, in Provo, Utah; Purdue University, in West Lafayette, Indiana; Georgia State University, in Atlanta; University of Denver, in Colorado; North Carolina State University at Raleigh; Maricopa Technical Community College, in Phoenix, Arizona; Miami University in Oxford, Ohio; and the University of Florida in Gainesville.

Because advisers cannot be expected to store all necessary information in their heads, a comprehensive, attractive, indexed adviser handbook is an indispensable tool for good advising. Such a handbook might include statements of policy, descriptions of campus resources and procedures, information on advising skills and techniques, information on academic requirements, and samples of documents used in the advising process. Ford (1983) provides an excellent discussion of the basic elements necessary in an advising handbook.

Whether it involves evaluation or providing information, there is simply no substitute for strong administrative support for academic advising. Without such support, the other factors discussed in this chapter are not likely to make a significant difference in the institution's attempt to improve the delivery and quality of advising on campus. Consideration of each of these elements is critical to upgrading advising on campus. With the proper administrative support and a developmental emphasis, academic advising can provide students with a needed and valuable service that enhances their growth and development as well as their commitment to the institution and the higher education experience.

References

Baldridge, J. V., Kemerer, F. R., and Green, K. C. *Enrollments in the Eighties: Factors, Actors, and Impacts.* American Association for Higher Education—Educational Resources Information Center/Higher Education Research Report, no. 3, Washington, D.C.: American Association for Higher Education, 1982. (ED 222 158)

Beal, P. E., and Noel, L. *What Works in Student Retention.* Iowa City, Iowa: American College Testing Program and National Center for Higher Education Management Systems, 1980. (ED 197 635)

Bonar, J. R. "Developing and Implementing a Systems-Design Training Program for Academic Advisers." *Journal of College Student Personnel*, 1976, *17*, 190–198.

Bostaph, C., and Moore, M. "Training Academic Advisors: A Developmental Strategy." *Journal of College Student Personnel*, 1980, *21*, 45–50.

Crockett, D. S. "Academic Advising Delivery Systems." In R. B. Winston, Jr., S. C. Ender, and T. K. Miller (eds.), *Developmental Approaches to Academic Advising.* New Directions for Student Services, no. 17, San Francisco: Jossey-Bass, 1982.

Crockett, D. S. *Academic Advising Audit: An Institutional Evaluation and Analysis of the Organization and Delivery of Advising Services.* Iowa City, Iowa: American College Testing Program, 1983.

Crockett, D. S., and Levitz, R. S. "Current Advising Practices in Colleges and Universities." In R. B. Winston, Jr., and Associates, *Developmental Academic Advising: Addressing Students' Educational, Career, and Personal Needs.* San Francisco: Jossey-Bass, 1984.

Crockett, D. S., and Silberhorn, C. J. "A Partnership to Enhance the Advising Process," *National Academic Advising Association Journal*, 1982, *2* (2), 24–29.

Ender, S. C., and Winston, R. B., Jr. "Training Allied Professional Academic Advisors." In R. B. Winston, Jr., S. C.

Ender, and T. K. Miller (eds.), *Developmental Approaches to Academic Advising.* New Directions for Student Services, no. 17, San Francisco: Jossey-Bass, 1982.

Ford, J. "Producing a Comprehensive Academic Advising Handbook." *National Academic Advising Association Journal,* 1983, *3* (2), 61–68.

Forrest, A. *Increasing Student Competence and Persistence: The Best Case for General Education.* Iowa City, Iowa: American College Testing Program National Center for Advancement of Educational Practices, 1982.

Gordon, V. N. "Training Professional and Paraprofessional Advisors." In R. B. Winston, Jr., and Associates, *Developmental Academic Advising: Addressing Students' Educational, Career, and Personal Needs.* San Francisco: Jossey-Bass, 1984.

Grites, T. J. "Training the Academic Advisor." In D. S. Crockett (ed.), *Academic Advising: A Resource Document.* Iowa City, Iowa: American College Testing Program, 1978.

Grites, T. J. *Academic Advising: Getting Us Through the Eighties.* American Association for Higher Education—Educational Resources Information Center/Higher Education Research Report, no. 7. Washington, D.C.: American Association of Higher Education, 1979. (ED 178 023)

Habley, W. R. "Academic Advisement: The Critical Link in Student Retention." *National Association of Student Personnel Administrators Journal,* 1981, *18* (4), 45–50.

Habley, W. R. "Organizational Structures for Academic Advising: Models and Implications." *Journal of College Student Personnel,* 1983, *24,* 535–540.

Kramer, H. C. "The Advising Coordinator: Managing from a One-Down Position." *National Academic Advising Association Journal,* 1981, *1* (1), 7–15.

Larsen, M. D., and Brown, B. M. "Rewards for Academic Advising: An Evaluation." *National Academic Advising Association Journal,* 1983, *3* (2), 53–60.

Murry, J. P. "The Comparative Effectiveness of Student-to-Student and Faculty Advising Programs." *Journal of College Student Personnel,* 1972, *13,* 562–566.

Academic Advising

263

Noel, L. "Increasing Student Learning and Retention: The Best Case for Advising." National Academic Advising Association annual meeting, St. Louis, Mo., Oct. 1983.

O'Banion, T. "An Academic Advising Model." *Junior College Journal*, 1972, *42* (6), 62, 64, 66–69.

Polson, C. J., and Cashin, W. E. "Research Priorities for Academic Advising: Results of Survey of NACADA Membership." *National Academic Advising Association Journal*, 1981, *1* (1), 34–43.

Standards of the Council for the Advancement of Standards for Student Services/Development Programs. Iowa City, Iowa: American College Testing Program, forthcoming.

Teague, G. V., and Grites, T. J. "Faculty Contracts and Academic Advising." *Journal of College Student Personnel*, 1980, *21*, 40–44.

Thomas, R. E., and Chickering, A. W. "Foundations for Academic Advising." In R. B. Winston, Jr., and Associates, *Developmental Academic Advising: Addressing Students' Educational, Career, and Personal Needs.* San Francisco: Jossey-Bass, 1984.

Walsh, E. M. "Revitalizing Academic Advisement." *Personnel and Guidance Journal*, 1979, *57*, 446–449.

Zunker, V. G., and Brown, W. F. "Comparative Effectiveness of Student and Professional Counselors." *Personnel and Guidance Journal*, 1966, *44*, 738–743.

14

Learning Assistance Programs

~~~~~~~~

Eric V. Gravenberg
John H. Rivers

Successful academic support programs for academically under-prepared students embody certain necessary and fundamental characteristics. Campuses that incorporate these characteristics in the goals and objectives of their support services are more likely to provide consistent and comprehensive assistance which promotes student success and appreciably increases overall student retention rates. In this chapter we will first consider how successful support efforts demystify the college experience, "decode" the environment, diagnose individual readiness, and develop academic preparedness. We will then look at three kinds of academic support efforts: early outreach programs, summer programs, and ancillary instruction. We will look at specific efforts taken at a number of institutions in California.

Demystifying the College Experience

As noted by Noel in Chapter One, academic underpreparedness, transition and adjustment difficulties, and unrealistic or uninformed expectations of college are major forces of attrition. Demystifying the process of applying, enrolling, persisting, and graduating from postsecondary institutions is an essential function of academic reinforcement programs and one that can effectively counter forces of attrition. A majority of underprepared students are the first in their families to attend college; for many of them, facing the new academic environment can be a frightening prospect. Because their parents are not in a position to assist them to prepare realistically for college life, this lack of a family history of association with higher education also accounts for many false and misleading assumptions and expectations. Consequently, academically underprepared students feel vulnerable upon entering college.

Although these new students may be initially unaware of their academic limitations and the inadequate preparation they received in secondary school, they soon begin to receive signals from college personnel that they are academically deficient. They then begin to view themselves as deficient academically, emotionally, and socially and incapable of functioning effectively in a college environment. Successful retention programs for academically underprepared students thus must provide information early—prior to or at the time of matriculation—to ensure that students understand what is expected of them early on in their experience and have a reasonable amount of time to adjust emotionally to these expectations. For unless there are mechanisms to demystify the college experience and ensure congruency between students' expectations and those of the institution, the transition for these students is extremely difficult. As Browne (1980, p. 7) notes, "A retention program is designed to curtail the amount of alienation that a student feels when matriculated at an institution."

As noted by Titley in Chapter Twelve, the information presented to students during orientation should be as concise and relevant as possible. Many orientation and retention programs make the mistake of overwhelming students with information that does not apply to their immediate concerns or to the decisions they are currently making. This only confuses and frustrates students who need information that is both simplistic and immediately relevant. Moreover, retention and orientation programs should provide students with an experience base through firsthand encounters with aspects of campus life that parallel and support the information provided. Such an approach provides them with prior exposure to and experience of the demands of college life.

Decoding the Environment

Acquiring the capability to decode institutional policies and regulations and translate them into understandable and manageable guidelines is a necessary stepping stone to effective academic and career decision making. As Gordon points out in Chapter Seven, lack of familiarity with the most simple regulations and procedures such as add and drop deadlines, course prerequisites, academic progress requirements, and departmental advising sessions contributes to students' anxiety and frustration, causing many to feel that dropping out is their only option. Given the plethora of such institutional policies and regulations, retention activities must help students develop the organizational deciphering skills necessary to succeed. Although such rudimentary skills are crucial to students' matriculation, persistence, and eventual graduation, decoding or deciphering skills often receive the least emphasis of all aspects of retention programs.

Compounding the decoding problem is the fact that, in order to get help, a student must first decide what type of assistance is needed and then select the campus support unit best equipped to provide that assistance. All too often, campus support services force students in need of comprehensive support to shuttle from one area to the next for assistance. This practice is neither efficient nor effective.

A number of campuses have redesigned and reconfigured their support services so that they work together in a more comprehensive manner. California State University, Fresno, has implemented a one-stop center where students can receive timely and relevant information about institutional procedures and be referred to the appropriate offices or departments. The center then monitors the referral process to ensure that the student referred to a support service actually receives the assistance needed. The effectiveness of such centers is enhanced by a high level of institutional support and commitment from senior administrative officials, academic departments, and student services offices.

Diagnosing Academic Difficulties Early

Successful retention programs also identify early on students who are experiencing academic difficulties. Properly diagnosing students' academic preparedness and their motivational and emotional readiness is essential to their success and persistence. Campuses employ a variety of standardized evaluation and measurement instruments, but these initial tests do not provide the ongoing monitoring which many academically underprepared students need. A number of campuses have therefore initiated early alert or academic monitoring systems. During the fourth or fifth week of classes, evaluation forms are sent to instructors of those students identified as being high risk. The instructors are asked to discreetly assess the student's performance level in the course. Specifically, the evaluation form may ask instructors to (1) verify student attendance (if possible); (2) estimate the student's grade at this point in the term; (3) indicate if assignments have been completed; (4) indicate if the student has taken tests, quizzes, and so on; and (5) make a recommendation and referral for additional support. The evaluation form is then returned to the office of origin which contacts the student and begins rendering the appropriate service or assistance.

The evaluation may uncover potential or hidden problems that are affecting the student's scholastic performance. The early alert evaluation at California State University, Northridge, for example, serves as a check on the vital factors of classroom participation and performance. In several instances, when an instructor indicates that a student has not attended class since the first day of classes, closer examination reveals that the student decided to drop the course by simply not attending instead of securing the proper forms to do so. If this information had not been ascertained, the student would have received an F at the end of the term, thereby jeopardizing his or her academic status.

Because faculty involvement in the response and referral process is integral to the success of an early alert system, the efficacy of such a system should be explained to faculty through departmental presentations designed to elicit their cooperation and support.

Developing Academic Preparedness

Successful reinforcement programs also promote the development of comprehensive developmental tools designed to bolster academic preparedness and provide students with a realistic opportunity to excel scholastically. Moreover, successful developmental efforts seek to provide academic reinforcement by motivating students to prosper—not merely to persist. Noel and Levitz (1982, p. 1) report that "by providing effective and efficient academic and personal/social support systems," institutions are able to maintain the integrity of academic standards and at the same time make certain that academically underprepared students are prepared to successfully meet those standards. While institutions employ a myriad of remediation and developmental services for academically underprepared students, the more successful programs adopt an underlying philosophy which says in essence that students begin from "where they are at" and under the guidance of the college attain the knowledge, skills, and experiences to prepare them to serve the needs of society (Rivera, 1970, p. 30).

Some educators have questioned the legitimacy of providing remedial assistance to students who should have—these educators believe—mastered basic skills in high school. Recently this debate over teaching basic skills and protecting institutional standards has been exacerbated by the sharp increase in the number of students requiring remediation and the current fiscal exigencies of higher education. Yet, with the kind of successes noted by Noel and Levitz (1982, p. 8) it is evident that interest in and commitment to serving academically underprepared students within postsecondary education is great and holds "the promise of extending the influence and resources of colleges and universities to meet significant human needs and to contribute to an enlightened society.''

Further, a growing number of faculty consider teaching underprepared students a refreshing and stimulating challenge. Teachers such as these, who strive to achieve excellence for and with their students, do so out of a dedication to helping these students learn; they take ''whatever actions are natural to an individual instructor to make that happen.'' (Roueche and Watkins, 1982, p. 23). Many underprepared students are intelligent people who simply lack essential academic skills. Therefore, as one instructor notes, ''the teaching techniques that are most effective go beyond the subject matter and, in essence, help students 'learn how to learn''' (Perry, 1983). To this end some institutions such as California State University, Sacramento offer workshops on time management, study techniques, term paper organization, and test preparation. Others such as Humboldt State University in Arcata and San Diego State University offer nonbaccalaureate credit for courses in basic mathematics, English, chemistry, and biology and regular student conferences, tutorial sessions, or laboratories emphasizing individualized drills. Integrated programmatic approaches for meshing skill-building activities with content development are described by Martin, Blanc, and De Buhr (1982), Weinstein (1982), and McCadden (1982).

Each of these functions of successful retention programs—demystifying the college experience, decoding the environment, diagnosing individual readiness, and developing academic preparedness—is vital both to the student and the institution. Overall, activities and programs established to accomplish these ends should be conducted as parallel, ongoing efforts which work in conjunction with traditional campus programs to guide academically underprepared students toward the most appropriate academic and career paths.

Admissions and Early Outreach

It is widely recognized among educators concerned about increasing campus retention rates that effective retention begins with effective recruitment. In recent years, recruitment strategies have proliferated and become increasingly more sophisticated. However, the more successful outreach programs have student graduation, not merely recruitment, as their goal. Rather than merely seeking to convey institutional expectations and guidelines to prospective students with promising academic and socioeconomic profiles, these outreach efforts attempt to identify prospective students with a variety of attributes. Although many of these students lack the necessary academic preparation, given the proper assistance and opportunity, they can succeed in pursuing their postsecondary aspirations.

The purpose of recruitment programs is thus to identify students who have the potential to succeed in college and to provide them and their parents with the information and assistance necessary to their successful transition to college. It is important to underscore the demystification procedures that outreach/recruitment programs should employ. Various nontraditional recruitment strategies such as involving parents through home visits, using faculty and students in recruitment, and offering financial aid information workshops and admissions application assistance can encourage participation, allay fears, deliver critical information, and help in diagnosing academic skills.

Targeting Feeder Institutions. Another proven method of academic reinforcement is a series of well-coordinated early outreach activities directed at feeder institutions. While many such early outreach programs are conducted by professional recruiters, it would appear that the most successful programs consist of structured and carefully coordinated activities involving selected staff from feeder and transfer institutions. Under such a program, faculty and student affairs professionals from both institutions work together to ensure that activities are known, supported, and successful.

The goal of such an early outreach program is for transfer colleges and universities to work with their counterparts at feeder institutions to establish a smoother transition process for high school and community college students. Such a program might include the following activities.

- Workshops on how to apply for financial aid and how to select an appropriate career
- Assessment in academic basic skills (writing, mathematics, and science)
- Early registration
- Early sign-up for major academic support services (that is, tutorial, ancillary instruction, part-time jobs, mobility services for handicapped students)
- Early contact with and academic advising from faculty advisers
- Campus visits
- Early exposure to college-level instruction

Usually an administrator is appointed from the transfer institution to coordinate the program and the feeder schools and colleges designate a staff member to serve on an ad hoc committee which plans and oversees the implementation of the program. An important element in the support strategy for the program, the committee discusses planning, program objectives, and implementation issues and makes decisions which represent commitments from the various interests represented on the committee. In this sense, the committee functions as a vehicle for promoting intersegmental cooperation between at least four branches of education: high schools, community and junior colleges, four-year colleges, and four-year universities.

The ad hoc committee develops a division of labor plan specifying responsibilities to be assumed by each segment. For high schools and two-year institutions, these responsibilities may include

- Provide facilities for small and large group meetings with students
- Identify students
- Arrange students' schedules to allow for adequate involvement in the program

For four-year and transition institutions, these responsibilities may include

- Plan and implement ongoing faculty guest lectures
- Plan and implement ongoing professional growth workshops for selected teachers in all segments of education
- Implement guidance classes taught by staff at the transfer institution which orient students to the expectations of the two- and four-year college experience
- Establish a process to provide feedback on the academic performance and persistence of students who have gone through the transition program

Model Program. Such an early outreach program for easing transition and transfer has been implemented in California. The institutions involved are Monterey and Pacific Grove unified school districts; California State Universities, Chico and Sacramento; San Jose State University; California Polytechnic State University, San Luis Obispo; and the University of California, Santa Cruz. The results of the California early outreach program are encouraging. Through exposing students to the demands of campus life in advance, before they are threatened by the usual academic penalties, early outreach programs ease the transition process for underprepared students and thus promote retention. The retention rate for program students in 1980–81 was 93 percent as compared with 65 percent for other students and the rate of transfer to a four-year institution for program students was 38 percent as compared with less than 10 percent for other students at Monterey Peninsula College ("Institutional Research . . . ," 1982).

One key factor in the early outreach program is the movement by transfer institutions to provide information about the benefits of academic support programs to students as early as the ninth grade. Yet another successful strategy is the emphasis on individualization. Each student in the program is expected to initiate a transition plan. In fulfilling the plan, students are exposed at each stage to the expectations and demands of the next step on the educational ladder. They are also given academic support such as tutoring and advising as deemed appropriate on the basis of their readiness to move from one step to the next. Lastly, the members of the ad hoc committee serve as advocates for students in the program, ensuring that proven academic support services are provided and students are continuously monitored during their tenure at the transfer institution. This monitoring process includes an exit step in which students leaving the institution are required to talk to a college official to ensure that an alternative plan for reentry is developed if appropriate.

Throughout this transition process, transfer institutions will be better able to respond to the specific academic support needs of students if they have the appropriate data for each student. For a significant number of newly admitted students, this data can be collected through the early outreach program. Careful analysis of the data can guide institutions in developing activities that can improve student retention.

Specific activities in each step of the transition process in the California program may be of interest and so are highlighted here. In April of each year, students are identified and nominated by mathematics and science teachers in the local unified school districts and two-year colleges. Counselors and other staff responsible for working with underrepresented groups also nominate students. Project staff (or often the coordinator for academic support services) interview each nominee and make a decision to accept or refer a nominee to other, more appropriate opportunities. Students selected for the program receive a formal letter of acceptance including instructions for the next step in the transition process.

Project staff (science instructor, academic support coordinator) work with students to identify their academic backgrounds, career goals, strengths and weaknesses in mathematics and science, and need for tutorial and other ancillary instructional support. The results of this assessment, which can be updated, serve as students' initial academic profiles. Students develop a plan for transition that will serve as the basis for monitoring and tracking their progress in achieving their transition objectives. The plans are designed to be updated at each step in the transition process. Students' activities are monitored to check on their progress and level of participation in the transition process.

Students may participate in the following support activities on an interest or need basis.

- Campus visits
- Academic advising from appropriate faculty—who receive academic and other personal information on these students before meeting with them—at the transfer institution
- Tutorial assistance if a need for extra help is demonstrated
- Enrichment workshops and forums conducted by mentors who explain some of the major issues in mathematics and science careers, and help students relate those concerns to their educational experiences and explore employment opportunities
- Academic and career counseling on required and appropriate support courses for their major

Students complete and mail their applications to transfer institutions. Attention is focused on meeting all important deadlines. Tracking and monitoring of students continues to ensure that the elements of students' transition plans are addressed. Updates and major changes in the plan can and most often will occur.

Staff at the transfer institution provide advance information and relevant advice on students' applications for admission and financial aid *before* a final, formal decision is made. Staff from both the admissions and the financial aid offices work with students to promote a positive admissions decision. In cases where the decision is negative, students receive help in developing an alternative transition plan which would enable them to overcome current obstacles. Students' progress is monitored for two years after enrolling in a transfer institution to ensure completion of goals.

Summer Academic Enrichment Programs: A Case Study

The more effective summer academic enrichment programs offer a collage of academic, environmental, and cultural experiences to prepare participants for the demands, pressures, and concomitant adjustments of being a college student. For academically underprepared students, this unique summer educational experience can be a vital academic bridge in providing skill development and acclimation to the university environment.

Collins (1982, p. 81) identifies objectives for prefreshman summer programs.

- Provide extended orientation to college life and requirements
- Evaluate student strengths and weaknesses
- Develop sound study habits
- Improve basic skills
- Improve attitudes and expectations about college work

In attempting to meet these and other objectives, many institutions employ a variety of strategies to maximize the efficacy of summer enrichment programs. Programs vary in duration, content, and intensity. Some programs are offered over a series of weekends during late summer. These weekend programs generally offer prospective students and their families an opportunity to visit the campus, tour various departments, receive academic advising, talk with faculty and student government leaders, seek and—it is hoped—secure housing, follow up on financial aid and admissions applications and preregister for fall courses. Usually, depending on campus and family fiscal resources, the program is residential. Campuses taking this generalized approach often provide many alternative dates in order to work around students' summer employment and family vacation plans.

A more comprehensive and more successful approach for academically underprepared students, however, is the four- to five-week residential program which emphasizes integrated language arts development. The summer educational experience program at California State University, Chico is a curriculum-based program focusing on reading, writing, and study skills. The curriculum package for each of these components is developed in conjunction with academic departments. The course is offered through the continuing education department, is assigned a unit value of eight, and can be taken as either a credit or a noncredit course.

Identifying Participants. Sixty to one hundred participants selected on the basis of demonstrated need, that is, academic underpreparedness and/or need for emotional support, are identified by the educational opportunity program outreach and admissions unit of the campus. These students are academically capable but, either because of environmental factors or poor academic preparation, need assistance to pursue their educational goals. The criteria for screening and selecting program participants include high school or community college transcripts, test scores, counselor recommendations, and an autobiographical statement or personal interview with program staff. When they are identified by the college outreach team, students are informed that participation in the summer program will enhance their ability to perform effectively in college. Some are informed that their admittance to the university is contingent upon participation in the program. This explicit statement at the outset of the goals, expectations, and anticipated outcomes of the program helps demystify the experience for students.

Integration of Course Work. The course is systematically planned so that teachers in each of the academic components are familiar with one another's teaching methods. The components use common and interrelated materials yet are organized to avoid unnecessary repetition and overlap. To integrate skills development with content course work, material for the skills areas is based on lectures in a variety of general studies areas to which students will be exposed while at the university. Lectures are offered from four disciplines (mathematics, geological sciences, political science, and humanities and fine arts), to correspond with weekly study formats.

Students attend classes a minimum of five hours per day, five days per week. In addition, attendance is required at one evening laboratory period of two and one-half hours per week in the student learning center. Students live in dormitories and attend specialized workshops on such topics as early career exploration, personal budgeting, and a general studies overview conducted by student services personnel one evening a week to introduce or reacquaint them with the survival skills necessary to decode and adapt to independent university living. On weekends, cultural and recreational activities provide a refreshing balance, ease alienation and boredom, as well as promote a cohesive group atmosphere among participants while acclimating them to the surrounding community and environs.

Assessing Students' Needs. Because diagnosis is a critical dimension of any support activity for academically underprepared students, assessment is a part of each component of the course and the results are used in counseling and advising sessions throughout students' development. The Informal Reading Inventory and the Stanford Diagnostic Reading Test, when used with other instruments, appear to be useful in improving the reading levels of students. Assessment results provide diagnostic tools which are discussed at week-in-review staff meetings during which common information is shared and formulas for treatment agreed upon and prescribed.

Funding. Funding for the course is generated through summer session full time equivalencies in the form of financial aid, parent support, and institutional contributions. Total cost per student for fees, room and board, books, supplies, and miscellaneous expenses is $1,100.

Evaluation. To evaluate the success of the program, longitudinal data on students' postsecondary experience is assessed and examined by the Educational Opportunity Program staff in consultation with campus testing office, learning center, continuing education, English, and education department personnel. In comparing the performance of academically underprepared students who have participated in the program with that of students with similar academic preparation who have not attended a program of this type, certain inferences can be drawn.

- Summer program participants outperform nonparticipants as measured by units attempted and passed and overall grade point average.
- Program participants benefit from their familiarity with the campus and community environment. Because their adjustment problems are less severe than those experienced by nonparticipants, program participants are more confident and self-motivated and seek assistance when necessary.

- After matriculation, program participants maintain a close relationship with one another. Often they tend to study together and reinforce each other academically and emotionally. This provides stability and promotes persistence.
- Program participants provide positive role models for other students with similar backgrounds. Often they become tutors, peer counselors, or learning assistant aides to help other students pursue their educational goals.

Statistical comparisons between these two groups are difficult to establish because of the lack of an adequate control group. Given past experiences and observations, we are confident, however, that summer academic programs such as the one at California State University, Chico and the nationwide Upward Bound Program have a major impact in reinforcing academically underprepared students' chances for success at the university level. Such programs are, therefore, cost effective, despite the fact that they are expensive and require a high level of institutional support and endorsement. Early planning is the key to effectively involving all segments of the university in summer enrichment programs which are most effective when everyone shares a sense of ownership and feels that they have an investment in this educational enterprise.

Ancillary Instruction

Monterey Peninsula College, a two-year institution, has implemented an intense learning experience—the Immersion Curriculum—in which academically underprepared students are immersed in a single course for a specific period of time. The goal is to improve the capacity of existing developmental courses to teach academic competencies necessary for successful entry into transfer colleges' mathematics, science, and English curriculum. Students select the immersion program by choice. Usually these students are academically underprepared or frightened of some or all of the courses. They are immersed first in a forty-hour mathematics and then a forty-hour science course during the semester. English competencies are taught in the mathematics and science courses using content and concepts from these disciplines. The Immersion Curriculum can be repeated until the student demonstrates the competencies deemed necessary by faculty for academic success. The decision to move into other college courses is made by the student and an instructor. Students who complete all the program requirements of the Immersion Curriculum have an 87 percent retention rate at the college, which is considerably higher than the norm for the campus.

Expectations. The courses are taught in a no-nonsense manner; the aim is to acquire specific academic competencies in each discipline. Upon completing the courses, students should:

- Know how to reconcile and apply principles and laws
- Know how to solve problems using mathematics and scientific methods
- Know how to perform basic and/or advanced arithmetical operations, fractions, percentages, and word problems
- Know how to communicate what is learned orally and in writing
- Know how to read when studying
- Know how to develop and organize thoughts and information
- Know how to write a complete sentence, paragraph, and essay
- Understand how to manage study time, use instructional resources, prepare for tests, and take suitable notes

Instructional Approaches. The program's instructional strategy employs two main approaches: the initiative method through which teachers design activities that encourage students to ask questions, become curious, imagine, and begin to initiate the need to know; and the instructive method through which teachers teach competencies and content. Students are active rather than passive in the courses. They observe, speak, demonstrate, produce, read, analyze, solve problems, and write. Teachers are also active and engage in the same activities as the students. The program includes films, guest speakers, and frequent visits to the college library as well as field trips to enrich learning. Classrooms feature pictures, symbols, designs, colors, and images that illustrate and reinforce mathematics and science concepts.

Another important and proven ancillary instructional method is structured tutorial laboratories in areas in which students are having problems. Such a laboratory is required of all students taking developmental mathematics courses at Monterey Peninsula College. The laboratory is directly under the control and direction of the classroom teacher who, in designing tutorial activities to help students overcome problems experienced in the course, works with the learning manager, usually a respected member of the faculty who supervises the laboratories. Teachers thus direct the learning manager as to what each student needs to work on. The learning manager sets up the tutorial session, directs the work of the tutors, and informs the teacher of each student's progress on a weekly basis.

The tutorial laboratory functions as a direct instructional resource for the classroom teacher who can both focus on the objective of the course and help students individually. Students are able to accelerate their learning as well as learn how to learn through the individualization of the laboratory format. Because the tutorial laboratories are a regular part of the divisional offerings and are controlled by the classroom teacher, they have the support of the faculty, a factor critical to the success of the program.

Ancillary instruction, when geared to the needs of the underprepared students and integrated into the school's curriculum, can do much to promote the success and retention of these students.

Conclusion

Each of the three approaches to academic reinforcement for academically underprepared students outlined in this chapter—early outreach, summer programs, and ancillary programs—can result in a solid, comprehensive academic support program which eases the transition process for these students. Perhaps the greatest drawback of these approaches is the professional and financial commitments which they require on the part of the institution (Turner, 1977, p. 204). In some cases, institutional structures may have to be modified to accommodate such a new approach. In any case, none of these approaches should be implemented without a clear understanding of these costs and a genuine commitment from staff and students. Although outcome data on the effectiveness of a particular approach may support continuation of a program once it is adopted, all programs should be constantly monitored and evaluated and modified when appropriate.

Future trends in academic support programs will certainly be based on a recognition of the advantages of early outreach programs and of the need for establishing functional partnerships between all educational systems as well as for innovative instructional approaches and aggressive academic assessment and counseling. In some cases, institutions will be forced to implement changes as the public demand for better educational outcomes and improved educational opportunity grows. Whatever the case, as colleges and universities continue to reexamine their mission within the current climate of educational reform, they will discover that academic reinforcement programs can provide effective support services to underprepared students which promote their success and boost retention rates.

References

Browne, L. F. "Midpoints Versus Endpoints: Recruitment and Admissions Versus Retention and Graduation." Pasadena: Office of Secondary Relations and Special Programs, California Institute of Technology, 1980.

Collins, W. "Developing Basic Skills Through a Learning Center Summer Program." In L. Noel and R. Levitz (eds.), *How to Succeed with Academically Underprepared Students*. Iowa City, Iowa: American College Testing Program National Center for Advancement of Educational Practices, 1982.

"Institutional Research Report on the Rate of Retention and Transfer." Monterey, Calif.: Office of Special Support Services, Monterey Peninsula College, 1982.

McCadden, J. "Team Teaching the Basic Skills." In L. Noel and R. Levitz (eds.), *How to Succeed with Academically Underprepared Students*. Iowa City, Iowa: American College Testing

Program National Center for Advancement of Educational
Practices, 1982.

Martin, D., Blanc, R., and De Buhr, L. "Supplemental Instruction: A Model for Increasing Student Performance and
Persistence." In L. Noel and R. Levitz (eds.), *How to Succeed with Academically Underprepared Students*. Iowa City, Iowa:
American College Testing Program National Center for Advancement of Educational Practices, 1982.

Noel, L., and Levitz, R. (eds.). *How to Succeed with Academically
Underprepared Students*. Iowa City, Iowa: American College
Testing Program National Center for Advancement of Educa-
tional Practices, 1982.

Perry, S. "Teaching Underprepared Students Without Com-
promising Standards." *Chronicle of Higher Education*, 1983, *26*
(14), 25–27.

Rivera, E., Jr., "New Programs for the Nitty Gritty College."
Black Academy Review, 1970, *1* (2), 30.

Roueche, J. E., and Watkins, K. "A Commitment to Great
Teaching." *Community and Junior College Journal*, 1982, *53* (1),
22–25.

Turner, M. E. *A Comparative Survey of Some Measures of Academic
Achievement and Retention Rates of Black Students in Two Predominately White Institutions of Higher Education*. Unpublished doctoral dissertation, Department of Education, Stanford University, 1977.

Weinstein, C. "A Metacurriculum for Remediating Deficits in
Learning Strategies of Academically Underprepared Stu-
dents." In L. Noel and R. Levitz (eds.), *How to Succeed with
Academically Underprepared Students*. Iowa City, Iowa: American
College Testing Program National Center for Advancement
of Educational Practices, 1982.

15

Teaching and Learning

John E. Roueche
Suanne D. Roueche

No matter the organizational or programmatic efforts made to set higher standards and to more closely evaluate educational outcomes, the unquestionable pivotal point in the educational system has been, and will always be, the teacher. Without that individual's determination to demand more of students, to make them work hard, and employ instructional strategies that provide a supportive and caring learning environment directed toward those ends, all of the rhetoric about improving our colleges will be for naught. As Ernest Boyer of the Carnegie Foundation for the Advancement of Teaching states: "All the talk about excellence is superficial unless we acknowledge that good teaching is at the very heart of good schools." ("Can the Schools Be Saved?" 1983). The teacher is the key.

Admittedly, teaching is a complex activity; it is, therefore, shortsighted and narrow-minded to assign simple cause and effect relationships to either successful or unsuccessful outcomes of the teaching process. However, it is clear that we now need to take a renewed interest in investigating what happens in the classroom and what variables appear to have the most impact on teaching and learning experiences. It is, after all, the knowledge of what works in the classroom and the ability to implement that knowledge that makes for effective teaching and the kinds of positive learning experiences that promote retention.

Since Rosenthal and Jacobson's (1968) isolation and analysis of the impact of teacher expectations on student performance, other studies have involved similar investigations, developing and expanding upon their initial findings. Although methodological and conceptual problems exist in such studies, it is clear that teachers significantly affect student performance by both verbally and nonverbally acting out their personal expectations of their students' abilities. For example, studies demonstrate that teachers tend to praise more frequently and in a different way those students to whom they assign higher levels of expectation than students from whom they expect less (Brophy and Good, 1970). Studies also determine that teachers give more attention to students whom they consider to be very bright (Rothbart, Dalfen, and Barrett, 1971). Teacher expectations do indeed correlate with level of student performance, indicating that these expectations provide some students with a psychological and academic boost but inhibit others.

Students enter classrooms with expectations of their own; these expectations influence how favorably they react to their instructors (Feldman, 1976). Accordingly, teachers are found to react to students' positive and negative expectations, performing (as could be expected) better in response to students' positive expectations (Feldman and Prohaska, 1979). The resulting phenomenon is obvious. Clearly, although the variables and related problems inherent in such studies are significant, these studies demonstrate that the impressions that students and teachers have of one another are important predictors of the performance of both.

Expanding upon this notion, numerous studies focus on the formal and informal interactions of students and teachers in and out of the classroom for clues as to what influences student persistence. While variables such as size of institution and students' aspirations and academic histories account for some variations in findings, it has been determined that: (1) informal outside-of-class contacts with faculty are positively associated with student satisfaction with the total college experience (Wood and Wilson, 1972; and Pascarella and Terenzini, 1976); (2) the quality of these informal interactions may be as important in influencing potential dropouts to remain as the frequency (Pascarella and Terenzini, 1976); (3) student-teacher informal contacts appear to make the most significant impact upon persistence when students are apparently withdrawal-prone (Tinto, 1975); and (4) informal interaction correlates with student satisfaction with classroom instruction, as well as with other variables in the college environment (Astin, 1977).

Although students enroll in courses for a variety of reasons, they share a common interest in receiving a passing grade for their work. Logically, the teacher and the institution also wish for grades that represent acceptable student performance. Numerous studies provide significant evidence that there is a strong correlation between academic success and persistence in the academic arena (Forrest, 1982; Aitken, 1982; and Bean, 1983). Students tend to remain in environments where they feel comfortable and satisfied; meeting personal and academic goals in those environments further strengthens commitment to the task at hand. Achieving the twin goals of retaining students and teaching them necessitates a look at teaching strategies that work toward the achievement of both goals at once.

In this chapter, we will explore three key human and professional qualities involved in teaching excellence (1) love and concern for others, (2) the ability to create a positive learning environment, and (3) commitment to teaching as a profession. Teachers who possess these qualities get students involved, make the classroom a place where students want to be, and provide an image of professional commitment to teaching. After first defining each quality, we will describe specific teaching behaviors and strategies that exemplify each of these qualities. These strategies work with the diverse student populations now arriving at open-door colleges as well as at the most selective institutions of higher education. The chapter concludes with a consideration of why, in light of the recent National Commission on Excellence in Education report (1983), these qualities are more important to good teaching today than ever before. With a keen eye toward retention, we must make conscious efforts to understand both the nature of good teaching and the special conditions that make teaching particularly challenging now.

Love and Concern for Others

The first quality of excellent teaching is the very basic human characteristic of love and concern for others; it is demonstrated by making an active effort to get involved with students. Rousseau's observation that, "In order to teach French to Johnny, it is imperative that the teacher first know Johnny," is no less true today than it was two centuries ago.

Involvement with Students. Efforts to get to know students, initially by name and then through more personal knowledge of their background and interests, demonstrate caring and concern. Instructors who spend the first day of class introducing themselves and introducing students to each other do not lose valuable time that might be spent covering content; rather they lay important groundwork whereby the students sense some tie to the class and to the teacher.

Students are a lot like people; they enjoy being called by their own names and being recognized as individuals. They are genuinely impressed when others remember seemingly unimportant pieces of information about them. Instructors who take the time to make this information a part of their general picture of the individual student become important persons themselves in the student's mind. Students will then have difficulty rejecting instructors' requests or not believing in their optimism for them; they will work harder to be worthy of the attention and interest offered.

Many of us have fond remembrances—especially those of us who have chosen teaching as a profession—of teachers who took a special interest in us and thereby affected our future career decisions. We have recollections of instructors who made content come alive. We remember others whose teaching skills may have been woefully inadequate but who made up for this and engendered interest in their subjects by demonstrating extraordinary personal kindness. The key to the impact of such interest is that such an obvious willingness on the part of a teacher to go beyond what is required is often unexpected.

Sam Postlewaite of Purdue University in West Lafayette, Indiana, developed a technique of standing at the door of his classroom for the first few days of class and greeting students as they came in, linking names and faces and learning something about each student. He was able, in this manner, to learn the names of all the students in very large lecture classes. Other activities to further reinforce linkages between student names, faces, and backgrounds can be conducted during the first days of class. Students can be asked to interview each other and report on their findings; the instructor can be included in the interview sessions. Information cards can be completed during the first class session, providing the instructor with pertinent information for student files: information about family and job responsibilities; prior course work, completion dates, and grades; current course work; nicknames; and hobbies or special interests. Additional information might include any remarks that the student wishes to make about the present course. Most importantly, information cards should include addresses and telephone numbers so that the students can be easily contacted.

Many students behave in ways that promote their own failure, such as missing class and not completing their work on time. Oftentimes this behavior is the direct result of a lack of faith in their own ability to be successful which leads them to decide not to try. They thus absent themselves from the learning process. It is the responsibility of the instructor to contact such students, either by telephone or by letter, outlining a strategy for their return to class, explaining the assignments that would bring their work up-to-date, making plans for completing the work, and getting a commitment from them to return to class at the following (or an agreed-upon) class period. Central Oregon Community College in Bend, reports dramatically improved freshman-to-sophomore year retention rates (222 percent) after implementing a faculty decision to contact absent students the very first time they miss a class (Weber, 1981).

It is extremely important, however, that this outside-of-class contact be kept confidential; that is, the instructor should talk directly with the student. Leaving a message about a concern over absences, tardiness, or incomplete work is unacceptable. No one but the student should have this information.

Another aspect of excellent teaching is that the instructor can make the classroom a place where students will want to be. Initially, getting involved with students will help set the climate for continuing strategies to keep the classroom environment a pleasant place in which to work. Teaching behaviors that promote positive experiences are merely extensions of careful thinking about what makes any experience pleasurable.

Celebrating the Experience. Teaching and learning should be a pleasurable experience. When the first universities were established, education was a lively, celebratory experience. Vestiges of those first celebratory experiences are often exhibited today in the teaching and appreciation of music, art, and drama as well as in a variety of other disciplines. Reminders of those first experiences also exist today at college football games: in the band, the cheerleaders, the thousands of fans, and in the excitement that such support brings to the players. Motivation of that magnitude happens rarely; players cannot ignore the enthusiasm, and their playing cannot help but be affected by the excitement.

Instructors must bring that same excitement to their work; they must practice the kind of celebration that clearly demonstrates a deep love of their subject and an interest in the teaching of it. Drumheller (1977) speaks of the interest and value of content as major contributors to that excitement; contending that instructors should ask themselves two questions every time they enter the classroom: Am I teaching anything of *value* to anyone today? Am I teaching anything of *interest* to anyone today? Negative answers to these questions probably mean that a most familiar student question, "Will I miss anything by not being in class today?" will also receive a negative response.

Nonverbal Behavior and Classroom Control. Instructors must be in charge of the classroom, which means maintaining eye contact with students, looking for inattention or boredom, and moving around the room or at least changing positions to give some animation to the lecture or discussion. This nontraditional behavior of moving around among students may be somewhat unnerving; students are more accustomed to distance between the instructor and the class. Yet the close proximity of instructor to student sharpens student alertness: moving about the class-room is a valuable way of keeping inattention to a minimum.

It is also important that the instructor control mannerisms that suggest nervousness or insecurity about the subject or the learning activity. Videotaping one's classroom may be painful, but analyzing one's own performance can produce valuable insights. Clenching fists or twisting jewelry can be distracting and, more importantly, can indicate that the instructors are not in control of themselves much less of class activity. Students respond more positively to instructors who demonstrate that they can maintain such control.

Model Behavior to be Respected and Imitated. Instructors should demonstrate behaviors that they wish students to learn and display. These behaviors include avoiding erroneous assumptions about a person's knowledge and ability, listening, showing respect for students as adults, being positive, and being dependable.

Instructors are human, too; they tend to carry around with them the baggage of stereotypes about dress, gender characteristics, age, race, and ethnicity. While making judgments is a natural behavior, applying these untested assumptions in the classroom can jeopardize student success. For example, ascribing strong self-concepts and responsible behaviors to older students on the basis of their age overlooks the strong likelihood that they are insecure about their ability to do well in their return to the classroom and are as likely to avoid the learning process by being absent or late with assignments as are much younger students. Tendencies to assign interests and values to particular ethnic or racial groups or to males or females on the basis of some assumed learned or instinctual bent are very risky. Expectations of tardiness or absences from particular students, beliefs that men and women naturally prefer different learning activities (for example, women prefer and will do better at writing assignments than will men; men will more likely perform better in mathematics or science-related tasks) are examples of such unfounded instructional judgments which, if acted upon, will alienate students.

Another problem is that instructors are not generally well regarded for their listening skills. Koile (1977) finds that teachers are among the poorest of listeners. Good listeners do not spend listening time merely planning their next comments. Good listening means that students know that they are getting through, that they are being heard, and that the instructor will respond in some meaningful way based upon what was heard. That is, the instructor is listening in an empathic manner and is manifesting genuine interest.

Attentive listening can also be demonstrated in the instructor's response to a student's written work. Writing assignments should not be made unless there is an accompanying commitment to read them. Written assignments deserve to be carefully and thoughtfully read, with instructors going beyond making determinations about the level of literacy demonstrated in the writing and considering the student's ability to think and conceptualize in print. Appropriate comments *throughout* the text will demonstrate to the student that the work has been read and given thorough, thoughtful consideration. In our extensive experience looking at returned student papers from all over the country, we find that many carry no comments beyond the first one or two pages, signifying woeful faculty inattention that translates into a lack of caring.

Respectful Behavior. Sometimes instructors, either in light conversation or in conference with a student, are negligent in demonstrating even the most basic of manners. A colleague passes by and the instructor fails to introduce the student, begins a conversation, and ignores the student altogether. Or, instructors unwittingly assign a special importance to the telephone and allow it to take precedence over a prearranged student conference. Taking the time to introduce students to colleagues and include them in the conversation briefly or holding all calls until the conference time is completed is another way of saying that the student is important and that the student has the instructor's complete attention for the time reserved.

Excellent instructors provide students a place in their adult world by treating them as they would any adult they care about or admire. Any demonstration—calling them by name on campus, spending time with them in informal settings, mentioning news that you have received about them or about their accomplishments—is a small but valuable way of acknowledging their importance.

Being Energetic. Students deserve to find a pleasant, energetic instructor in class every day. There are, obviously, occasions when that expectation is difficult to meet; however, as small an activity as spending the first few minutes just before or after class in small talk with students will often serve to provide the lift needed to continue. Laughter in the classroom is therapy; the old adage that learning is a grim and serious business is deadly, and all too often borne out in classroom behaviors. An instructor's willingness to laugh—oftentimes at himself or herself—and to encourage students to laugh is a wonderfully healthy way to lighten many class activities. Jokes, while not the only vehicle for promoting laughter in the classroom, are often the most memorable parts of a teacher's presentation, particularly when they are linked to more serious and important information.

Positive Learning Environment

Students deserve a positive environment for learning, a classroom free of negative and humiliating experiences. James Kinneavy, a distinguished professor of English at the University of Texas at Austin, is the project director of a national study analyzing writing assignments and instructors' written comments on students' papers. As Kinneavy finishes his three-year study, he is finding that most of the comments teachers write on students' papers are not very encouraging. They are generally negative, caustic, and as a result, act as de-motivators for ever writing again (Witte, Meyer, and Miller, 1982).

In the classroom a student should not be submitted to oral humiliation such as that involved in calling attention to mistakes, using punitive or teasing expressions to demoralize, or employing sarcasm to make a point. Humiliation, however, is not tied only to negative instructor behaviors; sometimes students can be humiliated by what appears to be very positive reinforcement. For example, a student who is easily embarrassed by being singled out would not receive a publicly extended compliment well. Such an expression of kindness may not be construed by the instructor as anything but a thoughtful, supportive act, but unless the student has demonstrated that such behavior will be acceptable, it is best to show support and approval in other ways. A safe guide is to use the student's own behavior as an indicator of acceptable instructor behavior; that is, if the student engages in friendly banter, if he or she jokes and exchanges small talk frequently, the chances are good that similar instructor behavior will be readily accepted and appreciated.

Finally, instructors should be dependable. They have a contract with students to be in class, to be on time, and to be available for out-of-class conferences. If teachers are late to their own classes, they can scarcely expect students to be on time and ready for work. Instructors also should be available for posted office hours. When they are unable to keep appointments, they should give appropriate notice to students and arrange for another meeting time. Students who fail to keep appointments or are tardy for instructor-student conferences are not well regarded; the reverse is equally true, with perhaps more damaging consequences.

Moreover, students have a right to expect their assignments to be returned promptly or whenever promised. While keeping commitments is behavior that is expected of students, it is a learned behavior that may well not be in the student's repertoire. It is thus the instructor's responsibility to teach it by modeling it and then demanding it.

Commitment to Teaching as a Profession

The third quality of great teaching is the commitment that teachers bring to their work. There is much talk today about professionalism having gone out of teaching. The news is replete with teacher unions negotiating for fewer hours in the classroom and for fewer hours to be spent in the grading of papers. There are indications that increasing numbers of college instructors have outside interests that have taken priority over their teaching. We at the University of Texas at Austin in the College of Education have a series of posters conspicuously displayed, all with one central theme: Nobody ever said that teaching was going to be easy. The posters typically picture a group of rowdy children in the classroom or a stack of ungraded papers on a teacher's desk, usually accompanied by a teacher sporting a woebegone expression. But no matter what the image displayed, the message is clear and true: *Nobody ever did say that teaching was going to be easy!* Yet there is real concern that the commitment to good—much less great—teaching is being slowly eroded. Powerful data suggest that teaching is losing its image as a profession.

Great teachers make commitments to great teaching; stated simply, they learn about student behaviors. They are interested in defining what conditions and what approaches promote learning, and they seek to apply this knowledge in the classroom. Furthermore, they seek to determine whether or not they have done a good job in their teaching by evaluating their own performance. Call it attention to their own professional growth and development if you will, but it is a commitment to improving their effectiveness as teachers. For our purposes here, we might call these qualities the commitment to effective instruction and to usable evaluation.

Effective instruction is more likely to occur when the instructor has confronted some of the major troublesome realities of student learning behaviors, realities which, if ignored, militate against student success in the classroom. Great instructors acknowledge these realities, then move to deal with them.

They acknowledge that it is realistic to expect a tremendous range of student skill development in any classroom. This is particularly true if the institution has no procedure for pre-assessment and mandatory placement in developmental courses for students who demonstrate poor skill development. Instructors will then be faced with an unmanageable diversity in the classroom and those students who are less prepared will be humiliated by their lack of success and will drop out. In such cases, unless other instructional interventions are applied, expectations that every student will profit from the same instruction and perform at acceptable rates will be unmet.

Another reality which must be confronted is that institutional time settings do not allow all students to meet the same requirements; some learn more quickly than others, and the time necessary to complete assigned tasks will vary considerably from student to student. Research has indicated that students also process information differently; that is, some may not learn as well from the printed page as from audiovisual activities. Such dissimilarities in learning styles require that the instructor be prepared to vary the presentation of content to accommodate each individual student. Other students bring with them a pre-possession for failure that causes them to view success as unde-served, and failure as unsurprising.

In general, students who are now enrolling in college do not read, write, or study as well as students have been tradition-ally expected to do; moreover, they do not listen well and tend to either stop listening or to begin taking notes indiscriminately. Their inability to listen well obscures the important points in lec-tures or discussions, and their inadequate processing of informa-tion results in an unthought-out, random selection of facts. It is in the face of these troublesome classroom realities that many instructors become perplexed and discouraged and entrapped, along with their students, in the Pygmalion phenomenon. In such cases, teacher expectations do much to encourage some students and to discourage others (Rosenthal and Jacobsen, 1968).

It is out of these difficult realities that instructors with an interest in great teaching will seek to provide structure in the classroom. At the base of such structure is the belief that great teaching, through creating a sense of involvement and a sup-portive environment, can make a difference to students. At the very heart of this structure is the belief that students can suc-ceed. Unless the crippling effects of teachers' and students' belief that failure is a given are acknowledged and dealt with in the educational design, attitudinal problems can undo even well-designed systems for learning. Crim (1983, p. 2) believes that students must feel that people who are important to them believe in their goals. This means that the goal of the instructor should be that each student be given every opportunity to learn and be provided with every support possible to meet course require-ments. Crim is faced with learned evidence that things cannot get better, yet he believes that if teachers demonstrate commit-ment, students will respond.

Thus it is that the structure of a class is at first best kept rather inflexible. Students should be required to be in attendance, given assignments with deliberate, built-in successful experiences as lesson components, and carefully monitored through frequent checks on their progress by reviewing daily assignments and testing for mastery. This inflexible approach can be referred to as individualized instruction, although it in no way suggests that students are to be allowed to progress at their own pace unattended for any period of time. Rather it is instruction that has the individual at its center, with the instructor always involved. It is instruction that allows students to progress through sequentially developed steps that move them from the simple to the more complex at a pace and at a level of mastery that both they and the teacher have agreed upon prior to beginning the learning process. Finally, this instruction has the built-ins necessary to help students get over their attitudinal impediments to success.

Individualizing instruction means designing sequential steps that can be attempted and completed at the student's own pace. It is important that the students have some say in selecting valuable and interesting material for that process. The learning activities should be varied to prevent boredom and should be relevant to other courses and to students' personal lives. Learning activities can include lectures, discussion, field trips, individual learning packets, and special projects that combine in-class and extracurricular activities.

Students may work best under an arrangement that allows them to structure their time either within or outside of regular class periods. Such a contract, however, should be very structured, ensuring that the steps for completing the assignments are specific and the completion dates are specified. The timetable can at times be made flexible to accommodate a complicated personal and work schedule.

Assessing Students. In order to know at what point students should begin, it is imperative to assess their skill development level or depth of knowledge about the course content or tasks. They can then begin at a point that will provide some success with the material early on and thus reduce their initial uncertainty about their ability to fulfill course requirements. In addition to assessing cognitive development, the initial information-gathering process should look into any personal or study skills problems that students might have that would negatively or positively affect their work. Open-ended questions with no one correct answer, questions about the kind of reading and figuring that students must do to negotiate daily living activities, are suitable for extracting such information.

Course Goals and Objectives. Students should have some broad-based ideas about what the course is about and the goals and objectives the instructor has for the class. It is not, however, imperative to share every detail; a thick syllabus will most likely scare away even the most motivated of students. Instructional wishes indicating that the student will begin to demonstrate some higher affective levels, including, for example, valuing, organizing, characterizing, are suitable. Cross (1976) identifies goals as the signposts by which students can better see where they are going and can know when they have arrived, thereby experiencing all of the excitement that is generated by reaching a goal.

Communication with Students and Instructors. Students must know that someone is aware of their progress—or lack of it. This takes the responsibility early on from the shoulders of the student and places it upon the instructor, who is responsible for recognizing problems and difficulties. The instructor can then intercede by arranging special conferences and special learning activities and perhaps looking into the student's past work to spot gaps in skills development. As the class continues, however, there will be more occasions to give increasing responsibility to the student to report problems and to become part of the problem resolution: that is, to take more responsibility for his or her own learning. Frequent testing of mastery is imperative; to allow a student to progress through materials that are half-learned is confusing and a waste of precious time and effort. Bloom (1976) speaks to the speed at which a student will process information when the initial tasks are clearly understood and completed. Cross (1976) addresses the danger of testing infrequently, maintaining that mid-semester or final examinations are poor times to discover that students are in trouble. Thus it is that designing a strong management system benefits both instructor and student and is a positive retention strategy.

Students who are having difficulties in one class may be having similar problems in their other courses. Centering upon insights about the student's behavior in other classes may well help avoid nonproductive discussions and give the instructor an effective tool for dealing with the student's problem. Collecting such information about the student's other course work and teachers at the beginning of the term can also provide an instructor with a support group with which to confer.

Attendance Policy. Students may exhibit irresponsible behavior by attending class irregularly. Instructors committed to providing good instruction must have learners to receive it, and it is their responsibility to advise students of their expectations for attendance. That is, students should be informed that tardiness and absences are not appreciated; in fact, those behaviors will produce immediate and decisive action—the student will be contacted, the instructor will expect the student to make up the time, and so forth. Expecting students to be on time necessitates the instructor's arriving on time; ending the class promptly is also indicative of the instructor's commitment to allow students time for between-class activities, provide time for chatting with students following the class period, and so on.

Evaluation. Another component of the commitment to great teaching is the instructor's evaluation of his or her own performance. No matter the quality of teaching being done, unless there is some effort to gauge its impact on students, to determine whether or not the effort made any difference, the excitement of teaching is surely reduced. Of course, the results may not always be as positive as one would wish; in that event, they may be used to improve instructional strategy. It is also important to know what appears to work best so that it can be repeated.

Student evaluation of the class activities, the content, the instructor's performance, and the student's achievement and feelings about the learning process are important. And such evaluation should not be obtained only at the end of the term; rather, frequent feedback from students provides valuable formative evaluation and gets around the time delay that Cross (1976) speaks to in her warnings about infrequent testing of subject mastery.

Instructors should, but rarely do, it appears, know exactly how many students started their class, how many dropped it, how many passed, how many failed, what happened to those who did well, and what happened to those who did poorly. In effect, there is little retention information generated by institutions or by instructors (Roueche, Baker, and Roueche, 1984). It is imperative to know—for the sake of parents, legislators, funding, and for all facets of program evaluation—how many students were able to progress successfully through the course, how many were not, and how well both groups performed in subsequent experiences.

A distinguished professor emeritus of educational administration at the University of Texas at Austin, C. C. Colvert, noted many years ago that he kept up-to-date records of every student he had ever had in his doctoral program; he knew where they were at virtually any moment, and he knew what they were doing. That is rare—in fact, unheard of outside of this wonderful caretaker. He cared for his best and for his worst students. It is easy to care about our successes but also instructive to know what has happened to all our students. This concern for outcomes, for the well-being of our students and for their lives beyond the classroom, must be a part of the teaching process at any level whether postsecondary, secondary, or elementary.

Conclusion

Those of us in the teaching profession who are aware of the research on teaching outcomes over the last ten or fifteen years were not surprised, only justifiably saddened, to learn that the National Commission on Excellence in Education (1983, p. 11) recently pronounced all of American education to be in real trouble. The commission reported that for the first time in our country's history, the current generation of students will not demonstrate the educational skills possessed by their parents. We have watched the downward spiral of standardized test scores since 1963. On a more personal level, as parents of school-age children, we observe a decrease in the numbers and the rigor of the academic courses required of high school students and note an appalling lack of reading, writing, and mathematic skills development, all of which are—remarkably—accompanied by rising grade point averages.

Unfortunately, few of us were particularly shocked by the commission's report. Yet surely no one was untouched by the feeling of panic that the downslide was more pervasive than we had thought and that the damage cannot soon or easily be repaired. Of the general recommendations formulated by the commission—recommendations regarding content, standards, and expectations, time, teaching, leadership, and fiscal support—those having to do with teaching may well be the most important. Undoubtedly, recommendations for attracting better candidates for teacher training, improving existing teacher training programs, and evaluating training outcomes will be given serious consideration; in fact, many states and institutions are, at this writing, involved in testing students prior to their entering teacher education programs and again prior to certification. Efforts to improve the quality of students who are entering the teaching field—to determine that they are literate and that they know their subject matter—are obviously important steps in improving educational outcomes in the future. The truth is, however, that beyond these efforts, there must be a change in traditional teacher training programs that are often bent on preparing teachers in narrow and restrictive content areas. We must broaden these programs to include the teaching of strategies through which teachers can more effectively transmit valuable content to their students and produce more positive and encouraging learning experiences in the classroom.

This discussion of these strategies, of the qualities of great teaching which promote improved retention, could no doubt be enlarged considerably (Roueche and others, 1983), but the points made here are each especially significant. It is our intent to draw attention to them as reminders of the myriad realities and variables that make teaching such a special—although certainly not easy—career. We hope that the career will reestablish itself as a profession. In order to make that happen, we must first make learning our most important product.

References

Aitken, N. D. "College Student Performance, Satisfaction, and Retention: Specification and Estimation of a Structural Model." *Journal of Higher Education*, 1982, *53* (1), 32–50.

Astin, A. W. *Four Critical Years: Effects of College on Beliefs, Attitudes, and Knowledge.* San Francisco: Jossey-Bass, 1977.

Bean, J. P. "Interaction Effects Based on Class Level in an Explanatory Model of College Student Dropout Syndrome." Paper presented at annual meeting of American Educational Research Association, Montreal, Canada, April 1983.

Bloom, B. S. *Human Characteristics and School Learning.* New York: McGraw-Hill, 1976.

Brophy, J. E., and Good, T. L. "Teachers' Communication of Differential Expectations for Children's Classroom Performance: Some Behavioral Data." *Journal of Educational Psychology*, 1970, *61*, 365–374.

"Can the Schools Be Saved?" *Newsweek*, May 9, 1983, pp. 50–58.

Crim, A. A. "Community of Believers." Paper presented at University of Texas at Austin, March 1983.

Cross, K. P. *Accent on Learning: Improving Instruction and Reshaping the Curriculum.* San Francisco: Jossey-Bass, 1976.

Drumheller, S. J. "Global Behavioral Objectives: A Foundation for Teacher Freedom, Instructional Efficiency, and Accountability." *Educational Technology*, June 1977, pp. 6–13.

Feldman, K. A. "Grades and College Students' Evaluations of Their Courses and Teachers." *Research in Higher Education*, 1976, *4*, 69–111.

Feldman, R. S., and Prohaska, T. "The Student as Pygmalion: Effect of Student Expectation on the Teacher." *Journal of Educational Psychology*, 1979, *71*, 485–493.

Forrest, A. *Increasing Student Competence and Persistence: The Best Case for General Education.* Iowa City, Iowa: American College Testing Program National Center for Advancement of Educational Practices, 1982.

Koile, E. *Listening as a Way of Becoming*. Waco, Texas: Regency Books, 1977.

National Commission on Excellence in Education. *A Nation at Risk: The Imperative for Educational Reform*. Washington, D.C.: U.S. Government Printing Office, 1983.

Pascarella, E. T., and Terenzini, P. T. "Informal Interaction with Faculty and Freshman Ratings of Academic and Non-academic Experience of College." *Journal of Educational Research*, 1976, *70*, 35–41.

Rosenthal, R., and Jacobson, L. *Pygmalion in the Classroom: Teacher Expectation and Pupils' Intellectual Development*. New York: Holt, Rinehart & Winston, 1968.

Rothbart, M., Dalfen, S., and Barrett, R. "Effects of Teacher's Expectancy on Student-Teacher Interaction." *Journal of Educational Psychology*, 1971, *62*, 49–54.

Roueche, J. E., Baker, G. A., and Roueche, S. D. *College Responses to Low-Achieving Students: A National Study*. San Diego: Harcourt Brace Jovanovich-Media Systems, 1984.

Roueche, J. E., and others. *Beacons for Change*. Iowa City, Iowa: American College Testing Program National Center for Advancement of Educational Practices, 1983.

Tinto, V. "Dropout from Higher Education: A Theoretical Synthesis of Recent Research." *Review of Educational Research*, 1975, *45* (1), 89–125.

Weber, J. "Bringing Them Back—By Phone." *Innovative Abstracts*, 1981, *3* (10).

Witte, S. P., Meyer, P. R., and Miller, T. P. *National Survey of College and University Teachers of Writing*. Technical report no. 4, Writing Program Assessment Project, University of Texas at Austin, 1982.

Wood, L., and Wilson R. C. "Teachers with Impact." *The Research Reporter*, 1972, *7* (2), 1–4.

16

Career Planning
and Counseling

~~~~~~~~~

Hazel Z. Sprandel

Considering the growing consensus in the literature in recent years that career relevance is a key factor in student retention, it is not surprising that many strategies currently being implemented to improve retention are specifically related to career planning and counseling. In a longitudinal, multi-institutional study of over 100,000 students from 358 two- and four-year colleges and universities, Astin (1975) identifies a number of factors that played a significant part in students' dropping out of school before completing their programs. In this chapter, I will emphasize two of the twelve possible reasons for dropping out of college presented to these students in a follow-up questionnaire: a change in career goals and poor grades.

A change in career goals was reported by 19 percent of the students in the study as a reason for not continuing at their institution. While this might indicate that these students had simply lowered their goals and were no longer seeking the same level of education, it could also be the result of a lack of clear career goals and a concomitant lack of any perceived reason for staying in school.

Poor grades were reported by 22 percent of the respondents as a reason for dropping out. While the exact meaning is difficult to interpret, some of the literature in the educational psychology field suggests that poor grades often result when students are unsure of their educational or career goals and, again, lack a real reason for going to school. In addition, the psychological trauma of poor achievement in college may cause students to question whether or not they belong in school. This is especially true of students who were successful in high school. Boredom with studying and with school was also identified as a reason for dropping out; this would seem to be related to a perceived lack of relevance or of any realistic understanding of the connection between the material being studied and the students' life goals. Again, students who have not yet identified career options may feel trapped and frustrated and may have little or no commitment to school.

In interpreting data from this study, Astin suggests that there is a direct relationship between the educational aspirations of students (the degree they desire to earn) and their career goals. Evidence indicates that students with higher educational goals and well-established career goals are more likely to persist to graduation.

Another factor linked to attrition is a lack of work opportunities, either on- or off-campus. Without such opportunities, students may drop out for financial reasons. Working can also increase persistence because a job can give students a better understanding of the world of work and thus help them set more realistic career goals.

Like Astin, Beal and Noel (1980) find that the student with limited educational plans and without any clear goals in pursuing a postsecondary education is more apt to drop out. In their study of student retention, they asked colleges and universities to report information about retention on their campuses. The factors reported as contributing most to attrition included indecision about major/career goals and limited educational aspirations. These factors had average ratings of 3.93 and 4.09, respectively, on a scale in which 1.00 was the lowest and 5.00 the highest.

Researchers have identified additional factors that may be directly correlated with retention. According to Erikson (1968), if students have not gained a sense of identity in the adolescent stage and have thus been unable to move on to adulthood with its sense of establishment in the world of work, in a family, and in the community, they may not be able to make appropriate use of the college experience. Super and others (1963) also feel that if the exploratory stage of vocational development is prolonged too long and a vocational goal not identified, students are more likely to drop out. Their theory stresses the necessity of the students moving from the exploratory to the establishment stage in order to achieve academically and vocationally.

Hillery (1978) outlines a number of ways in which career planning and counseling have a positive impact on retention. He believes that when educational decisions are made without a career plan in mind, curriculum and courses are often chosen impulsively, resulting in a lack of commitment to academic work. This may lead either to voluntary dropout or enforced dropout prompted by poor academic achievement. Hillery contends that those students who do make career decisions often base them on unrealistic, romanticized notions of what various occupations involve. These students' career plans may be overambitious, particularly if they choose to pursue prestigious careers without considering vocational or technical programs. When such students base their career planning on wish fulfillment rather than reality, confusion, doubt, and dropout are likely outcomes. It is important to make these students aware that they need to consider many factors in making their career plans, including their own values, interests, and abilities, as well as the economic and social realities of the world around them.

Some Basic Principles

It is possible to summarize some of the primary tenets of career planning and counseling that serve as the basis of many of the retention programs described in this chapter. These tenets are derived from the broad field of career development and vocational guidance as well as from studies by professionals in the field of student development (for example, Miller and Prince, 1976).

Career planning and placement services are concerned with offering a comprehensive program of counseling to students, from the freshman who needs guidance in deciding on career goals to the senior who seeks help in writing a résumé. Many of these career planning services base their approach on an explicit theory of career counseling. Crites (1969), for instance, bases his approach to counseling on his belief that emotions and reason enter into any vocational choice and that career choice is a process rather than a one-time event. Accordingly, students should be taught ways to make necessary career choices as they move through different stages of their lives.

Whatever theory of counseling is adopted, career planning should be viewed as a developmental process beginning in infancy and extending throughout life. The number of mid-career changers and persons returning to school in their thirties and forties illustrates this fact. However, because the college years are perceived as being the time that an initial career choice must and should be made, students who are unable to do so are often considered—by themselves and by others—to be deficient in some way. This poor self-concept is not conducive to success and persistence in school.

Experts in the field of vocational development and career counseling generally agree that there are three key areas of exploration involved in career planning.

1. Self-exploration: Who am I? What are my interests? My skills? My values?
2. World of work exploration: What's out there? How can I find out all about it? What written information can I get? Whom can I talk to? What experience can I get through volunteer work, internships, part-time jobs, summer jobs?
3. Decision making: How do I put it all together? How do I know what information is valuable, which options to consider? How do I implement a decision once I have reached one?

Despite the universality of these key career planning concerns, there is no *one* way to reduce attrition through career planning and counseling activities on a campus; each institution must look carefully at the characteristics of its students and of its campus in order to develop the best approach to serve its students.

This careful scrutiny may include a research study of the reasons some students leave the institution and others stay, a survey of existing programs and services on campus, and some decisions about what needs to be done to meet the needs identified through research.

Such a carefully planned and specifically tailored approach to career planning and counseling requires the support and involvement of everyone on campus, including faculty, administrators, students, and student service personnel. An advisory committee or task force appointed by the chancellor or president and including representatives from these four groups can provide this kind of support. This is especially true if those on the task force are persons who have demonstrated an interest in and concern about students' career development. The retention advisory committee of Saint Cloud State University in Minnesota, for example, focuses a great deal of its attention on the university's career resources because committee members regard career planning as a critical factor in increasing retention.

Just as there is no one way to effectively reduce attrition through career planning on an institutional level, there is no one way to work effectively with the career development of an individual student. Because students are not all at the same level of career development, a variety of approaches and programs may be needed.

Regardless of their stage in the career planning process, it is important for students to see the relevance of career development and counseling activities to their own career decision-making process. They need to be aware of the real world of life outside the campus and of how the courses and activities in which they are engaged as students are related to their future lives. The task of engaging students in planning, implementing, and evaluating their own future goals can be accomplished in two main ways: formal and informal learning situations in the classroom, and student services and counseling activities.

Curricular and Classroom Approaches

In writing about the need for change in education, Marland (1974) emphasizes that the concept of the usefulness of education is basic to what was then being called "career education." He believes that students should perceive learning as useful both to themselves and to society. It would seem that such a perception would encourage students to remain in school and complete their education. Marland also suggests that our curricula and schools have not been concretely related to individual learners' aspirations and that career education could assist in establishing this important link.

Hoyt and others (1974, p. 15) define career education as "the total effort of public education and the community to help all individuals become familiar with the values of a work-oriented society, to integrate these values into their personal value system, and to implement these values into their lives in such a way that work becomes possible, meaningful, and satisfying to each individual." This definition clearly delineates the role that an academic/career education approach to career planning and counseling can play in an institution's retention effort. As education becomes meaningful and more personally relevant to students, they are more likely to be persisters and to complete their education.

Since their curricular offerings are not explicitly related to career goals, colleges offering a liberal education have particular cause for concern when it comes to establishing the link between education and the work world. There is, however, a general consensus among educators that a liberal education can lead to a satisfying career. An annual alumni study conducted by Washington University of St. Louis, Missouri, demonstrates that the majority of arts and sciences graduates surveyed are gainfully employed five years after graduation. The results indicate that a significant percentage have entered professional (for example, law, medicine) or other graduate schools, and that they feel that their undergraduate education has prepared them well for this experience. Others find work in areas directly related to their undergraduate majors. The majority of this third group indicates satisfaction with their career options and feel their arts and sciences degrees have been of value to them.

The vocational success and satisfaction of these graduates can be attributed to the fact that many fundamental skills acquired through a liberal arts curriculum are transferable to the world of work. These include writing and analysis, the application of logic and reason, the possession of a historical sense and of cultural awareness, facility with other languages, and a knowledge of mathematics and science. Persons possessing these skills would seem to be well equipped to enter a wide range of careers, particularly if colleges have made special efforts to make them aware of how liberal arts training transfers to the work world.

Numerous postsecondary institutions across the country have implemented programs that combine a liberal arts emphasis with an emphasis on career relevance. Many elements of these programs can be adopted and used successfully by other institutions. One of the more surprising changes of the early seventies was made in the curriculum at Columbia University in New York City. Columbia's course offerings were changed to ensure that undergraduates would henceforth take courses that were more technical and career oriented and graduate students in professional training programs would devote more attention to the humanities. Undergraduates intending to enter the medical field, for example, would begin some of their professional courses as early as their sophomore and junior year, combining these courses with their ongoing liberal arts curriculum. Medical students would continue to take general education courses as well as the highly specific occupational and technical courses required for a degree in medicine. Such a well-rounded curriculum enables students to consider effectively the historical, legal, and ethical aspects of many questions related to the medical field such as eugenics and euthanasia. Columbia believes in the importance of a liberal education with a strong emphasis on the humanities and has found a way to integrate occupational or specialized curricula with its liberal arts curriculum. This innovation was the first major curriculum reform at Columbia since the school pioneered the concept of general education after World War I.

Other colleges and universities have recently initiated similar changes in curricula, all seemingly pointing to a new emphasis on establishing links between course work and careers. Claremont McKenna College in California now combines undergraduate and graduate training in law and business administration. Many other major colleges have adopted an interdisciplinary approach to subject matter.

A second method of combining liberal arts and career study is illustrated by a special project I conducted at Washington University. A booklet, entitled "Using Washington University Majors in Career Planning," was developed to illustrate the connection between career preparation and liberal learning. The booklet includes the following information for each of the major arts and sciences departments: general description of the discipline, possible areas of specializations, employment outlook for graduates, graduate school information, types of work to which this field of study might lead, and sources of additional information. The project also includes contact with graduates of the institution, business and industry leaders, faculty members, and student development personnel.

Chatham College in Pittsburgh, Pennsylvania, a women's college with a progressive liberal arts philosophy, articulates its belief in the connection among liberal arts, learning, and success in professional fields in its handbooks and bulletins. These publications emphasize the fact that the skills students develop in their rigorous training in liberal arts courses are invaluable in developing the ability to think critically, analyze assumptions, and communicate well—all skills valued by prospective employers in the business world and other fields.

Community colleges, judging from the inclusion of electives in their descriptions of two-year terminal programs, and from suggestions that students take some courses outside their career fields, recognize the value of a broad-based education.

Another way of introducing career planning into the classroom is to offer career planning courses. Beal and Noel (1980) indicate that 16 percent of the institutions in their survey offered some kind of noncredit course in career planning. Such courses are usually relatively short term yet comprehensive enough to cover the personal, academic, and economic aspects of careers. Still other institutions such as Marquette University in Milwaukee, Wisconsin, offer career planning courses on a credit basis. The amount of credit given for such courses usually ranges from one to three credit hours with the intensity and academic content varying accordingly. Some courses require both extensive self-study and study of the theoretical background of career planning, as well as research into various aspects of the work world; others are more like workshops, requiring little work outside of class. These courses, which may be taught by education, counseling, industrial psychology faculty or by counseling/career planning center staff members, are generally more readily accepted by faculty as legitimate academic offerings if they are offered under a departmental banner.

Acquiring work experience through curriculum-related plans is yet another particularly effective method of acquainting students with various careers. This work experience may include research, volunteer work, work-study assignments, and internships. Washington University, for example, offers a number of such opportunities for students:

1. An undergraduate research assistantship providing firsthand knowledge of and experience in the techniques of scholarly research in fields related to career interests is offered. Some students in this program have coauthored and published research articles before attaining their bachelor's degrees.

2. Volunteer work is arranged in a wide range of settings (medical, social service, law, and others) with credit possible. The student educational service and the campus YMCA-YWCA are both useful to students seeking volunteer experience.

3. Work-study assignments also provide some interesting and enlightening experience to undergraduates. If the work-study coordinator can, for instance, place prospective physics majors in the physics department as assistants or even as clerical workers, they will gain a better knowledge of what it is like to work in the field of physics. Although no credit is given for work-study jobs, students have been able to arrange internships or volunteer work opportunities with credit associated with them as a result of their work-study experience.

4. Internships or practicums are also available through various departmental programs. Typical of these are the internships offered by the Human Services Program and by the Urban Studies Department. In each case academic credit is available

for the internship and supervision is provided by both the agency in which the student is placed and the university.

5. Because a semester or even a year away from campus is an especially worthwhile learning experience, many Washington University students, particularly those interested in law and government, take a semester in Washington, D.C. These students are assigned to work in a government agency or in a legislator's office as aides, thus gaining firsthand knowledge of the governmental process and of a particular facet of government. There are a number of helpful guides to such internships on the market, including the *Directory of Undergraduate Internships* and the *Directory of Washington Internships*, both published by the National Society of Internships and Experimental Education. Some professional societies (for example, American Chemical Society) also publish lists of opportunities within their fields.

Northeastern University in Boston has long been known for its broad-based program of cooperative education. Under the cooperative plan to which the eight day colleges of the university are committed, five years are required to earn the bachelor's degree. After spending the freshman year in full-time study, students spend four years alternating between study and paid employment in business, industry, schools, hospitals, and social service and government agencies. While a full-time study option in liberal arts is available, the majority of students choose the cooperative education program. By the time they graduate, they have gained two years of experience in positions related to their career interests and have also earned a major portion of their own educational expenses.

Many community colleges have demonstrated particularly innovative planning in incorporating on-the-job experiences into their curricula. Lane Community College in Eugene, Oregon, is the career education center for a large part of the state, serving nearly 20,000 students each year. The college offers over forty different career-oriented fields of study, all designed to make the student ready for employment at the end of the program. Lane's concern for the needs of the individual student is demonstrated by the development of several hundred Vocational Instructional Packages (VIPs) stressing on-the-job experiences.

Designed by faculty members with the cooperation of professionals and experts in various occupational fields, each of the more than 800 VIPs allows students to proceed at their own rates, and to leave the program whenever they have met the requirements of the job they wish to enter.

Because many students have been exposed to few—if any—career settings, temporary positions can provide an understanding of new areas of the world of work. Part-time summer positions are also helpful to the student seeking vocational goals. Placement services should be encouraged to devote a significant part of their efforts to helping students secure such jobs. The job location and development office of Furman University in Greenville, South Carolina, publishes an annual list of summer employment opportunities, particularly in resort areas, including names, addresses, salaries, and living possibilities for students.

Student Services/Counseling Approach

While career planning is increasingly being integrated into the classroom and curriculum, it has traditionally been the responsibility of those working in student services areas including counselors, placement directors, residential housing directors, career specialists, and orientation directors. The range of student services and counseling approaches to assisting students in their career planning that has evolved over the years is quite extensive.

Many colleges and universities use various types of tests in their attempts to provide effective career planning and placement. These include the Strong Campbell Interest Inventory and Holland's Self-Directed Search to determine career interests; the Adjective Checklist to assess personality characteristics; the Myers-Briggs Type Indicator to provide a better understanding of personal likes and dislikes; and many other vocational interest and personality tests as well as aptitude or achievement tests. In most instances, the counselor shares test results with students and outlines additional information students need in order to make a decision or additional steps they might take to gain a better understanding of the world of work. At some universities, counselors videotape their interpretations of common test results and provide personal counseling.

In any case, care must be taken in interpreting test results for students. Sodetz and Vinitsky (1977) report on two commonly used approaches to Strong Campbell Interest Inventory test interpretation: the differentialist view and the developmental view. They prefer the developmental approach supplemented by Gestalt techniques to enhance and facilitate awareness. Such an approach can help students clarify conflict between what they want to do and what they feel they should do and can increase their awareness of their own self-concept, self-ideal, and decision-making style.

Workshops covering subjects ranging from personal values to résumé writing are another widely used approach to career planning. Washington University's career planning and placement services offer an extensive series of workshops including: basic interviewing skills, career alternatives for educators, effective résumé writing, interviewing for the business world, making career choices, summer jobs and internships, and others. Workshop offerings, which can be planned in response to specific student needs as identified from needs assessments or in response to student requests, should be scheduled at times convenient for students. Programs such as Walz's Life Career Development Systems can also be very effective.

Beal and Noel (1980) report that orientation programs often play a critical role in career planning and that early orientation efforts have proven helpful in reducing attrition, especially for students undecided about their educational goals. To encourage such students to seek help in vocational decision making early in their college lives, an introduction to career planning and counseling should be a part of orientation activities.

The use of media and other technological innovations has opened the door to exciting new possibilities in career planning and placement. There is a wide range of printed materials (brochures, books, publications, and so on), film strips, and videotapes about career options available offering a comparatively low-cost way to provide current information about the world of work.

The computer has made it possible to engage students in career planning in a way that appeals to them and provides them with the most current information. Particularly stimulating is a system that interacts with the user, like the American College Testing (ACT) Program DISCOVER system now in use at the St. Louis Community College at Meramec. DISCOVER's occupational file contains information about more than 400 of the nation's current vocations as reflected in over 1,000 job titles. The user can receive answers to a wide range of questions about each occupation, such as: What do these people do? Where do they work? What is the work setting like? What are ways of getting training? What is the salary range nationally? What is the employment outlook? These occupational files are updated annually as part of the license agreement; users can be assured they are receiving the latest information available.

A similar delivery system, the System of Interactive Guidance Information (SIGI), available through Educational Testing Service and in use in a number of postsecondary institutions, can provide career information and teach decision-making skills to large numbers of students.

Graduates of postsecondary institutions can also play a vital role in career planning and counseling for students. Washington University's ACCESS program and the career advisory network at Dartmouth College in Hanover, New Hampshire, have established systems whereby counselors can arrange connections between students seeking information about specific occupational fields and graduates working in these fields. Princeton University in New Jersey encourages its graduates to "adopt" entering freshmen so that they can talk to students and advise them about the world of work. Other institutions use their graduates' association to assist students in obtaining meaningful summer employment. The Cornell tradition summer program at Cornell University in Ithaca, New York, is an example of a program organized to provide both financial support and valuable work experience to undergraduates. This connection with persons who have graduated twenty to thirty years earlier can be of great value to undergraduates. It is unfortunate that some institutions fail to make effective use of the valuable resource that graduates can be; students gain from the relationship with an older graduate of their own school and graduates enjoy the opportunity to meet with a student interested in their profession.

The strategies described are typical of the kinds of career planning programs that institutions can implement for their students both inside and outside the classroom. A number of institutions have attempted to assess the effectiveness of their various career planning services through surveys of seniors and graduates. But it is often difficult to determine a cause and effect relationship between specific career planning services and reduced attrition rates. Self-report by students is one alternative method of assessment. In any case, institutions must continue to explore new approaches while continuously evaluating the impact and effectiveness of each aspect of their career planning services.

Some Thoughts About the Future

There are strong indications that postsecondary educators will continue to be concerned about the problem of retention in the immediate future. If economic conditions remain uncertain and education costs continue to rise, students will continue to question why they are in school and will need greater assurance that their education, be it in a liberal arts college or in a business school, will be useful and relevant in the real world. Thus, it will be ever more important to plan and implement career planning and counseling programs that provide this assurance and encourage students to stay in school. Such programs will include attempts to integrate career awareness into the classroom and curriculum in addition to the traditional student services counseling approach to career guidance.

At the same time, postsecondary institutions must undertake or continue ongoing attrition research through conducting follow-up studies of dropouts, stop-outs, and persisters. ACT's Withdrawing/Nonreturning Student Survey suggests the type of questions that need to be asked of students leaving an institution. The results from such research can suggest new approaches and delivery strategies for career development activities which can be initiated on a trial basis with a limited group of students before being implemented on a large scale. Many of the programs described here were first tried on a limited basis in response to identified student needs. Before SIGI was made available to the total student body at Illinois State University in Normal, it was first used with a group of seventy-two students (Cochran and others, 1977). In such trial runs, programs can be shown to be effective in increasing students' likelihood of staying in school and therefore economically cost effective.

In addition to conducting research on why students leave and why they stay, career planning and counseling professionals must stay abreast of the constantly changing nature of the job market. In fact, they should stay several years ahead of current trends so that they can predict job market trends for students as they enter postsecondary institutions. This is indeed a challenging task requiring the skill of an economist, the abilities of a statistician, the social scientist's understanding of human dynamics, and the seer's talent for prophecy. Sources like the *Occupational Outlook Handbook* are of some help in this task, as are many professional organizations which monitor numbers entering their profession and projected needs. Career counselors can also stay in touch with local needs by working closely with groups such as the chamber of commerce.

It is not enough, however, to be able to foretell trends four years hence; it is also necessary to prepare students for the fact that the world of work changes at a rapid rate and to make them aware that the person who is successful must be able to adapt to this rapid change. If, as Herr (1982) suggests, career development is a lifelong process, then decision-making skills are also of great importance. This suggests that postsecondary institutions need to continue to promote liberal arts programs which help students learn to better know themselves and to develop decision-making skills that will be invaluable at change points throughout their lives. Colleges and universities might also require students to take a decision-making course—under any name—to focus on the personal qualities that play an important part in decision making. *Decisions and Outcomes* (Gelatt and others, 1973), although written for high school use, contains effective exercises in setting priorities, determining personal values and skills, setting objectives, and making choices; it and other such materials can be very useful.

Colleges and universities should also continue to make good use of their graduates in the work world. Because industry and business can make significant contributions to career planning and counseling, the bridges between the educational, industrial, and business worlds should be strengthened.

Because career planning and counseling is important to student satisfaction and retention, it will continue to be a high priority of postsecondary administrators. There is nothing magical about any of the career planning methods described in this chapter but each of them has contributed to retention efforts at postsecondary institutions and may suggest programs and activities that other institutions can implement in their own campaigns to maintain enrollment. Helping students gain a strong feeling that their education is relevant to the world of work beyond the classroom is critical both to their success and to overcoming the attrition problem.

References

Astin, A. W. *Preventing Students from Dropping Out*. San Francisco: Jossey-Bass, 1975.

Beal, P. E., and Noel, L. *What Works in Student Retention*. Iowa City, Iowa: American College Testing Program and National Center for Higher Education Management Systems, 1980. (ED 197 635)

Cochran, D. J., and others. "Effects of Client/Computer Interaction on Career Decision-Making Processes." *Journal of Counseling Psychology*, 1977, *24*, 303–312.

Crites, J. O. *Vocational Psychology*. New York: McGraw-Hill, 1969.

Erikson, E. H. *Identity: Youth and Crisis*. New York: Norton, 1968.

Gelatt, H. B., and others. *Decisions and Outcomes*. New York: College Entrance Examination Board, 1973.

Herr, E. L. "Comprehensive Career Guidance: A Look to the Future." *Vocational Guidance Quarterly*, 1982, *30*, 367–376.

Hillery, M. C. "Maintaining Enrollments Through Career Planning." In L. Noel (ed.), *Reducing the Dropout Rate.* New Directions for Student Services, no. 3. San Francisco: Jossey-Bass, 1978, pp. 13-22.

Hoyt, K. B., and others. *Career Education: What It Is and How to Do It.* 2nd ed. Salt Lake City, Utah: Olympus, 1974.

Marland, S. P., Jr. *Career Education.* New York: McGraw-Hill, 1974.

Miller, T. K., and Prince, J. S. *The Future of Student Affairs: A Guide to Student Development for Tomorrow's Higher Education.* San Francisco: Jossey-Bass, 1976.

Sodetz, A. R., and Vinitsky, M. H. "Expanding Vocational Alternatives: Innovative Techniques for Interpreting the Strong Campbell Interest Inventory." *Vocational Guidance Quarterly,* 1977, *26*, 141-146.

Super, D. E., and others (eds.). *Career Development: Self-Concept Theory.* New York: College Entrance Examination Board, 1963.

17

Residence Halls
and Student Activities

❧❧❧❧❧❧

M. Lee Upcraft

From the beginnings of higher education in America, college administrators and professors have known that a student's education occurs as a result of what happens both inside and outside the classroom. Early American colleges educated students outside the classroom primarily through the concept of in loco parentis whereby colleges acted on behalf of parents, assuming that they must exercise total control over students both inside and outside the classroom if students were to develop good moral character and become truly educated.

For very different reasons, to be elaborated later in this chapter, today's colleges still assume some responsibility for students' education outside the classroom, although the rationale and methodology have changed. The first section of this chapter will review the educational impact of residence halls. I will discuss the powerful role the peer group plays and the ways in which residence halls should be structured to enhance retention, including: strategically assigning students; carefully selecting, training, and supervising residence hall staff; and offering educational programs. The second section will review the educational impact of campuswide—as opposed to residence hall—student activities programs and offer guidelines for developing educational programs. The third and final section will review a model of student development programming appropriate to both residence halls and campuswide student activities planning.

Residence Halls

Historically speaking, nowhere was it easier and more efficient for early American colleges to exercise total control over students than in college dormitories. The "dormitory rationale," as Rudolph (1965, p. 96) calls it, "made possible . . . the supervision and parental concern of the faculty for the well-being of their young charges . . . and taught responsibility." This rationale was basically unchallenged for the next two centuries. Rules and regulations became less restrictive, and the supervision of residents passed from the faculty to persons who were hired solely to keep students in line, such as housemothers, retired military officers, and football coaches (Hardee, 1964). Paid or volunteer students also helped supervise other students. The underlying thought was that there was something inherently good about living in dormitories.

Unfortunately, there was no commonly accepted definition of this assumed goodness and no evidence that living in dormitories in fact resulted in anything good or evil. Thus when students in the 1960s began questioning the concept of in loco parentis, they were successful in eliminating most dormitory rules that infringed on their personal freedom because the dormitory rationale had no evidence to back it up. Rules that infringed on students' privacy were thus eliminated and the freer association of the sexes permitted.

In spite of the lack of evidence, however, colleges still believed that residence halls provided educational advantages as well as a place to eat and sleep. The rationale now became student development and the methodology involved programs that promoted the academic and personal development of students. As this new developmental rationale emerged, housemothers and retired military officers gave way to professional residence educators with graduate training in student affairs and related fields. The role of student supervisors also changed; they could now help students maintain a good living environment, develop activities and programs, and counsel and advise students as well as enforce what few rules were left.

However, in spite of a new rationale and professionally trained residence educators, the inherent good of residence halls was still an assumption, not a fact. Not until the 1970s did research evidence of the educational benefits of residence halls emerge. Astin (1973) finds that students living in residence halls are less likely than commuters to drop out and more likely to attain a baccalaureate degree in four years. Chickering's (1974) highly controlled study involves nearly 170,000 students in one analysis and 5,400 in another. He concludes that even when background variables and other student characteristics prior to attending college are taken into account, students living in residence halls (1) exceed the learning and personal development predicted when their advantages in ability, prior education, extracurricular activities, and community and family backgrounds are considered; (2) are more fully involved in academic and extracurricular activities with other students; and (3) earn higher grade point averages, even when differences in ability are taken into account.

Astin's later study (1977) involved more than 225,000 students from 1961 to 1974. Astin concludes that the most important environmental characteristic associated with finishing college was living in a residence hall during the freshman year. With students' entering characteristics and other environmental measures controlled, living in a residence hall adds about 12 percent to a student's chances of finishing college. Astin concludes that students in residence halls (1) express more satisfaction than commuters with their undergraduate experience, particularly student friendships, faculty-student relations, institutional reputation, and social life; (2) are more likely to achieve in extracurricular areas, particularly in leadership roles and in athletics; and (3) show slightly greater increases in artistic interests, liberalism, and interpersonal self-esteem. Further, he concludes that men in residence halls are more likely to earn higher grades.

Thus, the relationship between residential living and educational benefits, including retention, is established. To be sure, not every student benefits from living in a residence hall. Indeed, some halls can develop a "zoo" atmosphere that may be very destructive. But in general, the evidence is clear: there *is* inherent goodness in living in residence halls, if one assumes that staying in college and graduating are inherently good.

Promoting Retention. Just why do residence halls help retain students? How does the influence occur and how might it be enhanced? The answers lie in students' interactions with one another and with the residence hall environment. Students, particularly freshmen, are susceptible to the press of their living environment, which is a function of architecture, propinquity, and the residents' collective attitudes, values, and needs. Mable, Terry, and Duvall (1980) identify shared goals, shared responsibilities, and shared communication as the basic ingredients for interaction between students and their living environment. These shared experiences are intensified because of the close proximity of large numbers of students to each other.

The scope of students' influence on one another is enormous, ranging from their academic lives to their personal lives. Feldman and Newcomb (1969, pp. 236–237) describe eight functions peer groups serve for students.

1. Help students achieve independence from home and family.
2. Support and facilitate or impede the institution's academic and intellectual goals.
3. Offer students general emotional support and fulfill needs not met by the curriculum, classroom, or faculty.
4. Give students practice in getting along with people whose backgrounds, interests, and orientations differ from their own.
5. Provide students support for not changing.
6. Provide students support for changing. Peer groups can challenge old values, provide intellectual stimulation, and act as sounding boards for new viewpoints, present new information and new experiences to students, help clarify new self-definitions, suggest new career possibilities, and provide emotional support for change.
7. Offer an alternative source of gratification and self-image

and reward a variety of nonacademic interests for students not satisfied academically. Peer groups can also discourage voluntary withdrawal from college for nonacademic reasons.

8. Help students' postcollege careers by providing general social training and developmental ties.

The peer group establishes norms and behavior guidelines that are enforced through direct rewards and punishments. As a result, students transfer some control over themselves to the group and become subject to its influence. In residence halls, friendships become a major influence. However, the most important interpersonal influence is a student's roommate, or, in some circumstances, roommates. Assigning two—or more—freshmen who do not know each other to a room is, indeed, a very strange practice. Persons who have developed over eighteen or nineteen years in a family environment in which they may even have had their own room are put into the unique situation of a residence hall and told to get along. The only other situations where persons are forced to live together this way are in the military and in prison. The resulting adjustment problems can have very powerful effects on students' academic and personal adjustment including the following.

1. Roommates challenge each other's confidence and self-understanding and force each other to become more tolerant and accepting (Heath, 1968).
2. Roommates force each other to express themselves more clearly and sharply (Heath, 1968).
3. Roommates affect each other's attitudes (Vreeland, 1970).
4. Highly dissatisfied pairs of roommates have significantly lower grades than do those roommates who have little dissatisfaction with one another (Pace, 1970).
5. A student's grades are likely to deviate from expectancy above or below in the same direction as those of his or her roommate (Murray, 1961).
6. Significantly higher levels of academic achievement can be attained by middle- and low-achievers by assigning them as roommates to above-average achievers (Blai, 1971; and Ainsworth and Maynard, 1976).

7.   Roommates affect each other's study habits (Hall and Willerman, 1963).

Given the tremendous influence of the peer group, one
might assume that the key to retention in residence halls is simply
putting students together in rooms strung along corridors, and
watching the peer group "do its thing." The evidence, however,
suggests something quite different. First, as seen, peer group
influence is a double-edged sword. Students can influence one
another's grades negatively, punish one another for healthy but
unacceptable behavior, and negatively affect one another's study
habits. Students often leave college because of a lack of success
in dealing with or befriending their peers or roommates. The
peer group in residence halls, left strictly to its own devices, can
be destructive.

Second, there is evidence that the way in which an institution structures its residence hall environment can influence
the academic and personal development of students. Essentially,
a college can affect the residential environment in three key
areas: assigning students to residence hall space; selecting, training, and supervising residence hall staff; and implementing educational and developmental programs and activities.

Assigning Students. The size and composition of a residence
hall floor including such variables as residents' gender, majors,
and academic abilities, as well as the assignment of roommates,
is very influential in personal and academic development. Yet,
too often, little attention is paid to these factors, and architecture and tradition play predominant roles in room assignments.
Just what is known about the different ways of assigning students to residence hall rooms?

Considerable evidence indicates that when students are
assigned by major, academic achievement is improved (Davidson, 1965; Taylor and Hanson, 1971; and Schroeder and Freesh,
1977), and scholarly orientation is greater (Morishima, 1966)
when compared with randomly assigned students. There is also
greater satisfaction with the living environment (Schroeder,
1980; and McKelfresh, 1980). However, if a floor is dominated
by one particular major, students not in that major will expe-

rience less social interaction and be less satisfied with college (Brown, 1968).

There is some evidence that when high-ability students are assigned to the same floor, they earn higher grades than high-ability students assigned randomly (DeCoster, 1966). They report that their living environments are more conducive to study, that they have more informal educational discussions, and find their accommodations more desirable (DeCoster, 1968). They also report their environment as more stimulating and academically oriented (Kaplan, Mann, and Kaplan, 1964).

There is no demonstrated difference in academic achievement between students in coeducational and segregated halls (Linnell, 1972; and Brown, Winkworth, and Braskamp, 1973). However, in just about every way, coeducational halls are better. Students in coed halls, compared to those in segregated halls, have a greater sense of community and more actively participate in hall programs (Linnell, 1972). They also report greater satisfaction with their social lives, have more informal social interaction in the living environment (Corbett and Sommer, 1972; and MacInnis, Byrne, and Fraser, 1980), and are less likely to perceive the other sex in terms of traditional sex-role stereotypes (Young, Campen, and Ray, 1980). However, these researchers report no differences in frequency of sexual intercourse and little dating among residents, refuting the myth popular among some skeptics that coed halls are havens of sexual promiscuity.

Generally, it is not a good idea to create all freshmen floors or to assign freshmen to floors where upperclass students are in an overwhelming majority. A mix of freshmen and upperclass students provides a better living environment, but the evidence regarding academic achievement is mixed (Beal and Williams, 1968; Schoemer and McConnell, 1970; and Upcraft, Peterson, and Moore, 1981).

Every fall thousands of students are placed in overcrowded conditions such as three-person rooms, study lounges, and recreation areas. There is evidence that overcrowding is detrimental to students' privacy, roommate relationships, general satisfaction with the living environment, academic achievement, and retention (McNeel, 1980; Karlin, Rosen, and Epstein, 1979; and Schuh, 1982).

Generally, if roommates choose one another rather than receive random assignments, there is less likelihood of difficulty (Hall and Willerman, 1963). Sharing common socioeconomic backgrounds can lessen incompatibility (Lozier, 1970). Roommates assigned on the basis of preferred characteristics stay together longer and express more satisfaction than randomly assigned pairs (Roby, Zelin, and Chechile, 1977). However, assigning roommates according to self-ratings and ideal ratings (Wetzel, Schwartz, and Vasu, 1979), by birth order (Schuh and Williams, 1977), or by parents' educational level, size of high school enrollment, church attendance, smoking habits, and predicted grades yields no significant differences in compatibility when compared to randomly assigned roommates (Gehring, 1970).

Selecting, Training, and Supervising Staff. Most residence halls are staffed by a professional staff headed by a resident director, head resident, or area coordinator who is assisted by paraprofessional staff, typically known as resident assistants or resident counselors. The professional staff select, train, and supervise these resident assistants, help plan programs, assist students with their problems and concerns, and may even be responsible for overseeing the maintenance of the buildings.

It is the resident assistants, however, who have the direct responsibility for creating a good living environment. These frontline troops who interact daily with residents are typically part-time employees (at worst, volunteers) pursuing an academic career full time. They are not true professionals when one considers their age, experience, amount of time available, and the training they usually receive. But they are typically enthusiastic, eager to learn, and filled with potential.

Resident assistants are asked to do a lot, including (1) provide personal help and assistance; (2) manage and help groups; (3) facilitate social, recreational, and educational programs; (4) inform students about campus life or refer them to appropriate resources; (5) explain and enforce rules and regulations; and (6) maintain a safe, orderly, and relatively quiet environment.

This is a very tall order for twenty-one-year-old juniors and seniors who are also full-time students. They are, in effect, expected to create an environment conducive to personal development and retention; in short, to fulfill the educational objectives of residence halls. Can they do it?

Unfortunately, in many institutions, dedicated young people cannot get the job done because they are not properly supported. This results in an even greater disservice to residents as there is evidence that when resident assistants are doing their job effectively, residents' academic development is enhanced. For example, Upcraft, Peterson, and Moore (1981) find that students who are compatible with their resident assistant earn significantly higher grades than those who are incompatible.

The key to effective resident assistant performance is proper selection, training, and supervision. Unfortunately, selection usually involves a few interviews in the semester prior to taking the job. Training is often nonexistent, or merely entails a few days of covering "nuts and bolts" issues just before classes begin. Supervision may also be nonexistent, amounting to letting resident assistants "do their own thing" with little or no accountability until a crisis develops.

There is some evidence, however, that when selection, training, and supervision are done properly, resident assistants become more effective. A comprehensive selection, training, and supervision model has proven effective in improving resident assistant performance (Upcraft and Pilato, 1982; Upcraft, Pilato, and Peterman, 1982; and Peterman, Pilato, and Upcraft, 1979).

Together with Pilato (1982), I argue that the best way to select resident assistants is to conduct a preliminary screening of candidates and then train them before making a final hiring decision. Professional staff who supervise resident assistants should conduct the selection/training program, which should begin at least six months before the positions open. Training should be conducted in small groups, consist of at least forty classroom hours, and focus on self-awareness, student development, interpersonal skills, and group leadership skills. Each training unit should be approximately two hours in length, highly structured, and consist of several experience-based learning exercises.

There are many advantages of including training in the selection process. First, the wealth of information gleaned about candidates' skills, abilities, and attitudes far exceeds what might be gained in typical selection interviews. Second, resident assistants are better prepared. Once they are on the job, it seems that there is never enough time for adequate training. Third, professional staff can gain information and insights that will be helpful in supervising resident assistants once they are on the job. Fourth, candidates are more highly motivated during training sessions because their performance determines whether or not they are hired. And fifth, because candidates enter the position better prepared and more confident, they get off to a better start.

However, resident assistants, even if properly selected and trained, are only as good as the supervision they receive. They should be held accountable for their effectiveness, or lack of it, and monitored using fair and equitable supervisory techniques.

Just how can this be done? Effective supervision involves two key ingredients: competent supervisors who know and understand their supervisory roles; and a formal system of evaluation that is open, fair, and valid. Supervisors should have effective interpersonal skills and be familiar with student development theory as well as with theories about the impact of residence hall life. They should also know how to select and train resident assistants; establish and interpret job functions; provide information, advice, and support; evaluate resident assistants' job performance; serve as advocates for resident assistants; and represent other student concerns. Supervisors should also develop effective supervisory techniques including frequent individual conferences, group meetings, training sessions, direct involvement with resident assistant tasks, and informal interactions with resident assistants. And finally, they should have effective group leadership skills.

But most importantly, supervisors should provide a very clear understanding of job expectations and develop ways of collecting information to determine if these expectations are being met. Although many sources of evaluative information should be used, by far the most important is students themselves. A formal, written evaluation of resident assistants by students should be used by supervisors as the most important basis for evaluating and improving performance. Such evaluations also let students know that the institution is serious about creating a positive environment in its residence halls.

Offering Educational Activities and Programs. The third way in which institutions can influence their residential environment is through educational programs. Over the past twenty years, there has been considerable emphasis on developing such programs. But is there any evidence that educational programs and activities have any impact on students' development?

Generally speaking, the answer is yes. For example, living-learning residence halls, where classes are held and faculty offices located, appear to have advantages over other halls. Living-learning residents demonstrate significantly improved personal adjustment, intellectual growth, and have more positive attitudes toward their college experiences (Nosow, 1975). These residents are also more likely to complete their college programs (Gordon, 1974; and Pascarella and Terenzini, 1980). Faculty-student relations are also enhanced by this living arrangement (DeCoster, 1968).

Unfortunately, most institutions do not have the resources to create living-learning programs. Most residence hall programming involves one-shot attempts to educate students in a particular subject or to create certain types of social or educational interaction. However, getting students to attend such programs is like pulling teeth because there is great skepticism about their value. Do they make a difference? There is little evidence in the literature that they do, with one exception.

Upcraft, Peterson, and Moore (1981) compare the grades, retention rate, and personal development of students who attended selected educational programs with those students who did not attend, controlling for academic ability, sex, major, parents' income, and race. Although no differences in academic achievement or retention were noted between attenders and non-attenders, there were some differences in personal development over the course of the freshman year. For example, students who attended these programs improved their intellectual and socio-emotional development significantly more than nonattenders. In general, social, educational, and sexuality programs had the most impact, along with intramurals and programs involving faculty.

Thus it appears that living-learning programs and selected individual programs are effective and should be promoted in residence halls. It is interesting to note that faculty are involved in both. There is evidence that faculty participation in residence halls is a very positive influence on residents and should be promoted for its own sake (Magnarella, 1979; and Pascarella and Terenzini, 1980).

In conclusion, it is clear that the positive influence residence halls can have on academic achievement, retention, and personal development does not just happen naturally. It occurs when institutions structure their residential environments through carefully assigning students, rigorously training and evaluating the residence hall staff, and developing educational programs and activities.

Campuswide Student Activities

In a sense, creating a residential environment that enhances retention is much easier than creating a total campus environment which does so. The residence hall is a much more controlled environment and can be structured by properly trained and supervised staff to enhance retention. Students in residence halls are captive audiences for whom the power of the peer group is amplified by propinquity and architecture. But a majority of American college students do not live in residence halls. Many do not even have the opportunity because of overcrowding or personal reasons such as finances or family commitments. So for many institutions, creating campuswide student activities and programs which enhance retention is the only means outside of the classroom of influencing student retention.

Compared to residential impact, the impact of student activities on academic achievement and retention is much less specific. There is considerable evidence, however, that active participation in the extracurricular life of a campus can enhance retention. However, as is the case with residence halls, participating in activities is a double-edged sword. Excessive involvement can have a negative impact on retention (Hyatt, 1980).

Several specific types of student activities participation have a positive impact on retention. Establishing close friends (Billson and Terry, 1982; and Fiedler and Vance, 1981) is important to academic success, especially during the first month of enrollment (Simpson, Baker, and Mellinger, 1980). Once again, freshmen have a need to affiliate with one another and participation in student activities fulfills this need and enhances retention.

There is also substantial evidence that participation in orientation programs and activities enhances retention (Lenning, Sauer, and Beal, 1980; Ramist, 1981; Beal and Noel, 1980; and "University of California . . . ," 1980). From summer preenrollment programs through programs and services offered upon arrival, it is clear that orientation programs help students get off to a better start and result in a better finish. It is unclear, however, just what specific orientation programs have an impact, since most programs are a potpourri of social, athletic, academic, and informational activities.

Other activities that enhance retention include (1) belonging to student organizations (Billson and Terry, 1982); (2) involvement in social activities (Jeanotte, 1982; and Terenzini, Pascarella, and Lorang, 1982); (3) involvement in cultural activities (Winter, McClelland, and Stewart, 1981); (4) attending lectures (Hyatt, 1980); (5) using campus facilities (Churchill and Iwai, 1981); and (6) general participation in extracurricular activities (Lenning, Sauer, and Beal, 1980; Ramist, 1981; and "University of California . . . ," 1980).

One of the problems in interpreting this evidence of the impact of involvement in student activities on retention is the lack of specificity. Some extracurricular activities occur spontaneously as a result of students themselves and need no institutional support or encouragement (parties, dances, and other informal gatherings). Others, such as lectures, concerts, cultural events, and orientation programs, require institutional support, planning and involvement, not to mention funding. It is therefore difficult for an institution to determine which activities specifically affect retention. Although further research is necessary, institutions can proceed under the assumption that an active student activities program will enhance retention.

As in residence halls, the reason for the positive relationship between participation in activities and retention is most likely the influence of students on one another. And just as in residence halls, this influence must be structured and channeled by the institution. But there are some fundamental differences. Because the campus as a whole is not a captive audience, staff supervision is indirect rather than direct. Whereas residence halls can influence students through assignment, staff, and programming, student activities must rely on programming only and very often depend on volunteers instead of paid staff.

So what can be done? First, activities must be heavily publicized. Every possible effort using print media, bulletin boards, radio spots, and word of mouth must be made to make students aware of the opportunities available. Programs must be ''sold'' through attractive and informative promotional techniques.

Second, organizations such as student government, special interest organizations, fraternities, sororities, and other groups must be heavily involved in the development, promotion, planning, and implementation of student activities programs. It may be necessary to organize special programming groups such as student union programming committees or orientation planning groups. If students are involved, the programs will be better promoted and more likely to be relevant and interesting to other students.

Third, the facilities of the institution must be available and used to their maximum. Almost every institution has a student union or common area where students ''hang out.'' Programs might be held in either of those locations. Programs that are easily accessible to students are more likely to succeed, especially if they are offered at convenient times. For example, it is very difficult for commuter colleges to attract students to programs for which they would have to make a special trip back to the campus. Commuter colleges should make every effort to offer programs at times when students are most likely to attend.

Fourth, student activities programming cannot occur without the strong support of creative professionals who know how to work with students and promote, as well as develop, programs and who are in tune with the needs and interests of the students in their institution.

Fifth, the many resources of both the institution and community must be mobilized to develop student activities programming. Of course, a strong effort must be made to involve faculty and administrative staff. Often community resources such as lawyers, physicians, politicians, laborers, clergy, business people, and others are overlooked as programming resources, when, in fact, they could be very helpful.

And, sixth, the institution must provide adequate resources to develop a strong student activities program. Many times the student activities program is the first to feel the effects of budget cutbacks. This is very unfortunate, for if there is a relationship between student activities and retention, such reductions may, in fact, increase the likelihood that students will withdraw.

In summary, the conventional wisdom that students should study hard at first and then get involved is simply untrue. To enhance retention, students must be encouraged to work at their social adjustment through active involvement in student activities just as hard as they work at meeting classroom demands.

Educational and Developmental Programs and Activities

Too often, programs and activities are offered on a hit or miss basis. That is, we offer programs that have worked in the past and count on high attendance or we cater to some real or imagined student interest or fad. Even when programs are based on some systematic assessment of student interests, they may miss the mark. To be sure, programs should be attractive and interesting to students, but they should be based on real student developmental needs, not on the whims of students at some moment in their lives.

Because students talk about their college experiences more as a series of events rather than as psychological or sociological processes, it is probably more useful to develop programs and activities based on a student development model, rather than on a theory. Upcraft, Finney, and Garland (1984) identify six major developmental issues that students must confront and resolve during their college years: (1) developing intellectual and academic competence; (2) establishing and maintaining interpersonal relationships; (3) developing a sex-role identity and sexuality; (4) deciding on a career and life-style; (5) maintaining personal health and wellness; and (6) formulating an integrated philosophy of life. These issues may overlap (deciding on sexual behavior, for example), and not all students deal with all these issues all the time. But if educational programs and activities are to be developmentally based, a further elaboration of each of these dimensions is in order.

Developing Academic and Intellectual Competence. If asked what they fear most about going to college, most students will probably say, "flunking out." Although most students come to college to prepare for a career, many soon recognize that education involves something more than acquiring knowledge. They can learn how to learn and to synthesize, integrate, criticize, and analyze what they learn. They can consider the moral, ethical, and spiritual implications of what they learn, and develop an appreciation for the esthetic, political, and social sides of life. (Chickering, 1969; Lenning and others, 1974; Krathwohl, Bloom, and Masia, 1964; Bowen, 1977; Baird, Hartnett, and Associates, 1980; Heist and Yonge, 1962; Warren, 1978; and Morrill, 1980).

Programs which enhance intellectual and social development range from study skills and tutoring to seminars on important social issues. Cultural programs featuring drama, art, and music are also important, as well as programs that explore the moral, ethical, and spiritual dimensions of life. Outside speakers, performing groups, or exhibits should be brought to campus. Faculty involvement in and support of all these activities is especially important.

Establishing and Maintaining Interpersonal Relationships. The other frequently mentioned worry of students when they first enroll in college is finding new friends. As I have mentioned, there is evidence that establishing effective interpersonal relationships is an important element in college success. All students must develop interpersonal support systems among their fellow students and learn how to relate to faculty and other persons in the collegiate environment. There may be roommates to live with and—perhaps for the first time—students must relate to persons who have different cultural backgrounds, sexual preferences, life experiences, physical disabilities, or skin colors.

Programs which promote interpersonal relationships range from social activities such as parties, mixers, and dances to race relations workshops. Others include assertiveness training, roommate relationship training, various support groups for selected student subpopulations (returning adults, minorities, women, the disabled, children of divorced or separated parents), intramural activities, and encounter groups.

Developing a Sex-Role Identity and Sexuality. Erikson (1964) argues that one's sense of identity is fully developed when one's inner self is consistent with one's meaning for others. An important source of one's general sense of identity is one's sexual identity. Students come to college from backgrounds that have advocated sexual identities ranging from traditional to liberated. Because traditional sex roles are currently being challenged, many students become confused and uncertain about their roles as men and women in our society, while others may become strong advocates for a more androgynous identity (Deutsch and Gilbert, 1976). Further, students must contend with the role of sexuality in their interpersonal relationships, learn how to develop healthy and positive sexual relationships, and avoid the negative consequences of sexual activity.

Programs that help students develop a clearer sex-role identity include women's and men's consciousness raising groups, seminars on changing sex roles, and various support groups. Programs that help students develop their sexuality include seminars on contraception and sexually transmitted diseases, as well as programs which help define sexuality in a relationship, discuss sexual orientation, and analyze sexual morality.

Deciding on a Career and Life-Style. Most students come to college with some career goal in mind. The fact that a large percentage of them change their major is some indication of the instability of that initial career choice. Matching careers with interests, abilities, and more recently, economic expectations, is a major task of college students. Programs which help students with this issue include seminars for undecided students; career fairs where representatives from various occupations discuss their work with students; decision-making and problem-solving workshops; résumé writing seminars; interview skills workshops; and workshops for special student subpopulations such as minorities, women, returning adults, and disabled students. Faculty may also offer presentations on careers in their fields.

Maintaining Personal Health and Wellness. Students should be aware of the impact of their life experiences on their physical and emotional well-being; in other words, on their state of wellness. Wellness is defined as: (1) being free of symptoms of disease and pain in so far as possible; (2) being able to be active enough to do what one wants and what one must at the appropriate time; and (3) being in good spirits most of the time. Wellness is an ongoing process in which one develops and encourages every aspect of one's body, mind, and feelings to interrelate harmoniously as much of the time as possible (Edlin and Golanty, 1982).

Although stress can be a positive motivating force in students' lives, encouraging them to satisfy their needs, too much stress can lead to problems such as alcohol and drug abuse, psychosomatic illnesses, depression, new or increased dependence on cigarettes, nutritional disorders, sexual disorders, and even to suicide (Selye, 1975). Wellness programs should encourage positive health and wellness habits such as good nutritional habits, regular physical activity, and responsible alcohol use for those who choose to drink.

Formulating an Integrated Philosophy of Life. Chickering (1969) sees college as a time when students develop a clearer sense of purpose and clarify personally valid sets of beliefs which have internal consistency and provide a guide for behavior. Both Perry (1970) and Kohlberg (1971) describe stages of ethical and moral development of students. Students must consider what is right and wrong, their priorities in life, their religious and spiritual beliefs, and how they fit into the larger order of things in the universe. Some students will rethink and reformulate their values and beliefs, while others will affirm them. But regardless of their response, most students will leave college with values, beliefs, and self-concepts that are internalized and integrated. That is, these values, beliefs, and self-concepts are "owned" by the student and have internal consistency.

Of all the developmental issues described in this section, formulating an integrated philosophy of life is probably the most difficult to integrate into a residential or student activities program. It is a lifelong process, and not easily approached by students who may have—what are to them—more important things on their minds. Nevertheless, programs on values clarification, religious beliefs, morality, philosophy, and major social issues should be offered.

Conclusion

There is very clear evidence that residence halls and student activities have a positive impact on retention, but only if institutions support and structure student participation to positive ends. Left alone, residence halls become zoos, student activities do not happen, and there is no impact on retention. And for the most part, the enrichment of residential and campus activities and programs can be accomplished with very little additional funding. What is needed is a strong institutional commitment and the support and collaboration of students, faculty, and staff.

There is a problem, however. Even though the relationship between residence halls, student activities, and retention has been clearly established in the literature, an awareness of this fact has not yet become an important part of the retention strategies of most institutions. In fact, as dollars become scarcer and enrollments decline, extracurricular programs are often the first to be drastically reduced. Institutional decision makers often still consider such programs to be icing on the cake. This is a very shortsighted view because institutions that reallocate limited resources to classrooms and faculty may find their classrooms empty and their faculty reduced in force. Yet it is very difficult to convince a budget committee that student activities and residence halls should be funded ahead of replacing a history professor. However, in the long run, persons responsible for the survival and effectiveness of institutions must have the courage to make such decisions if students are to be retained and given the opportunity to successfully complete their educational goals.

References

Ainsworth, C., and Maynard, D. "The Impact of Roommate Personality on Achievement: An Exploratory Study and Model of Analysis." *Research in Higher Education*, 1976, *4*, 291–301.

Astin, A. W. "The Impact of Dormitory Living on Students." *Educational Record*, 1973, *54*, 204–210.

Astin, A. W. *Four Critical Years: Effects of College on Beliefs, Attitudes, and Knowledge.* San Francisco: Jossey-Bass, 1977.

Baird, L. L., Hartnett, R. T., and Associates. *Understanding Student and Faculty Life: Using Campus Surveys to Improve Academic Decision Making.* San Francisco: Jossey-Bass, 1980.

Beal, P. E., and Noel, L. *What Works in Student Retention.* Iowa City, Iowa: American College Testing Program and National Center for Higher Education Management Systems, 1980. (ED 197 635)

Beal, P. E., and Williams, D. A. *An Experiment with Mixed-Class Housing Assignments at the University of Oregon.* Columbus: Ohio State University, Association of College and University Housing Officers Research and Information Committee, 1968.

Billson, J. M., and Terry, M. B. "In Search of the Silken Purse: Factors in Attrition Among First-Generation Students." *College and University*, Fall 1982, *58*, 57–75.

Blai, B., Jr. "Roommate Impact upon Academic Performance." Bryn Mawr, Pa.: Harcum Junior College, 1971. (ED 052 228)

Bowen, H. R. *Investment in Learning: The Individual and Social Value of American Higher Education.* San Francisco: Jossey-Bass, 1977.

Brown, R. D. "Manipulation of the Environmental Press in

a College Residence Hall." *Personnel and Guidance Journal*, 1968, *46*, 555–560.

Brown, R. D., Winkworth, J., and Braskamp, L. "Student Development in a Coed Residence Hall: Promiscuity, Prophylactic, or Panacea?" *Journal of College Student Personnel*, 1973, *14*, 98–104.

Chickering, A. W. *Education and Identity*. San Francisco: Jossey-Bass, 1969.

Chickering, A. W. *Commuting Versus Resident Students: Overcoming the Educational Inequities of Living Off Campus*. San Francisco: Jossey-Bass, 1974.

Churchill, W. D., and Iwai, S. I. "College Attrition, Student Use of Campus Facilities, and a Consideration of Self-Reported Personal Problems." *Research in Higher Education*, 1981, *14*, 353–365.

Corbett, J., and Sommer, R. "Anatomy of a Coed Residence Hall." *Journal of College Student Personnel*, 1972, *13*, 215–217.

Davidson, M. B. "Educational Outcomes and Implications of Academically and Vocationally Focused Small Groups of Undergraduate Students in a Women's Residence Hall." Paper presented at American Personnel and Guidance Association meeting, Minneapolis, Minn., April 1965.

DeCoster, D. "Housing Assignments for High Ability Students." *Journal of College Student Personnel*, 1966, *7*, 19–22.

DeCoster, D. "Effects of Homogeneous Housing Assignments for High Ability Students." *Journal of College Student Personnel*, 1968, *9*, 75–78.

Deutsch, C. J., and Gilbert, L. A. "Sex-Role Stereotypes: Effect on Perceptions of Self and Others and on Personal Adjustment." *Journal of Counseling Psychology*, 1976, *23*, 373–379.

Edlin, G. P., and Golanty, E. *Health and Wellness: A Holistic Approach*. Boston: Science Books, 1982.

Erikson, E. H. *Childhood and Society*. New York: Norton, 1964.

Feldman, K. A., and Newcomb, T. M. *The Impact of College on Students*. Vol. 1: *An Analysis of Four Decades of Research*; Vol. 2: *Summary Tables*. San Francisco: Jossey-Bass, 1969.

Fiedler, D., and Vance, E. B. "To Stay or Leave the University: Every Student's Dilemma." Paper read at American Psychological Assocation meeting, Los Angeles, August 1981.

Gehring, D. D. "Prediction of Roommate Compatibility." *Journal of College Student Personnel*, 1970, *11*, 58–61.

Gordon, S. S. "Living and Learning in College." *Journal of General Education*, 1974, *25*, 235–245.

Hall, R. L., and Willerman, B. "The Educational Influences of Dormitory Roommates." *Sociometry*, 1963, *26*, 294–318.

Hardee, M. "The Residence Hall: A Locus for Learning." Paper presented at research conference on Social Science Methods and Student Residence, University of Michigan, Ann Arbor, November 1964.

Heath, D. H. *Growing Up in College; Liberal Education and Maturity.* San Francisco: Jossey-Bass, 1968.

Heist, P., and Yonge, G. *Omnibus Personality Inventory, Form F Manual.* New York: Psychological Corporation, 1962.

Hyatt, S. A. "Facilities Planning for Academic Results." *Planning for Higher Education,* 1980, *9* (2), 10–13.

Jeanotte, L. D. "A Study of the Contributing Factors Relating to Why American Indian Students Drop Out of or Graduate from Educational Programs at the University of North Dakota." Paper read at American Educational Research Association, New York City, March 1982. (ED 214 737)

Kaplan, S., Mann, S. C., and Kaplan, R. "Honors Housing at the University of Michigan." *Superior Student*, 1964, *7*, 14.

Karlin, R. A., Rosen, L. S., and Epstein, Y. M. "Three into Two Doesn't Go: A Follow-Up on the Effects of Overcrowded Dormitory Rooms." *Personality and Social Psychology Bulletin*, 1979, *5*, 391–395.

Kohlberg, L. J. "Stages of Moral Development." In C. M. Beck, B. S. Crittendan, and E. V. Sullivan (eds.), *Moral Education.* Toronto, Canada: University of Toronto Press, 1971.

Krathwohl, D. R., Bloom, B. S., and Masia, B. B. *Taxonomy of Educational Objectives Handbook 2, Affective Domain.* New York: McKay, 1964.

Lenning, O. T., Sauer, K., and Beal, P. E. *Student Retention Strategies.* American Association for Higher Education— Educational Resources Information Center/Higher Education Research Report, no. 80, American Association for Higher Education, 1980.

Lenning, O. T., and others. "The Many Faces of College Success and Their Nonintellective Correlates: The Published Literature Through the Decade of the Sixties." Monograph 15, Iowa City, Iowa: American College Testing Program, 1974.

Linnell, R. *Coeducational Housing at Colleges and Universities.* Los Angeles: Office of Institutional Studies, University of Southern California, 1972.

Lozier, G. G. "Compatibility of Roommates Assigned Alphabetically Versus Those Assigned According to Educational Goals or Extracurricular Plans." *Journal of College Student Personnel*, 1970, *1*, 256–260.

Mable, P., Terry, M. J., and Duvall, W. H. "Student Development Through Community Development." In D. A. DeCoster and P. Mable (eds.), *Personal Education and Community Development in College Residence Halls.* Washington, D. C.: American College Personnel Association, 1980.

MacInnis, M. C., Byrne, T. P., and Fraser, J. A. H. "Opinions of Students, Parents, Faculty, and Community Concerning Coeducational Residences." *Journal of College and University Student Housing*, 1980, *10* (1), 30–34.

McKelfresh, D. A. "The Effect of Living Environments on Engineering Students." *Journal of College and University Student Housing*, 1980, *10* (2), 16–18.

McNeel, S. P. "Tripling Up: Perceptions and Effects of Dormitory Crowding." Paper read at American Psychological Association, Montreal, Canada, September 1980.

Magnarella, P. J. "The Continuing Evaluation of a Living-Learning Center." *Journal of College Student Personnel*, 1979, *20*, 4–9.

Morishima, J. K. "A Preliminary Report: The Effects on Student Achievement of Residence Hall Groupings Based on Academic Majors." In C. H. Bagley (ed.), *Research on Academic Input: Proceedings of the Sixth Annual Forum of the Association for Institutional Research.* Athens: Institute of Higher Education, University of Georgia, 1966. (ED 044 786)

Morrill, R. L. *Teaching Values in College: Facilitating Development of Ethical, Moral, and Value Awareness in Students.* San Francisco: Jossey-Bass, 1980.

Murray, M. E. "The Effect of Roommates on the Scholastic Achievement of College Students." *Dissertation Abstracts*, 1961, *21*, 2195.

Nosow, S. "An Attitudinal Comparison of Residential College Seniors with Other Seniors." *Journal of College Student Personnel*, 1975, *16*, 17–23.

Pace, T. "Roommate Dissatisfaction in Residence Halls." *Journal of College Student Personnel*, 1970, *11*, 144–147.

Pascarella, E. T., and Terenzini, P. T. "Student-Faculty and Student-Peer Relationships as Mediators of the Structural Effects of Undergraduate Residence Arrangement." *Journal of Educational Research*, 1980, *73*, 344–353.

Perry, W. G. *Forms of Intellectual and Ethical Development in the College Years.* New York: Holt, Rinehart & Winston, 1970.

Peterman, D., Pilato, G., and Upcraft, M. L. "A Description and Evaluation of an Academic Course to Increase Interpersonal Effectiveness of Resident Assistants." *Journal of College Student Personnel*, 1979, *20*, 348–352.

Ramist, L. "College Student Attrition and Retention." College Board Report, no. 81-1, New York: College Entrance Examination Board, 1981. (ED 200 170)

Roby, T. B., Zelin, M. L., and Chechile, R. A. "Matching Roommates by an Optimal Indirect Technique." *Journal of Applied Psychology*, 1977, *62*, 70–75.

Rudolph, F. *The American College and University, A History.* New York: Vintage Books, 1965.

Schoemer, J. R., and McConnell, W. A. "Is There a Case for the Freshman Women's Residence Hall?" *Personnel and Guidance Journal*, 1970, *49*, 35–40.

Schroeder, C. C. "The Impact of Homogeneous Housing on Environmental Perceptions and Student Development." *Journal of College and University Student Housing*, 1980, *10* (2), 10–15.

Schroeder, C. C., and Freesh, N. "Applying Environmental Management Strategies in Resident Halls." *Journal of the National Association of Student Personnel Administrators*, 1977, *15* (1), 51–57.

Schuh, J. H. "The Influence of Temporary Residence Hall Assignment on Students: Another Look." *College Student Affairs Journal*, 1982, *4* (3), 12–18.

Schuh, J. H., and Williams, O. J. "The Effect of Birth Order on Roommate Compatibility." *College Student Journal*, 1977, *11*, 285–286.

Selye, H. *Stress Without Distress.* New York: Signet, 1975.

Simpson, C., Baker, K., and Mellinger, G. "Conventional Failures and Unconventional Dropouts: Comparing Different Types of University Withdrawals." *Sociology of Education*, 1980, *53*, 203–214.

Taylor, R. G., and Hanson, G. R. "Environmental Impact on Achievement and Study Habits." *Journal of College Student Personnel*, 1971, *12*, 445–454.

Terenzini, P. T., Pascarella, E. T., and Lorang, W. G. "An Assessment of the Academic and Social Influences on Freshman Year Educational Outcomes." *Review of Higher Education*, 1982, *5*, 86–110.

"University of California Undergraduate Enrollment Study." Report of Task Group on Retention and Transfer, Berkeley: University of California, June 1980.

Upcraft, M. L., and Pilato, G. T. *Residence Hall Assistants in College: A Guide to Selection, Training, and Supervision.* San Francisco: Jossey-Bass, 1982.

Upcraft, M. L., Finney, J. E., and Garland, P. "Orientation: A Context." In M. L. Upcraft (ed.), *Orienting Students to College.* New Directions for Student Services, no. 25. San Francisco: Jossey-Bass, 1984.

Upcraft, M. L., Peterson, P. C., and Moore, B. L. "The Academic and Personal Development of Penn State Freshmen." Unpublished manuscript, Pennsylvania State University, 1981.

Upcraft, M. L., Pilato, G. T., and Peterman, D. J. *Learning to Be a Resident Assistant: A Manual for Effective Participation in the Training Program.* San Francisco: Jossey-Bass, 1982.

Vreeland, R. "The Effects of Houses on Students' Attitudes and Values." In J. M. Whiteley and H. Z. Sprandel (eds.), *The Growth and Development of College Students.* Washington, D.C.: American College Personnel Association, 1970.

Warren, J. R. *The Measurement of Academic Competence.* Berkeley, Calif.: Educational Testing Service, 1978. (ED 174 649)

Wetzel, C. G., Schwartz, D., and Vasu, E. S. "Roommate Compatibility: Is There an Ideal Relationship?" *Journal of Applied Social Psychology,* 1979, *9,* 432–445.

Winter, D. G., McClelland, D. C., and Stewart, A. J. "Understanding the Effects of 'Ivy College': An Integrated Model." In D. G. Winter, D. C. McClelland, and A. J. Stewart, *A New Case for the Liberal Arts: Assessing Institutional Goals and Student Development.* San Francisco: Jossey-Bass, 1981, 118–150.

Young, D., Campen, J., and Ray, J. "Selected Personality Variables of Students in Single-Sex and Coeducational Residence Halls." Paper read at American Educational Research Association, Boston, April 1980. (ED 185 932)

18

Using a Systematic Approach to Assessing Retention Needs

~~~~~~~~

Randi Levitz
Lee Noel

"Staying ahead of change means anticipating the new actions that external events will eventually require and taking them early, before others, before being forced, while there is still time to exercise choice about how and when and what" (Kanter, 1983, p. 64). Effective retention research can provide just the vehicle colleges need to stay ahead of and cope with the changing environment of the eighties and beyond.

Given the environment for higher education as it is now and as it is predicted to be into the next decade, it becomes apparent that there are three imperatives which can give direction to retention research efforts on campuses: emphasize performance, design appropriate indicators of measurement, and provide data that validate performance. First, performance must be emphasized instead of growth. As has been well documented, the decades of tremendous growth in higher education have passed. The strength of our institutions' competitive posture in the future will be dependent upon how directly we focus on our distinctive mission and how successfully we communicate to potential students the value and worth of our enterprise. For, when price has limited adjustability, success and even viability become heavily dependent on clarity and quality.

In many ways, this environmentally pressured change in emphasis in higher education parallels what happened in the U.S. automobile industry. As recently as 1975, fifty-five U.S. auto executives participating in structured interview sessions talked almost exclusively of outputs—the number of units produced and moved—with few words devoted to the quality of their product or to their mission, that of providing the best possible transportation (Clifton, 1985). It was only when faced with increasing competition from Japan, that American car manufacturers began mounting campaigns to improve quality and enhance the image of their products, emphasizing service and backing up their claims with guarantees. Just as American automakers had to redefine their objectives in the face of changing market conditions, so it is time for colleges and universities to determine whether our business is to run institutions or to deliver student learning.

In addition to facing competition with other colleges and universities, we in higher education are now in competition with what Hodgkinson (1983) describes as the second system of education, a $50 billion industry that provides the learning that occurs daily in this country outside of college and university classrooms in corporate training programs, community centers, YMCA–YWCAs, and so on. If we are to successfully counter competition from this sector (involving a dollar amount matched only by the budgets from all American colleges and universities combined), we must place renewed emphasis on performance by explicitly stating what it is we do well.

The second imperative is to construct indicators of quality, concrete measures of performance, that are capable of evaluating the levels of achievement we have attained. Outcome measures need to be tied directly to the mission of our institutions. One of the most readily agreed-upon principles in all of management is that measurement improves performance (Clifton, 1980, p. 6). Without such direction, we tend to lose focus, relying upon input measures to assess the quality of our efforts rather than evaluating the outcomes of the operations, activities, and efforts themselves.

Presenting data that will clearly indicate that the performance-achievement indicators have been satisfactorily reached is then the third retention research imperative. Astin (in Keller, 1983, p. 132) says that institutions "must monitor what they get paid to do. It is irresponsible for an institution not to know what the students are learning, what impact the college is having, what suggestions the students have for change." Data that will have the desired impact will be those that go beyond the simple listing of activities, processes, and easily countable inputs. The new generation of research will measure and confirm outcomes that are deemed desirable by those most interested in assessing outcomes: our students, the clients who buy our product, and those who pay for it—students, parents, legislators, taxpayers, and graduates, as well as those responsible for corporate and private giving.

It is not the purpose of this chapter to provide a how-to guide. Rather, this chapter sketches out a results-oriented approach for assessing the current campus environment based on key outcome indicators. This approach can provide direction for new and continuing effort designed to enhance the likelihood of student success and persistence.

After first considering the objectives and scope of a retention research program, three key phases in such a program will be closely examined: analysis of enrollment behavior, assessment of student-institution interactions, and evaluation of program effectiveness. Finally, because the ultimate purpose of a comprehensive retention research program is the provision of data for decision making, for making those informed choices about how and when and what, we will consider how retention data can be used as a trigger for action on campus.

Researchers have had a difficult task to date, because certain critical outcomes—such as what is supposed to happen to students who spend one or two or four years on campus—have not been explicitly stated. Our outcome measurements have often been highly imprecise and often based on subjective impressions, such as "I know an educated person when I see one." Further, when we have looked at outcomes, we have often relied upon measures—course grades and grade point average, for example—without data confirming that learning has actually taken place, that student achievement is actually attributable to student involvement in the class. The National Institute of Education report, *Involvement in Learning* (1984, p. 40), stresses the importance of an outcomes orientation for faculty as well as students. "Publication of a widely known and understood list of academic expectations for students should also improve classroom instruction and facilitate the integration of college curricula. Faculty typically focus on their particular subject matter and often lose sight of the ways in which [it] contributes to the entire curricula. By clarifying the capacities students are supposed to develop . . . faculty remind themselves of what they are supposed to be doing in their own classes."

Making These Research Imperatives Operational

Following the imperatives just outlined, Forrest's research (1982) focuses on the performances of colleges and universities, clearly defines outcomes of general education, establishes key performance indicators, and validates the extent to which they are achieved. He links the operation of the institution to student achievement outcome indicators: student growth in general education knowledge and skills and persistence to graduation. As a result of his findings, Forrest slates six significant operational features for campuses interested in making institutional changes designed to make general education work better.

- Substantive academic advising and orientation
- Sufficient depth and breadth of general education component
- Instruction focused on relevant skill development
- Student-oriented goal statements and proficiency examinations
- Campus-centered environment during the freshman year

- Evaluation of the institution's ability to increase student competence

It is fascinating to find that the features Forrest finds to be least related to increased student learning and persistence to graduation are features we so often automatically associate with quality in an institution, such as the number of books in the library, the college's student-faculty ratio, the percent of faculty with doctoral degrees.

In the past we have used these traditional measures to judge quality by proxy. While there are critical levels of each that must be maintained, going beyond certain levels may not produce any additional outcome gains. Forrest's outcomes assessment seems to indicate that the results we get are more heavily dependent upon what we do with students in our classrooms and elsewhere on campus than they are on the input or measures that have received so much attention. Though Forrest's data base is small (based on forty-four two- and four-year, public and private, large and small institutions), his results nonetheless provide important focal points for campus-based researchers interested in outcomes assessment. As the general level of interest in the outcome of educational expenditures continues to grow, creative researchers will be able to provide exciting, substantive data that demonstrate our value and worth and move us far beyond mere accountability.

Research Focused on Retention Outcomes

It has been said that we are where we are more by accident than by design. A myth that is continually refuted as we examine efforts to improve student success and retention on campuses is that good ideas succeed on their own merits. As detailed by Smith, Lippitt, and Sprandel in Chapter Nineteen, and by Noel, Levitz, and Saluri in Chapter Twenty-two, organizational change requires concerted and planned effort. In our experience, we have found that retention improvement efforts are highly dependent on planned changes in practice, attitudes, and behavior and that impetus for such change stems from taking a sharper look at the way an institution serves students. Astin (in Keller, 1983, p. 132) indicates that the high-quality institution, the one that knows its students, "has a method for gathering and disseminating [information about students], enabling it to make adjustments in programs or policies when the student data indicate that change or improvement is needed."

To this point, retention research has often been narrowly conceived, both conceptually in the literature and operationally on campuses. The focus has primarily been on the phenomenon of attrition, with the emphasis on either designing studies to calculate and catalogue attrition rates or identifying patterns of withdrawal to determine who has dropped out and why. Yet throughout this book we have seen that the forces and factors influencing student success and persistence are far reaching, encompassing virtually every program, activity, service, and person on campus. This holistic view of what it takes to create a staying environment on campus demands a similarly comprehensive approach to retention research. The future success of our colleges and universities will be dependent on gathering and using data on students and from students today.

Objectives of a Comprehensive Retention Research Program

The overriding objectives in constructing a retention research program and making it a priority on campus ought to be

1. To study success—to find out what the institution is doing well in order that it may do more of it
2. To pinpoint campus services that need further attention so that they may become the type of student resources of which the institution can be proud
3. To determine the type of intervention programs and practices that are linked to student success and student persistence
4. To follow those students who receive special attention or participate in special programs to determine whether the intervention is having the desired impact

5. To target students who will benefit from interventions known to have a positive impact
6. To provide validation of the outcomes the institution is striving to achieve

The underlying assumption behind each of these objectives is that one cannot get better at what one is doing if one does not know *how* one is doing. For an institution to be more effective in carrying out its mission and meeting students' needs, it must gather more information about what it is and is not doing well. Retention research then ought to be undertaken with the spirit of becoming as good as possible instead of seeing what is wrong now. It ought to be an ongoing process, not a one-time event. And finally, the data that are collected should serve as triggers for action as well as for administering rewards.

Effective retention research involves more than assembling periodic head counts and determining who has dropped out and why. Retention research should be viewed broadly as a comprehensive process through which the institution, its personnel and its activities are examined to

1. Identify the scope and dimensions of the attrition/retention situation on campus
2. Provide baseline data against which gains can be measured
3. Identify those areas of the institution that are functioning well and those areas that are not functioning as intended
4. Guide action to institute changes where necessary
5. Determine effectiveness after changes have been made and validate claims

As Gene Amdahl, president of Amdahl Corporation has said, "It's impossible to really innovate unless you can deal with all aspects of a problem. If you can only deal with yolks or whites, it's pretty hard to make an omelette" (Kanter, 1983, p. 156). Retention research must be similarly comprehensive in scope if we are going to use it as a tool in our efforts to create a staying environment for students.

Three Major Research Phases

There are three major phases to a comprehensive retention research program that meet these objectives.

1. Analysis of student enrollment behavior
2. Assessment of the multidimensional interactions that occur between students and the collegiate environment
3. Evaluation of outcomes—program effectiveness and/or intervention impact

These phases, which parallel the retention improvement efforts we, singly and together, have viewed on many campuses, will each be discussed in turn and the purposes, objectives, and research questions for each phase outlined.

Phase One: Enrollment Behavior. Phase one research centers on student behavior and first examines students' actions and interactions as they make an initial commitment to the institution and recommit with each subsequent registration. "When" and "at what rate" are the questions that need to be addressed at this point. Is there a gap between admission and enrollment? Do students leave after the first week, or the first three, or six weeks? Is the last day for drop/add a common point for withdrawal? Do students fail to return after vacations, or after the first term, or first year? It is important to establish the critical junctures for student withdrawal, whether official or behavioral (that is, observed lack of recommitment).

Our experience with hundreds of individual institutions suggests that attrition is likely to be most severe after the first year of study, that students often use the break after their first year as the time to make the decision to leave the institution. An elementary, but critical point is that retention rate calculations must be as accurate as possible, following individual students by name or identification number. Tracking students in any other way may artificially inflate or deflate attrition rates. In general, our experience leads us to believe that the attrition rate in four-year institutions decreases by half with each passing year. For example, an institution admitting 1,000 freshmen might find 680 returning for the sophomore year, 520 for the junior year, and 440 for the senior year. With an additional slippage of some 40 students during the senior year, the resulting attrition rates are 32 percent, 16 percent, 8 percent, and 4 percent with an approximate graduation rate of 40 percent. It is easy to imagine what this rate of attrition costs an institution over time.

We have found a somewhat different trend, however, in some women's colleges where the sophomore-to-junior year attrition rate is higher—in some cases even double—than the freshman-to-sophomore year rate. In many cases this unusual pattern has been ascribed to parental pressure to attend a single-sex institution for the first two years of college.

Among community colleges, attrition ideally should be checked each term, measuring against student objectives at point of registration/matriculation. Tinto's point in Chapter Two about the importance of using individual student objectives as the ultimate test of attrition is well taken. As institutions of all types become more sophisticated in their efforts to track retention/attrition data, efforts to encompass such individual-specific points of reference should be made. Attrition in senior institutions most often occurs at the end of the school year. In community colleges, attrition is very often acute between the first and second term. First-to-second term attrition rates of 60 percent and higher are not uncommon. There are, however, critical points other than the end of the year or term when students consider dropping out. These points should be identified by individual institutions and viewed as critical junctures at which some meaningful contact with a caring representative of the college may result in a positive outcome.

A cautionary note: it is also important to consider the gap that often occurs between a student's decision to drop out and the point at which he or she actually does so. Many students decide after the first six weeks, or first three weeks, or perhaps even after the first three days, that they are unhappy and want to return home. However, actually doing so may take more courage, more resolve, and more maturity than they are then able to muster. So, even though the decision to leave has been made, they are likely to wait until a convenient moment to reintegrate themselves into their home environment—perhaps during the Christmas vacation or between terms.

Once these withdrawal patterns have been determined for a given campus, decisions about interventions can be made and interventions made prior to these critical junctures can be tested. For example, many campuses use a student's failure to pre-register as an early warning signal of dropout proneness. Other campuses take a more active approach, sending a very brief postcard questionnaire to all students mid-term asking about their plans for the following term, and what type of assistance they will need prior to registration. Whatever the method used, the purpose here is to identify the dimension and scope of the attrition problem and to begin to identify points at which interventions may be warranted or at least their feasibility examined.

The next step in this first phase of retention research is to draw profiles of persisters, students who have been successful on campus, and of nonpersisters, reviewing their characteristics. Among characteristics that may be included in this profile are measured ability at entry (American College Testing [ACT] Program/Scholastic Aptitude Test [SAT] scores); demographic data; and variables related to college attendance including grade point average, the course attempted and completed ratio, college major, resident versus commuter status, number and type of activities in which the student has been involved, whether or not the student has voluntarily or mandatorily participated in a special college program; the amount and type of financial aid received; whether or not the student has held a job, and if so whether it was on or off campus.

These variables may discriminate between dropouts and persisters and help predict which students are likely to need some additional or individual attention to enhance the likelihood of their success. Methodologies used for these studies may be of two types. Initially, a retrospective analysis may be conducted by pulling at random the files of a number of students who entered the institution within the past six or seven years. Within a small college, 100 files may be sufficient for a study of this type, while in a very large institution, 500–1,000 files should probably be examined. Second, longitudinal studies may be conducted beginning with the next entering class. There are many good books and articles highlighting appropriate research designs for predictive studies so we will not spend time on methodological approaches in this chapter. (For example, see Patrick, Myers, and Van Dusen, 1979; and Terenzini, 1982.)

Phase Two: Assessment of Student-Institutional Interaction. Questions guiding research in this phase of retention research center on the extent to which student expectations are congruent with their experiences on campus.

- Do students feel that they are learning what they need to be learning, that they are experiencing the kind of teaching they had hoped to experience, and that advisers and counselors are providing the kind of direction and guidance they need?
- Do enrolled students use, and are they satisfied with, the institution's services, program, approaches, and facilities?

In addition to the perceived quality of classroom instruction and faculty-student interactions, how do graduates view their experience at the institution in terms of their personal, educational, intellectual, career, and social development? A complete assessment of student opinions should also touch on all major areas of the living/learning environment, such as

- The library
- Dormitory rooms and food services
- Commuter lounges
- Classroom and laboratory facilities
- The learning assistance center
- Tutorial assistance
- Career planning and placement activities
- Personal safety on campus
- Recreational facilities
- Student activities and organizations
- Admissions process
- Financial aid
- Rules, regulations, and procedures

Research in this area is attitudinal, measuring utilization, behavior, and opinions. Yet, despite inherent shortcomings, it provides critical information on student perceptions that must not be overlooked. As Peters and Waterman (1982) emphasize in their book, *In Search of Excellence*, we must stay close to the customer. Asking our students, allowing us to see our work through their eyes, provides powerful and important data; without it, we are blinded to even the most obvious of necessary changes. Survey data of this type can help campuses really tune in to what organizational behaviorists call the performance gap and identify, from a student's perspective, just where and how big the discrepancies are between what is and what ought to be.

As student-institutional interactions are assessed in this second phase, opportunities for data collection closely follow the path of students as they move into and through the institution. An institution's need for information on students begins at the point at which students first come into contact with the institution. At this point, institutions must examine prospective students' objectives for the immediate future by determining their most important reason for attending in a given semester or year, their enrollment plans for the future, the degree to which they are certain of their educational plans, and the areas in which they need assistance. In community colleges in particular, or in those institutions with a great many part-time students, it is essential that students' objectives be clarified and that those objectives be used in measuring student retention/attrition.

For example, statements gathered at point of admission can be terribly important bits of information concerning the students and the areas in which they need help. Student needs vary widely, ranging from the needs for financial assistance, employment, or day care; to the needs for help in choosing a major or career, and bolstering reading, mathematics, or other academic skills; to the needs for advice in how to get along with roommates or feel comfortable in adjusting to a new setting. It is critical to note that from the student's vantage point there is no difference between real and perceived needs. If a student feels a need exists, the institution must do all that it is capable of to help the student fulfill that need and maximize the chance that he or she will feel satisfied with the campus experience.

Once students are enrolled, the place to begin is with a survey of currently enrolled students to examine the quality of interactions between students and the institution. Most campuses want to begin with exit interviews which are, in our opinion, problematic. First, we have found that many institutions feel they can "save" a few students at this point. Yet, on far too many occasions, campus staff members have reported to us the plaintive student response: "This is the first time that anyone in this college has appeared to care about me, to talk to me, to see what I need . . . and now it's just too late." Second, when surveying withdrawing students through live interviews rather than mailed surveys, it is essential that the interviewer be especially empathetic, caring, and able to build friendly, trusting relationships quickly if accurate information is to be gathered. Without such a sensitive interviewer, the viability of data exit interviews' yield is very questionable. Third, the major problem with mailed surveys seems to be the expense involved in obtaining a usable number of responses that are truly representative. Response rates are typically very low, with return rates of 10 to 20 percent not uncommon.

There is no doubt in our minds that the very best, most accurate data obtainable comes from currently enrolled students. Student opinion surveys ought to be administered toward the end of the first term of the freshman year, preferably during class time to achieve the best response. These responses may be kept and used very effectively as proxy exit interviews. If the student's identification number is affixed to the survey, responses may be held for a term (in a community college) or for a year (in a senior institution) and then sorted by enrollment status—continuing student versus dropout. By comparing responses, it is possible to draw a very accurate picture of the institution from the perspective of these two groups.

Surveys of graduates also provide critical data which ought to be carefully examined and used in institutional decision making. This type of research is conducted too infrequently and, when conducted, too little used. Satisfied graduates mean a great deal to an institution, and not only in terms of later financial donations. As most colleges know, graduates can be extraordinarily useful recruiters. But what many colleges seem not to realize is the tremendous amount of informal recruiting that goes on, especially in community-based institutions. When an institution is turning out satisfied graduates and has the data to back it up, it has a powerful recruiting tool. Several effective college admissions publications that we have examined make creative and prominent use of graduate survey results.

Overall, much of this phase of research and its focus on student-institutional interactions has to do with one word: expectations. Embedded in the demographic and attitudinal data collected nationwide each year are some startling views of freshman expectations. As reported in *The American Freshman* (Astin, Hemond, and Richardson, 1982), 55 percent of almost 190,000 freshmen who entered college in the fall of 1982 indicated that the chances were very good that they would be satisfied with college. That leaves nearly half the class expecting to be somewhat dissatisfied by that college experience. Yet, of the total group, 74 percent indicated that they were attending their first-choice college and 20 percent their second-choice college.

Other questions focused on expectations concerning the likelihood of transferring to another college and whether students planned to complete a degree on time. Plans to transfer to another college were reported by 11 percent of the new students. Further, it is astonishing to note that 95 percent of entering freshmen indicated that they planned to graduate on time. Recent national graduation data (Noel and Levitz, 1983) based on colleges' self-reported graduation rates demonstrate just how unrealistic are those expectations. The data indicate that, on average, only 40 percent of students graduate within three years from two-year institutions, and 57 percent within five years from four-year institutions. In each case rates would be lowered about 10 percent if we were to use standard completion times of two and four years. These data indicate a strong need to learn more about students, their expectations of themselves within the college setting that they have selected, and of the college itself, if we are to do more in creating a climate conducive to student success and student satisfaction. Further, research points to the need to help students develop realistic expectations of themselves and of their college.

We must first be aware that students bring a variety of expectations and objectives to campus, just as they bring different individual skill levels; social, political, and intellectual orientations; and levels of motivation, drive, or need for an education. At the same time, the external demands on their time, energy, and financial resources vary tremendously. The extent to which these individual differences successfully mesh with the institutional offerings is the extent to which a fit has been achieved and a given student will be successful, satisfied, and persistent in a given institution.

In many ways, students come to campus in a testing mode. Those 45 percent of students indicating some less-than-optimal level of anticipated satisfaction with college are testing—themselves as well as the institution—whether another choice might be more desirable. In some cases this tentative behavior is observable. We see it in the students who rarely venture out of their rooms, who come on campus only to attend classes and then return to their homes in the community, the students in residence halls who invest little of themselves in their new home—putting up little on the walls, knowing or hoping that it will come down all too soon. For these students each negative interaction on campus is logged with a small "Aha! . . . I was right. I'm not going to like this place."

An example of this recently came to light as a residential college attempted to use such behavioral cues to measure students' expectations. In the first week of the fall term they counted the number of items freshmen put up on the walls of their rooms. At the beginning of the next fall term they determined that students who had not returned for a second year had put up, on average, only half as many items as the students who had returned for the second year. Behavioral cues may be used to trigger interventions from a caring member of the faculty or staff. We have opportunities to alter student expectations if we reach out to them, determine their needs, and then, in a positive and sensitive way, use the resources of the institution to meet those needs.

In short, in designing our research efforts we must bear in mind that students bring to college a host of expectations regarding their ability to succeed in the classroom, in the dormitory, in maintaining the dual role of child-student or parent-spouse or student-worker. The degree to which these expectations or fears or hopeful anticipations meet with reality—the extent to which the college's offerings meet, exceed, or fall short of a student's expectations—is likely to be the extent to which we see persistence behavior on the part of the student.

Phase Three: Outcomes Assessment. The third phase in retention research focuses on the outcomes that we set out to achieve. In this stage we must determine whether the programs or practices that we have designed are having the desired impact. The key criteria for this phase of research should be outcomes oriented—student learning, competencies, and skill levels; student persistence; student and graduate satisfaction levels; and measures of student development (self-concept, self-confidence, attitudinal change, and so on). Other criteria such as college grade point average and course attempted/course completion ratios are somewhat less useful because of their relative nature.

Study designs may be cross-sectional, or controlled, using current or retrospectively matched control groups. Assessment criteria must focus on desired outcomes, avoiding the confusion of inputs and outputs, and should be concerned with absolute performance or the amount of change students experience.

There are a variety of reasons for conducting outcomes assessment.

- To monitor—is implementation parallel to the design?
- To assess impact and validate our outcome claims—is what we are doing making a difference?
- To identify areas for change—what aspects of our program are not meeting the established goals?
- To analyze cost-benefit—what is the balance between effectiveness and efficiency?

Again, the question behind this type of assessment ought to be: How can we do what needs to be done better—striving constantly for that near-perfect performance—because when students are most successful, the institution is most likely to be successful.

As an example, an effective program assessment was designed to determine the outcomes of a program to increase the retention of science majors by assigning freshmen science majors rooms in proximity to one another in residence halls. The study found that prospective science majors who were housed close to other science majors were more likely to remain in their major for two years and remain at the college than were science majors who were housed at random. Many other controlled institutional studies we have reviewed have examined the effect on persistence of student participation in orientation, advising, career-planning, and developmental education programs. A particularly well-designed study documenting the relationship between persistence, achievement, and student participation in a program of supplemental instruction is presented by Martin, Blanc, and De Buhr (1982). Further, we are finding many institutions using similar assessment data at critical decision-making junctures when resources are being allocated or reallocated.

Data as a Trigger for Action

Institutional retention data, when properly presented to faculty and staff, can serve as an effective trigger: a catalyst spurring action and further study. These attention-getting triggers are often needed initially to emphasize not only the magnitude of the problem, but also the fact that it is one which will ultimately affect every person on campus. Colleges use many methods of alerting their faculty, staff, and administrators about the attrition rate of students. Recently, one community college sent flyers to all faculty and staff with graphics and captions indicating that for three years running, six of ten students who enrolled in the fall did not return one year later. On many campuses where we have worked, faculty and staff have been unaware of the attrition problem on campus until confronted with the hard facts during a campuswide workshop on the topic. At one selective state university, many faculty were startled by and attentive to the following fact: Their academically talented entering freshman class, as measured by ACT scores and high school grades that put them over the 90th percentile in a very large national sample of college-bound students, were, on average, earning freshman college grade point averages that put them only at the 63rd percentile of grades earned by entering freshmen nationally. This disparity deserves the attention of faculty and administrators, and may have direct policy implications for course placement and prerequisites if retention is to be improved.

Other campuses have used a dollars-lost approach to initially draw attention to the problem. One private university calculated how much tuition was lost in one year due to attrition across four classes; the figures are shown in Table 1. Based

Table 1. Tuition Loss Statement.

Class	Number of Dropouts	Number of Quarters for Which Tuition Was Lost	Tuition Dollars Lost (Based on Tuition of $1,200/Quarter)
Freshman	441	9	$4,286,520
Sophomore	247	6	1,600,560
Junior	99	3	320,760
Senior	99	1	106,920
Potential Tuition Loss for One Year			$6,314,760

on tuition of $1,200 per quarter, the net loss was in excess of $6 million! As campuses begin retention efforts, data such as these serve as an effective trigger for action in planning for a maximum effect. Some of the items to consider include those on the following start-up checklist.

1. What data are already available—in admissions or advising folders, registrars or financial aid offices, or standardized reports provided to the college by ACT, College Board, Cooperative Institutional Research Program—that might trigger attention and action?
2. What other data will be needed to substantiate the points highlighted by already existing data?
3. Whose attention do we want to capture?
4. Who else needs to be aware of what we are planning?
5. What is the best form or forum for distribution of these data?
6. Can these data be effectively presented by a faculty or staff member, or would they be better received by the audience we want to reach if presented by an external consultant?

However, in presenting research findings, care must be taken not to do so in a way that seems to place blame on any particular segment of the campus community. The retention plan implementation guide presented by Noel, Levitz, and Saluri in the last chapter of this book further explores the role that data collection and data reporting play in a retention improvement effort.

Overall, retention data can remind everyone on campus of what we too often tend to forget: colleges should, after all, exist at the behest of their students.

Conclusion

Ultimately, retention rates are a relative, campus-specific matter. Care must be taken before judgments are made about individual campus attrition rates. There are two key variables to be taken into consideration. First, academic ability of students is an important control variable. As Noel highlights in Chapter One, there is a clearly demonstrated relationship between ability as measured by ACT/SAT scores and freshman attrition. Second, the relationship between the function that the institution serves and student expectations can have a dramatic impact on attrition rates. Individual student objectives may not include the completion of a program of study at the institution they first enter. The transfer plans of students before entry effectively turn some community colleges and regional state universities into one-year schools.

While the national dropout data outlined at the beginning of this book serve as useful benchmarks against which institutions can make initial comparisons, ultimately the real test has to do with degree of improvement. The challenge for retention researchers on campus is to provide starting-point data— where we were when we began to pay attention to student success and student retention—against which we can document the rate of improvement. Effective retention research, then, is not a one-time event but a process that serves to integrate the multi-faceted approaches to dealing with students on campus, from admissions through orientation and initial advising to ongoing interactions with teachers, advisers, staff, and administrators. It is a way of cataloguing the quality of the experience our campuses have to offer; of assessing the level of satisfaction of students, graduates, and withdrawers; of focusing on problem areas; of studying the success of targeted students who are predicted to benefit from appropriate interventions. It further provides a mechanism for zeroing in on problem areas, for diagnosing and prescribing needed changes.

Retention research data must be outcome centered. Used as part of an accountability program to demonstrate worth by validating our mission, it can also be employed to justify the existence of campus programs, secure additional resources, and generate good public relations by creating a successful image both within the college community and for external funding sources. However it is used, it is critical that retention research data become decision-making data, that the process becomes a part of the institution's ongoing evaluation and planning activities and celebratory sense of its own success.

References

Astin, A. W., Hemond, M. K., and Richardson, G. T. *The American Freshman: National Norms for Fall 1982.* Los Angeles: Higher Education Research Institute, University of California, 1982.

Clifton, D. "Varsity Management: A Way to Increase Productivity." Lincoln, Nebr.: Selection Research, 1980.

Clifton, D. "Principles of Varsity Management." Presentation delivered during Advanced Retention/Enrollment Management Concepts and Practices Conference, Chicago, Ill.: February 1985.

Forrest, A. *Increasing Student Competence and Persistence: The Best Case for General Education.* Iowa City, Iowa: American College Testing Program National Center for Advancement of Educational Practices, 1982.

Hodgkinson, H. L. "Guess Who's Coming to College: A Demographic Portrait of Students in the 1990s." *Academe*, 1983, *69* (2), 13–20.

Involvement in Learning: Realizing the Potential of American Higher

Education. Final report of Study Group on Conditions of Excellence in American Higher Education. Washington, D.C.: National Institute of Education, Oct. 1984.

Kanter, R. M. *The Change Masters: Innovation for Productivity in the American Corporation.* New York: Simon & Schuster, 1983.

Keller, G. *Academic Strategy: The Management Revolution in American Higher Education.* Baltimore, Md: Johns Hopkins University Press, 1983.

Martin, D., Blanc, R., and De Buhr, L. "Supplemental Instruction: A Model for Increasing Student Performance and Persistence." In L. Noel and R. Levitz (eds.), *How to Succeed with Academically Underprepared Students.* Iowa City, Iowa: American College Testing Program National Center for Advancement of Educational Practices, 1982.

Noel, L., and Levitz, R. "National Dropout Study." Iowa City, Iowa: American College Testing Program National Center for Advancement of Educational Practices, 1983.

Patrick, C., Myers, E., and Van Dusen, W. *A Manual for Conducting Student Attrition Studies.* rev. ed. Boulder, Colo. and New York: National Center for Higher Education Management Systems and College Board, 1979.

Peters, T. J., and Waterman, R. H. *In Search of Excellence.* New York: Harper & Row, 1982.

Terenzini, P. T. "Designing Attrition Studies." In E. T. Pascarella (ed.), *Studying Student Attrition.* New Directions for Institutional Research, no. 36. San Francisco: Jossey-Bass, 1982.

19

Building Support
for a Campuswide
Retention Program

Laurence N. Smith
Ronald Lippitt
Dorian Sprandel

Readers of the first three parts of this book might well be wonder-
ing how the material presented relates to their own professional
responsibilities as well as to their own campuses. They may be
considering how certain ideas can be adapted to their own institutions. And they may be thinking about ways to awaken
their colleagues and key leaders on campus to the importance
of creating a campuswide program designed to improve quality
of life and thus retention.

However, as Kanter (1983) demonstrates, the ability to
change, either as an individual or as an institution, is a complex phenomenon. Various degrees of readiness for change exist within us as individuals, within our respective organizational
units such as departments and divisions, and within our institutions as a whole. The degree to which readiness exists or can

be fostered increases and expands the potential for change to take place. Because readiness for change is a systems concept, it occurs with varying intensities within the different individuals, departments, and divisions that ultimately constitute the institution's overall potential for growth and development. In some institutions there is a strongly recognized need for change, but a lack of readiness or knowledge about how to change. At other institutions where readiness for change has been acted upon, there is an understanding that as readiness evolves into action and change, new levels of readiness must be continuously developed and acted upon to maintain the momentum critical to fully achieving desired goals.

This chapter focuses on the challenge of stimulating and focusing readiness to work on planned change. It examines the change process in a complex system and considers ways of diagnosing system readiness and of overcoming the obstacles and conditions involved in moving from readiness to action. Since institutions must continually redevelop and reestablish readiness in order to achieve new levels of change as they pursue their goals, we conclude with a consideration of the readiness characteristics necessary for maintaining momentum and spreading change throughout the entire system.

Whether or not we want change to occur, change takes place, triggered by a myriad of internal and external forces. This chapter, however, discusses only planned change—purposeful, deliberate change—recognizing that the increased retention of students directly depends on making carefully considered changes that improve the quality of campus life. Changes in attitude and practice—in programs beginning with admissions and continuing in orientation, advising, and career planning as well as in the classroom as students move in and through the institution— will have to occur on many campuses in order to create a more positive and staying environment.

In order for such planned change and retention efforts to be successful, the various subparts of a campus must work together. Because our colleges and universities tend to be hierarchically structured and administered through structural units such as departments, divisions, schools, and, in our larger institutions, colleges, it is difficult to develop the rich, collaborative networks necessary to improve the quality of campus life and create a strong sense of campus community. We must adopt a strategic planning process involving all units, programs, activities, and services in order to bring about the preferred change required for institutional renewal (Palola and Padgett, 1971).

Briefly, the key interdependent parts of our higher education system are

1. A vertical set of relations between system levels: trustees, administrators, faculty, support personnel, and students
2. A horizontal set of relations between departments, peer managers/administrators, peer teachers, student leaders, student organizations, and so on
3. Relations between elements of the past (traditions, mission statement, reputation), the present (morale, standards, procedures), and the future (goals, perspectives, and so on)
4. Relations between the system and its environment (economic, political, physical factors, and others)

Under this system of interrelationships, instead of developing the collaborative structures necessary to best achieve our goals, much of our energy is focused on pursuing the interests of competitive factions, a situation that has been exacerbated in recent years by increased competition for declining resources (Dressel, 1981). Launching a change effort requires new strategies for overcoming the negative impact of this rigid, competitive compartmentalization and departmentalization. It also means replacing, where it exists, the rigid communications characteristic of limited vertical interaction with truly collaborative mechanisms that will replace both the vertical and horizontal networks characteristic of politically appointed committees, task forces, and councils.

Table 1 contrasts noncollaborative actions with collaborative patterns of action. While collaborative patterns are emerging on many campuses, there is a great deal of evidence that many noncollaborative, ineffective patterns of problem solving also exist among administrators and faculty. These negative

Table 1. Noncollaborative and Collaborative Patterns.

Noncollaborative	Collaborative
Focusing on problems and "system pain"	Focusing on images of future and potentiality
Forcing solutions	Searching for alternatives
Requesting resources added-on	Reallocating current resources through consensus
Using segmented approach	Using a systemic approach
Making closet decisions	Involving everyone in ideas, commitments
Guarding territory	Exploring, sharing, pooling, exchanging
Using departmental problem solving	Using interdepartmental problem solving
Maintaining old patterns	Scanning for simplification of existing models or developing new models
Assigning overload work	Restructuring roles, retraining
Operating within traditional and bureaucratic decision-making structures	Using temporary, voluntary participative structures

patterns grow out of institutional impersonalization, individual isolation and mistrust, and anxiety about the future in difficult economic times. Yet it may be that it is precisely the existence of these ineffectual patterns, coupled with conflict and frustration, that is stirring a new readiness among faculty and administrators to bring about the collaborative structures that will make us the beneficiaries of—not the victims of—change.

Retention has always been a problem on American campuses. What is different now is the increasing readiness to look at retention in terms of enrollment stabilization as the number of students available from the traditional sending markets dramatically declines (Smith and others, 1981). In our experience over the past few years, we have now come to recognize clearly that retention cannot be improved without involving the total campus system. This means involving everyone in a planned change effort that will improve the quality of campus life by drawing upon our institutional ability to function as a strong community.

Forces for Change

First among the forces producing this new climate of readiness for change at today's colleges and universities is the recognition that highly centralized, top-down bureaucratic administrative structures and styles have not been efficient or successful in solving attrition problems (Riley and Baldridge 1977). An important force is the growing realization by leaders in industry and business, as well as in higher education, that attention to the quality of work life and to employee involvement is critical to success. As a result, there is an increased willingness on campus to experiment with organizational development strategies and their applications. Where there has been significant planned change activity, an awareness has emerged that pro-active is better than reactive, collaborative is better than adversarial, and planning on an institutionwide basis is most successful. There is also an increased awareness that quality is a critical factor in creating consumer loyalty.

In addition, there is growing concern about the fact that a college education no longer guarantees employment or employment at a level parallel to the education and ability of the graduating student. U.S. Department of Labor statistics ("Tomorrow's Jobs: Overview." 1982–83, p. 3) show that 25 percent of those who entered the labor market between 1969 and 1978 were underemployed because professional, managerial, and technical occupations could not expand rapidly enough to accommodate the increased supply of college graduates. As Noel points out in Chapter One, the fact that the traditional view of a college degree as a guarantee of success has not been matched by reality is stimulating reexamination of the most basic claims and practices of higher education. On many of our campuses, faculty and administrators find this to be a very discomforting situation.

There is also an increasing awareness among educators of the growing competition from courses, workshops, and institutes conducted by professional organizations and associations. Coupled with rapidly growing corporate-based educational programs, these activities constitute a serious challenge to the nation's unresponsive colleges and universities.

Recent developments in technology have also produced forces for change on campus. Computer-based instruction is only one of a growing number of emerging possibilities. Anxiety about these alternative instructional delivery methods and about the possibilities arising from innovations in information technologies has prompted many educators to confront the necessity for change.

Still another major force for readiness to change has been the increased recognition that retention programs conserve human as well as economic resources.

Obviously, campuses with existing strong traditions of faculty and student involvement are best able to respond to these forces. Other campuses may be threatened but can survive by changing.

Assessing Readiness for Change

The forces just described are creating a new readiness for change in our complex college and university systems. Regrettably, most desires for change do not result in a systems change process because of a lack of understanding of the various elements of readiness and how to diagnose and use them. The major source of change readiness in any system is "system pain," which occurs when any part is experiencing discomfort with the functioning of the total system or over its role in influencing the total system. "System pain" may cause this readiness because people are motivated by pain and respond to it instead of to symptoms. Or an image of a new potential or improved circumstance may cause this readiness. The critical ingredient for change readiness comes when the part of the system experiencing the discomfort recognizes influence on and from other parts of the system. What is critical at this point is how this readiness energy, this desire for change, can be used to influence critical leaders within the institution who are at the appropriate power levels to activate a process resulting in an institutional commitment to goal setting and the change effort.

Once the need to change is widely agreed upon and there exists the readiness potential to bring it about, just waiting for that potential to develop into action on its own will not suffice. For when change occurs on its own without the requisite planning, it has usually been forced on the institution by dramatic events. Because it generally involves piecemeal solutions, such forced change exacts a large and unnecessary price for correcting a problem, often resulting in an even worse situation in the long run.

Properly diagnosing an institution's readiness to act is a critical step in the change process. In many institutions there may be a need for change but no one who feels the responsibility or has the authority to make change happen. Obviously, if one were to ask around campus, one would find very few colleagues who would not support the notion of improving retention (especially if it meant retaining highly qualified students) by enhancing the quality of campus life. But, if one were to ask these colleagues for their help in creating widespread campus awareness of the opportunities inherent in these activities, their response would give ready support to the notion that there can be agreement about the need for change without the willingness or readiness to respond to this need.

Readiness to change thus exists both as potential energy and actual energy. For the most part, because of our limited vantage point within our own institutions, we are unaware of or cannot adequately assess the change potential that exists. We thus must make our diagnosis on a speculative basis or try to motivate others into action through the use of political or bureaucratic structures or altruistic emotional appeals. Our frustrations mount as we realize our colleagues often are comfortable with and have vested interests in keeping things the way they are.

The response to appeals for change made to those at higher authority levels is usually equally unsatisfactory. Their failure to respond may stem not so much from disagreement about the desired end results, but from not really understanding what role is being asked of them. They may be reluctant to be involved in creating something they cannot understand or to endorse a new approach to problems they feel are already being responded to within the institution. Their unwillingness to make a commitment could even indicate a legitimate reluctance to start another top-down process, no matter how good it may be for the long-term survival of the institution. Equally important is the fact that key administrators often lack knowledge of existing grass-roots support for systematic change and are reluctant to order programs that cut across the boundaries of the several vertical and horizontal levels in their institutions. In many situations, a less-than-enthusiastic response from the administration may stem not from a lack of support or a failure to recognize the need for change, but from an inability to understand how to bring about the desired change (Meltzer and Nord, 1981).

It is not only top administrators who have difficulty assessing grass-roots readiness for change. A common complaint in colleges and universities is the lack of efficient formal structures for communicating between peers and peer subsystems to exchange information, create new opportunities, or even to discover common areas of disagreement. Because our institutions' organizational structures are usually developed along divisional or departmental lines, our major adherence is to those structures in which we are based and through which we receive our rewards.

Faculty and staff have diminishing contact with their colleagues and each other as institutions increase in size and interaction involves crossing the boundaries from one department to another or from one division or college to another. In many instances, just being in a different building or on a different floor is enough to block interaction from occurring. As a result, each of us has very few ways to really assess the readiness of other parts of the institution to approve of and invest in change efforts.

When an idea for change emerges, usually in the shape of a response to a problem or, more accurately, a symptom of a problem, we tend to respond by establishing a committee. Because committee members are usually appointed on the basis of a bureaucratic/political view of who can do the most for a particular unit or vested interest, they do not often respond to problems in terms of what is best for the campus as a whole (Lippitt, 1980). Unfortunately, most of our formal linking across departmental and individual lines on campus grows out of serving together on such factional committees, task forces, and councils. As important as these committees are as linking mechanisms enabling us to conduct daily business, the very nature of their charges and structures limits their effectiveness in establishing the proper collaborative climate for change readiness.

As we noted earlier, since our institutions are constituted as a complex set of social, administrative, and operational systems, one of the most difficult tasks is to adequately assess the quantity and quality of readiness for a successful retention start-up. Because the structures which evolve from these systems often are barriers to change and there are an infinite combination of individual and organizational dynamics involved, readiness assessment can become an overwhelming problem which in itself can block a successful change effort.

Four Levels of Readiness

What conditions must prevail for nurturing readiness potential and converting it into readiness for action? Taking into account the need to oversimplify the complexities of campus systems, a model of retention readiness can provide a self-appraisal tool for identifying readiness characteristics and determining an institution's degree of readiness to begin a planned change effort. There are four levels of increasing systemwide readiness which are preconditions for successful start-up: Level One: Latency; Level Two: Awareness; Level Three: Intention to Act; and Level Four: Energy.

Latency is the most common state of retention readiness at our institutions. At this level, there are several persons within the institution who wish to influence systemwide retention efforts. Among these persons, there are at least a small number who are significant formal or informal influencers within the institution. Frequently this group includes persons who are innovators and tend to operate outside the formal decision-making apparatus of the system.

During Latency, there is no top-level systemwide sanction, though there may be verbal reinforcement to the effect that
retention has merit and is important. Generally at this point
the chief executive officer has little or no notion about how to
plan and execute a systemwide retention activity.

Perhaps the most obvious and widespread characteristic
of the Latency stage is individual and group efforts to remedy
system pain, which usually appears in the form of chronic, acute
organizational dysfunction.

Most frequently the remedies prescribed at the Latency
level reflect a segmented rather than a systemic approach. During this phase, diagnosis and prescription typically are focused
on specific offices, functions, or subparts that are viewed as major
problem areas in the system with virtually no consideration of
causes and effects within the larger system. Continuing in this
partial mode not only inhibits the ability to move to higher levels,
but produces resistance to change, resulting in cosmetic camou-
flage, displacement of the source of the system pain, and participant passivity. Most unfortunate, any improvments which may
result from such surface changes are usually vitiated by the more
basic and enduring systematic problems. It is thus not unusual
for an institution to deplete its ability to move to higher levels
of system readiness at this stage. This is all the more regret-
table since the next three levels of readiness may be passed
through within a period of a few months if the change process
is planned and carefully managed.

One special feature characterizes movement to Level Two,
the Awareness level, and that is understanding that retention
remedies require systemwide or systemic efforts. Usually this
level of readiness cannot be achieved without inside or outside
consultative assistance. The key is to link the institution's most
ready persons in a collaborative design for power and information sharing as they move toward initiating and sanctioning a
tentative conception of the system's preferred future.

This last element, initiating a view of a new future for
the system, requires special emphasis because it represents a
powerful passport for moving from Level One to Level Two.
Simply stated, movement from the Latency level to the Aware-

ness level usually can be successfully achieved by convening a
meeting involving no more than ten to twenty influential campus leaders for a campuswide futuring effort in which they envision what it would be like if they joined together in providing
leadership for a campus renewal campaign. Other primary features of Level Two readiness are

1. Developing public advocates for specific retention activities by
   a. Placing retention on the formal agendas of the institu-
      tion's governing board and top-level administrative
      councils
   b. Stimulating commentary and establishing points of
      view in student and staff newspapers
   c. Reporting retention information and data to the cam-
      pus community and to specific departments
   d. Conducting special campus meetings through already
      established constituent structures for faculty, students,
      staff, executive officers, and trustees
2. Discussing the institution's budgetary commitment to retention by focusing on such matters as
   a. The high cost of dropouts
   b. The significant gains that might easily be made to en-
      hance the campus environment and improve student
      services
   c. The immediate need for a small budgetary allocation
      to conduct a preliminary diagnostic study of the cam-
      pus retention situation
3. Establishing intentions to develop written proposals by
   a. Organizing into special ad hoc task forces and work
      groups
   b. Sending select, interested persons to retention work-
      shops and conferences
   c. Initiating a systematic inventory of what similar insti-
      tutions are doing about retention
4. Developing leadership awareness while assuring there is
   deliberate constrained use of the full powers of the president to

a. Appoint retention committees and ad hoc members without making specific assignments of accountability for the tasks to be achieved

b. Sanction retention activities without direct and active participation in them

c. Support retention efforts without directly planning them

d. Sponsor retention initiatives without actually deciding upon them

While it is difficult to distinguish exactly where the actual transition occurs between Level Two and Level Three, it is not difficult to identify Level Three's distinguishing qualities. At this readiness level there is a strong degree of publicly expressed leadership support. And within constituent parts there is an ever-increasing willingness to participate in a systemwide retention effort and to become voluntarily involved in preparing for it. Usually top-level formal sanctioning occurs during Level Three following executive involvement in the Level Two meeting.

As with the transition between Level Two and Level Three, there is no distinct line of demarcation between Level Three and Level Four, the Energy level. What is most notable is the process's high energy at this point. Optimism is spurred by a confident expectation of curing age-old ills. Fostering the institution's good health by engendering new visions of the system's potential generates enthusiasm and a snowballing level of interest. Unfortunately, the mild euphoria characteristic of this phase also can stimulate actions which seriously hinder future success.

One common pitfall involves the executive who is eager for results and attempts to use administrative power to order the desired change. When this occurs, the net effect is the activation of overt resistance as well as undercurrents of resistance to change which can seriously undermine activities and doom the change effort to failure. During the Energy phase it is critical that executives demonstrate patience, restraint, and faith in the collaborative process, maintaining a moratorium on directives and the use of their vertical power. Failure to do so de-energizes the necessary collaborative process by stimulating competitive, segmented, and vested-interest behaviors. Normally the intensity of the Energy level will be clearly evident and will provide the best clue as to when retention start-up should begin.

Obstacles to Retention Readiness

Retention readiness is vulnerable, and there are constant threats to its greater development. Readiness can be severely diminished at any of its four levels and even after a successful start-up campaign has been launched. Whenever system change is begun, specific generic issues and obstacles inevitably evolve.

One of the first obstacles is resistance; this can be a major readiness problem. Whenever a system's quasi-stationary equilibrium or homeostasis is in peril, resistance will result. It is a natural and predictable system phenomenon, whether involving the individual, the group, interlocked institutional subparts, or the larger systems of which the institution is a part. The key is to use resistance as a positive force rather than to try to overwhelm or fight it (Bennis, 1961). The following are suggestions for using resistance positively at any readiness level and at any time in the change process.

- Always maintain two-way communication.
- Never punish resistance because punishment only strengthens it.
- Fact gathering and fact finding should be conducted by persons most affected by the proposed changes and consequences.
- Do not predetermine that major resistance is illegitimate because it often can be a source of valuable information which can guide the change process.
- Take the initiative to promote communication directly aimed at confronting, sharing, and probing the negative feelings and opinions of resisters in order to clarify issues, identify alternatives, identify points for negotiation, and provide a useful mechanism for venting feelings.

- Look for opportunities to forge compromises and to negotiate win-win solutions.
- Provide learning opportunities designed to build participant confidence and competence in dealing with situations and tasks.

A second obstacle to readiness is the form of participation involved. As we have seen, the most common form of participation within the campus community is based on representation of various subparts or vested interests. This political mode of participation adversely affects both the quality and quantity of involvement. Instead of relying on this representative structure, opportunities must be designed for all persons to directly participate in the change process through face-to-face interaction with others. This enhances opportunities for shared learning, team building, and collaboration as well as easing the implementation of eventual changes. One of the most effective ways for involving the community's real movers and shakers is nominating volunteers through special invitation.

A third obstacle to readiness is failing to maintain an open and ongoing change process. New participants should be welcome at virtually any point in the process. For success to be maintained, there must be ongoing orientation as well as opportunity for full involvement for all new entrants. Otherwise new participants will be marginal contributors who will drop out as they become frustrated, confused, and bored. Unless they can become involved, their behavior will debilitate rather than enhance readiness.

Inadequate participation skills are a fourth readiness obstacle. Many forces all too often push participants into roles for which they are not prepared. The consequence is resistance and low-quality involvement. Frequently role playing and simulation are used to provide opportunities for skill practice and risk-taking rehearsal. Promoting a sense of confidence and competence about new situations and tasks is one of the most effective ways to promote readiness and reduce resistance.

A fifth obstacle is ambivalence to system change. Initiation of the possibility of system change inevitably activates individual and group ambivalence toward both the process and content of potential change. Positive and negative feelings can then push toward each other to impede readiness. However, from these expressions of doubt and caution can come valuable information which can assist in identifying blind alleys and unexpected alternatives. Ambivalence only remains an obstacle when the activated underground of ambivalence is ignored or misjudged as resistance which must be fought. It is normal for persons to be ambivalent when they are considering making a commitment to change which entails the use of personal energy and resources. The way to keep this natural ambivalence from becoming an obstacle is to provide widespread opportunities for the open expression of concerns, anxieties, hopes, and expectations.

The sixth obstacle to readiness is failing to mobilize energy and maintain momentum. Many leaders unknowingly create an undercurrent of resistance by mandating involvement rather than establishing the opportunity for persons to volunteer energy and time and then rewarding their efforts. Momentum will also be lost and a "snap back" or backsliding, possibly past the beginning point, will occur if a new normalcy or homeostasis is not established.

Conclusion

Finally, there is an essential set of conditions which facilitates converting readiness potential to readiness action.

- Planning for change is established and sanctioned at the top level as a systematic process with supporting management goals. It is also recognized and rewarded as an important activity throughout the institution both at the unit and staff levels.
- Planning is future oriented and pro-active. It allows for a strategic blending of what we want to hold on to and what we want to leave behind, but most importantly it is firmly rooted in the framework that develops from envisioning what we want to become.

- Planning is collaborative, not a top-down management activity involving only the central administration. Collaborative planning involves communication and legitimization of feelings and values between and among all parts of the campus system. It involves those who will be responsible for implementing goals or who will be affected by the planned change. The collaborative process reduces the threat to individuals because they can see where change will lead and how they will benefit from it.
- Approaches and commitments reflect a campus stewardship which always assumes "we" instead of "I." The structure of power is flattened by decentralizing responsibilities and centralizing crucial coordination and linking functions. This is necessary for collaborating, networking, planning, and successfully implementing change.
- The change process is managed by those who personally or as part of the management team have access to other professionals with skills and experience in planning, organizing, and managing change.
- The process respects the uniqueness of the campus culture and is tailored accordingly. By so doing, unnecessary resistance is avoided and higher levels of readiness are promoted.
- The change process is open, documented, and evaluated. In this way all members of the campus community have access to information about all events, successful practices, and activities as well as about any failures.

In summary, when it is properly structured, the group activity necessary to initiate planned change involves more than a collection of individuals representing various interests. Instead, new forces and new properties are created through the planned and spontaneous interaction that occurs when persons work toward a common goal. It is this collective spirit arising out of collaborative efforts that can make the difference in instituting a plan for organizational change and development which enhances the quality of student life and learning on campus and hence increases retention.

References

Bennis, W. G., and others (eds.). *The Planning of Change.* New York: Holt, Rinehart & Winston, 1961, 501–512.

Dressel, P. L. *Administrative Leadership: Effective and Responsive Decision Making in Higher Education.* Jossey-Bass, 1981, 42.

Kanter, R. M. *The Change Masters: Innovation for Productivity in the American Corpoation.* New York: Simon & Schuster, 1983.

Lippitt, R. S. "Life and Death of Committees." *Human Resources Development Journal,* 1980, *4,* 2–5.

Metzer, H., and Nord, W. R. *Making Organizations Humane and Productive: A Handbook for Practitioners.* New York: Wiley, 1981, 463–474.

Palola, E. G., and Padgett, W. *Planning for Self-Renewal: A New Approach to Planned Organizational Change.* University of California, Center for Research and Development in Higher Education, 1971, 65–101.

Riley, G. L., and Baldridge, J. V. (eds.). *Governing Academic Organizations: New Problems, New Perspectives.* Berkeley, Calif.: McCutchan, 1977, 11.

Smith, L. N., and others. *Mobilizing the Campus for Retention: An Innovative Quality-of-Life Model.* Iowa City, Iowa: American College Testing Program National Center for the Advancement of Educational Practices, 1981, 3–4.

"Tomorrow's Jobs: Overview." Reprinted from *Occupational Outlook Handbook.* 1982–83 edition. Washington, D.C.: U.S. Department of Labor, 3.

20

Increasing Faculty Involvement
in Retention Efforts

∿∿∿∿∿∿

Terrence J. Toy

It may be the talk about fiscal problems and the possibility of faculty and staff reductions. It may be the report showing that only one-half of the entering freshmen will eventually graduate, or the data indicating that attrition from one's department exceeds the average for the institution. It may be the realization that a tenure contract does not mean very much if one's entire program is eliminated for financial reasons. Or perhaps it is learning that Ann Marie Kelly, the best student in ten years of teaching, has transferred to another college to pursue the same major. In any case, sooner or later, the retention issue touches most faculty. Might there have been something that one could have done differently? Indeed, there probably was in the past, and there probably is in the present and future.

While research has sometimes produced confusing or even contradictory results about the factors contributing to retention and attrition, there is apparent unanimity regarding the role of the faculty. In their review of several research studies, Pantages and Creedon (1978, p. 79) find that the quality of the relationship between students and their professors is of critical importance in determining satisfaction with the institution. In a nationwide survey, the data compiled from 944 responding institutions provided a rank-order tabulation of the factors thought to influence retention positively. As Beal and Noel (1980, p. 19) report, the retention factor considered most important by all types of institutions (two-year public, two-year private, four-year public, and four-year private) was "caring attitude of faculty and staff." In an overview of the research, Smith and others (1981, p. 88) find that "the most important features of the holding environment have to do with the faculty and the instructional staff." Based upon a statistical examination of the Cooperative Institutional Research Program's data base which includes longitudinal information for more than 200,000 students at more than 300 institutions of all types, Astin (1977, pp. 223 and 233) concludes: "Student-faculty interaction has a stronger relationship to student satisfaction with the college experience than any other involvement variable, or, indeed, any other student or institutional characteristic. Students who interact frequently with faculty are more satisfied with all aspects of their institutional experience, including student friendships, variety of courses, intellectual environment, and even administration of the institution."

Because initial impressions seem to significantly influence student opinion of an institution, the early reception given students by faculty is particularly important. As Noel observes in Chapter One, experiences during the first six weeks on campus are critical to students' impressions of the institution. The results of a survey administered to freshmen in their seventh week of attendance at the University of Denver in Colorado indicate that they sometimes held negative opinions of student service offices with which they had probably had no personal interaction (Toy, 1980, pp. 173-220). It appears that conversations with the sophomores, juniors, and seniors who make up the bulk of the student grapevine had to some extent effectively conditioned freshmen's perspectives. The importance of first impressions supports the contention of Pantages and Creedon (1978, pp. 95-96) that we need to find new ways to maximize faculty-student interaction during the freshman year, including greater faculty involvement in the orientation program and more care in the assignment of faculty advisers.

Although most student-faculty interaction centers around the academic function of the institution, there is substantial evidence that contact outside of the classroom is also important. Citing several references, Tinto (1975, p. 109) asserts: "It is not surprising that a number of studies have found that social interaction with the college's faculty is related to persistence in college." (See Chapter Two.) According to Noel (1978, p. 97), "Students make judgments about their academic experience on the basis of such factors as quality of instruction, freedom to contact faculty for consultation, availability of faculty for consultation, and faculty involvement outside the classroom." Beal and Noel (1980, pp. 91–93) identify action programs employed by various colleges attempting to improve retention rates and report that the first subheading listed in the category of most influential involvement experiences was "Faculty Outside the Classroom." Finally, Spady (1971, pp. 38–62) suggests that interaction with faculty outside the classroom not only increases social interaction and, therefore, institutional commitment but facilitates the student's academic integration as well.

It is clear then that the performance and attitude of the faculty both in and outside of the classroom is a significant variable in the complex equation by which students form an opinion of a particular institution. In examining the influence that these factors have on retention rates, this chapter will consider the key role the faculty play in the academic milieu and in the generation of a staying environment; discuss various faculty responses to retention projects; and offer some suggestions for building greater faculty support for and participation in such projects.

Because it seems apparent that our attrition rates are not founded upon institutional successes, it is essential to view the role of the faculty with candor. As Noel (1978, p. 87) observes, "A concerted effort to increase student retention forces an institution to examine itself closely and what is observed will not always be pleasant or easy to accept." Some faculty will greet retention efforts with enthusiasm; this interest should be nurtured to the greatest extent possible. However, it doubtlessly will be necessary to convince some of the more skeptical faculty of the value of retention efforts in order to obtain their cooperation. To promote such faculty involvement it is first necessary to appreciate the faculty's position and to recognize their many roles on campus.

Role of the Faculty

The centrality of faculty to student satisfaction with a college or university is likely a consequence of the variety of functions they perform. As Roueche and Roueche point out in Chapter Fifteen, foremost, faculty are teachers. The level of faculty performance in classroom teaching is critical to campus health. Learning is the principal reason for attending college; the faculty are the chief catalysts in this process. "It is the instructors who ultimately make the educational system effective and relevant" (Flannery and others, 1973, p. 6).

Faculty are also mentors. Frequency of contact and shared interests draw students to the faculty of particular disciplines. "Student interaction with faculty appears to be more important in the student's major area than it is in other areas not only because of the former's proximity to the interests of the student but also because of its potential impact upon the student's future occupational mobility" (Tinto, 1975, p. 110).

Faculty are advisers. In Beal and Noel's study (1980, p. 21), improvement of academic advising is the most often-cited action program undertaken by institutions to improve retention. Fisher (1978, p. 73) contends that "faculty members clearly make the best advisers. They can be assisted by other staff and students; but . . . the core of a good advising program is the regular faculty members." In an article entitled, "Academic Advising: A Cornerstone of Student Retention," Crockett (1978, p. 30) concludes that "students receiving effective academic advising tend to feel positive not only about the process but the institution as well; and this positive attitude can be a strong contributing factor to student persistence." (See Chapter Thirteen.)

Faculty are a liaison between the student and the institution, connecting the student with academic, counseling, and extracurricular resources. In this capacity, faculty often have the opportunity to interpret procedures for students. Sometimes merely explaining the rationale behind a particular policy, rule, or regulation is sufficient to assuage a student's frustration.

Faculty are role models. Both as professionals in a specific discipline and as exemplary citizens, they are expected to embrace the highest ethical and moral standards—indeed, standards which generally represent an ideal rather than the norm for the society-at-large.

Faculty are friends. The college years are a period of social adjustment, and social problems may become a major source of student dissatisfaction with the institution in general. Many students seem to greatly value faculty friendships, perhaps because they see their instructors as survivors in the academic struggle in which they are currently engaged. Perhaps they respect the expertise and intellect of the faculty. Perhaps the faculty function as surrogate parents from time to time, mature adults with whom students can discuss serious issues. Probably, all of these factors and more are involved.

Although research has produced somewhat conflicting results concerning the peer-group influence on retention (Pantages and Creedon, 1978, pp. 70–71), it seems permissible to suggest that the support of a "faculty member as friend" can fulfill a student need during the development of peer-group alliances.

Beyond all of these roles, the faculty are representatives of the institution. Because classroom contact makes them the most accessible agents of the college or university, the performance and attitudes of the faculty may be taken as a reflection of institutional attitudes and the character of the faculty as a group may be a fairly accurate model of the strengths and weaknesses of the institution as a whole.

As a consequence of their multivariate role, faculty members establish a measure of credibility with students rather easily. This credibility allows them to substantially influence the attitudes of many students about the quality of their school and education through their verbal and nonverbal communications both in and outside of the classroom. Faculty comments and behavior may reinforce student perceptions or cause them to question their impressions. Further, violations of this trust may have a devastating impact on high-risk students. A faculty which uniformly lauds and reinforces the quality of the institution and of its personnel and graduates constitutes a powerful force in the development and maintenance of a staying environment. For students, such reinforcement makes temporary frustrations easier to bear.

In performing their various roles, faculty have access to the knowledge about student concerns which can provide direction for retention programs. Frequently it is the classroom teacher who first learns of the problems, anxieties, and concerns of the student body, and in the most explicit terms. Although such knowledge is not a substitute for periodic surveys of student opinion, recurring themes from student-faculty conversations often can furnish the specifics of student concerns and may uncover some problem areas overlooked by even the most carefully constructed survey instrument.

In this capacity as information sources, attentive faculty may also function as part of an early warning system to identify potential dropouts: those students in need of counseling. Sheffield and Meskill (1974, p. 42) advocate an early alert system involving faculty, peers, and administrators trained to watch— especially during the first eight weeks—for those who do not talk; who sit in the back row; who take no notes; who resist advising; and who show signs of hostility, withdrawal, and anxiety. Noel (1978, p. 95) suggests that early in the term instructors be given a form for use in identifying students with observed behavior patterns that could indicate a potential problem. The bulk of the referrals can then be handled in a manner that requires minimal effort on the part of instructors and allows for timely intervention by the institution's support services.

It is not uncommon for students to specifically discuss plans to withdraw or transfer from school with a faculty member prior to making a final decision. Sometimes this threat is a thinly veiled plea for assistance. As retention project coordinator at the University of Denver, I had several experiences of this sort: the students were not seriously contemplating withdrawal but merely seeking help and through consulting faculty members had discovered an institutional sensitivity virtually guaranteed to generate action in their behalf.

If the numerous roles which faculty play were recognized, it would follow that any successful effort to improve retention rates would be founded upon faculty support, cooperation, and participation. Yet Beal and Noel (1980,pp. 50-51) find that only 18 percent of the responding 944 institutions cited faculty/instructional development among the action programs restructured or introduced on their campus in a specific effort to improve retention. Only 3 percent of the responding institutions provided retention activity reports which described in some detail the nature of faculty/staff development programs. This neglect in acknowledging the key faculty role in retention may stem from a misconception about the significance of faculty or simply from a penny-wise-and-pound-foolish attitude that can be devastating to the success of a retention effort.

Faculty Response to Retention Projects

The initiation of a retention project on campus will elicit a spectrum of faculty responses at most institutions. Some will be highly enthusiastic, some will appear apathetic, and others will exhibit resistance and opposition. As a broad generalization, one might suspect that the proportion of faculty in each category would vary by institutional type. Institutions predominantly engaged in teaching would seem likely to include a greater percentage in the first group. Those with a substantial research component to their mission would most likely include a greater percentage in the second and third categories. There are surely exceptions to these generalizations, but there appears to be some research support. Astin (1977, p. 89) reports that his findings "clearly confirm the stereotype of the large multiversity as an impersonal institution that discourages direct contact between faculty and students." Beal and Noel (1980, p. 98) find that "public four-year institutions know they are likely to lose students who are not satisfied about either their academic advising or their contacts with faculty; yet these institutions are often 'locked into' higher student-faculty ratios and research activities."

Given the importance of retention to every college and university, it may seem surprising that any faculty member at any type of institution would ignore or oppose a retention project. It must be obvious that most common faculty concerns such as tenure, promotion, salaries, fringe benefits, and working conditions are of secondary importance when the economic survival of the school is in doubt. Nevertheless, nearly everyone who undertakes a retention project encounters some degree of faculty resistance. Beal and Noel (1980, p. 49) find that 20 percent of the responding 944 institutions cited "Lack of Faculty Support" among the factors inhibiting retention efforts on their campuses.

Although potentially unpleasant, we must address this problem with candor; it is not likely to go away by itself. The reasons for faculty reluctance to support retention projects include: simple inertia, a belief that retention is someone else's responsibility, a negative history of faculty involvement in other campus projects, the variety and extent of faculty expectations, and the structure of the institution's reward system.

Let us consider the question of inertia. Many faculty are rather conservative with respect to institutional change. Even seemingly minor fine-tuning of programs occasionally requires lengthy debate, resulting in considerable lag time between the initiation of a proposal and its implementation. While an atmosphere of well-being and security at an institution can provide an environment more conducive to change and risk taking, the fact that many faculty have a deep respect for the history and traditions of the school should not be overlooked: their years in residence usually exceed those of most students, staff, and administrators.

On nearly every campus there are likely to be some faculty members who regard the retention issue as someone else's responsibility—it is a great idea, but it is not my job. Enrollment is frequently regarded as an administrative problem; the feeling is that admissions officers are paid to maintain the body count. There may also be a few faculty familiar with the statistical correlations derived from retention studies who will cite the relationship between retention and past academic performance in high school and suggest that retention would improve if the admissions office would recruit only those students congruent with the college's academic standards. Faculty might also suggest that the attrition rate would drop if recruiters would refrain from over-selling the institution, a practice which ultimately results in disappointed and dissatisfied students. In addition, faculty might list various other offices on campus which in their view are responsible for retention. These may include the office of student affairs, the office of counseling and placement, or, perhaps, an office of retention. Surely, it is the responsibility of these people to handle this retention matter. But retention cannot be regarded as the responsibility of a single office or a single individual. A staying environment is based on the premise that the quality of student life on campus is everyone's concern.

Another obstacle to gaining faculty support is the fact that retention programs are sometimes perceived by faculty as attempts to cater to the whims of students. Does the highly significant relation between attrition and first-semester grades (Pantages and Creedon, 1978, p. 64) mean that the faculty are supposed to abandon their academic standards? Of course not! In fact, there is considerable evidence that students require academic challenge. Astin (1977, p. 171) finds that academic involvement is the main factor in student satisfaction with the academic environment: "Whatever the explanation, the student's own involvement is a more important determinant of satisfaction with the intellectual environment than any objective characteristic of the institutions themselves." It would seem apparent that lax academic standards and grading practices demand less academic involvement from the student than fair but rigorous standards and thus promote attrition rather than retention.

Another factor in faculty resistance is their history of involvement in other projects at the institution. Does past experience indicate that faculty participation has significantly influenced the final decisions and results? Or does it seem that the opinions of experts, brought in from the outside for relatively short time periods have overshadowed the findings of the faculty who have examined the same issue?

A very important factor is the variety and extent of demands made on the faculty. We have all attended meetings called to discuss a set of specific problems where the solution to each came to rest with the faculty, requiring still more of their time. It is thus commonly the case that the dynamic and knowledgeable faculty members whom we wish to involve in a retention project are already extensively committed to other campus projects. Another problem is that those faculty members who do participate in retention projects are often relieved of teaching assignments, thereby removing a number of the best instructors from the classroom, and thus undermining retention efforts.

While most institutions conduct inventories of various sorts with some regularity, comprehensive delineations of what is expected of faculty are less common. Such delineations are useful in assessing the amount of faculty time available for additional involvements. It should also be remembered that most faculty have family responsibilities and some will insist upon a modicum of leisure time.

Perhaps the most important factor in the faculty response to retention efforts, the reward system, has been reserved for last. In their chapters on academically underprepared students and on teaching, Moore and Carpenter and Roueche and Roueche propose various ways of recognizing and rewarding good teaching. I would like to approach this subject by way of analogy. Most of us are familiar with the concept of "economic man," a term applied to business persons, male and female, who possess perfect knowledge of the variables affecting their enterprises and the capabilities to manipulate these variables, and who always behave rationally to achieve the single goal of maximizing their profits. While this represents an ideal, most business people must bear some resemblance to the model if they are to remain solvent. Similarly, we could consider both male and female faculty members under a concept of "academic man." This term could be applied to those faculty who possess perfect knowledge of the variables affecting their achievement in academe and the capability to manipulate those variables, and who always behave rationally to achieve the single goal of academic advancement. Doubtlessly, this also represents a somewhat idealized paradigm; however, most faculty must bear some resemblance to the model if they are to survive and flourish at any institution.

Different faculty activities carry different weights in faculty evaluations on various campuses. In determining the priorities for the allocation of their time, faculty members are likely to emphasize those activities which seem to be most valued in their department and on campus. At most large institutions, some of the faculty will ask, publicly or privately, whether or not their participation in retention efforts will be weighed as heavily as another publication, preparation of a grant proposal, or presentation of a report at a professional meeting in determining tenure, promotion, and salary increase. Often, published statements of institutional priorities are less important in establishing actual priorities than perceptions gained by an examination of tenure and promotion lists. If improving the retention rate is a serious objective at an institution, then activities most directly related to the enhancement of a staying environment must truly carry the greatest weight.

The retention committee at the University of Denver asserts that: "If the reduction of attrition is a priority, then the reward system must include consideration of activities such as classroom performance, student-faculty interaction, and so forth, which appear positively correlated with retention. Every effort must be made to effect congruency between the performance of priority activities and the subsequent reward" (Toy, 1980, p. 30). In describing student-faculty interaction at large multiversities, Astin (1977, p. 89) observes that the formal or impersonal atmosphere created by the complex administrative superstructure may discourage direct contact between faculty and students. Further, in institutions emphasizing research and departmental affiliations, paying attention to undergraduates is often given lower priority than departmental research activities or concern for graduate students.

As one respondent cited by Smith and others (1981, p. 4) remarks, "If they're serious about this teaching system, they better get serious about changing the reward system too." A clearly defined reward system for quality teaching must be developed, for until then, most faculty will remain skeptical about the real value that the institution places upon this time commitment (Toy, 1980).

As to the problem of rewarding faculty participation in academic advising, Mayhew (in Pantages and Creedon, 1978, p. 91) points out that not only are faculty not trained for counseling, but quite often their teaching and research activities do not leave them the time necessary for counseling students. Spilka (1980, p. 14) observes: "Though individual motivations by potential and actual faculty advisers have always been a major influence on how advising prospers or wanes, institutional policy provides the context within which the process takes place. By neglect, usually benign as evidenced by silence from higher quarters, many evaluate their priorities and match them with those of department chairpersons, deans, and other officials." Later in the same report (p. 15) he contends: "It is dubious that much can be accomplished with the present reward system. Apparently even those who expect much of their life satisfactions to come from intrinsic motivation reach a point where the extrinsic becomes very meaningful." Forrest (1982, p. 44) recommends that faculty advisers be specifically selected, trained, and compensated.

According to Pantages and Creedon (1978, p. 96), "Faculty promotion criteria might be modified to include the ability of a given member of the faculty to establish easy, friendly, supportive relationships with students that are not restricted to just the high achievers or those who are graduate-school bound." Despite the difficulties of assessing such a quality this is certainly an interesting prospect.

Though the reward system appears to be an important link between what is expected of faculty and performance, there is some question as to which rewards are most effective. Austin (1981, pp. 123-124) finds two distinct groups of faculty perceptions of inducements which would encourage them to improve their advising efforts. Advising must be rewarded, but in different ways for the different groups of faculty. In Austin's study, arts and sciences faculty perceive a reduction in teaching load as the single most influential inducement, followed in descending order by consideration in salary, promotion, and tenure decision-making processes, and general recognition awards. Faculty in the college of business administration reorder the importance of inducements, placing recognition awards first, followed in descending order by consideration in the promotion, tenure, and salary decision-making processes. There is clearly a need for further research to more specifically define the type of reward which will motivate specific faculty at specific types of institutions to perform specific tasks.

Those who have carefully examined the issue of student retention over the years have demonstrated that the faculty are a key to improving the retention rate on most campuses. Their universal participation and support should not be assumed. It is for this reason that an enthusiastic faculty member should be regarded as a prized commodity. Many more can be drawn into the fold with proper incentives, encouragement, and management.

Building Faculty Support

Two fundamental points have emerged from the foregoing: faculty support is likely central to the success of any concerted effort to improve retention, and faculty support is not necessarily given at the outset of a retention project. Consequently, it seems worthwhile to offer some suggestions for garnering greater faculty cooperation based upon past experiences and the available literature.

First, the faculty must be convinced that attrition is a serious matter. Because on some campuses it seems that there is one disaster after another throughout the year and faculty are somewhat calloused to cries of wolf over the years, it should be made clear that retention is a high priority in the eyes of the institution and will remain so well into the future. And accordingly, the faculty should be presented with credible motives for supporting and participating in the program.

Not uncommonly, retention projects are presented as alternatives to retrenchment. While fear is a great motivator, it seems preferable to stress the positive consequences of a successful retention program. If it appears that job security is threatened or that the very survival of the institution is in doubt, some faculty may conclude that their time will be best spent updating their résumés in anticipation of a job search. Some of the more mobile faculty will not remain to see if the vessel can be repaired but will jump ship for employment elsewhere. Certainly the financial welfare of the institution provides one justification for retention efforts. However, as noted earlier, it is often easy for faculty to hold others responsible for balancing the budget and to cite recent expenditures in areas of perceived secondary importance: If we are in so much financial trouble, why are we now redecorating the president's home?

There are, however, many noneconomic inducements for participation in retention projects which are likely to appeal to faculty. If retention efforts increase enrollment, it may well be possible to tighten admissions standards and improve the quality of the students with whom the faculty interact. This is the reverse of the common faculty suspicion that an emphasis on retention leads to a lowering of academic standards. And, as the size of the student body increases, there will also eventually be a need to hire additional faculty, bringing new life and resources into the institution. Sometimes I believe faculty feel that retention programs are designed solely to retain students at the lower end of the intellectual-capacity scale. Clearly this is not the case. Recall our disappointment upon learning that Ms. Kelly was not returning this year. A successful program will also retain a number of better students who would have otherwise transferred.

Because successful retention programs thus tend to improve the overall quality of life on campus, faculty can expect generally better working conditions and greater job satisfaction. "The faculty and administrators of collegiate institutions also benefit from the successful performance of the task of increasing student competence and persistence. They have the professional satisfaction of achieving the major mission of nearly all institutions—enhancing the general competence of the students who come to them for assistance" (Forrest, 1982, p. 6). According to Smith and others (1981, p. 85), "Retention should not be viewed as the only result or outcome of a total campus renewal project. Improved fund raising, enhanced faculty morale, stronger external communications, increased community appreciation, and cost effective use of campus resources will surely result as well."

Increased enrollment also may mean higher salaries, better fringe benefits, more support staff and services, and improved facilities. Declining enrollments reduce the likelihood of achieving these advantages regardless of the extent to which the faculty are deserving.

A second point in securing faculty support is that faculty must believe that their involvement really matters. Because most faculty are quick to sense insincerity or an element of tokenism in their participation, they must believe that their recommendations will be given every consideration in the final program. At this point, the history of faculty involvement with various institutional projects becomes important.

To ensure that faculty understand that they are central to retention project success, they should be provided with the results of past retention research. Some care, however, should be exercised in the presentation of this information. It must not appear that faculty are entirely to blame for the existing retention problem nor that they are entirely responsible for its solution. As Noel (1978, p. 96) observes: "Everyone must be a retention agent—the president, instructors, librarians, the staff in the cafeteria, the business office, and the custodial personnel in the dormitories."

Third, the faculty must be assured that a retention project and the subsequent programs have demonstrable institutional support. Beal and Noel (1980, p. 90) point out that such support is the most critical aspect of a retention effort and on many campuses, "academic administrators are most likely to carry the clout that is necessary to effect institutional change in areas involving the faculty."

I suspect that tenure, promotion, and salaries are generally more important forms of reward than non-negotiable certificates of appreciation and wall plaques, although these are important symbols of achievement. If retention-related activities are adequately rewarded, the faculty will find time for them. Otherwise, they will merely take a subordinate position in the perceived hierarchy of priorities of the institution.

In addition to these three considerations, attention must be directed toward maintaining the interest of faculty during the initial period of designing the retention project. Because efficient use of time is a fundamental concern of many faculty, three factors would seem important: direction, progress, and prospect. The specific objectives and alternatives of the project should be set forth at the beginning of deliberations. As time passes, it should be apparent that some progress has been achieved. Structured meetings with prepared agendas are very useful in helping the meeting chair adhere to a program and avoid the time-sinks of endless war stories and other diversions. Finally, as time passes, it should become apparent to faculty that their input constitutes a real contribution. Any evidence of growing campus support should be reported. Implementing some suggestions even before the completion of the initial design phase of the retention project can provide a very valuable form of positive reinforcement.

Those involved in garnering faculty support should be aware of the sequence of steps involved in drawing faculty into a retention effort. On every campus, a number of faculty will show immediate interest; these constitute a core group of faculty who usually volunteer their services. They are often those closest to student affairs and may exhibit a nearly chauvinistic loyalty toward and affection for the institution. The size of this group might be one measure of faculty morale. It seems preferable that these initial participants in the design of the retention project be volunteers; although it is possible to mandate attendance at meetings, it is much more difficult to mandate enthusiasm and action.

After forming the core group, the next objective will be to motivate other faculty to join the cause. There are at least two routes to this goal. The first depends upon generating campuswide interest and excitement surrounding the subject of retention by disseminating information on the benefits for faculty of improved retention and the centrality of the faculty role. A bandwagon effect will set in as retention becomes a topic of faculty discussion throughout the institution.

The second, more focused route is to send a personal invitation to certain faculty members requesting their participation. Depending upon the dispositions that prevail at a particular school, this solicitation could come from the executive officers, the director of the retention project, or from already committed colleagues. As retention project coordinator at Denver University, I generally had little difficulty recruiting associates for retention committee membership.

One final factor to note in involving faculty is that parenthood may alter the attitude of some faculty concerning the importance of the quality of campus life, classroom instruction, and student-faculty interaction. The questions become: Is this the kind of college I would like my children to attend? Is this the kind of classroom experience I would like my children to have? Am I the kind of teacher I would like my children to have?

Regardless of attempts to gain their confidence, a few faculty will probably remain incorrigible. Just as it is unrealistic to expect 100 percent retention rates, so we cannot expect 100 percent faculty support. As the success of the retention program and the derived benefits become evident, enthusiasm will become infectious and support will grow.

In launching a retention effort, it is important to remember that the conditions contributing to attrition did not emerge overnight but evolved through time. Similarly, the solutions to the problems, including faculty support, must also be given time to develop. Patience and continual encouragement are necessary on the part of the retention project coordinator and the institution in general.

Conclusion

Faculty are a critical part of any retention program but their support should not be assumed. On every campus, they are subjected to a wide variety of pulls, each involving an investment of their time. It is usually necessary for them to select from among the available alternatives those with which they will become involved and to what extent. For the most part, the highest priority will be given to those tasks perceived to carry the greatest weight in the reward system. To make retention a serious matter at any institution, retention-related activities requiring faculty input will thus have to be given a degree of prominence in the decision-making processes for tenure, promotion, and salary increases.

Threats of financial exigency may not be sufficient to enlist faculty cooperation. In fact, they may have the opposite effect in some cases. However, there are several positive incentives for involvement which the faculty are likely to find appealing such as an improved quality of life for both students and faculty.

At every institution, there will most likely be a core group of dedicated faculty eager to participate in the retention project. Members of this group should be treated as prized commodities and viewed as a foundation upon which to build a program. In the proper setting and given the proper incentives, the number of committed faculty will grow quite rapidly as faculty become aware of the seriousness with which retention efforts are viewed and of the benefits to be derived from making constructive changes on campus.

References

Astin, A. W. *Four Critical Years: Effects of College on Beliefs, Attitudes, and Knowledge.* San Francisco: Jossey-Bass, 1977.

Austin, P. O. "Faculty Perceptions of Student Academic Advising and Factors Which Influence Those Perceptions." *Dissertation Abstracts International*, 1981, *42*, 1956A–1957A. (University Microfilms order no. 8121426)

Beal, P. E., and Noel, L. *What Works in Student Retention.* Iowa City, Iowa: American College Testing Program and National Center for Higher Education Management Systems, 1980. (ED 197 635)

Crockett, D. S. "Academic Advising: A Cornerstone of Student Retention." In L. Noel (ed.), *Reducing the Dropout Rate.* New Directions for Student Services, no. 3. San Francisco: Jossey-Bass, 1978, 29–35.

Fisher, J. L. "College Student Retention from a Presidential Perspective." In L. Noel (ed.), *Reducing the Dropout Rate.* New Directions for Student Services, no. 3. San Francisco: Jossey-Bass, 1978, 65–75.

Flannery, J., and others. *Final Report from the Ad Hoc Committee to Study Attrition at Miami-Dade Community College, North Campus.* Miami, Fla.: Miami-Dade Junior College, 1973. (ED 085 052)

Forrest, A. *Increasing Student Competence and Persistence: The Best Case for General Education.* Iowa City, Iowa: American College Testing Program National Center for Advancement of Educational Practices, 1982.

Noel, L. (ed.). *Reducing the Dropout Rate.* New Directions for Student Services, no. 3. San Francisco: Jossey-Bass, 1978.

Pantages, T. J., and Creedon, C. F. "Studies of College Attrition: 1950–1975." *Review of Educational Research,* 1978, *48,* 49–101.

Sheffield, W., and Meskill, V. P. "What Can Colleges Do About Student Attrition?" *College Student Journal,* 1974, *8* (1), 37–45.

Smith, L. N., and others. *Mobilizing the Campus for Retention: An Innovative Quality-of-Life Model.* Iowa City, Iowa: American College Testing Program National Center for Advancement of Educational Practices, 1981.

Spady, W. G., Jr., "Dropouts from Higher Education: Toward an Empirical Model." *Interchange,* 1971, *2* (3), 38–62.

Spilka, B. *Undergraduate Advising II: Freshman Experiences with and Perceptions of the Advising Process at the University of Denver.* Denver, Colo.: University of Denver, 1980.

Tinto, V. "Dropout from Higher Education: A Theoretical Synthesis of Recent Research." *Review of Educational Research,* 1975, *45* (1), 89–125.

Toy, T. J. *Final Report of the Retention Project.* Denver, Colo.: University of Denver, 1980.

21

Case Studies
and Successful Programs

~~~~~~~~~~~~

Diana Saluri

Throughout this volume the authors stress the fact that retention is a practitioner's art. They speak not only as theorists but as practitioners—teachers, advisers, counselors, and administrators. And as practitioners they remind us that retention efforts must grow out of the particular concerns and characteristics of the individual campus, noting that merely grafting strategies and approaches from one campus to another will most likely result in frustration and disappointment.

This chapter illustrates how individual retention efforts have grown out of specific concerns at specific campuses by presenting case studies of highly successful retention strategies at thirteen institutions. The case studies were drawn from Noel and Levitz's forthcoming study of the nation's campuses that have the most noteworthy retention programs. This study focuses on two types of institutions, those with high self-reported freshman-to-sophomore year retention rates and those in which there was a self-reported improvement of 10 percent or greater in freshman-to-sophomore year retention rates in three years' time. There were 270 two- and four-year institutions in the first category and 143 institutions in the second.

Three Categories

The innovative practices presented in the case studies fall into three categories: comprehensive, campuswide programs; those dealing with academic advising; and those dealing with ways to initiate or mobilize a campuswide retention effort.

Comprehensive Programs. A word about the three programs presented in the first or comprehensive category will pull together some common themes that run throughout the case studies. Two of the schools in this category, Notre Dame and Harvard, have remarkably low attrition rates: 1 percent at Notre Dame and 3 percent at Harvard. We might sum up what their approaches to retention have in common by saying that they both emphasize front-loading in the freshman year; that is, they focus heavily on programs and services that promote the personal, social, and academic adjustment of freshmen. These include intensive orientation programs, having a dean of freshmen, extensive initial and continuous adviser training with frequent informal contact between advisers and students, and a team approach to meeting the needs of freshmen. It would seem that the key factor in all these front-loading activities is involvement: they are ways to immediately involve the student in the life of the campus. The third school in this category, Jefferson Community College, provides an excellent, comprehensive example of how all segments of the campus community can be involved in the development of a retention effort. Citing the "creation of an awareness of the interrelatedness of all college activities" as one of the major outcomes of the retention project, the case study demonstrates how a successful retention effort can result in a more productive and cooperative involvement of everyone on campus—students, faculty, and staff—in the life of the institution.

Academic Advising. Involvement is also the key in the case studies presented in the second category, academic advising. Each of the institutions represented in this category employs a centralized, intrusive approach that draws students into the advising process. At Duke University's premajor advising center the emphasis is on aggressive identification and follow-up of students who need help in adjusting to the university and of those who will benefit from guidance in developing special talents or pursuing particular interests on campus. In Western New Mexico State University's general college the approach is intrusive with students required to meet with advisers at regularly assigned times and to attend a learning center if they need remedial help. In South Dakota State University's college of general registration, a specialized college for undecided students, students are required to take a career planning course and meet with advisers at specified times. In order to help students think beyond the most popular and obvious career choices, State University of New York at Albany's center for undergraduate education encourages students to postpone declaring a major and focuses on informing them of the wide variety of options available to them. In each of these programs, students are actively drawn into the advising process in innovative ways so that they can be encouraged to explore options and to take full advantage of the resources the institution offers them.

Campuswide Retention Efforts. In the case studies presented in the third category, the emphasis is on ways to initiate campuswide involvement in and responsibility for retention efforts. At Boston University this effort relies on two key factors: a network of campus committees, each investigating specialized areas of campus life, and an emphasis on a solid research foundation for action. Eastern Michigan University uses a matrix accountability model to draw all segments of the campus community into the retention effort. In order to achieve a comprehensive campuswide report on which retention efforts could be based, Denver University first divided its retention effort into two phases; the short-term phase involved the investigation of specific situations on campus that were suspected to be influencing retention, the long-term phase involves the formation of student, faculty, and administrative action committees. The success of Louisiana Tech University's campuswide retention program, which grew out of previous, more localized successful retention efforts on campus, is based on an emphasis on communicating retention information and on acceptance of a diversity of retention concerns and approaches among the various campus factions represented on the committee. The University of South

Carolina at Spartanburg achieves decentralization of its retention efforts by ensuring that retention planning takes place at both the university-wide and academic unit level through the use of advisory groups that require faculty participation. By combining six student services units into an office of student affairs, Bradley University has achieved a unified approach to student affairs which stresses a marketing approach that emphasizes identifying and meeting specific student needs. In short, each of the institutions in this category has taken its individual needs and characteristics into consideration in working out an effective way to draw all segments of the campus community into a retention effort.

Successful Practices Catalogue

Following the case studies, a catalogue of successful retention practices, also drawn from the Noel and Levitz forthcoming study, is presented. This catalogue illustrates the variety of innovative approaches institutions are taking to better serving their students and improving the quality of campus life for students, faculty, and staff.

Comprehensive Programs

Freshman Year of Studies
University of Notre Dame

Emil T. Hofman, Dean
Peter P. Grande, Associate Dean

At the University of Notre Dame, located in South Bend, Indiana, freshmen (approximately 1,800 students) spend their first year in the Freshman Year of Studies (FYS) program, then move into the college of their choice as sophomores. Notre Dame did not consciously undertake a campuswide retention effort. FYS grew out of a desire to develop two elements: (1) a freshman curriculum which would provide for strong general education and give freshmen the opportunity to explore before making a commitment to a major, and (2) support systems appropriate to the needs of freshmen. The subsequent development of such a curriculum and of suitable support systems produced as a by-product a freshman attrition rate which has been at only about 1 percent for the last ten years, with only about .5 percent attributable to academic failure.

The dean and associate dean are responsible for all policies in FYS. An assistant dean serves the special needs of minority and handicapped students. Seven advisers, the director of the learning resource center, and thirty senior interviewers complete the FYS staff.

Basically, there are four functions involved in FYS: (1) the curriculum was designed by the university committee and details of the program are examined annually; (2) each freshman is assigned to a guidance team, which includes an adviser-director and several undergraduate senior interviewers, to receive counseling on personal adjustment, academic survival, and career planning; (3) the learning resource center offers freshmen tutoring and special programs at no cost. Advisers work very closely with the center director to ensure that the freshmen receive the assistance required; and (4) special projects such as snow parties, trips to Chicago, and freshman date nights help freshmen to adjust socially and to learn to enjoy and like the campus.

The structure of FYS might not be radically different from similar programs at other universities, but the approach and spirit are unique. The program is characterized by a strong communication system which includes a special orientation program for parents; an aggressive counseling program; a dean's newsletter for freshmen, and another for parents of freshmen; regular contact by the FYS staff with faculty concerning the progress of students and regular contact between FYS and residence hall staffs. It is not uncommon for an FYS adviser to take a freshman to lunch. In fact, the dean takes a different freshman to lunch virtually every day during the academic year. Through this emphasis on communication, in general, freshmen become aware that the FYS staff is genuinely concerned with their progress and that the university wants their success and happiness and will do everything possible to help them achieve their goals.

As significant as this emphasis on communication is, the core of FYS is the freshman curriculum. All freshmen take the same course format, but not necessarily the same courses. The freshman curriculum includes required general education courses and three electives. The nature and level of the mathematics, natural sciences, and language courses depends upon the student's background and interests. Because many courses in the freshman curriculum provide a good foundation in specialized education for majors with a strong structural sequence, freshmen interested in these majors are able to take courses to affirm their interest and to start specialized study toward their majors. On the other hand, for students who might not yet have a strong commitment to a particular program, general education courses can be the springboard to a program of specialized study.

There is evidence that FYS is on the right track. The very low attrition rate in FYS (about 1 percent) establishes a pattern for the remaining three undergraduate years. The attrition from freshman through senior year is under 8 percent. Because some students not enrolled in the eighth semester later complete their degrees, the final attrition rate is closer to 6 or 7 percent.

The individual attention given freshmen in FYS makes it virtually impossible for them to simply leave the university. An elaborate withdrawal procedure requires an exit interview with the dean of FYS, who will have received information about the student from faculty, residence hall staffs, and the office of student affairs. Through this procedure, the problem the freshman is experiencing frequently is resolved and he or she decides to stay.

FYS is responsive to the uncertainty characteristic of many entering freshmen. During the past twelve years, about 60 percent of the freshmen changed their intended program at least once during the freshman year. The freshman curriculum, the aggressive and effective counseling program, and the assistance offered through the learning resource center have converged to create a climate in which substantial numbers of freshmen are able to work through their uncertainties and to advance confidently to the sophomore year.

A Decentralized Advising System for Undergraduates
Harvard College

Mack I. Davis II, Assistant Dean

Harvard College's undergraduate population of 6,000 men and women come to Harvard and Radcliffe in Cambridge, Massachusetts, with a variety of interests, prior intellectual experiences, and goals. The organizational structure that has developed is designed to maximally support this rich diversity of students by administering a separate freshman year experience, a three-year field of concentration sequence which begins in the sophomore year, and a housing system for groups of approximately 375 students living with teaching faculty during the junior and senior years.

This highly decentralized system offers any number of entry points for undergraduates who need academic advising. There are staff members in each setting available and responsive to students who need a variety of advising services. The system of services therefore does not reside in any single organizational structure. It is purposely structured to allow students access throughout their four years and from a number of vantage points. The system or network of services is thus at once very intrusive and somewhat unobtrusive by virtue of its decentralization.

Although an oversimplification, it is fair to say that the largest concentration of intrusive policies is applied in the freshman year. It is extremely important in our academic setting to start undergraduates in the proper courses and to provide informational services which clearly describe the total community. The combination of these two factors—a concentration of resources in the first year and a conscious attempt to provide a number of entry points for sources of help—makes for the smoothest transition to the college experience. The tasks are then to coordinate staff and services so that individual students or small groups of undergraduates receive exactly what they need. The network attempts on an annual basis to anticipate those needs as the academic environment changes and to readjust services according to the faculty's wishes.

In the freshman year, a full set of advising services is made available by the dean of freshmen and a staff of over seventy full- and part-time advisers. In addition, some faculty and senior administrative staff appointed in the faculty of arts and sciences serve as nonresidential advisers and as members of the board of freshmen advisers. Every entering freshman has a designated adviser (either resident in the student's freshman dormitory or nonresident) who works with the student in academic counseling, personal support, and referral to whichever resources may be necessary to ensure the smoothest transition to the life of the college.

The dean of freshmen and the dean's staff of senior advisers provide a wealth of services and information for the entire freshman-year advising staff. In addition to housing freshmen prior to matriculation and coordinating a full week of orientation activities for students, this senior staff holds an annual retreat for all advisers, produces a handbook for freshman advisers, and represents freshmen to the administrative board of Harvard College. Weekly luncheons are scheduled for nonresident advisers and evening meetings where a variety of topics and personnel are made available to the advising community are regularly scheduled.

A primary aspect of the support services for first-year students involves preparation for entering the sophomore year. Life changes radically for rising sophomores. Since there is a three-year concentration (other institutions call this the major), a key aspect of first-year advising involves extensive preparation for choosing the field of concentration at the end of the first year. This selection is supervised by an associate dean of freshmen in conjunction with the students' advisers and with the head tutors who are faculty members in the various fields of concentration. It involves planning and consultation with both the freshman adviser and representatives from the fields through informal departmental visits and finally via a series of formal meetings where the intricacies of study in a given discipline are fully discussed. Once the field is selected, advising is carried out by the head tutor's office. Upperclass students are ordinarily assigned and/or choose a departmental adviser in the field who serves for the next three years.

There is a fairly extensive course placement process for foreign language and mathematics study. Freshman advisers routinely receive the results of these tests and advise accordingly for proper course selection. There is an advisory system coupled with the departmental apparatus in mathematics and the natural science fields such as physics and chemistry. In these fields, proper placement is stressed and curricular adjustments are made in light of placement testing, the bulk of which takes place during the early weeks of the freshman year.

The freshman year is directly administered by the dean of freshmen and, along with the senior tutors (who are based in the residence halls and may be faculty, deans, or others) and the administrative board, supervised by the dean of Harvard College. There are two other support offices, both with professional counseling staffs, that are also under the direct supervisory umbrella of the dean of Harvard College. The bureau of study counsel offers a variety of academic and personal support services: a centralized file of trained undergraduate tutors; a faculty-nominated group of undergraduate tutors who are directly supervised by the bureau's professional staff who work with other students requesting tutorial assistance; a multidisciplinary team of ten professional counselors who provide short- and long-term counseling services for both academic and personal issues; a noncredit reading and study strategies course and a parallel set of short modules on time management and research paper writing focused for first-year students but made available upon request in the houses or for subgroups of undergraduates such as athletes or minority group students; a mathematics refresher for students who need precalculus review; and individualized consultative services to the twelve residential house staffs.

The office of career services and off-campus learning provides services to assist students in making career choices, learning how to get a job, applying to graduate and professional schools, arranging work or study abroad, or planning leaves of absence or summer jobs.

Because the college is highly decentralized and is as well a part of a large faculty of arts and sciences with a graduate school, considerable fiscal resources are earmarked for newsletters, brochures, and other printed matter which inform students of these services. This publication effort is required to assure that students know about the resources available to them by channels other than word of mouth.

In summary, the support services network in Harvard College does not reside in any single structure. Services of various kinds are made available by the component parts of the network as described. Staff in these offices are trained and continually informed about the best places to refer students for particular services such as personal counseling, extra tutorial help with courses, or career planning. The combination of these efforts makes it possible to provide services which maximize student success in the college experience.

A Recruitment, Retention, Attrition Program
Jefferson Community College

Ronald J. Horvath, Director

Jefferson Community College (JCC) in Louisville, Kentucky, is an open-door institution with inner-city and suburban campuses and an enrollment of approximately 7,000 students. The genesis of JCC's Recruitment, Retention, Attrition (RRA) program in 1978 can be traced to two events. First was the development of a data base which showed that 40 percent of JCC students were failing or withdrawing from classes for which they were registered (in-class attrition). Second, a slight downturn in enrollment for fall of 1977 and spring of 1978 foreshadowed a 22 percent loss of students (approximately 1,000) for fall of 1978 with competition from area colleges accounting for most of this loss.

Fortunately the college had already begun to address the attrition problem a few months prior to the calamitous enrollment drop. The spirit of the retention program emanated from a challenge—Could we reduce JCC's in-class attrition below the 40 percent national average?—and from outright fear—What will the budgetary impact of the loss of 1,000 students be?

A quick review by the college director of the attrition

literature resulted in an equally quick conclusion: dealing with semester-to-semester attrition (causes, preventive measures, effects) was like trying to hold quicksilver in one's hands. Developing a profile of past dropouts was an equally impossible task because most of our students exhibited dropout characteristics when they *entered* JCC. Furthermore, shifting the responsibility for retention to the college counselors or advisers (a tactic many colleges adopt) also seemed futile inasmuch as failing or withdrawal grades were an academic problem. Thus, with a quick and easy solution nowhere to be found, it seemed that any workable solution would require collegewide brainstorming.

At the invitation of the college director, approximately fifty (one-third) of the key faculty and staff members attended an in-house student retention conference. We decided that we would become our own problem solvers, rather than inviting others in to write a prescription for us. Small group discussions explored the theme of the day-long session: What were we as an institution doing to encourage attrition and what were we doing to minimize it? Faculty were forthright in identifying factors which contribute to attrition such as weak teaching techniques, ineffective support programs, an outdated advising system, and a lack of sufficient developmental sections.

All in all, this first retention conference was a success because faculty and administrators were involved in a major effort to provide direction for the college. Most importantly, however, a sense of unity evolved because no fingers were pointed, and no castigations made. One unanimous recommendation did surface: additional workshops should be scheduled during the year to address specific issues such as successful teaching techniqes, recruiting, and advising.

The key ingredients of the organizational process for a successful retention program began to emerge.

1. Identifying the existence of a problem in its early stages and developing data necessary to determine the nature of the problem
2. Defining what kind of attrition (in-class, semester-to-semester, entry-to-graduation, or dropout) the college will address

3. Involving the college community from president to faculty to clerical staff in finding workable solutions
4. Burying the knee-jerk tendency to blame someone or some program
5. Providing a model which can be used to assess systematically the problem from a holistic point of view
6. Following through by constantly informing faculty of results

The most tangible effect of the focus on in-class attrition through the spring semester of 1984 has been the reduction of failing/withdrawal grades from 40 percent to 30 percent and a marked increase in our semester-to-semester retention rate from 60 percent to approximately 66 percent.

Another effect has been that the faculty has produced several pamphlets—including *Full Classrooms: 95 Practical Suggestions to Guarantee Student and Teacher Success*, *Black Students—Special Problems/Special Needs for Retention*, and *Used Books: 54 Suggestions to Increase Library Use*—that pinpoint practical solutions to problems. Faculty emphasis on using the library has resulted in a 70 percent increase in library use among students.

Other indicators of success in the five-year RRA program include tangible outcomes or products and serendipitous outcomes or by-products. Among the products of RRA are

1. Higher course completion rates: ten consecutive semesters of higher passing grade percentages (increasing from 60 to 70 percent)
2. Improved semester-to-semester retention rates: percentages of returning students have increased from 60 to 66 percent
3. Improved public image and increasing use of campus facilities by community groups
4. Improved registration, orientation, advising, and teaching
5. More positive faculty and staff evaluations of administrators, greater explicit administrative concern for the teaching/learning process, greater faculty involvement with administrative processes
6. Expanded developmental courses and sections
7. Improved faculty/staff development program

By-products of RRA include

1. Creation of an awareness of the interrelatedness of all college activities and of a sense of unity and purpose among faculty, administrators, and staff.
2. Encouragement for the college to reexamine its missions and priorities
3. Provision of leadership opportunities for many faculty
4. Expansion of the conceptual role faculty have of themselves
5. Perception of the whole college as being greater than the sum of its parts (programs)

RRA produced these intended and unexpected positive outcomes because the program was initiated by and involved the entire college community. This campuswide initiative has demonstrated to students, faculty, and staff that JCC's renewal project genuinely belongs to everyone involved and benefits all.

Academic Advising

Personal Attention in a University: The Trinity College of Arts and Sciences Premajor Advising Center
Duke University

Elizabeth Studley Nathans, Director
Assistant Dean of Trinity College

Duke University in Durham, North Carolina, enrolls approximately 5,800 undergraduates in its Trinity College of Arts and Sciences and School of Engineering. Duke is a growing institution committed to retaining in the undergraduate college of arts and sciences many features of a smaller college.

The intrusive, centralized approach of the premajor advising center is at the heart of this individualizing process. Concerted efforts by the staff to identify early those who may encounter problems in adjusting to the university, to establish appropriate referrals even before students matriculate, and to follow up intensively thereafter lie at the heart of the center's success in working with students. Particularly in the freshman and sophomore years, close personal attention is readily available to any student who will accept it—and to some who actively resist. Aggressive identification and follow-up both of students with special problems and of those with special talents has unquestionably enhanced Trinity College's remarkable success in retaining its students.

Students enter Trinity College without declaring majors, though expressions of academic interests are welcomed and advising assignments based on students' interests. Students may declare majors at the end of the freshman year, or wait until as late as the end of the fourth semester. By recent faculty decision, students in the arts and sciences will devise a long-range plan for their undergraduate years when they declare their majors. Despite the administrative burdens it will impose, the requirement is viewed as an impetus to students to postpone declaring majors and to think early and broadly about their undergraduate experience and as a way to prevent the narrow preoccupation with semester-by-semester course selection in which too many students indulge.

The premajor advising center is centrally located and staffed by the professional staff and ten to sixteen of the nearly eighty faculty members and administrators who serve as advisers. The center serves as a point of first call for many students (and parents) with a variety of concerns and deals as often with nonacademic as with academic matters. Because the director addresses parents of incoming students during orientation, and because information on the center's services is included in an orientation publication mailed to matriculating students and their parents, parents as well as students tend to regard the center's staff as the fount of all knowledge about the university. While this assumption of omniscience adds to the pressures under which staff members work, it ensures that the center receives information about most major concerns which arise involving the students it serves.

Identification of those who may be at risk as they begin their college careers begins when accepted students judged by the admissions staff to be relatively weak candidates are presented to a review committee. Before admissions letters are mailed, students may be designated to participate in the college's semester-long academic support program or in a summer support program. The committee may require or simply urge participation.

A more comprehensive review occurs the summer before students arrive on campus. Matriculating students choose courses by mail, and during the registration period, admissions folders are sent to the college offices. Course requests and other information are reviewed by the director or assistant directors in the premajor center, and note made of students who seem likely to encounter difficulties.

Typically, the list thus assembled is far broader in scope than the roster presented to the admissions review committee earlier. It includes students whose socioeconomic backgrounds markedly differ from the campus norm; those with major academic weaknesses, including those whose academic interests differ sharply from their apparent academic strengths; those whose classroom performance has consistently failed to equal their abilities; and those with serious family or personal problems. Minority and international students are automatically included, as are scholarship athletes. Special situations are flagged for the attention of the student affairs division or of the dean for minority affairs. Also flagged for special notice are outstanding students who need help early to secure appropriate course placement and to meet outstanding faculty members. Such students are matched with experienced faculty advisers in their fields of academic interest.

All students identified during the prematriculation review meet during their first three weeks on campus with senior members of the center staff and with their faculty advisers. These meetings allow early assessment of how well each student is adjusting and provide a base for future contacts; in addition, they provide many students with the internal permission needed to bring problems to the staff if they arise later in the semester.

Because students and advisers meet at least three times each semester after orientation, the staff can easily follow students' progress. Those who repeatedly break appointments, those whose appearance changes markedly over the semester—

who gain or lose weight, who seem unusually unkempt or tense—are immediately obvious. Paraprofessional staff, who visit informally with students in the waiting area to elicit information about how things are going, come to recognize students by sight. Students who appear to need further attention are flagged for the attention of senior staff and immediate follow-up is arranged. And because the center's staff consciously solicits the cooperation of instructors in large freshman-sophomore courses, the university's mid-term grade report is supplemented for the center's staff by faculty members who bring to the center director after each major test or paper, lists of students who are in academic difficulty.

This process of identification is now over 95 percent accurate in alerting the staff to students who have special needs. There are virtually no surprises when the lists of students in difficulty and outstanding students appear at the end of each term. This aggressive identification policy is reflected in the academic college's freshman-to-sophomore year attrition rate (attrition due to insufficient academic progress) which never exceeds 1.0 to 1.5 percent annually. And in a university which for many students was a second choice behind one of the Ivy League colleges, attrition for other causes is remarkably low. Only rarely does a student who has met regularly with his or her adviser voluntarily transfer from Duke. Many inquire, and several apply to other schools each year. But in the end most remain, having developed during the routine of conferences the first two years, the personal ties with faculty, senior staff, and fellow students that make leaving Duke difficult.

Intrusive Advising and Retention
Western New Mexico University

Robert E. Glennen, Former President
Dan M. Baxley, Dean, General College

Western New Mexico University (WNMU) in Silver City has an enrollment of 1,900 students, with 48 percent minorities, mostly Hispanic. For eleven years, statistics revealed that WNMU averaged between 62 percent and 65 percent freshman attrition and 30 percent to 40 percent sophomore attrition. These figures exceeded the national average considerably and affected annual legislation appropriations.

An evaluation of the causes of attrition revealed that students were not receiving enough individual attention; were confused about degree and program requirements; were in need of a guidance and testing program, more vertical degree options, and developmental programs; and, most importantly, were reluctant to take advantage of many of these services should they be offered. This hesitancy on the part of students to seek out assistance became a key consideration in the design of the general college which was created to ensure student participation in needed services by taking an intrusive approach, particularly in advising.

Based on the philosophy that institutions should not wait for students to get into trouble before they begin receiving counseling, the general college's intrusive system calls students in right from the beginning of the year for advising, letting them know that there are people on campus who are concerned about them and who want them to succeed.

The general college exists parallel to WNMU's four other colleges and, in addition to being the college of record for all entering freshmen, encompasses all sub-baccalaureate degrees and programs, developmental studies programs, and the counseling and advisement center. It is housed in a new facility designed solely to support its activities.

Students in the general college have the advantage of exploring and taking courses in a variety of areas before selecting a major and are not allowed to declare a major until the end of their first year. Until then they are asked to state a planned major for the purpose of assigning an adviser. After the conclusion of their freshman year and the accumulation of thirty-one credits, students declare a major and move forward to the upper division college of their choice. Those who are still undecided may elect to remain in the general college until the end of their sophomore year.

Two components of the general college exist primarily to address the attrition problems at WNMU: the learning resource center and the counseling and advisement center. The learning resource center is staffed by a director who supervises faculty who teach developmental skills courses. Tutors assist students with their course work. Freshmen who are scheduled into remedial courses on the basis of American College Testing Program (ACT) scores must complete all required developmental courses before leaving the general college. The counseling and advisement center is staffed by a director and trained advisers and professional counselors. Faculty advisers provided by the colleges on a release-time basis usually number ten or fewer depending on the demand. Consultants representing fields throughout the university are always on call to provide more in-depth information.

Although the general college at WNMU is in its infancy, evaluation thus far indicates that the following results have been obtained.

- There were university record enrollment increases of 18.1 percent for fall of 1982; 18.8 percent for spring of 1983; 13.4 percent for fall of 1983; and 14.6 percent for spring of 1984.
- The attrition rate for freshmen was reduced from 66 percent in fall of 1981 to 48 percent in fall of 1982 to 23 percent in fall of 1983.
- Freshmen who enrolled in fall of 1981 (after initiation of the general college) enrolled for a significantly higher number of semester hours than before the general college's initiation.
- Freshmen had significantly higher completion rates of semester hours attempted than the previous class.
- Freshmen had significantly higher mean grade point averages than before.
- Freshmen with high semester hour loads achieved higher mean grade point averages and higher completion rates than those enrolled prior to the general college.

In one year the number of counseling and advising sessions increased as follows: (1) advising interviews from 595 to 1,087, (2) test administrations from 211 to 792, and (3) vocational/career counseling from 106 to 383.

The counseling contacts for all categories increased by 43.8 percent. There was a decrease in personal/social counseling from 855 sessions in 1980–81 to 279 in 1981–82 (possibly indicating that intrusive advising reduces the need for psychological counseling). Tutoring contact hours increased from 476 to 632. The percentage of freshmen who entered with low ACT scores (composite of 10 or less) who were still enrolled at the end of the semester increased from 71 percent in 1980–81 to 98 percent in 1981–82. The percentage who completed the semester with honors increased and the 87 percent who completed the year had an average grade point average of 2.27.

These results are being fortified by data from second-year studies which have revealed that freshman attrition has been further reduced and enrollment has increased to a record high of 1,900 students.

Obviously, WNMU was in a critical situation because of its student attrition problem. Its concerted effort to improve retention through the general college and its intrusive adjustment system has produced dividends for the institution and for its students.

General Registration: A Specialized College
for Undecided Students
South Dakota State University

Arnold J. Menning
Former Dean of the College of
General Registration

At South Dakota State University (SDSU) in Brookings, approximately 1,000 of the 6,500 undergraduates are enrolled in the College of General Registration (GR). GR was established in 1974 to accommodate undeclared majors, pre-professional students, and nontraditional students. The major factors contributing to this decision were:

1. Academic survival. The American College Testing Program (ACT) report for 1974 showed that 52 percent of entering

SDSU students expressed a need for assistance in choosing career goals and/or improving academic skills.

2. Enrollment projections. Enrollment in the liberal arts and in education was declining while the number of undeclared majors was increasing.

3. Student retention. Undeclared majors were exit-prone and a system was needed to improve career assistance programs.

4. Need for attachment to academic affairs. It became apparent that many career planning efforts needed extensive coordination with academic departments.

Entering students may either enroll directly in one of the six degree granting colleges or in GR. Enrollment in GR is limited to two years. GR students can take courses meeting general university requirements and explore possible majors in courses offered by the other colleges of the university.

At the heart of GR is the Career Academic Planning (CAP) center where students questioning whether college is a viable alternative for them receive help in exploring career goals and interests. The center is staffed by seven faculty members from the degree granting colleges, one full-time coordinator, and three student assistants. Faculty advisers have no advisees from their own colleges and are in the center several hours a day only during peak advising times such as preregistration.

The center's approach to advising is pro-active. Of entering GR students, 85 percent choose to be assigned to CAP advisers. Students choosing the center's pro-active approach are required to take a one credit course in career planning their first year and to meet with their advisers at least twice each semester. Those GR students (15 percent) preferring a more traditional advising approach are assigned to one of a group of such GR advisers.

All staff are kept informed of GR program activities and results. A total campus commitment from academic as well as student services units has allowed us to effectively meet students' needs. The following specific procedures have contributed to the success of GR.

1. Admissions brochures are specifically developed to inform prospective students and their parents about GR program offerings.
2. Summer orientation-registration programs enhance student and parent understanding of program objectives.
3. Individual sessions are arranged with students experiencing academic difficulties and with those who did not register.
4. Program costs are minimal. Student services staff teach tuition-generating career planning classes and conduct workshops.

One of the most significant results of the GR program is the perceived differences between participants and other students in understanding of self and academic programs. Faculty advisers report that CAP center students better understand the rationale for taking specific courses, are well prepared for advising sessions, more knowledgeable about careers, and expect advising assistance that goes beyond the clerical role of signing course registrations.

There are also several quantitative indicators of program success. Attrition (from spring to fall semesters) of this rather exit-prone group of undeclared students has steadily decreased from 29.1 percent in 1974 to 12.8 percent in 1982. Freshmen and special GR student enrollment has stabilized at 1,000 with most students choosing their major before their sophomore year. And less 1 percent of GR students who declare majors subsequently change their majors. Students in GR select particular majors in the same proportion as do students regularly enrolled in the degree granting colleges.

Second and third members of the same family are now beginning their college careers in GR. The stigma of being undecided has been reduced. Parents and students speak of the advantages of delaying choosing a major until students have achieved greater understanding of their abilities and interests and of career opportunities. Faculty acceptance of GR and referral of students enrolled in other SDSU colleges to the CAP center continues to increase.

Providing Options and Alternatives Through Advising
State University of New York at Albany

Richard L. Collier
Coordinator of Advising Services
for Undergraduate Education

The State University of New York at Albany (Albany) enrolls 16,000 students. The large number of applicants allows us to enjoy a well-prepared and highly motivated freshman class, approximately two-thirds of whom initially intend to major in business, accounting, the natural sciences, computer science, mathematics, or economics.

The Center for Undergraduate Education (CUE) has its roots in University College which was created in the mid-sixties to provide generalist advising services to freshmen and sophomores. The goal was to offer the kind of advising that would encourage students to keep an open mind about possible majors and to become well informed about the options available to them. Encouraging this openness to alternatives has become increasingly important on a campus where over half of the students who enter with an expressed intention to major in a quantitative area such as computer science or accounting either opt out or are forced out of their first choice due to academic problems.

CUE provides advising for all freshmen, students waiting for acceptance into restricted majors (business, accounting, computer science, economics, social welfare, and criminal justice), and undecided students. CUE also serves as the advising center for all undergraduates and coordinates advising services for law and health career programs, independent study and internships, and interdisciplinary majors, minors, and courses.

In addition to the many checklists and information sheets CUE provides for students, it regularly sends packets of updated information, extended course descriptions, detailed explanations of policy, and so on, to faculty advisers of declared majors. CUE also publishes data and attendant observations and recommendations concerning course enrollment figures and trends, and over- and underenrolled course and program problems.

Prior to orientation, new students are sent *Major Decisions*, a lively, informal booklet which expresses the philosophy behind CUE. It begins with a straightforward explanation of advising services and goes on to explain the practical goals and functional skills of a liberal education and the common myths versus realistic concerns of career planning.

The section on advising includes a description of how to work with one's adviser, a list of the questions advisers can and cannot answer, and a planning form to focus the first advising session. The discussion of the value of and rationale for a liberal education is written in terms meaningful to students. First-semester courses, appropriate minors, and graduate school opportunities are listed for each major, as is the name, office location, and telephone number of a faculty member to contact for further information.

Major Decisions and a separate sheet listing priorities given to advisers indicate that the student's first task is to sample courses for possible majors, then to pursue other interests and electives, and finally, if time allows, worry about meeting any general requirements not already fulfilled. Unless students need to take a writing course, many will benefit from postponing their general education courses until after they have decided on a major. They can then often fulfill the requirements through specific courses which relate to their major.

This emphasis on flexibility and exploration is particularly important for those students who come to Albany with an expressed intention to major in such restricted areas as computer science, business, or accounting and who later find they cannot meet the admissions requirements in these areas. Taking exploratory courses can give these students alternative interests to fall back on when they either are screened out or opt out of their first choice. They thus have an alternative to total discouragement and dropping out.

The May 1983 statistics indicate that 89 percent of our freshmen continue as sophomores, 77 percent of our freshmen continue into their junior year, and a fairly steady 60 percent of our freshmen receive a baccalaureate degree from Albany within four and one-half to five years.

Our real success may better be summarized thusly: students, at times naively, are attracted to the more practical of our disciplines in overwhelming numbers. After being encouraged to sample alternatives, the majority change their major, having found one much more suited to their goals, abilities, and interests. Most of these students have also come to truly like and trust Albany and, when we offer the particular program they wish to pursue, remain here. They and we have retained integrity and quality and our respect for one another, and the resulting competition among programs for these savvy and hardworking students can only be considered salubrious to the campus as a whole.

Campuswide Retention Efforts

First Steps in a Retention Effort
Boston University

Brendan F. Gilbane
Dean of the College of Basic Studies

The problems related to retention at an institution the size of Boston University are as complex as the expectations of its 27,724 students who enrolled in the fall of 1983. These expectations can be differentiated into those of the 18,727 full-time students and the 8,997 part-time students. Or they can be identified by geographical region (70 percent of the 1983 freshmen typically came from the northeast corridor stretching from Boston to Washington, D.C.). A poll of students has indicated that all these differing expectations relate directly or indirectly to the cost of attendance: $8,300 tuition and $3,780 basic room and board in 1983.

Against this profile, retention at Boston University, as at other Northeast schools, has assumed major significance in view of the demographic declines predicted for the 1980s (a 20 percent drop in the eighteen-year-old population nationally with a more formidable 40 percent decline projected for the Northeast) combined with the inevitable increases in the costs of quality higher education.

The approach to retention that has evolved at Boston University in response to these dire predictions relies on two factors: a network of campus committees and subcommittees and an emphasis on research as a basis for establishing priorities. In 1980 Boston University President John Silber charged a newly appointed enrollment management committee to formulate recommendations. The committee, organized by the vice-president for university relations and the assistant vice-president for enrollment services, and including an academic dean, two faculty members, and two administrators, agreed upon a division of labor into subcommittees on positioning, publications, financial aid, and retention.

The subcommittee on positioning soon recommended that a major survey be undertaken by a leading marketing research firm to refine the institutional fit between the universiy and its prospective student populations. The subcommittees on publications and financial aid also made recommendations in their own areas.

The subcommittee on retention—expanded to include the dean of student life, the assistant dean of liberal arts, and staff from the offices of enrollment services and analytical studies—reviewed the retention literature and then began its research into factors contributing to attrition. With support from all academic units, the subcommittee quickly instituted a standardized, university-wide exit interview procedure administered through the office of the dean of student affairs to replace the haphazard procedures established over the years by some of the schools and colleges. The subcommittee then decided to use a recent alumni office freshman/sophomore opinion survey to evaluate the university's programs as the basis for a more comprehensive questionnaire to be sent to the entire undergraduate population after final examinations in May 1983. A drawing for a one-week vacation in London funded by the alumni office increased the response rate. The survey results which suggested areas and degrees of student satisfaction and dissatisfaction have been reported to the parent committee and to the individual colleges of the university, all of whom had appended their own specific sections to the instrument.

In the meantime, faculty and staff awareness of the retention effort has gradually spread. In response to the president's request, retention has been made an item of reporting at university-wide faculty meetings and college representatives on the faculty council solicit ideas from individual faculty members on how faculty can contribute to retention. The university's council of associate deans appointed its own committee on student retention which set as its major goal the streamlining of the university's administrative procedures. And upon the recommendation of the subcommittee on retention, the president approved the establishment of an office of enrollment planning and retention within the enrollment services area.

In summary, the retention effort received its initial impetus from the president, who has continued to offer financial and staff support, and is spearheaded by the enrollment management committee and its subcommittee on retention. Top priority was given to the accumulation of research data in order to formulate retention priorities. Data drawn from the two student opinion surveys and the exit interviews have been analyzed by the university office of analytical studies with separate analyses done for each of the undergraduate schools. Deans and faculties of those schools will soon begin their own internal discussions of retention strategies within their units.

The next step then is discussion at both the university and college levels of the short- and long-range changes indicated by the data. While resistance to some of these recommendations for change is inevitable given the scope and the complexities of the evaluation (touching on academic services, library, housing, campus life, support services, and the like), an atmosphere of acceptance of change has been created among faculty and staff by the research-oriented approach of the retention committees. A strategy of change by panic could have been misleading and counterproductive for the university. Patient administrators and faculty now have the data and the analyses to inform their debates on how to establish an effective effort to retain quality students whose academic and personal priorities coincide with those of the university. Those debates are about to begin.

Increasing Student Success and Persistence:
A Matrix Accountability Model
Eastern Michigan University

John W. Porter
President

Eastern Michigan University (EMU) in Ypsilanti enrolls 19,000 students. EMU's current retention effort has grown out of initiatives developed over the past several years during which the university has undergone thorough assessment and change. The driving force has been shrinking enrollments and the obvious need to be more competitive. Anticipating enrollment difficulties before they became common to other institutions or retention became a fashionable concern enabled EMU to increase its enrollment during the past five years by more than 8 percent. During the remaining years of its "Decade of Advancement," the university plans to stabilize its enrollment at 19,000 students.

Recognizing that retention is a by-product of improved quality of campus life, EMU's approach was to develop a matrix accountability system which integrates the university's retention effort with its accountability process. This approach parallels the approach suggested in *Mobilizing the Campus for Retention* (1981) coauthored by two EMU administrators, Smith and Sprandel, along with Noel and Lippitt. Initially, a series of campuswide workshops and reports about retention created awareness and support for change. Widespread grass-roots involvement along with key administrative sanction resulted in a cross-divisional university committee for implementing student retention programs. Cochaired by a representative from both the academic affairs and student affairs divisions, the committee collected retention data and reported findings in a special newsletter. As a result of the findings of these efforts, the university appointed a coordinator of student retention.

With this committee structure in place, the president, in 1979, developed six accountability goal areas under which university activities could be clustered. A strategic plan was developed for each of the six goal areas and qualitative and quantitative indicators of success and productivity determined. Each vice-president, in turn, had responsibility for examining the relationship of his or her division to these goals. At monthly meetings each goal area and its indicators were critically examined to assess progress. This not only provided an opportunity for step-by-step monitoring and evaluation, but allowed for making timely adjustments as needed.

In developing an accountability model, three assumptions were made: (1) the retention program's success would be enhanced by developing a matrix which would allow the assigning of accountability to organizational units of the institution; (2) this process would be most successful if it cross-linked the existing retention program with the students' primary holding factors; and (3) the university should express this interest in retention in a tangible manner.

When the eligible-to-return undergraduate student population was examined, seven population clusters emerged. They were categorized by segment, numbers, area accountable, and primary holding factor. For example, the provost's office is accountable for the academically talented segment of 1,000 students with the primary holding factor being academic scholarships and honors programs, while the financial aid office is accountable for the 3,000 high-financial-need students with the holding factor being work-study positions. These segments were not by definition mutually exclusive and computer runs by individual name were necessary to make sure that students were assigned to only one category. Each accountable area worked with the coordinator of retention to ensure accuracy.

Underlying this effort was the intention to help the students consciously make a decision about whether they intended to return. A series of deadlines was established for identifying students in each segment and a second series established for contacting them. A third series of deadlines guaranteed students that if they did not plan to enroll (expressed by not preregistering), the university would commit itself to meeting the terms of the primary holding factor. Students who were identified as not intending to return were referred to the responsible follow-up person in one of the seven segments to determine what the university could do, if anything.

EMU's retention goal was to improve retention by 10 percent. After identifying those not returning because of graduation or other uncontrollable factors, it was determined that an indicator of success for the 1983–84 academic year would be a reenrollment of 10,250 undergraduates for the fall of 1983 semester. The goal was exceeded when 10,467 students returned.

What is important about the matrix accountability approach is that by developing a system which integrates the university's retention effort with its accountability process, all members of our university community are carefully linked together and with our students. This fosters a strong sense of commitment on the part of the university to the student, and in return, on the part of the student to the university. As a result, we have both improved the quality of campus life at EMU and reached our enrollment goals.

Organizing a Retention Project
University of Denver

Terrence J. Toy
Department of Geography

The University of Denver (DU) in Colorado enrolls 8,300 undergraduate and graduate students. There were three motivating factors for the first comprehensive examination of student retention at DU, conducted from January 1, 1979 through June 1, 1980: (1) earlier in-house reports concerning student attitudes in general and retention in particular, (2) a consultant's report indicating a significant attrition problem, and (3) the prospect of a continuing decline in enrollments. Ample financial support and the full cooperation of the university's administrative staff were made available to the retention project director, a tenured member of the faculty who was given one year of release time to spearhead the effort.

The purpose of the retention project was to organize the institution for an assault upon the attrition rate and, in the process, create an awareness and a readiness on the part of those whose participation would be necessary. Toward this end, the following objectives were chosen: determine the severity of the attrition problem, identify probable causes, and provide recommendations for improving the retention rate.

The project began with the appointment of a director by the chancellor of the university and a thorough review of both internal and external reports related to retention as well as attendance at an American College Testing Program (ACT) retention workshop. There were two major components to the project: the short-term and long-term programs.

The short-term program involved the investigation of specific situations or problems which were thought by the director to be influencing retention. The issues addressed included (1) compilation of retention data by longitudinal tracking and statistical analyses, (2) review of the adequacy of available financial aid packages, (3) evaluation of the academic challenge offered by DU with particular focus upon the possibility of grade inflation, and (4) an examination of campus morale from both student and faculty perspectives.

It soon became apparent that additional research would be required. The objectives of this research were (1) to determine the chronology of the decision to withdraw from the university (when does the student typically decide to drop out?), (2) to compare student expectations and subsequent perceptions about various aspects of DU, (3) to formulate a methodology to provide for early recognition of probable dropouts so that they might be targeted for interventions, and (4) to develop computer programs for extracting and manipulating student information contained on master-file computer tapes. Research proposals were prepared by the director, while the actual research was conducted by others within the university.

The long-term program involved the formation of student, faculty, and administration committees. The groups were organized in May 1979, provided with summer reading materials, and began regular meetings at the start of the next academic year. Each independently constructed an agenda prioritizing the items that they felt most influenced retention. The director chaired every meeting and the conclusions of the three committees were synthesized into a final report. Lastly, a decision was made to employ a consultant to evaluate the adequacy of the project and provide an objective opinion of our attrition problem.

The results of both the short- and long-term programs were assembled in a 300-page document. A list of specific recommendations derived from the document was itself nearly 13 pages long. The report was presented to a meeting of interested students, faculty, and administrators; distributed to administrative offices; and placed in the library where it was available to all. Following completion of the initial phases of the retention project, responsibility for further retention efforts was assigned to special assistants to the chancellor and the director returned to a full-time faculty assignment.

It appears that there are at least five factors which determine the success realized in organizing a campus to confront the issue of retention: (1) institutional climate; (2) definitive objectives; (3) a well-conceived strategy for achieving these objectives; (4) involvement of influential students, faculty, and administrators; and (5) specific and realistic recommendations.

Clearly defined goals help determine strategies and offer benchmarks against which the success of the project may be evaluated. Because each institution is unique, the precise nature of the operational milieu should be given full consideration in identifying these objectives.

Although many reports assert that implementing retention programs requires the participation of virtually the entire institutional community, the initial organizational phase is likely to include a relatively small proportion of this community. Among the characteristics of those persons with the greatest potential value to the retention project would seem to be (1) knowledge of student concerns and behavior, (2) clout and credibility within the institutional decision-making mechanism, and (3) time to attend regularly-scheduled meetings.

Finally, the recommendations emerging from the retention project must be clearly expressed and feasible within the institution's financial constraints. Proposals which are not feasible will encourage the notion that retention efforts are futile. In retrospect, I would also submit that the number of recommendations should remain rather modest. Lengthy lists may overwhelm those charged with implementation.

At the meeting where the final report was discussed, procedures were established so that in the future retention data can be compiled whenever needed. Numerous probable causes of attrition had been identified by the participants, and recommendations for improving these situations offered.

Perhaps of equal importance, several preconceptions were proven invalid. Statistics produced by the longitudinal tracking of students revealed that the attrition rate was generally not dissimilar to that of similar institutions. Females did not constitute a disproportionate share of the dropouts. Grade inflation did not appear to be a significant problem. The extended hiatus between autumn and winter quarters did not seem to be the time when the decision to withdraw was usually made.

At DU, our objectives were achieved because a sound foundation had been constructed upon which effective retention programs could be built.

Readiness, Data, and Diversity in Mobilizing
a Retention Effort
Louisiana Tech University

Maribel S. McKinney
Director of the Counseling Center

Although enrollment figures at Louisiana Tech University in Ruston where current enrollment is 11,172 show an annual increase for the past ten years, the attrition rate is still of concern. The registrar's office has conducted attrition studies periodically in recent decades and colleges and departments have gathered data on students not completing their programs. Motivated by an attrition study and a desire to assist students in meeting their nonacademic needs, the division of student affairs established a student retention program in 1976. Designed for entering freshmen residing on campus, the program deals with communication skills, value clarification, and helping students adjust to life away from home. An annual report on figures and attitude changes of participants is distributed to administrators across campus.

In 1979, because of the success of this student affairs program, a campuswide retention program was initiated to increase awareness of retention needs and to coordinate new and existing retention programs. The chairperson of the student affairs retention program was appointed as coordinator of the campuswide retention program by the vice-president of student affairs and as chair of the twenty-two-member campuswide retention steering committee.

One factor contributing to the success of this campuswide program was the university's readiness for such an effort, stemming from previous retention studies and activities. Other factors include an emphasis on collecting and distributing data and an openness to a diversity of concerns.

Campus support has been phenomenal. Minutes of retention steering committee meetings, with each participant's comments identified, are sent to the president and other top administrators, and the president has commended committee members individually and as a whole. The council of academic deans has provided funding for a campuswide survey of nonreturning students. Faculty and staff have been involved in programs recommended by the committee such as career days and exit interviews.

Communicating retention information across campus has been a highly positive factor. Committee minutes and follow-up reports on activities are distributed across campus and a university twelve-month desk calendar pad with retention messages for each month keeps faculty and staff members informed of current retention projects.

A final factor in the success of the program has been the acceptance of a diversity of retention concerns. Committee members, although all very retention oriented, present different, sometimes contradictory views as to where the greatest needs lie and how to approach these needs.

The success of the retention organizing efforts can best be documented by the following actions taken by the committee and implemented by the university:

- A quarterly printout and address labels of all students who do not reenroll in the following quarter are prepared for each academic college.
- An American College Testing Program survey of withdrawing/nonreturning students and a survey of continuing students

provide statistically sound data on student opinions about the university which have been requested by several departments across campus.

- A program has been set up to provide accurate tracking data on all enrolled students.
- Results of an exit interview questionnaire completed by students as they receive their dean's signature on a withdrawal form are distributed annually.
- A career emphasis program in which undecided students are invited to visit department heads on designated days has been initiated.

The campuswide retention program has had a dramatic impact on the retention awareness level of the university. All academic colleges have either established retention committees or have incorporated retention topics into their departmental meetings. A next step will be to evaluate retention efforts in terms of student persistence.

A Decentralized Approach to Retention
University of South Carolina at Spartanburg

Ron G. Eaglin
Vice-Chancellor for Student Affairs

The University of South Carolina at Spartanburg (USCS) is a commuter campus with 2,700 students enrolled. The central force in USCS retention efforts has been the faculty. An initial retention program in 1972, conducted by faculty, offered special classes and guidance for students with low achievement scores and poor high school performance. From 1975 on, a new approach to retention has evolved during a period of rapid enrollment growth. The faculty has tripled in size, but its early interest in retention has remained.

This is largely due to a decentralized organizational structure which encourages faculty participation in the retention effort. Care is taken by the administration to reinforce individual efforts and to ensure that all faculty and staff share in "ownership" of university-wide programs.

To achieve this decentralization, retention planning takes

place at both the university-wide and academic unit level. A university-wide committee chaired by the assistant vice-chancellor for academic affairs and made up primarily of faculty members, has functioned as an ad hoc retention committee since 1976. While the university committee does make recommendations on university-wide programs, the strength of the USCS retention effort is at the unit committee level. Faculty on the committee form retention committees within their schools or divisions which initiate most retention activities.

Advisory groups also encourage "ownership" of university-wide programs. In addition to helping design orientation, advising, and developmental programs, faculty, along with staff and students, serve on advisory groups which make ongoing evaluations of these programs. Suggestions made by local advisory committees that have been implemented by individual faculty are contacting students who are absent two consecutive times, meeting with freshmen advisees outside of formal advising sessions, and coordinating the curricula of developmental and regular classes. One school has created a learning resource center for its majors, and an office is now open until 7:00 P.M. to help evening students.

Factors important to the success of student retention efforts at USCS include the following:

1. Retention is viewed as a general goal in all academic units and not as the goal of a single unit such as student affairs.
2. The student affairs division supports all retention efforts at the university and unit level; for example, orientation, tutorial laboratories, counseling, career guidance, and so on.
3. School and division committees have contact with students on a regular basis.
4. Special attention is given to freshmen by providing academic advising through the freshman/sophomore center.
5. A clear institutional mission statement was developed by the faculty and is, from time to time, amended by them.
6. An effort is made to provide useful institutional research data to analyze attrition problems.

At USCS, an institution whose students have all the indicators of high-risk, dropout-prone students, a staying environment has been developed through the cooperative efforts of faculty and staff. The attrition rate has dropped from 42 percent in 1977–78 to 32 percent in 1982–83. The decentralized approach to solving campus problems has not only increased retention but has been responsible for many other activities that promote the general health of the institution such as implementation of a faculty peer review system, student evaluation of instruction, and teaching demonstrations for prospective faculty. This progress indicates that at USCS retention is not an end in itself but merely a by-product of good teaching and advising, solid institutional research, and the creation of an awareness of student needs among faculty and staff.

A Unified Marketing Approach
to Student Affairs
Bradley University

Thomas Huddleston, Jr.
Former Associate Provost for Student Affairs

Located in Peoria, Illinois, Bradley University is an independent, four-year institution which enrolls 5,600 undergraduate and graduate students. Recognizing that the student life area has a powerful influence on student development, in 1982 Bradley formed a division of student affairs, bringing together six student services units under a unified philosophy of service. The units include career development, co-curricular and organizational development, educational development, financial assistance, residential life and student judicial system, and undergraduate admissions. This configuration encompasses most campus services outside of the classroom and reflects a redirection of the university's intention to meet specific, identified needs of both prospective and current students. Bradley thus identified the important benefits its primary markets were seeking and established a model of organization to deliver these benefits.

The division of student affairs grew out of a move toward consolidation of services begun in 1975 when it seemed that student and parent attention was being increasingly focused on nonacademic areas such as admissions, financial aid, and career assistance. Students' primary questions included: "What interests me about college? If admitted, can I afford to attend? Will I succeed in college? Will I find a good job after college?" Bradley recognized that students were trying to cope with a changing society and a changing university without adequate self-awareness and without a plan. Some believed they never had a chance to discover what they desired or for what they were best qualified.

To provide a more meaningful environment for these uncertain young people, the university created a unified administrative component to formally monitor the needs of students and translate their findings about these needs and how they are being met to both the university community and the community at large. Student services personnel also felt that by combining their functions into one formal structure with readily identifiable responsibilities, they could compete more effectively for the institution's limited financial resources. Dominant throughout the division is the underlying philosophy of the marketing concept. Identifying and meeting students' needs is foremost and required annual marketing plans and marketing audits are commonplace in each office of every unit.

The division of student affairs sponsors two major communications efforts. Student representatives from major campus organizations, publications, and living units meet monthly with top student affairs administrators to exchange ideas and discuss campus concerns. And a monthly divisional newsletter is distributed to the university community highlighting activities in each of the major program units.

Structurally, student affairs enjoys the distinctive position of reporting to the provost and vice-president for academic affairs; this has resulted in opportunities for the division to interact positively with faculty, thus increasing its visibility and credibility with them. Division members also have the opportunity to participate in the development of programs on a larger scale, rather than being limited to smaller, individual efforts. There is also an opportunity for greater shared use of resources such as staff, equipment, ideas, and publications.

Since 1975, freshman applications have increased by more than 42 percent and transfer applications by more than 75 percent. New student enrollments have increased by more than 10 percent and admissions standards have continued to rise despite declining numbers of graduating high school seniors throughout Illinois and the Midwest since 1976.

The American College Testing Program composite score has risen from 21 in 1975 to 24 in 1983. Scholastic Aptitude Test entrance scores have increased by more than 100 points. New students' rank in class has increased significantly. Freshman and university retention rates have improved. Currently, 65 percent of entering freshmen are graduating or still enrolled four years later compared to 53 percent in the early 1970s at Bradley. Approximately 91.8 percent of freshmen are returning to the university their sophomore year.

Through bringing together various services under one unified division, commonalities have been strengthened and a unified philosophy of service now pervades the student life area. Much of the progress made in each major student services unit has been enhanced by the assistance of others working in the larger family of the division of student affairs.

A Catalogue of Successful Practices

The practices presented in this section are drawn from the Noel and Levitz report (forthcoming) which identifies programs that seem to be influential as part of a larger effort to maintain or improve retention rates.

Academic Alert System

"The single most important factor in an early warning system is some type of 'search and rescue' team responding to early notification of students' nonattendance in class."

Larry S. Haverkos
Dean of Students
Urbana College, Ohio

- All students tracked every three weeks in all courses to discover academic problems early. If difficulties are noted, students are contacted by advising office. (Grinnell College, Iowa)
- A freshman hour incorporated into the first-year schedule functions as an early warning to identify first-year problems associated with academic regulations, study habits, grading systems, and so on. (St. Louis College of Pharmacy, Missouri)
- Class lists contain the names of students' advisers, enabling faculty to contact them should problems arise. (Molloy College, Rockville Centre, New York)

Academic Advising and Career Guidance

"Academic advising is the core of a retention program. Do whatever it takes to make it work."

Anna Wasecha, Assistant
Dean of Student Affairs
Hamline University
St. Paul, Minnesota

- Personalized letters are sent by faculty to parents of their newly assigned advisees. (McPherson College, Kansas)
- A special core of faculty whose advising responsibilities center on freshmen attend summer orientation sessions where they receive special training and then meet with incoming advisees in formal group and individual sessions and then in less formal settings such as discussion groups and cookouts. (Assumption College, Worcester, Massachusetts)
- The career development center working through six peer counselors interviews all undecided students during the first term and urges use of the center's services. Seminars relating liberal arts to career goals are held throughout the year. (Wartburg College, Waverly, Iowa)
- Special career awareness course and the assignment of faculty mentors to seventy-five undecided freshmen who opt for such services. (State University of New York College at Potsdam)

Campuswide Collaborative Efforts and Research

"Frequent consciousness raising sessions about the problem (opportunity?) are necessary . . . memories are short!"
> Gerald Gaither, Director of
> Institutional Research and
> Planning, California State
> University, Northridge

• Dialogue Day. Classes are cancelled. All faculty, staff, and students are required to attend and organized into groups of twelve. Group activities include describing one's ideal college; listing positive characteristics of the college, then negative characteristics; prioritizing each list, then focusing on what can be done to increase positive experiences and reduce negative ones. Since the initial dialogue day, shorter dialogues on specific topics have been conducted. (McPherson College, Kansas)
• Year-end report required from each college summarizing the efforts made by that college to improve retention. (Arkansas State University, State University)
• Program marketing plans designed by faculty with retention in mind result in yearly contract objectives for individual faculty. (Oklahoma City Community College)
• Self-report data used to determine student perceptions of their needs and the degree to which these needs are being met. (State University of New York Agricultural and Technical College, Canton)

Communication with Students

"Taking a close look at the covert messages the institution is sending via its policies and practices, correspondence and materials, and so on is helpful. Actually, socialization for retention begins in the material sent to students following acceptance."
> Wendy G. Winters, Dean
> Smith College
> Northampton, Massachusetts

- Publicity department publishes a special issue of the student newspaper each summer and mails it to prospective and current students. Articles are designed to keep students informed about and interested in the college and to introduce prospective students to one another. (McPherson College, Kansas)
- Freshmen applying for admission to a restricted admission program are sent a letter providing specific information about the program's admissions standards and procedures to make it clear what is expected of them when they arrive on campus. (Northern Illinois University, De Kalb)
- Entering students are sent extensive introductory information during the summer to help them set reasonable expectations for what lies ahead. (Carleton College, Northfield, Minnesota)

Involvement Experiences

"Think through appropriate ways to bond the freshmen to the campus . . . freshmen who are involved tend to stay unless there are family crises that are serious."

Sister Sue Miller
Academic Dean
Saint Mary College
Leavenworth, Kansas

- Leadership intern program for freshmen in the fall. (Saint Mary College, Leavenworth, Kansas)
- An effort to expand campus employment to develop psychological ties to the campus and individual departments has resulted in about 410 students out of 1,150 being employed on campus. (Wartburg College, Waverly, Iowa)
- A music department with a philosophy of participation has resulted in nearly 40 percent of the student body being involved in the music program, either playing in an ensemble or taking lessons. Nearly the same number of students are involved in varsity or club sports, not to mention intramurals. (Gustavus Adolphus College, Saint Peter, Minnesota)

Learning Assistance/Support

"Acknowledge the need of remediation without attaching a stigma to those participating in such programs. Using titles such as 'Skills Improvement' provides access without labeling students."   Sister Patricia Morris, Vice-
President for Academic Affairs
Molloy College
Rockville Centre, New York

- Faculty selected on the basis of their teaching/advising skills teach required tutorial to twelve freshmen. The emphasis is on writing, speaking, and research skills. Faculty tutor continues to advise students until a major is selected. (Grinnell College, Iowa)
- The academic support services program has a full-time director who coordinates a staff of fifteen student tutors (called A + tutors) and additional departmental tutors. The A + tutors are each associated with a residence hall where they run study skills, time management, and examination preparation workshops. (Wellesley College, Massachusetts)
- In the special English tutorial program, freshmen are carefully selected on the basis of admissions credentials to work with upperclass students. (Tufts University, Medford, Massachusetts)
- Before students are admitted on probation, they must take placement tests in reading and mathematics. Students then meet with a probation adviser to discuss terms of a probation contract which may include required remedial courses. (University of Arkansas at Little Rock)

Orientation

"The atmosphere created by freshman orientation is one of a friendly community. This idea of community continues throughout the first year and allows the student to feel a part of the university at an early stage."
                                    Frank G. Persico, Dean of
Students, Catholic University of
America, Washington, D.C.

- Freshman Week. Freshmen arrive on campus a week prior to the start of the fall term. All resources of the university are devoted to their needs. Freshman seminar begins during this week and continues to meet three times per week throughout the first semester. (University of Redlands, California)
- Five-day orientation program which includes opportunities to sample classes by attending faculty presentations, exposure to academic support services, diagnostic testing for course placement, two meetings with a faculty adviser, and a variety of social gatherings. (Carleton College, Northfield, Minnesota)
- Freshman Seminar. Two-semester course focusing on introduction to the liberal arts and the tradition of great Western literature while developing writing and communication skills. (Saint Mary College, Leavenworth, Kansas)

Out-of-Class Contact with Faculty

"When we design programs deliberately to increase retention, they usually are aimed at creating a sense of belonging to the institution by encouraging a personal relationship with a member of the faculty or staff."

> Barbara H. Palmer
> Assistant Dean of the College
> Brandeis University
> Waltham, Massachussetts

- Dinner with Twelve Strangers. Eight students, two faculty members, and two graduates share in the cost of a dinner. The participants' names are drawn from lists of people interested in participating. Anyone may host the dinner. (Marquette University, Milwaukee, Wisconsin)
- Cognitive Cuisine. Small groups of students go to faculty homes for dinner. (Brandeis University, Waltham, Massachusetts)
- Free cafeteria lunches are provided to faculty one day each week for those interested in meeting and talking with students. (Biola University, La Mirada, California)
- Fifty dollars is available each semester to each member of

the faculty to entertain students in his or her home. (Smith College, Northampton, Massachusetts)
- Life Skills and Communiversity. Two major programs of mini-courses reflecting the avocational interests of faculty, staff, and students provide short-term instructional opportunities and a chance for informal interaction. (Brandeis University, Waltham, Massachusetts)

Peer Support

"Upperclassmen need to share the responsibility for the success and persistence of new students."

Cynthia O. Bruckman
Coordinator, Freshman
Program, Florida Institute of
Technology, Melbourne, Florida

- New Student Days. Three hundred student volunteers help new students move into residence halls and become acquainted with the university. (Northern Illinois University, De Kalb)
- Peer academic counselors, who receive a week of formal training before freshmen arrive, work with a group of freshmen in formal weekly sessions for eight weeks focusing on study skills and attitudes for success in college. Weekly meetings continue for the rest of the semester focusing on topics selected by the group. (Saint Mary College, Leavenworth, Kansas)
- Upperclass students who serve as part of a student support network during orientation participate in training sessions held in the previous spring semester and just prior to the beginning of fall session. In August, each freshman receives a personal letter from the head of freshmen of the residence hall in which she will be living. (Smith College, Northampton, Massachusetts)

Residence Halls

"Our resident assistants are important resources. They

are carefully selected and trained to help ensure that the freshman year is a positive experience.''

James W. Davis
Vice-Chancellor
Washington University
St. Louis, Missouri

- Selected, specially trained tutors are placed on residence hall
  floors that house large numbers of freshmen. (Tufts University, Medford, Massachusetts)
- In addition to foreign language floors, there are special interest residence hall floors for such groups as computer
  science, science majors, and honors program participants.
  (Northern Illinois University, De Kalb)
- Study skills clinics are set up in residence halls as well as
  in the student center. (State University of New York Agricultural and Technical College, Canton)
- All freshmen in a residence hall take one course in common.
  (Saint Lawrence University, Canton, New York)

Structure

"Build a strong network of services for first-year students
and articulate an information-sharing system for undergraduates
which helps them quickly identify sources of support.''

Mack I. Davis II
Assistant Dean
Harvard College
Cambridge, Massachusetts

- Office of dean of freshmen sponsors an advisory council of
  freshmen to work with the dean. (Bradley University, Peoria,
  Illinois)
- Campus information center offices reorganized into a one-
  stop campus center where students can get financial aid,
  enroll, pay bills, pick up checks, and have questions answered. (McPherson College, Kansas)
- The freshman dean is the coordinator of orientation and remains the primary academic adviser for all freshmen, con-

ducting group meetings and one-to-one advising sessions on a full-time basis. (Wellesley College, Massachusetts)

• A dean of student affairs coordinates academic advising, residential life, student activities, and personal counseling. This uniting of curricular and co-curricular activities has brought a new awareness of the importance of the integration of the student into the college community. (Skidmore College, Saratoga Springs, New York)

References

Black Students—Special Problems/Special Needs for Retention. Louisville, Ky: Jefferson Community College, 1982. (ED 237 179)

Full Classrooms: 95 Practical Suggestions to Guarantee Student and Teacher Success. Louisville, Ky: Jefferson Community College, 1980. (ED 237 184)

Noel, L., and Levitz, R. "Reporting on the 'Best of the Best'— the Nation's Most Noteworthy Retention-Wise Campuses." Iowa City, Iowa: Noel/Levitz Centers for Institutional Effectiveness and Innovation, forthcoming.

Smith, L.N., and others. *Mobilizing the Campus for Retention: An Innovative Quality-of-Life Model.* Iowa City, Iowa: American College Testing Program National Center for the Advancement of Educational Practices, 1981.

Used Books: 54 Suggestions to Increase Library Use. Louisville, Ky: Jefferson Community College, 1982. (ED 237 178)

22

Getting Retention Results:
A Blueprint for Action

～～～～～～～～

Lee Noel
Randi Levitz
Diana Saluri

The scope and depth of the ideas presented in this volume make clear that retention is a campuswide issue covering every aspect of campus life. This recognition that retention is not solely the responsibility of the student services office is a big step forward in the work that needs to be done on our campuses. While acknowledging the wide scope of the issues and solutions set forth here, we can, however, draw together some common underlying themes, principles for action, and strategies for practice, and finally, with these insights behind us, look ahead to future directions.

Despite very pressing and difficult environmental factors, the contributing authors all clearly believe that the picture on campus is not as bleak as some think. Whatever the area of expertise, the authors make it clear that, to them, what retention is really about is serving students better and promoting their success in learning. The theme that Noel introduces in his chapter on outcome measures in general education—improved

448

quality means improved persistence—is picked up by each author and runs throughout this volume. Retention is thus presented in terms of the positive aspects of improving the quality of education, of upgrading the experience we provide for students both in the classroom and out.

In his chapter on the link between student learning and persistence, Forrest demonstrates that the college that can clearly identify student growth in terms of outcomes; the college that is truly in the talent development business will have a decided advantage in recruiting and retaining our increasingly consumer-oriented students. This emphasis on outcomes means that in the future we will move away from more traditional indicators of quality and instead take student growth and development as our one standard for excellence. In this chapter we will review the authors' analyses and suggestions and then look ahead to future directions. Our emphasis will be on the programs that can, and above all the people who can achieve this excellence, deliver the kind of learning and life experiences that will ensure student success.

The authors agree then that the way to increase the productivity and performance of faculty and staff, and hence retention, is to put renewed emphasis on responding to the individual student and his or her needs. In fact, the entire student-centered thrust of this volume can be seen in Tinto's statements in Chapter Two. In defining dropout, he makes it clear that all forms of student departure in some fashion reflect the unique experience of a particular individual with given intentions, commitments, and skills within a particular institutional environment characterized by distinct academic and social communities.

The authors make clear that, to them, putting the emphasis on achieving success with the individual student primarily means shifting our thinking from an institutional to a student perspective. We shall see in this chapter that this means first of all defining dropout according to the student's educational objectives, not institutional record-keeping convenience. This focus on the individual student is also apparent in the authors' call for a greater awareness of the needs and characteristics of new dropout-prone student populations and in the intervention strategies the authors propose. We shall see that the focus of these strategies, both inside and outside the classroom, is developmental and intrusive—reaching out to the individual student in whatever developmental stage he or she may be.

Finally, we will consider the mechanisms the authors present for redirecting the energies on our campuses to make them more student-centered by *mobilizing* and *organizing* for action and change. After considering each of these factors, we will conclude with a detailed blueprint for action: ten basic steps for implementing a campuswide retention effort.

A Shift in Perspective

To make this shift in our retention viewpoint from an institutional to a student perspective, we must begin by redefining our notion of what dropout means. In his chapter, Tinto makes it clear that we need to look at attrition from the student's point of view, concluding that the label *dropout* should be limited only to "those situations in which there is failure on the part of both the individual and the institution, a failure of student to achieve and of the institution to facilitate the achievement of reasonable and desired educational goals."

Anderson also takes up the student's view by advocating a force field analysis of the factors at work on each individual student as he or she makes the decision to attend a particular institution and the decision to stay or leave. Stewart, Merrill, and Saluri, in their chapter on commuters, and Pappas and Loring, in their discussion of adult students, point out that no longer can we view higher education as a set two- or four-year process. All agree that when a student has achieved the self-defined goals that he or she sets out to achieve, then he or she is a success, not a dropout. We must then begin by viewing retention in terms of student success, individually defined, and not in terms of dropout statistics.

A New Perspective on the Dropout Prone

Keeping this student-centered perspective on retention in mind, we can look at the characteristics and needs of dropout-prone populations of students—low-income, underprepared, undecided, commuting, and adult—in a new light. Clearly, all the authors are well aware that we in higher education are no longer faced with a homogeneous student population of eighteen- to twenty-two-year-old residential students. As Valverde points out, the emphasis on equality of opportunity in the sixties and seventies has opened the door to many new groups of students whom we have now placed under the umbrella of the term "nontraditional." The authors agree that these special populations of nontraditional students will be dropout prone unless we respond to their special characteristics and needs. Valverde maintains that colleges and universities must be aware that their students vary in background, future aspirations and abilities, motivation, and academic skills.

Learning to view these special populations as individuals with their own unique purposes and goals is the focus of the chapters on low-income students, underprepared students, and commuting and adult students. In their chapter on underprepared students, Moore and Carpenter fault researchers for chasing after a typical student who no longer exists. They maintain that the academically underprepared students of the late seventies and the early eighties represent a diverse population that includes older widowed and divorced women, veterans, career changers, workers whose jobs have changed or been eliminated, and workers in fields experiencing rapid technological change.

Moore and Carpenter argue that the truly innovative way to deal with this diversity is to move away from a tendency to blame the victim and focus on ways our institutions can make the accommodations necessary to serve the diverse needs of these students. The key is to emphasize improving the quality of instruction through institutional change and true innovation rather than emphasizing the psychosocial characteristics of underprepared students.

An Individualized Developmental Approach

This focus on serving the individual student extends to the authors who deal with institutional interventions. As we have noted, their approach is developmental and intrusive, stressing the need to reach out to serve students in new and more flexible ways. The importance assigned to the role of support services in retention is best summed up by Tinto's model which points out that intellectual as well as social integration is necessary for students to feel at home on campus and persist.

Admissions and Financial Aid. In their chapters, Ihlanfeldt and Martin demonstrate that this student-centered emphasis on promoting individual student success begins with two main areas that serve as points of entry into an institution: admissions and financial aid. In an outcome-centered emphasis that allows for a diversity of student characteristics, the focus in these areas will be on achieving the best fit between the institution and the individual student's needs. Ihlanfeldt recommends an approach to admissions that is success oriented both for the student and the institution, an approach that will benefit the institution and ensure that students choose to attend institutions at which they are most likely to flourish and succeed. This brings us back to outcomes. To achieve this best fit, an institution must be able to interpret for a prospective student the exact nature of the product it has to offer. By measuring outcomes through institutional assessment, a college can reposition itself in relation to competing institutions.

In his chapter on financial aid, Martin takes up the question of how to carry this emphasis on student success into financial aid packaging. He advocates a flexible aid packaging policy appropriately bolstered with follow-up support services such as money management training, job placement, and counseling geared to individual students' needs.

A Continuing Process. In line with putting student needs before institutional convenience, Titley stresses that orientation must be more than something we do at the beginning of a term, an initial activity. Instead, it should be a continuing process so that the individual student encounters information as the need for it arises. In her chapter on career planning, Sprandel points out that career counseling should be individualized by beginning at the developmental stage where students are and going from there. She also demonstrates how career planning can move outside the career planning office and become a part of the curriculum.

In his chapter on residence hall programming, Upcraft

maintains that "Because students talk about college experiences more as a series of events rather than as psychological or sociological processes, it is probably more useful to develop programs and activities based on a student development model rather than on a theory."

Crockett carries this developmental emphasis to academic advising, pointing out that the link between advising and improved student retention is not surprising if advising is viewed developmentally. Once advising goes beyond being a mere course-scheduling activity and becomes a decision-making process designed to facilitate student growth and development, it becomes a means of not only helping students to select courses but to synthesize life and career goals.

The Classroom. Roueche and Roueche, in their chapter on teaching strategies, advocate an approach to teaching that puts the individual student at the center of the teaching process. This means that instructors will need to be willing to face and deal with "troublesome realities of student learning behaviors, realities which, if ignored, militate against student success in the classroom." These difficult realities include a range of student skill levels, diverse learning styles, and time restrictions. To teachers who are willing to acknowledge and work around these realities, the term "individualized instruction" takes on a special meaning. It does not mean a freewheeling approach to letting students move at their own pace indefinitely. "Rather it is instruction that has the individual at its center, with the instructor always involved. It is instruction that allows students to progress through sequentially developed steps that move from the simple to the more complex at a pace and at a level of mastery that both they and the teacher have agreed upon prior to beginning the learning process."

The emphasis then in all the intervention strategies—both inside and outside the classroom—that the authors propose is on promoting the success of each individual student by first helping him or her find a goal and then pursue it. Because when students are clear about their purposes and how an institution can best serve those purposes, they are more likely to succeed and persist.

Mobilizing for Change

Now that we know what we want from our campuses—a
student-centered, outcome-oriented staying environment—how
do we go about generating the changes we need to make, changes
successfully made at the campuses noted by Saluri in Chapter
Twenty-one. Smith, Lippett, and Sprandel, and Toy agree with
us that the key is to elicit total community involvement in the
change process on campus. Smith, Lippett, and Sprandel discuss, from an institutional perspective, how we can involve the
total campus community in creating readiness for change, maintaining that to promote change efforts we need to develop a collaborative structure in place of the traditional hierarchical structure that exists on most campuses. Toy focuses in on one key
element in gaining campus support for the change process: the
faculty. Based on his experience, he emphasizes the importance
of gaining faculty confidence in order to overcome misunder-
standings about and resistance to change. The research dimension as presented by Levitz and Noel provides an approach for
gathering data which serve to gain a common awareness, spur
and guide action, and evaluate progress. As we consider the
ideas that have been put forth in the preceding chapters, what
is yet uncharted are the steps needed to actually implement a
campuswide retention effort.

Before describing the ten basic steps in mobilizing a campus for action, we note that as a campus embarks upon a retention effort there are two factors to consider. First, a retention
effort should be viewed as a kind of gigantic, campuswide problem-solving exercise. It then naturally follows that there are certain steps that are logically and inevitably taken. Second, the
essential task is to find a way to mobilize the collective wisdom
that already exists on campus. The best solutions to the problems on a campus—and solutions do exist—for the most part
reside with its own people. The task of mobilizing the campus
thus involves bringing together the best people and the best ideas
that already exist right on the campus.

The real question for an institution initiating a retention
effort then becomes: How can we get a collaborative effort go-

ing and benefit from the wisdom that resides throughout the campus? In essence what needs to be done is to initiate and maintain an internal dialogue about what the institution does well, what it does not do so well, and which students it is best equipped to serve.

The purpose of this collaboration is twofold: to mobilize the collective wisdom and energy that already exists on campus and to build a sense of ownership and commitment to the plans and activities designed to improve retention. After first considering the importance of faculty support and of collecting appropriate data, the balance of this chapter will present ten steps to establishing such a collaborative process. Each step is designed to draw together an ever-widening circle of participants in a campuswide renewal effort while establishing a commitment to change. The three conditions necessary for change are that (1) the benefits of change are clearly established, (2) the leaders have a clear image of a desired state, and (3) the leaders have a clear picture of some practical first steps. Bringing about these change-oriented conditions on a campus involves the successful application of theories of organizational development and planned change, rigorous self-assessment, and an ongoing monitoring and evaluation process. These processes are incorporated in the ten steps outlined later in this chapter.

Faculty Support as Key

Before delineating these ten steps, we might first consider a major source of resistance to change on campus: faculty misconceptions about retention efforts. In the 1982 survey reported in *Organizing the Campus for Retention*, campus personnel who were actively involved in a retention effort stated the key advice they would give to those beginning a retention project. The advice most often stated (34 percent of the respondents) was "Do what is necessary to get faculty support, that is the number one key" (Noel, Levitz, and Kaufmann, 1982).

The premise behind the ten mobilizing steps we present is that support grows out of a feeling of being involved; involvement leads to ownership, ownership leads to commitment. In order to create that initial sense of involvement among faculty, we must first dispel a myth that is pervasive on campus. One of the keys to creating faculty acceptance and support is to make clear to faculty early on that we are not asking them to sacrifice standards, that in fact what we are really talking about is doing a better job for the students, doing those things that will cause students to achieve more and to be more successful and more satisfied. Rather, our approach will be to help students into a position where they can meet our standards, not to smash them against the standards. This approach leads to results in student retention. Faculty should understand that retention is not the goal, but only the by-product, the result of improved programs and services for students. This idea that increasing student learning is the key to attracting and retaining students is now empirically supported by Forrest's study (1982), which demonstrates that persistence is linked to student learning, that the more students learn, the more likely they are to stay. (See also Chapter Four.)

Another obvious benefit of a retention effort for faculty is job security. As Marchese (1983, p. 7) says, speaking of a fictional state university embarking on a retention effort, "Don't be afraid to put dollar signs on the result. A five percentage-point gain in 'State's' year-to-year retention rate recaptures $750,000 in lost revenue. Figures like that command attention." A less obvious benefit, perhaps, is the improvement in student and faculty morale brought about by the creation of a more stimulating learning and work environment. A still less obvious benefit which may not have occurred to many faculty is that improved retention increases the pool of students for advanced courses. Upper division and even graduate faculty sometimes forget that freshman attrition concerns them also.

Importance of Data

The importance of collecting data throughout each of these ten steps should be emphasized. As the two examples in this section illustrate, collecting and analyzing data is a way of making a case for doing something about attrition and spreading the awareness of the need for studying conditions on campus.

A four-year private college we recently worked with had a freshman dropout rate of 39 percent, very high for an institution which is reasonably selective. Enrolling students had American College Testing Program test scores that ranked them in the 70th percentile of college-bound students, and there was some indication that they were achievers because they were earning a high school grade point average that put them in the 90th percentile of college-bound students. Yet at the end of their freshman year at this institution, these students earned grade point averages that put them in the 28th percentile of college freshmen nationally.

When these data were presented to the college's faculty, the initial response was to become very defensive: "I'm proud of that record; that means we have standards. There's nothing wrong with a good C. It's an average grade and there's nothing wrong with being average." But after awhile they began to understand that they ought to take a look at the data, to ask themselves: "Is this a justifiable record for students in our freshman classes?" And they particularly began to see this in light of their understanding of the fact that they were dealing with a group of students that had been conditioned to achieve. It became apparent, not surprisingly, that these students responded to unexpected low performance by dropping out. Further investigation led us to four instructors in freshman courses whose highest average course section grade point average was 1.6. In presenting such data to faculty and staff, it is important to avoid hasty judgments. Rather than immediately identifying those four teachers as the source of the problem, it is important to consider the possibility that the course placement system may be at fault or that a prerequisite should have been required for the courses involved. Data such as these should be used as a trigger for further study and attention.

Another example: In the fall of 1980 a two-year college system had 150,000 students enrolled in 363,999 individual courses; the average student took just under three courses. On average the grades given out were 18 percent A's; 19 percent

B's; 17 percent C's; 5 percent D's; 3 percent F's; 2 percent I's (incompletes); and 35 percent W's (withdrawals). They had an unwritten college policy that if students just stopped coming to class or missed the final examination and made no attempt to reschedule they were reported as withdrawn. Simply highlighting the fact that 45 percent of the grades given out to students were nonproductive grades (D's, F's, I's, and W's) made the school's attrition rate come into sharper focus.

However, in interpreting such data, we need to be careful about where we place the blame. There are many reasons why students in the first example performed at the 28th percentile or why 45 percent of the students in the second example did not earn a productive grade. It may or may not be due to poor teaching in the classroom. It may simply be for lack of an assessment program that places students in the appropriate course levels. It is possible to identify a number of reasons. The point is that such data can point up the need to study attrition at a systematic, conscious level. After all, not many enterprises can succeed if 45 percent of the product is substantially below acceptable levels of completion.

The Ten Steps

Step One: Decide to Act. Creating an awareness of the benefits to both students and faculty of improving the quality of learning on campus—the decision to act or institutional internalization—is the first step in a retention effort. The initial task is to identify the appeals and benefits that will accrue if, in fact, something is done to improve the quality of campus life. As noted, appeals may be made to the desire of faculty and staff to maintain or upgrade academic quality, to maximize student development, or to counteract the effect of economic forces caused by declining enrollments such as a high dropout rate and the declining number of high school graduates. This can be done in brainstorming sessions in which participants compile a list of all the possible benefits of a campus renewal effort.

Step Two: Create Need. Once the beneficial outcomes of a retention effort are established, the second step is to begin the process of creating an awareness on campus of a need for action. At this stage the task is to identify and pull together committed supporters, those who feel things could be improved. These might be the risk takers, the early innovators. Oftentimes they come from within one department or one division on campus. At this stage, participants should examine the institutional data they have available and compare the data for their campus with national data, cite basic blunt facts about conditions on campus, and quote external authorities on the impact and benefit of retention efforts.

It is important to note that these first two steps do not have to be taken in a formal way; any one person or small nucleus of concerned individuals can initiate them. Anyone on campus, the director of admissions, vice-president for student affairs, director of academic advising, or a concerned faculty member can get inspired and begin to spread awareness of the need for change.

Step Three: Identify Supporters. Once the initial interest in and support for a retention effort is generated, it is helpful to have a wide base of support. Hence the third step is to identify an ad hoc start-up committee among the committed supporters. In forming the committee, efforts should be made to ensure that all key campus constituents and units with a stake in campus renewal are represented. One way to do so is to ask: "Who ought to be here who is not here?" In many ways the very act of expanding the start-up committee can spread awareness throughout the institution.

Step Four: Assemble Start-Up Committee. The fourth step is to assemble the newly formed start-up committee and share campus retention data. At each step in the process as new members are added to the group, it is important to go back and review the data with them, in effect, to re-present the rationale by emphasizing the necessity for studying and acting on needed retention improvements. The committee should next determine what additional data are needed to determine such factors as who drops out when and why, and the opinions and level of satisfaction of enrolled students. Since the goal is to promote involvement, commitment, and ownership at all stages of the process, it is important that participants feel they can request additional data at any point.

At this stage, the start-up committee should also provide a retention literature review, brainstorm campus strengths and weaknesses, take a "futuring trip" as detailed in Smith and others (1981) to determine desired campus images of the future, and finally, arrive at a consensus on the need for a conscious, organized retention effort. If it is agreed that such a need exists, a recommendation should be made to the president that a formal retention project be initiated.

It should be noted that some institutions, a large university for example, may not begin a retention effort by organizing the entire campus at once. It is almost inconceivable that a large institution would organize according to the model presented here. But a college within a university might organize in this fashion, and that college's initiative and success would have a spreading effect, carrying over to other colleges and departments.

Step Five: Formalize Effort. After the ad hoc committee establishes the need for a retention effort, the fifth step is to officially create a formal campus committee for retention. This group can be called a task force or a steering committee; the important thing is that it ought to be apparent that this is something other than just another committee.

The key factor in creating this impression is presidential commitment and support. The president should appoint the committee with some fanfare, and with some indication that the work it is about to undertake is of high priority for the campus. The act of appointing the committee thus should do more than merely indicate a determination to act. It should create an awareness of the president's commitment to improving retention as a priority that is consistent with the goal of increasing the quality of the learning life on campus. It should be evident that the president is pledging his or her support as well as the financial resources necessary to ensure the success of the retention effort.

The president's next task at this stage is to identify a retention coordinator. If we attend carefully to the advice campuses involved in retention efforts give us as to what is important, it is clear that there is no substitute for appointing a coordinator who has a high degree of credibility with key campus faculty and administrators. A great deal of the work required in the institution is going to demand and depend upon that support. The advising process, the assessment and course placement policy, the level of academic support services provided cannot be changed without such support. On some campuses, student personnel administrators enjoy this type of credibility on campus. In most instances, however, a highly respected faculty member or academic administrator may be in the best position to serve as an effective coordinator. In a few instances, we have observed successful efforts headed jointly by representatives from academic and student affairs. It can be helpful if the coordinator emerges as a committed supporter of the original start-up committee.

Aside from enjoying the confidence and support of the president and the campus, the retention coordinator must have the organizational skills necessary to facilitate a collaborative campuswide change effort. He or she should be able to facilitate decision making, spur action, and have a good understanding of the dynamics and politics of the organization. These skills are requisite if change is really to take place on campus.

The president, in consultation with the coordinator, will next appoint the task force members. The task force should include broad-based representation from the expanded start-up committee and should be made up of the opinion or informal leaders on campus as well as the formal leaders. It should also include members who can facilitate data collection and analysis as well as members with expertise in organizational development, planned change strategies, staff training, and development. Table 1 provides a sample listing of the composition of a possible task force.

While balance is of critical importance in determining the composition of the task force, priority should be given to the academic side of the campus with faculty, academic deans, and academic affairs administrators thoroughly represented. In selecting representatives from other areas of the campus, it is not always necessary to select the chief administrator of a unit.

Table 1. Retention Task Force—One Possibility.

Faculty Members	40–60%
Deans (assistant or associate deans)	
academic	10–20%
student affairs	5–10%
Campus Area Representatives	20–40%
institutional research	
computer center	
registrar	
counseling center	
academic advising	
admissions	
orientation	
financial aid	
housing/food service	

Note: At a small college, a workable size task force would include 8–12 members; a task force at a large college may include as many as 18–24 participants.

Because the primary role of the task force is to spearhead needed changes, whenever possible, innovators or risk takers who represent the areas listed should be selected.

A key department such as academic advising should always be represented, but in determining the composition of the task force, it is important to make judgments relative to the individual institution. A private residential institution, for example, might want to include a representative from the housing staff since on such a campus, housing touches the lives of all or almost all students.

In assembling the task force, some provision should be made to include significant student input. Whether students actually serve on the committee is a question for each campus to decide. The important point is that there be some opportunity for direct input from students or some means of addressing student opinions. We have sometimes found that if a campus is having serious attrition problems, it may be counterproductive to bring students into the early soul-searching or data analysis phase when the sources of various problems are being determined. The type of students selected has also been problematic. On many campuses, government leaders may not be representative of the student body; consider what percentage of the students participate in elections. Further, student government leaders are often so busy with other personal agendas that they have little time to become actively involved with the task force. If students are to participate formally, a random method for selection may have the best outcome.

   Step Six: Convene Committee and Display Data. Convening the newly established retention task force is the sixth step. As at any point when new partipants are brought into the process, the first step should be for the whole committee to review all existing data, including the results of the strengths/weaknesses brainstorming exercise and the futuring trip, with the new members. Those interested should be appointed to a separate data subcommittee because data are so critical in driving a retention effort. Then further data collection needs can be determined and assignments made.

   At this point the task force should devise strategies to expand to an even greater extent the awareness of retention needs and activities across campus—strategies to foster a deeper understanding of the forces of persistence and a heightened awareness among staff members of how they influence the quality of life on campus. In developing these strategies, the guiding principle should be to generate awareness and support. Awareness and support are the precursors to involvement, which is necessary for the development of ownership of the problem and its solutions.

   In furthering awareness at this stage, it is important that the task force keep up a steady flow of information in order to maintain a high degree of visibility on campus. Little is accomplished by setting out everything that is known in one session or in one document and then being left with little new to present from that point on. A continuous information flow not only piques attention but allows time to process the implications of the data as well as to address problems in manageable chunks.

   Step Seven: Begin Implementation. After formulating strategies for creating campuswide awareness of the need for change, the next step is to begin to implement these strategies. There are two basic techniques to build momentum for implementation. First, institutions can use an external retention authority as a catalyst to initiate the campus effort. An external authority brought to campus should be able to

1. Create a broad-based awareness that student success, satisfaction, and retention rates are the responsibility of faculty, staff, and support personnel campuswide.
2. Provide the latest research data on why students leave, why they stay, and what makes the difference.
3. Identify critical factors from the institution's own data base that shed light on the nature of their retention situation.
4. Destroy the myth that increasing retention means lowering standards.
5. Reinforce the importance of competent, caring, and enthusiastic faculty and advisers.
6. Document the positive impact that student support services can have on student success and persistence.
7. Highlight educational practices that have been successful at those campuses that are the "best of the best" as far as retention.
8. Build momentum for an organized, concerted campuswide retention effort and outline next steps for action on the campus.

Second, campuses can undertake collaborative involvement-building activities designed to involve larger segments of the campus community. Working through mobilization exercises at this stage can bring together the collective wisdom, energy, and enthusiasm that exist on campus. Involving persons who are affected by change builds a sense of ownership and commitment to the plans and activities designed to bring about the desired future state. These exercises (detailed in Noel, 1984) include identifying current strengths and weaknesses, sharing successful practices, and defining desired outcomes and directions.

Some campuses have successfully begun the implementation process using their own personnel. Most, however, find it advantageous to use an experienced, external authority, having found it is difficult to be an expert in one's own backyard. Sequencing these two techniques has worked effectively for many institutions.

Step Eight: Establish Priorities for Action. The next step is to determine priorities and establish action subcommittees, with the priorities growing jointly out of the committee's data base and the important messages culled from the external authority or extracted from the collaborative mobilization exercises. Possible priorities for action might include

- Institute strategies for improving classroom instruction.
- Increase frequency and quality of out-of-class contact between faculty and students.
- Improve delivery of freshman intake services, that is, orientation, course placement, and life/career planning.
- Expand scope and effectiveness of academic advising program.
- Respond systematically to needs of transfer students.
- Provide for awareness among and in-service training for classified support staff in relating to students.
- Identify and implement strategies to meet needs of academically underprepared students.

Detailed information on each of these areas is presented in earlier chapters of this book.

Most institutions should select a limited number of priorities for immediate attention, and then establish action subcommittees that parallel priorities selected. Membership of the subcommittees should be extended beyond the basic retention task force. The major role of the subcommittees should be to take a penetrating look at what is currently happening and determine how it should be improved. Their analyses and recommendations should be presented to the task force for consideration.

Step Nine: Gain Top-Level Support. Once an understanding of action needed has been reached, the ninth step in our ten-step process is to seek administrative support and sanction for the proposed changes. In making recommendations to decision makers, whether to a faculty senate or to the president, it is critical that each be specific and linked to the impact it will have on student learning and/or persistence. In addition to building the case for the desired change, the task force should also highlight the outcomes/benefits of the planned action and quantify the financial support that will be needed.

Step Ten: Assess Impact. The tenth and final step is to evaluate and continuously review to determine if the efforts have had the desired impact and are still on track and to highlight those efforts that need to be intensified. The findings of this evaluation process should be shared with the total campus community. Celebration of successes achieved is also important. "Celebration is an integral part of the institution's renewal and growth cycles. How a campus celebrates its success is one of the indicators of its quality of life" (Smith and others, 1981, p. 61). And finally, the very fact that there is an ongoing renewal and evaluation effort can be taken as a vital sign that things are working well on campus.

Conclusion

The principles of planned change that run through each of these ten mobilizing steps are to involve critical parties in collecting data and understanding the implications, dramatize the findings, gain access to opinion leaders and decision makers, build momentum through involvement which leads to broad-based ownership and commitment, focus on specific actions needed, and use data to support and reinforce actions taken.

The important point in any retention effort, as Marchese (1983, p. 8) points out, is to get started, to overcome the inertia that frequently bogs down committee work, to *do* something: "Let's say all the data aren't in hand, there's no budget yet, the ultimate program is not in view; in short, there's all the reason to do what most committees do, nothing. Fine; get started! The costs of doing nothing—to the institution, to individual students, to the committee itself—are always greater than those of a good stab at a couple of well-chosen targets!"

Achieving the planned change necessary to bring about a campuswide retention improvement effort first involves creating an awareness of the need for change and then encouraging widespread participation in the change effort. The entire campus mobilization process goes back to the question posed earlier: What kind of process can be advised that will promote an internal dialogue on campus? This is what a successful retention effort is about—organizing to bring the resources of a campus to bear on solving its problems. Ensuring that there is a commitment on campus to working collectively is the best way to maximize student success and persistence.

References

Forrest, A. *Increasing Student Competence and Persistence: The Best Case for General Education.* Iowa City, Iowa: American College Testing Program National Center for Advancement of Educational Practices, 1982.

Marchese, T. J. "Memo to a Retention Committee." *American Association for Higher Education Bulletin*, 1983, *35* (8), 7-9.

Noel, L. "Steps for Mobilizing a Campuswide Retention Effort: Implementation Guide." Iowa City, Iowa: American College Testing Program National Center for Advancement of Educational Practices, 1984.

Noel, L., Levitz, R., and Kaufmann, J. "Organizing the Campus for Retention: Report of a National Study." In L. Noel and R. Levitz (eds.), *Organizing the Campus for Retention.* Iowa City, Iowa: American College Testing Program National Center for Advancement of Educational Practices, 1982.

Smith, L. N., and others. *Mobilizing the Campus for Retention: An Innovative Quality-of-Life Model.* Iowa City, Iowa: American College Testing Program National Center for Advancement of Educational Practices, 1981.

Name Index

Subject Index

for undecided students, 132–133
Outcomes: and admissions, 184; measuring, 21–23; as research phase, 349–350, 360–361; and retention, 2–3, 10, 24, 62–63

P

Peers: as advisers, 251; functions of, 322–323; and retention practices, 445
Pell Grants: and adult students, 151; as foundation program, 209
Persistence and achievement: and achievement activities, 58–60; of adult students, 145–152; analysis of, 44–61; background on, 44–45; barriers to, 46–50; conclusion on, 61; correlation between, 285; and decision to attend college, 45–46; external forces on, 45–46, 47–48; and financial aid, 204–206; force field analysis of, 50–55; internal forces on, 46, 48–50; of low-income students, 82–83; and persistence activities, 56–58; profiles of, 354–355; promoting, 55–60; socioeconomic influences on, 52–55
Princeton University, career planning at, 314
Psychological variables, for adult students, 148–149. *See also* Developmental approach
Purdue University, computer-assisted advising at, 260

R

Recruitment: as orientation, 226; for undecided students, 125. *See also* Admissions
Redlands, University of, retention practices at, 444
Remedial courses: issues of, 103–104; in learning assistance programs, 268–269
Research: analysis of, 345–365; background on, 345–348; conclusion on, 363–364; data from, as action trigger, 361–363; enrollment behavior

phase of, 352–355; imperatives for, 345–347; importance of, 456–458; objectives of, 350–351; and operational features, 348–349; outcomes assessment phase of, 360–361; phases in, 352–361; and retention outcomes, 349–350; student-institution interaction phase of, 355–360
Residence halls: adjustment problems in, 323–324; analysis of, 320–330; assigning students in, 324–326; background on, 320–322; benefits of, 321; educational activities in, 329–330; impact on retention by, 322–324; staff for, 326–329; successful practices with, 445–446
Resident advisers, selecting, training, and supervising, 326–329
Retention: and academic advising, 244–263, 403–404, 415–425; of academically underprepared students, 95–115; action blueprint for, 448–467; and admissions, 183–202; of adult students, 138–161; analysis of challenges in, 1–27; and attrition themes, 10–15; background on, 1–3, 448–450; campuswide responsibility for, 15–21, 91–92, 366–382, 404–405, 425–439, 441; and career planning and counseling, 302–318; case studies of, 402–447; collaboration for, 464; committee assembled for, 459–460; committee meetings for, 463; of commuter students, 162–182; comprehensive strategies for, 90–91, 403, 405–414; conclusions on, 23–24, 466–467; as continuing process, 452–453; coordinator for, 460–461; creating conditions for, 62–77, 458–459; critical factors in, 15–16; critical time period for, 20–21; and deciding to act, 458; and enrollment management, x, 1–2; evaluation of efforts at, 466; external authority for, 464; faculty involvement in, 383–401, 455–456; and financial aid, 203–220; focus of, xiii; formalized effort for, 460–463; goal of, 29; guidelines and models for, 345–467; and higher education